Suffering in Silence

The Human Rights Nightmare of the Karen People of Burma

Karen Human Rights Group

Edited by

Claudio O. Delang

With an introduction by

Kevin Heppner

Universal Publishers
Parkland

Suffering in Silence, The Human Rights Nightmare of the Karen People of
Burma/ Edited by Claudio O. Delang
1. Human Rights
2. Karen
3. Burma
4. SLORC
5. SPDC
6. KNLA
7. DKBA

Cover photo: Villagers in Papun District living in hiding in the forest after their
villages were shelled and burned down by SPDC troops who are driving all
civilians out of the region. Just before this photo was taken, word came that a
large SPDC column was passing nearby and the villagers were preparing to flee
further into the hills. Villagers are shot on sight by SPDC troops patrolling the
area. [Photo: KHRG]

Published by
Universal Publishers
Parkland, USA • 2001

ISBN: 1-58112-704-9

www.upublish.com/books/delang.htm

Contents

PART II - CAUGHT IN THE MIDDLE
The Suffering of Karen Villagers in Thaton District

PART III - BEYOND ALL ENDURANCE
The Breakup of Karen Villages in Southeastern Pa'an District

Introduction

Despite being one of the most populous countries of Southeast Asia, in a highly strategic position at the juncture of Southeast Asia, India and China, and steeped in history, diverse cultures and traditions, Burma is a complete enigma to most people in the outside world. Even the peoples of its immediate neighbours have very little concept of what is happening there. To people from more distant countries, it sometimes brings with it vague allusions to World War Two, brutal Japanese occupation and the Death Railway, though more recently they may have heard of Daw Aung San Suu Kyi winning the Nobel Peace Prize and the struggle against a military junta. To Burma's people, to its exiles and refugees, and to those whose work brings them in regular contact with what is happening there, this lack of awareness is a steady source of frustration, particularly when looking at newspapers full of articles about countries where the suffering is not nearly so severe. At times it seems the military junta's policies closing off the country and restricting access to most of it have been successful in wiping it from the world's consciousness.

Burma is home to an estimated 50 million people, somewhere around 50 percent of them being ethnic Burmans (though the junta uses falsified figures to claim 67-70 percent dominance) and the remainder made up by at least 15 major ethnic groups such as the Karen, Shan, Mon, Kachin, Chin, Rakhine, Wa, and others. It is a large country of forests, huge rivers, plains rich in rice, and lower population density than most of east Asia, and until the 1800's various local kingdoms struggled for control of different regions. The British conquered it in the 1800's and made it a single entity, a province of British India. It was occupied by Japan in World War Two, then was given independence by Britain in 1948. Since then it has never ceased to be embroiled in civil war, with Burman-dominated central governments fighting a host of ethnic-based resistance groups and (until 1989) a Communist insurgency. It has been ruled by a military dictatorship since 1962, which transformed itself into a military junta in 1988. This junta was called the State Law & Order Restoration Council (SLORC) until 1997, when it changed its name to the State Peace and Development Council (SPDC). In 1989 the military junta changed the country's name from Burma to 'Myanmar', a name change which is seen by the non-Burman ethnic groups as an act of ethnic cleansing and by the country's elected government (which has never been allowed to assume power) as an illegal act by an illegal regime. Those who do not recognise the military junta as a legitimate government continue to use the name Burma, and this book will do so as well.

This junta has no particular ideology except 'holding the country together' and maintaining itself in power. When faced with massive uprisings for democracy in 1988, it massacred thousands of unarmed demonstrators - a year before Tiananmen Square, and many more people died, but with much less coverage in the outside world. The junta held elections in 1990, only to ignore the results when it lost, and continues to deny every basic freedom to its people. In rural non-Burman areas the situation is much worse, with the Army conducting mass forced relocations, using civilians for forced labour, using torture, rape, summary execution, and the destruction of villages and food supplies as weapons of control.

While the pro-democracy activists in the cities have managed to gain at least some attention in the outside world, the rural villagers who make up most of Burma's population and the poorer sectors of the townspeople have no such voice. Even now it is shocking to see how many people in the outside world have detailed knowledge of the SPDC's harassment of Daw Aung San Suu Kyi and the National League for Democracy, but no knowledge whatsoever of the forced labour, Army extortion, arbitrary detention, looting, rape, killings and other abuses which are the daily lot of the general population of Burma. As a volunteer teacher in an opposition-held area of Karen State, I began to come into contact with this reality in 1991 through talking to villagers who had fled forced porterage for the Burmese Army, villagers who had been arrested and tortured, women who had been gang raped by troops, and people whose villages had been destroyed for no clear reason. When a Burmese military offensive destroyed the village where I taught, I was shocked to see the foreign journalists coming only to ask about military advances and take photos of people firing weapons, none of them interested in talking to the villagers. This is what led to the formation of the Karen Human Rights Group in 1992 - the need, in whatever limited way we could, to help the voices of the villagers to be heard in the outside world.

In the beginning, we scribbled down or recorded the words of villagers, translated them into English, banged them up on an old typewriter with candlelight and carbon paper, and handed them to whomever we could make contact with. Now we have a network of Karen volunteers scattered throughout Karen State, recording hundreds of interviews on tape for processing, gathering SPDC order documents and snapping photos for evidence, all to be processed on computers by a translation and editing staff, then published and distributed to agencies throughout the world in print form, by email and on the World Wide Web. KHRG is and always has been apolitical and completely independent of any other organisation. Though focused on Karen regions, we have also repeatedly documented the situation in other areas throughout rural Burma. Our direct distribution now reaches people and groups ranging from the UN Special Rapporteur on Burma, the International Labour Organisation, and a range of embassies and governments, to international human rights organisations, trade unions, Burma activist groups, journalists and academics. Though our processing, distribution and the appearance of our reports have changed, their content remains essentially the same. Those first reports contained little but the raw translated texts of villagers' stories, and this year's reports are still based entirely around the same type of testimonies, translated sentence by sentence from cassette tapes recorded in the field. To round out the reports and make them more meaningful to those in the outside world, we now add a significant amount of analysis, and also publish Information Updates, summaries and Commentaries on a regular basis to look at trends and relate our detailed regional reports to the broader situation. The purpose remains simple, to provide a conduit for the villagers to get their voices to the outside world so that others can better understand their situation.

This book has come about as an additional way to further this purpose, by providing the reader with a digestible sample of some of our reports in the hope that this can provide an overview of the struggles of rural villagers, and maybe stimulate a further interest. Claudio Delang approached KHRG with the original idea in 1999, and then followed through by doing almost all of the work to make it happen, including selecting and editing the most representative reports, maps and photos, doing all of the formatting and arranging for publishing. Both KHRG and myself are extremely grateful to Claudio for all of his work on this. Months of correspondence by email followed, and you now hold the end result.

The book is based around three of our 1999 regional reports: *"Death Squads and Displacement"* (May 1999), *"Caught in the Middle"* (September 1999), and *"Beyond All Endurance"* (December 1999), which document in detail the situation in three different Karen regions. Taken together, they give the reader a broad spectrum idea of the abuses being inflicted on villagers and their struggle to survive in the face of these abuses, both in areas where opposition armies are active and where they are not.

"Beyond All Endurance" describes the situation of the villagers in a classic conflict area, eastern Pa'an District of Karen State, where the Karen National Liberation Army (KNLA) is in active guerrilla resistance

to the SPDC junta's forces. The SPDC has responded by forcing villagers into the centre of villages, destroying many villages, rounding up both local villagers and townspeople from afar as military porters for frontline operations, and forcing these civilians to march in front of their columns as human mine detonators and shields against ambush across one of the most heavily landmined patches of ground in all of Asia.

"Death Squads and Displacement" speaks with villagers from Nyaunglebin District, not far northeast of Rangoon. This region is divided between the SPDC-controlled Sittaung River plains in the west and rugged hills in the east where there is extensive KNLA activity. The two types of terrain have brought about two very different SPDC strategies for control. In the hills, SPDC forces have had difficulty rounding up the villagers, so since 1997 they have pursued a campaign of systematically shelling and burning villages with no warning or provocation. Approximately 200 villages have been destroyed in this area and neighbouring Papun District since 1997, and the troops have followed up by trampling or uprooting crops in the fields, burning rice storehouses, and shooting villagers on sight in the fields and forests where they have fled into hiding. Further west in the SPDC-controlled plains, there is little guerrilla activity but the SPDC is still engaged in a struggle to control the civilians, in this case by forcibly relocating entire villages to military-controlled sites and constantly using villagers for forced labour on roads and other infrastructure, at Army camps and as porters. As a further weapon of intimidation, the regime introduced the 'Guerrilla Retaliation' execution squads in the plains in 1998. These small squads have the sole purpose of executing anyone, Karen or Burman, with any perceived past connection with the Karen opposition. The squads have already executed many former village elders, and their methods are brutal - dragging victims into the forest to cut their throats, and sometimes displaying severed heads as a warning to other villagers. As a result, people of the plains have been fleeing to the hills, where the hill people are already living in hiding, in hungry desperation in the forests, their villages destroyed.

"Caught in the Middle" gives us a glimpse of an area more firmly under SPDC control, where there is little opposition guerrilla activity. Yet even in this area, villagers are finding it difficult to survive under the burden of forced labour, extortion and other demands imposed by SPDC forces in the area. At the same time, there is just enough of a perceived guerrilla presence in the area to bring heavy SPDC punishments and retaliations on the heads of the villagers on a regular basis.

To place these reports within a broader context and give the reader some background information, we have begun the book with the chapter *"Understanding Burma"*, which gives a brief summary of Burma's history and an overview of the mentality and tactics currently used by the regime in controlling the civilian population.

For those already interested in Burma or those who develop an appetite for more information on the subject, there are many places to look. The Karen Human Rights Group web site (**www.khrg.org**) is regularly updated with all of our published reports and photo sets. For other information about the Karen people, a good starting point is **www.karen.org**. To find links to many other web sites covering various aspects of the Burma situation from widely differing perspectives, start with **www.freeburma.org** or **www.soros.org/burma.html**. To see a regular (several times a week) news roundup on Burma, go to **www.burmanet.org**, which also tells you how you can subscribe to a free regular email newspaper on Burma.

Finally, I would like to acknowledge all of the difficult and dangerous work of our people in the field, without whom none of this reporting would be possible, the patient and endless efforts of our office staff, who have to handle such a mass of information coming in that we can never catch up with it all, to our contacts and supporters worldwide who keep up our morale by using our material so effectively, and to Claudio Delang for putting together this book and making it possible. Most of all, though, it is the villagers in Burma themselves who need to be acknowledged, not only for their courage in struggling to survive in the face of a myriad of abuses, but even more for their courage in refusing to be silenced, in trying to get their story to the outside world. Many people have asked me how we manage to convince villagers to talk despite their fear of retaliations by the junta, and the answer is that in the vast majority of cases no persuasion is required or used, because the villagers are eager to have their story heard. For many it is one of the only ways they can release their sadness, their frustration, their grief and their anger after a lifetime of suffering and fleeing.

As in any situation, there is no shortage of people in the outside world who readily pontificate on the solutions to Burma's problems without ever having listened to the voice of a villager. Many government and corporate leaders in the outside world argue that we should 'engage' the military junta in Burma, to seek an accommodation with them, because isolation and sanctions 'don't work' or because the junta is too entrenched to lose its grip on power. Using this logic, one could also argue that because the rule of law has never 'worked' to eradicate organised crime, we should abandon the law and seek an accommodation with organised criminals - which is essentially what Burma's generals are. Perhaps rather than trying to dictate to the people of Burma what is best for them, what 'works' or 'doesn't work', foreign leaders should listen to what the people of Burma want. Stop listening to the generals, and start listening to the villagers. Diplomatic protocol has taken precedence over the loss of innocent lives for far too long already. In my experience, once people hear a group of villagers describe how the junta holds on to power around their village, they want to do something about it. If it affects you this way, you can make a difference. Go to your political leaders, your corporate executives, those who say they have no time to hear the voices of villagers, and make them hear it whether they like it or not. You may not bring about change in Burma single-handed, but your action will not go unnoticed and you may be surprised by how much effect it will have. It will also make you feel good, strong, and alive, because you will be on the side of the villagers. And they will appreciate it - just listen to them.

Kevin Heppner
Coordinator
Karen Human Rights Group
June 2000

Understanding Burma

In order to fully understand the day-to-day suffering of Burma's villagers and the mentality of the ruling junta, it is essential to have some idea of the country's ethnic makeup and its historical development. This chapter presents a brief summary of Burma's people and historical development, followed by a summary of the current human rights situation. For more detailed historical background, see the suggested readings listed at the end of the chapter.

A Land of Ethnic Diversity

Burma is a country of great ethnic diversity, its estimated population of 48-50 million being divided between at least 15 major ethnic groups, many of them with several distinct subgroups. These groups come from very different origins: for example, the Muslim Rohingyas of Arakan (Rakhine) State are related to Bengali and Indian traders of centuries ago, the predominant Burmans originally migrated from the Indo-Tibetan region, the Shan are a Sino-Thai race originating from what is now China, the Karen, Karenni and Pa'O originated from the region of Mongolia, and the Mon are closely related to the Khmer of Cambodia. The extent of these differences is partly visible in the differences in culture and language, with languages such as Burmese, Shan and Karen having virtually no similarities at all. There is no reliable census data for Burma at present, because the last real census was conducted in the early 1930's and all of the census data since British colonial days has been collected by Burman-dominated regimes keen on exaggerating the dominance of the Burmans; for example, in many areas anyone with a Burman name (which many people adopt to avoid official discrimination) and anyone who is Buddhist has been listed down as a Burman. Using data collected this way, the SPDC and its predecessor regimes have claimed that 67-70% of the population is Burman, while in reality it is more likely that at most half the population is Burman, with 50% or more of the population divided among the other ethnic groups. After the Burmans, the most populous groups are the Karen with an estimated 6-7 million (when taken including the Karenni and Pa'O), and the Shan and Mon with about 4 million each.[1]   Even these figures, however, can only

---

[1] For more details on population figures and breakdown see for example Smith, Martin (1999) "Burma: Insurgency and the Politics of Ethnicity" Bangkok: White Lotus/Zed Books, chapter 2, especially page 30.

be taken as rough estimates.

Kingdoms and Colonisation

There is a great deal of debate over who arrived in Burma first, this honour being claimed by the Burmans, Mon, Karen and Rakhine, among others. Most of these claims appear to be based more on racist dogma than on available historical evidence, particularly the claims of the Burmans and Rakhines, but the oral histories of the Karen and Mon appear to coincide more closely with the historical records and artifacts available. According to the Karen version, their people arrived in Burma, a region which at that time was virtually unpopulated jungle, approximately 2,500 years ago (the current year 2000 is 2739 on the Karen calendar) after a migration in several stages from the region of what is now Mongolia, and settled in what is now the Irrawaddy and Sittaung basin of central Burma. Other groups began arriving at around the same time, possibly shortly before or after, particularly the Mon/Khmer. The Mon/Khmer began imposing their feudal kingdom structure on the other peoples, most of whom had little or no political structure. This began the movement of peoples like the Karen from the central lowlands out into the hills. The Shan also had a strongly structured hierarchical society and in time began dominating what is now Shan State, while the Rakhine kingdom dominated what is now northwestern Burma. The Burmans (whose current calendar year is 1362) were probably among the latest groups to arrive, but over the centuries their kingdoms gradually defeated the Mon and the Rakhine. For hundreds of years until the 1800's, there were various warring kingdoms trying to eat away at each other's territories, while less-organised or more peaceable peoples were gradually driven further into the hills toward the peripheries of what is now Burma. In 1767, the armies of the Burman king Hsinbyushin even conquered much of Siam (Thailand), sacking the capital at Ayutthaya and extracting tribute from the existing dynasties. However, none of these kingdoms were ever strong enough to occupy and hold all of this territory, so once they had conquered they generally had to withdraw and life went on.

The British took over what is now Burma piece by piece in 3 wars: 1824-26, 1852-53, and finally in 1886, when 'Burma' became part of the British Empire as a province of British India. Until that time, no one had looked on this diverse region as a single geographic unit, and this is an important point in understanding the historical argument for autonomy or independence of the non-Burman peoples. The British systematically eradicated the structure of the Burman kingdoms, but at the same time allowed the continued existence of the Shan princedoms and the Karenni *sawbwa*'s. These local rulers were allowed some autonomy because they were seen as less of a threat and because the British did not want to allocate the resources necessary to control such vast and far-flung territories, preferring to gradually implement an indirect rule enforced through local leaders. For peoples such as the Karen, Karenni and Kachin, British colonialism was partly a liberation from the repression of the Burmans, and it gave them their first access to education and some forms of development. British and American missionaries had a great deal of success with some of these peoples, gradually converting a sizable minority of Karens to Christianity (mainly Baptist), many Kachin, Chins (also known as Zo) and Naga of northwestern and northern Burma to Baptist and other Christian faiths, and a large proportion of the Karenni to Catholicism. As opportunities opened, many people from these groups joined the colonial administration, civil police force and army. Although in these colonial institutions they were heavily outnumbered by Burmans (for example, in 1938 the civil police force was 71% Burman and only 8.7% Karen[2]), many Burmans remained resentful of British rule and were not very well trusted by the colonisers compared to the other peoples.

Nationalism, Japanese Occupation, and Independence

In the first half of the 20th century, the Burman feeling against the British began to take tangible form in the beginnings of nationalist liberation movements, particularly the *Thakin* movement in which Aung San was a leader. Over the years the *Thakin*s looked to outside countries for military help in overthrowing the British, culminating in the trip of Aung San and the '30 Comrades' to Japan for military training in early 1941. By the end of 1941, they had returned and put together an 'army' of a few thousand in Siam, and followed the invading Japanese into Burma. In the face of the Japanese advance, the British Army retreated to India. During the ensuing 3½-year Japanese occupation of Burma, Aung San's 'Burma Independence Army' acted as enforcers for the Japanese forces, and attracted a mixture of nationalists seeking independence and riffraff who wanted to loot villages. A wide range of atrocities were perpetrated by the BIA against Karen villagers and other ethnic peoples, as many Burmans finally had their opportunity to vent their frustrations against peoples they perceived as British 'collaborators'. In areas such as the

---

[2] Taylor, Robert (1987) "The State In Burma", London: C.Hurst & Company, p. 101

Papun hills, Karen villagers feared the BIA much more than they did the Japanese occupation forces.

At the same time, some Karen, Kachin and others had left for India with the retreating British forces, later to parachute back in, and a few British officers had remained behind in Burma. Villagers were organised into resistance units and armed to fight the Japanese and BIA, and the villages suffered heavy retaliations as a result.[3] In 1944-45, when the Allies re-entered Burma, the Karen, Karenni and Kachin were instrumental in helping them to recapture Burma by systematically harassing and creating havoc among the retreating Japanese.[4] In return for their loyalty they hoped for independence from the Burmans after the war, but it never came. By 1944, Aung San and the BIA had realised that the Japanese had no intention of granting real independence and that the tide of the war was turning, so they switched sides and also fought the retreating Japanese. After the war, Aung San approached the British for independence. The non-Burmans protested that they should be granted freedom from the Burmans, and the British convened the Frontier Areas Commission of Enquiry (FACE) to hear testimony, particularly from Karen regions, on their views. However, as more and more villagers testified of BIA atrocities, the British began to regret the experiment and after the Commission closed they wiped much of the testimony off the record. In the end, independence was granted under Aung San's plan, with a unitary government which would clearly be Burman-dominated.[5]

Realising that some kind of accommodation would have to be made with the non-Burmans, Aung San engineered the 1947 Panglong Agreement, whereby some representatives from the Shan, Chin and Kachin hills signed their willingness to cooperate with his government and not to seek secession for at least 10 years. No representatives of the Karen, Mon, or any other peoples were present. Even so, Panglong appeared to be a good starting point, but its spirit was wiped out a few months later when Aung San was assassinated by his Burman political rivals. When independence came in January 1948, U Nu became Burma's elected

---

[3] For a detailed account of this period see Morrison, Ian (1946) "Grandfather Longlegs", London: Faber & Faber

[4] See Field-Marshal (Viscount) William Joseph Slim, "Defeat into Victory", London: Cassell, (1956); London: Papermac (1986), 576p.

[5] Harold Klein, the son of missionaries to Burma and a missionary himself, has produced very detailed unpublished research on this period which exposes much of the reality about the Frontier Areas Commission of Enquiry and the tactics of Aung San and the British Government.

leader. He immediately faced a Communist rebellion which threatened to topple the government, and was largely saved by non-Burman units of the former colonial army. However, behind their backs he was raising his own Army, and he soon turned it against the Karen and other non-Burman units. At the same time the Karen and others began rising for some form of independence or federalism, first in large peaceful demonstrations, but when this didn't work they went into armed rebellion. In 1949, the newly independent government faced armed uprisings not only by the Communists, but the Karen and others as well.

Civil War

Through the 1950s, U Nu's party managed to hold power and bring about some economic progress in the central Burman cities despite facing several armed opposition groups in the countryside. However, Gen. Ne Win, whom U Nu had made head of the Army, seized the government first in 1958-60, and then again in 1962, when he established a full military dictatorship and began stripping everyone in the country, Burman or otherwise, of their rights.

Through the 1950's and 1960's, more and more ethnic armed groups rose against the regime until by the late 1970's there were well over a dozen armed opposition groups controlling something like 20-30% of Burma's entire land mass. The Communists had become entrenched in large areas of Shan State, while ethnic-based armies controlled much of the hill territory near all of the country's land borders. Ne Win's response was to increasingly militarise the country and make his repression of all freedoms more and more systematic. He introduced the Burmese Way to Socialism, which essentially meant state control of everything, and he was the state. He largely cut off the country from international trade or contact, which only strengthened the hand of the armed opposition groups and drove the country into abject poverty. In the early 1970's he introduced the Four Cuts policy, aimed at cutting off all supplies of food, funds, recruits and intelligence to opposition groups; in practice, it meant undermining the opposition by systematically driving into destitution the civilian population supporting it. Forced relocations, forced labour and all forms of abuses against the civilian population became the order of the day.

Gradually the opposition to Ne Win's rule became almost universal. In the cities, major demonstrations broke out in 1974 but were put down by the military with many arrests and killings. In 1976, nine of the ethnic-based armies united to form the National Democratic Front (NDF) alliance. However, Ne Win's rule continued until 1988, when a sudden demonetisation which had wiped out many people's savings triggered mass uprisings in Rangoon, Mandalay and most provincial towns. Hundreds of thousands of people hit the streets, led by university students and Buddhist monks, only to be raked with machine gun fire or charged with bayonets by combat troops. Anywhere from 1,000 to 3,000 people were killed nationwide, and for the first time Burman pro-democracy activists fled to ethnic-held areas in the hills, where they formed their own pro-democracy organisations and allied themselves with the ethnic armies to form the Democratic Alliance of Burma and other alliances. In Rangoon, Ne Win stepped down but eventually hand-picked a junta, which assumed power in September 1988 and called itself the State Law & Order Restoration Council (SLORC).

The SLORC and the SPDC

The SLORC inaugurated its rule by massacring more civilian demonstrators, then immediately began implementing more draconian measures than Ne Win had ever imposed. However, the regime was hungry for international funds and support, particularly the foreign aid which the international community had cut off in its horror at the massacres. In an attempt to appease both international and domestic criticism and to obtain financing, the SLORC began to make a show of opening markets and announced democratic elections for 1990, calculating that it could control the election results by keeping the opposition divided. Unfortunately for them, Daw Aung San Suu Kyi, the daughter of General Aung San (who is an 'independence hero' to most ethnic Burmans), had returned from England to tend her sick mother in 1988 and had been dragged into the political whirlpool. She became the General Secretary of the National League for Democracy (NLD), a new opposition party, and the electoral opposition parties began rallying around her. To put a stop to this the SLORC put her under house arrest in 1989, but when the polls were held in May 1990, the NLD won 82% of the parliamentary seats, its allies 16%, and the SLORC's 'National Unity Party' only 2%. The junta immediately began taking steps to ignore the election, and never did honour the result. Daw Aung San Suu Kyi was held under house arrest until 1995, and even now is so restricted in her movements that she remains under virtual house arrest. Elected Members of Parliament have been harassed, arrested, disqualified, or forced or coerced to resign. Some have died in prison, while others fled to areas held by the ethnic resistance groups and formed a parallel government.

In the ethnic-held areas, agreements were made between ethnic and pro-democracy groups wherein most of the ethnic armies dropped independence from their objectives, and in return the pro-democracy groups agreed to the concept of a federal system with some autonomy for the ethnic states. The SLORC changed the country's name to 'Myanmar Naing-Ngan', a name essentially meaning 'Burman Country' in the Burmese language, which the Burmans had used historically to refer to their kingdoms of the central plains; at the same time changing all other names to their Burmese language versions such as 'Rangoon' to 'Yangon'. This was seen by the ethnic nationalities as part of ethnic cleansing and by the Burmese pro-democracy groups as the act of an illegal regime, so all of these groups rejected the name change.

The SLORC stepped up its military offensives against the ethnic armed opposition and its repression of the civilian population. In 1989, the Burmese Communist Party imploded when the ethnic Wa soldiery rebelled against the mainly Chinese leadership, and then formed the United Wa State Army. The SLORC saw an opening and negotiated ceasefires with the Wa and several small groups within Shan State, promising SLORC Army support for drug trafficking operations in return for 'joining hands with the government'. Burma rapidly became the world's largest supplier of opium and heroin. The regime then used military offensives, large-scale forced relocation of civilians, the complicity of neighbouring countries, and finally buy-offs of the leadership to force other armed opposition groups into ceasefire deals, none of which addressed any of the political or human rights concerns of those groups. After each deal, the SLORC sent more military to effectively surround the ceasefire groups, making it impossible for them to consider a resumption of hostilities. Human rights abuses against the civilians, such as forced labour for the SLORC military, continued.

The SLORC presented these ceasefires internationally as evidence that it was creating 'peace', and claimed that it had secured ceasefires with 7 of 9 opposition groups; then 9 of 11; then 11 of 13; then 14 of 15; and at present, 17 of 18 opposition groups. The reality is that many of the groups in the list are SLORC creations, while at least 5 groups continue to fight the regime (the Karen National Union, the Shan State Army, the Karenni National Progressive Party [which the regime includes in its 'ceasefire' list], the Chin National Front, the National Socialist Council of Nagaland, various Arakan Rohingya groups, etc.). The SLORC continued to offer business opportunities in return for international political support, and gained admission to the Association of Southeast Asian Nations (ASEAN) in 1997, while still keeping China as its principal political and military backer. In late 1997, the regime changed its name to the State Peace and Development Council (SPDC).

Most of the armed groups fighting the SPDC have given up their control of territory in the face of mass military offensives, and now fight entirely using guerrilla tactics. In areas where there is still armed opposition, the SPDC is demanding the outright surrender of the opposition groups, backing this with military offensives and by implementing the Four Cuts policy more systematically than ever before, forcibly relocating hundreds of villages at a time, systematically torturing and executing any villagers suspected of having any links to the opposition, and forcing the civilian population to do labour and provide all the material needs of the Army. In rural areas where there is no conflict, the Army and administration demand regular forced labour on infrastructure and money-making schemes, extort money out of farmers until they have to flee their land, and force them to hand over large proportions of their crops to support the Army. In the cities and Burman areas, the regime keeps most of the universities closed, all freedom of expression and association is denied, unauthorised access to fax machines, foreign radio or the internet is punishable by long jail terms with hard labour, high school students have been sentenced to 20 years imprisonment for handing out pamphlets, and corruption and official extortion are rampant. The economy is destroyed, with a worthless currency, spiralling inflation, billions in foreign debt incurred by building up the military and almost no foreign exchange reserves.   Politically the situation is at a stalemate, with the SPDC refusing to negotiate with the NLD, Daw Aung San Suu Kyi or representatives of the ethnic nationalities; the regime appears to believe that if it can simply continue holding power, the international community will give in and give it the financial and political backing it needs in return for access to Burma's resources and extremely cheap labour.

The Present Day: Junta Policy in the Rural Areas

The Karen people of today mainly inhabit southeastern Burma, consisting of Karen State (see map on page 29), where they form the majority, Tenasserim Division in Burma's far south, where they form the majority in the hills but not along the sea coast, the Irrawaddy Delta west of Rangoon, where they make up about half the population while Burmans make up the other half, and areas of eastern Pegu (Bago) Division and outlying parts of Rangoon.

Farming villages are the main social and economic unit throughout rural

southeastern Burma.   Most of the villagers are subsistence farmers,
growing rice and/or cash crops such as fruit, sugar cane or betelnut in
several small fields handed down within families.   On flat land, wet
paddy cultivation is practised, but in many areas little or no flat land is
available so families practice swidden agriculture, rotating each year to
another of their hill fields on an 8 to 10 year cycle, cutting and clearing
the trees which have grown since the field was last used and growing
hillside rice in the rainy season. Villages in flat fertile areas can be as
large as several hundred households, while in remote hill areas some
villages have as few as 8 or 10 families.

Families operate on a subsistence level, growing enough rice and
vegetables for their own use, raising some chickens, pigs and cattle, and
fishing for their own consumption. Cash crops or extra rice or livestock
are sold in surrounding villages or the nearest market town to obtain
some money for other goods, but the local economy within the village
operates largely on barter, loans and payments often being made in rice.
This ancient system is very delicate because there is little or no safety net
in hard times; if one family has troubles the village can pitch in to help
them, but if an entire year's crop fails the village goes hungry for the
following year.   There is also no built-in capacity to deal with the
scenario of several Army battalions moving into the area, restricting the
movements of villagers and demanding food, labour, and building
materials. However, under the rule of the State Peace and Development
Council (SPDC) this is what the farming villages are being forced to deal
with.

The SPDC itself is a classic case of a paranoid military junta; its leaders
restrict even the most basic freedoms in the belief that any freedom
whatsoever will be used to oppose their rule. They may be right, because
unlike repressive regimes in many parts of the world, the SPDC
represents no political faction or ideology other than pure militarism and
has no constituency among the general populace. The result is a regime
which focuses most of its energies on controlling the civilian population.
This is especially true in the rural areas, many of them populated by the
non-Burman ethnic nationalities which together make up approximately
50% of Burma's population. Ethnic-based armed resistance movements
have been seeking autonomy by fighting the central regime for the past
50 years, and the SPDC and its predecessors have believed since the
1970's that the best way to destroy these groups is to destroy the ability
of the civilians to support them.

This approach gave rise to the official Four Cuts policy, intended to deprive opposition groups of food, funds, recruits and intelligence. In practice, this is implemented by systematic intimidation and repression of the civilian population until they no longer dare support the opposition, and by making them so destitute that they are unable to provide any material support. In other words, undermine the opposition by directly attacking the civilians who support them, often referred to as 'draining the ocean so the fish cannot swim'.

The Four Cuts have been official policy since the early 1970's, but the present State Peace and Development Council (SPDC) military junta has made their implementation much more systematic than ever before. Using military offensives and large-scale forced relocations, the junta has managed to force many of the ethnic resistance groups into military ceasefires which do not address any political or human rights issues. However, several resistance groups continue to fight, particularly in Karen, Karenni (Kayah) and Shan States. In these areas, the junta's main tactic is now mass forced relocations of the civilian population. In the past forced relocation was used as a military tactic but only on a localised scale, a few villages at a time; however, in 1996 the junta began delineating regions where any form of resistance occurs, and forcing hundreds of villages at a time to move to Army-controlled sites. Between 1996 and the present, at least 1,500 villages in central Shan State have been ordered to move and destroyed, affecting at least 300,000 people; since 1997, 200 villages covering the entire map of Karenni (Kayah) State have been forced out and burned; since 1997, close to 200 villages in Papun and Nyaunglebin Districts of northern Karen State have been shelled and burned without warning, driving the population into hiding in the forest; between 1996 and 1997 over 100 villages in southern Tenasserim Division were forced out and destroyed, followed by a mass military offensive which is still destroying more villages now; and since December 1999 the SPDC has ordered that over 100 villages throughout Dooplaya District of central Karen State hand over their entire rice harvest to the Army and then move to Army-controlled sites or face being shot on sight. In hill villages throughout Karen State, villagers are now being ordered to move into the 'centre' of their villages, meaning they cannot stay near their fields, and are only allowed to leave the village between dawn and dusk under threat of being shot if they are out after curfew. This disrupts the entire crop cycle, because villagers are used to staying in field huts far from the village for much of the growing season to do all of the intensive labour which is required. Many of them find that they can no longer produce their own food.

Many of the villages ordered to move do not even have any contact with opposition groups, but they fall within an area where the SPDC believes the opposition can operate. The villagers are usually given no more than a week to move, after which they are told their homes and belongings will be destroyed and they will be shot on sight if seen around their villages. After the relocation deadline the Army usually sends out patrols to destroy the villages, and particularly to hunt out and destroy any food supplies. The villagers are usually ordered to move out of the hills, to larger Army-controlled villages or sites along roads. They have to bring their own food and building supplies because nothing is given to them; in many cases they even have to hand over their rice to the Army and have it rationed back out to them day by day. Once in the relocation site, people have few or no opportunities to return to their fields and must survive by foraging for food or looking for local day labour. At the same time, the Army uses them as a convenient source of unpaid forced labour at local Army camps and along the roads, making it almost impossible for them to support themselves. After a few months, many people find they have little option but to starve or flee.

These days most people know what awaits them at the relocation sites, so when they are ordered to move they simply flee into hiding in the forests surrounding their farmfields. They then try to survive from hidden rice supplies around their villages, planting small patches of crops in several different places and fleeing from place to place whenever SPDC Army patrols come around. Tens of thousands of people are presently living this way in central Shan State, throughout Karenni (Kayah) State, in Toungoo, Papun and Nyaunglebin districts of northern Karen State and eastern Pegu Division, and Tenasserim Division of southern Burma. They have little food and many are starving, there is no access to medicines and many die of treatable diseases, their children have no access to education of any kind, and they live under the constant risk of being captured or shot by passing SPDC patrols who also seek out and destroy their food supplies and crops in the fields. Many of them have been living this way for two to three years already. Eventually, finding they can no longer survive this way, a steady stream of them try to make their way to the border with Thailand to become refugees.

This desperate lack of options is most clearly reflected by the statements of villagers included in the **'Death Squads and Displacement'** chapter below. In the remote hills of eastern Nyaunglebin District, villages have been shelled and burned without warning and villagers hiding in the forests are hunted on sight. In the western plains of the district, which are close to the Sittaung River and under SPDC control, the villages have been forced into relocation sites where nothing is provided, and the SPDC has created new execution squads which have been systematically killing any villagers who have ever helped the opposition in the slightest way. As a result, villagers from the western plains flee into the hills, while villagers in the hills are themselves fleeing into the forests or toward Thailand - a trip that involves passing through northern Papun District, where even more villages have been systematically destroyed and the situation is equally as bad.

Forced relocation is not the only thing ripping the villages apart. Even in villages which have not been forced to move it has become almost impossible to survive. Village leaders living in conflict areas have described their lives as 'standing in a leaky boat which is being rocked from both sides'. They are forced to support opposition armies, such as the Karen National Liberation Army (KNLA), the Karenni National Progressive Party (KNPP), or the Shan State Army (SSA), with food, porters and recruits, and then they are severely punished for this by the SPDC Army. While most of the villagers support the aims of the opposition, they find it difficult to provide material support and they often ask local guerrilla commanders not to attack the SPDC in their area, because whenever SPDC columns are ambushed they respond by torturing the elders and burning homes in the nearest villages, accusing them of not providing sufficient intelligence. The dilemma facing village elders in this situation exists in all of the regions covered in the later sections of this book, but is perhaps most clear in the voices of villagers from Thaton District included in the section **"Caught in the Middle"**, because the SPDC is largely in control there. A typical SPDC written order sent by Infantry Battalion #26 to a Karen village in a similar area of Toungoo district in 1999 reads, *"do not give paddy, rice or 'set kyay ngwe' [protection money] to the enemy. [We] will burn and relocate the villages who give these. [We] will decree them to be hard core."*[6] However, villages have no choice but to provide these things, and they constantly face retaliations by SPDC commanders for it. At the same time, it must be said that the opposition armies do not engage in the brutal abuses of the SPDC Army, and when the worst abuses are occurring the villagers often flee to the opposition troops for some form of protection.

---

[6]   See **"SPDC and DKBA Orders to Villages: Set 2000-A"**, Karen Human Rights Group, February 2000, Order #3, available on the KHRG web site (www.khrg.org)

Landmines have become an added threat to villagers, particularly over the past 3 to 4 years. In Karen State, landmines are now being laid heavily by at least 3 groups: the SPDC, the KNLA, and the Democratic Karen Buddhist Army (a Karen splinter group allied to the SPDC). None of the mines are mapped, and though the KNLA tells the villagers which pathways are mined the information often doesn't get to everyone. Most of the casualties are villagers, particularly because of the SPDC practice of using villagers to march in front of their columns as human minesweepers and human shields against ambush. This form of abuse is on the rise in central Karen State, and many SPDC columns are specifically choosing to use women and children for it. According to research done by Non-Violence International for the September 2000 Landmine Monitor (the publication of the International Campaign to Ban Landmines), the estimated number of landmine casualties in Karen State rose in 1999 to well over 1,000, more than the reported landmine casualties for all of Cambodia during the same time period. With landmine use increasing every month, Burma is beginning to be seen as Asia's new landmine hotspot. On the ground, this is reflected in the testimony of villagers, many of whom say that the main thing making them flee their villages was fear of being taken by the SPDC to clear mines. Pa'an District of central Karen State is now one of the most heavily mined areas in all of Burma, and this is reflected in the feelings of villagers from the area recorded below in the chapter **"Beyond All Endurance"**; a few years ago, villagers interviewed from this area knew little or nothing of landmines, but now the issue permeates their consciousness and their fears.

Even this is only another factor in a whole range of suffering which combines to make life in villages impossible. In conflict areas, villagers face daily or weekly demands from all of the SPDC Army camps and mobile patrols in their area. At any given time, a village has to provide an average of one person per household for a whole range of forced labour: forced porters, guides and human minesweepers for military columns, messengers and sentries for Army camps, building and maintaining Army camp fences, trenches, booby-traps, and barracks, cutting and hauling firewood, cooking and carrying water to soldiers, building and rebuilding military supply roads, clearing scrub along roadsides to minimise the possibility of ambush, standing sentry along military supply roads, growing crops for the Army on confiscated land, and engaging in profit-making activities for the officers such as brick-baking, rubber planting or digging fishponds. Every Army unit demands most of these things from the surrounding villages, and every village is surrounded by three, four or five Army units. The forced labour is usually demanded on a rotating basis; a specified number of villagers must go for a day or a week with all their own food and tools, and they are not released until their replacements arrive for the next shift. Nothing is provided for them, and they often have to work under guard. Conditions for porters are especially brutal; forced to carry loads of rations or ammunition weighing 30 kg / 60 lb or more, they are marched in front of soldiers to detonate mines and kicked or beaten if they are too slow. If they become ill or cannot continue they are killed or left behind, and many porters die either during portering or afterwards, from disease complicated by physical exhaustion and malnutrition.

In addition, mobile patrols often grab farmers on sight in their fields or in the villages to be porters or to do forced labour at the local Army camps. Because of this, villagers usually run as soon as they see an Army patrol coming - and the Army considers anyone who runs as a rebel and immediately opens fire on them. To avoid forced labour, the village men in many conflict areas leave the village to stay in hiding in their field huts or in the forest while the women, children and the elderly remain behind in the village to protect the house from looting by soldiers and to carry on some semblance of family life. The men only sneak back into the village for food and to visit when SPDC patrols are not around. This system makes the women particularly vulnerable, because SPDC patrols arriving at the village often rape them on seeing that the men are not around. In the absence of men, they often take the women as porters, or accuse them of being married to 'rebel soldiers' and hold them hostage pending the return of their husbands.

In northern Karen State some villages in conflict areas have tried to appease the SPDC by making their own 'peace' agreements; they promise to abide by all SPDC demands and not contact the resistance if their village is not forced to move. They are subsequently labelled 'peace' villages, but even in these villages the demands for forced labour, money, food and materials usually become so intense that the village elders cannot keep up with them all. They are then arrested and tortured for failure to comply, houses are sometimes burned and many villagers flee just as though there had never been any agreement.

Abuses in the Non-Conflict Areas

It is a common misconception to think that forced labour and other abuses only occur in Burma's conflict areas. Many people are finding that they cannot survive in their villages even in areas where there is no opposition activity at all. As explained above, the SPDC tries to control the life of every civilian with its Army, so the non-conflict areas have almost as many Army units as the conflict areas.   With the rapid expansion of the Army in recent years to its current strength of over 400,000 troops, villagers who have never seen fighting now find their villages surrounded by 3 or 4 Army camps within one or two hours' walking distance. The officers in these camps see the civilian population as little more than a convenient pool of forced labourers and a source of profit.   Villages receive a constant stream of orders demanding their forced labour as Army camp servants, messengers and sentries, cutting and hauling building materials for camp construction, building and maintaining the camp.   They are also taken as porters, because even where there is no fighting the Army still needs people to haul rations and supplies from roadheads to hilltop Army camps, or from the Battalion bases to faraway outposts in the middle of conflict areas.

Where they are in complete control, the SPDC also uses villagers as forced labour to improve the road networks and build infrastructure such as railways and hydro dams.   Conditions on such projects can be brutal, with one person per family demanded on rotating one or two week shifts; in rainy season the adults have to work the fields, so the children often have to go and work in dangerous conditions with frequent mudslides. Once completed, the power from these dams goes only to the Army camps and to businessmen who can pay off the Army, while the villagers are often forbidden to take their bullock carts on the roads they have built with their own labour.   The roads, usually only dirt, are badly engineered by Army officers and wash out every monsoon season, causing many villagers to refer to the period November to January as 'road building season', when they are forced to rebuild the roads each year.

For Army officers, a posting in the countryside is an opportunity to make a great deal of personal profit in a short time.   Officers in areas where there is no opposition usually occupy themselves by ordering villagers to cut logs and bamboo, claiming it is for the Army camp but then selling it on the market for personal profit.   Other such schemes include forcing villagers as well as rank and file soldiers to bake bricks or dig and maintain fish ponds.   All profit goes to the officers, who also confiscate most of the rations intended for their soldiers and approximately half of the soldiers' pay in the name of various 'fees' and 'contributions', then sell the rations on the market and tell the soldiers to get their food from the villages.   This situation has become even worse since 1998, when the SPDC in Rangoon cut back severely on rations to units in the field and ordered them to produce more of their own food or take it from the farmers.   The result has been the systematic confiscation of much of the best farmland by Army units. The farmers are not paid any compensation; worse yet, they are called out for forced labour farming their confiscated land, from planting to harvesting, and the officers then take the entire harvest. Some villages report that they even have to provide the seed for planting these fields.

In addition to forced labour, villagers face constant demands for cash, food and materials from every SPDC Army unit in their area. On average, a family must hand over anywhere from 100 to 3,000 Kyat per month to the Army in cash as extortion which masquerades under the names of 'porter fees', 'servants' fees', 'development fees', 'pagoda fees', and so on. In theory, this money is supposed to be used to hire people for forced labour or to support projects in the area, but in reality it is pocketed by the officers and forced labourers are not paid. Villagers must also pay to avoid forced labour when they are ill or cannot go, at rates of 100-1,000 Kyat per day of labour missed. Cash is very hard to come by for most subsistence farmers in rural Burma because they do not operate in a cash-based economy, but if they do not pay these fees they are arrested. Every farmer in areas firmly controlled by the SPDC must also hand over a quota of every crop to the SPDC authorities for next to nothing. Usually this quota amounts to approximately 30% of the entire crop, but after the farmer deducts the portion of his harvest required for seed stocks, payments in rice for previous loans, use of other villagers' buffaloes to plough, etc., the quota amounts to 50% or more of what is left. Quotas have been increasing in recent years, and no exceptions are made for bad crop years such as the disasters caused by droughts and floods in 1997 and 1998. The farmers often have no option but to buy rice on the market to fulfil the quota in such years, while the family goes hungry. The price paid for quota is less than half of market price, but corrupt SPDC officials take out so many 'deductions' for themselves that the farmers usually receive no more than 10-20% of market price for quota rice. Even with little or no rice left to feed their families, the farmers still face regular demands for rice and meat to feed the local Army camps, and armed patrols often enter villages to loot rice, livestock and valuables.

The SPDC provides very few social services in the villages which it controls. In some villages it sanctions the construction of a primary or middle school, but usually it is the villagers who must pay the cost of building it as well as the salary of the state-supplied teacher. More remote villages usually cannot afford to do this, so many have opened their own primary-level schools with their own volunteer teachers. Since the beginning of 1999, the SPDC military has been ordering the closing of many of these village primary schools in areas such as Pa'an and Thaton districts of Karen State, telling the villagers that only state-sanctioned schools are allowed. Many villagers cannot afford to send their children to state schools, however, and they also complain that in the state schools the teaching of languages such as Karen, Mon, Kayah, or Shan is strictly forbidden, causing children to grow up illiterate in their mother tongue. As a result, fewer and fewer children in the rural areas of Karen State have any opportunity for education. The same applies to rural medical clinics. Even in places where the regime has allocated some funds for the establishment of some basic social services, the local military and SPDC authorities use these services as an excuse to extort even more money from the villagers by force, usually amounting to several times the worth of the services being provided.

Even where schools are available, many children are pulled out of school as soon as they are big enough to work because of all of the demands for labour and money which their families have to face. Families sell their valuables to pay the SPDC fees and pay to avoid forced labour so that they can work in their fields or do day labour to make money. However, there are so many fees that the money does not last long, and many families send small children to do the forced labour so that the adults can still work the fields. Eventually they sell all of their belongings and livestock to pay all of the fees, and when they are still ordered to go for forced labour or pay money they have no option but to flee the village or face arrest, torture and possible summary execution. Trials are not held in rural areas, villagers are simply tied up and taken to Army camps where they are held in mediaeval-style leg stocks or pits in the ground, tortured and interrogated until the Army officer decides what to do with them. They are often held for ransom, held for months under torture without charge, or simply executed without any record existing of their arrest. To avoid this, villagers in areas all over Burma have fled to the towns where they become beggars or cheap labour, to the hills, or to neighbouring countries.

The overall result is that the subsistence farming village, the basic unit of society throughout all of rural Burma, is losing its viability under military control. The classic image of internally displaced people and refugees is that they have fled military battles in and around their villages, but this is far from the case in Burma. In thousands of interviews conducted by the Karen Human Rights Group since 1992 with villagers who have fled their homes, approximately 95% say they have not fled military battles, but rather the systematic destruction of their ability to survive caused by demands and retaliations inflicted on them unilaterally by the SPDC military. When they do have to flee fighting it is only for a day or two, because the war in Burma is a fluid, hit-and-run affair which villagers can dodge by hiding for short periods in the forest. However, once the SPDC occupies the area around their village the suffering is inescapable. The village, rooted as it is to the land, is just too defenceless and vulnerable. It can be forced out to work, looted, retaliated against, all with complete impunity.

Loss of Hope: The People and the Army

The population has largely lost hope and sees almost no way out of the present situation. In the urban and central Burman areas, people are too afraid to make any move to oust the regime because of the massacres they know would result. In the ethnic nationality regions, the opposition groups can no longer offer protection to the villagers, who cannot see any way to organise against the regime and see no option but to flee the SPDC Army whenever it is around. Anywhere from 2 to 4 million people are internally displaced in Burma, at least 1 million of these in the ethnic nationality areas, surviving in hiding in the forests or as beggars in the towns. Approximately 110,000 Karen and Karenni refugees are registered in camps in Thailand, with more arriving each week. An estimated 800,000 to 1 million additional refugees and economic migrants are scattered throughout Thailand in the illegal labour market. The entire situation in Burma is clearly unsustainable, but the regime absolutely refuses to lessen its grip on power in any way and there is no way of knowing for how long this situation can continue.

The Army, known as the *Tatmadaw*, has no real ideology and no constituency within the society that supports its rule, but it appears to have been successful in entrenching its rule more than ever before by entrenching fear and hopelessness in the minds of the people. Even its junior and mid-level officers work mainly only for purposes of their own power or wealth, or because being an Army officer is one of the few viable careers in today's Burma. As for the rank and file soldiers, many are conscripted in forced lotteries, while others are coerced or misled into believing that the Army provides an escape from personal trouble or protection for their families. Once in the Army, they are dragged into the cycle of human rights abuses by officers who force them to take their food from the villagers and round up forced labourers or be punished. Even after years in the Army, they are not allowed to leave unless they round up 5 or 10 new recruits, which they do by coercing young boys they find at the markets and schools. As a result, most of the recruits to the Burmese Army are underage.

Though the SPDC junta has very few supporters within the population or even within its own Army, it is a mistake to pretend that the leaders of the SPDC junta are outsiders or aliens with no connection to the society in which they live. They may be deluded, but they did spring from Burmese society and they have succeeded in gaining and holding power over it. Essentially, their power is rooted in the deep racism that has permeated Burmese society since its beginnings; not only the racial supremacy complex which many Burmans are brought up with, but the racism of the Karen against the Burmans, the Burmans against the Shan, the Shan against the Wa, the Wa against the Shan, the Mon against the Burmans, the Rakhine against the Rohingyas, the Burmans against the Chinese, the Christians against the Buddhists, and everyone against the Muslims. The list goes on and on, and the military has always exploited it to turn people against each other and thereby increase its power. SPDC propaganda encourages a blind racist nationalism, full of references to 'protecting the race', meaning that if Burmans do not oppress other nationalities then they will themselves be oppressed, 'national reconsolidation', meaning assimilation, and preventing 'disintegration of the Union', meaning that if the Army falls then some kind of ethnic chaos would ensue. The non-Burman political groups are frequently just as guilty, relentlessly persecuting racial, regional and religious minorities within their own populations while demonising the Burmans, thereby preventing the very understanding among peoples which is so necessary to bring an end to military rule. A transition to democracy alone will not be enough to prevent the people tearing each other apart, particularly if it is a unitary, non-federal democracy. The first and biggest step in bringing about an end to the racism problem is to admit that it exists and to recognise its scale, but sadly there appear to be few people on any side of the struggle today who are willing to do so. Until they are, Burma will remain a country at war with itself.

•

Suggested further reading

Aung San Suu Kyi (1991) "Freedom From Fear and Other Writings", London: Penguin Books, 338 pages
A collection of writings by Aung San Suu Kyi.

Aye Saung (2000) "Burman in the Back Row: Autobiography of a Burmese Rebel", Hong Kong: Asia, 296 pages (First edition Bangkok: White Lotus, 1989)
The autobiography of a Burmese rebel who spent several years in the 1970s and early 1980s with Communist-affiliated organisations as well as the Shan State Army.

Cady, John F. (1958) "A History of Modern Burma", Ithaca and London: Cornell University Press, 682 pages
A comprehensive look at Burmese history.

Lehman, Frederick K. (1981) "Military rule in Burma since 1962", Singapore: Maruzen Asia, 83 pages
Six essays on modern Burma.

Lintner, Bertil (1990) "Land of Jade: a Journey through Insurgent Burma" Edinburgh: Kiscadale Publications; Bangkok: White Lotus, 315 pages
An account of an 18-month trek, from Oct. 1985 to April 1987, through rebel-held areas in Sagaing Division, Kachin State and Shan State.

Lintner, Bertil (1990) "Outrage: Burma's Struggle for Democracy", London: White Lotus UK, 208 pages
Detailed account of the 1988 uprisings.

Lintner, Bertil (2000) "Burma in Revolt: Opium and Insurgency Since 1948", Chiang Mai: Silkworm Books, 558 pages (First edition: Westview, Boulder, Colorado, 1994. 515 pages)
Political history of Burma since World War 2, with particular focus on north and northeastern Burma and the effects of the drug trade on events.

Morrison, Ian (1946) "Grandfather Longlegs", London: Faber and Faber
Account of the situation in Karen State under the Japanese occupation, based around the life of Major H.P. Seagrim, a British officer who stayed with the Karen through the war and was executed by the Japanese in 1944. Written in 1946, gives a good view of the real situation during the

war including BIA atrocities against civilians and the life of villagers under the occupation.

Owen, Frank (1974) "The Campaign in Burma", Dehra Dun: Natraj Publishers, 165 pages
An account of the Allied campaign to recapture Burma from the Japanese.

Peers, William R. & Brelis, Dean (1963) "Behind the Burma Road: The Story of America's Most Successful Guerrilla Force", Boston: Little, Brown and Company, 246 pages
About Detachment 101 and the US-trained Kachin guerrillas during World War Two.

San C. Po, Dr. (1928) "Burma and the Karens", London: Elliot Stock, 94 pages
Written by a prominent, pro-British Karen who argues that the Karens need a country of their own.

Selth, Andrew (1996) "Transforming the Tatmadaw: The Burmese Armed Forces since 1988", Canberra: Australian National University, Strategic and Defence Studies Centre, 207 pages
An account of the expansion of Burma's armed forces since the 1988 pro-democracy uprising.

Silverstein, Josef (1977) "Burma: Military Rule and the Politics of Stagnation", Ithaca and London: Cornell University Press, 224 pages
An introduction to modern Burmese politics.

Slim, William Joseph (Field-Marshal - Viscount) (1986) "Defeat into Victory", London: Papermac, 576 pages (First edition London: Cassell, 1956)
An account of the British campaigns in Burma in World War Two, by one of the British commanding officers.

Smith, Martin (1999) "Burma: Insurgency and the Politics of Ethnicity", Bangkok: White Lotus / London: Zed Books
Detailed reference on Burmese political development particularly since World War 2.

Smith-Dun, Gen. (1980) "Memoirs of the Four-Foot Colonel", Ithaca, New York: Cornell University Southeast Asia Programme, data paper no. 113, 126 pages

A history of the Karens by the first chief of the Burma Army, a Karen himself.

Yawnghwe, Chao Tzang (1987) "The Shan of Burma. Memoirs of a Shan Exile", Singapore: Institute of Southeast Asian Studies, 276 pages
A study of the Shans, their history and rebellion against Rangoon.

Yegar, Moshe (1972) "The Muslims of Burma", Wiesbaden: Otto Harrassowitz, 151 pages
A history of Burma's various Muslim communities.

Map of Karen Districts

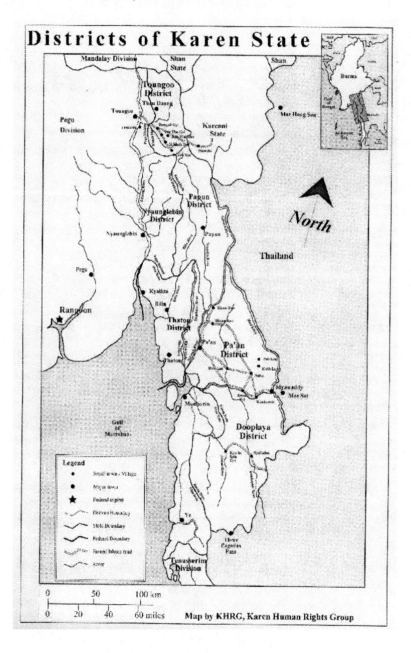

Terms and Abbreviations

Bowl/Pyi	Volume of rice equal to 8 small condensed milk tins; about 2 kilograms / 4.4 pounds
DKBA	Democratic Karen Buddhist Army, Karen group allied with SLORC/SPDC
IB	Infantry Battalion (SLORC/SPDC), usually about 500 soldiers fighting strength
Kaw Thoo Lei	The Karen homeland, also used as slang for KNU/KNLA
KNLA	Karen National Liberation Army, army of the KNU
KNU	Karen National Union, main Karen opposition group
Kyat	Burmese currency; US$1=6 Kyat at official rate, 300+ Kyat at current market rate
LIB	Light Infantry Battalion (SLORC/SPDC), usually about 500 soldiers fighting strength
loh ah pay	Forced labour; literally it means traditional voluntary labour, but not under SPDC
nga pway	'Ringworm'; derogatory SPDC slang for KNU/KNLA people
PDC	Peace & Development Council, SPDC local-level administration (e.g. Village PDC [VPDC], Village Tract PDC, Township PDC [TPDC])
set tha	Forced labour as messengers and errand-boys
SPDC	State Peace & Development Council, military junta ruling Burma
SLORC	State Law & Order Restoration Council, former name of the SPDC until Nov. 1997
T'Bee Met	'Closed-eyes'; DKBA slang for KNU/KNLA people
Viss	Unit of weight measure; one viss is 1.6 kilograms or 3.5 pounds

('Some details in the text below have been omitted or replaced by 'xxxx' where necessary to protect villagers.)

PART I

DEATH SQUADS AND DISPLACEMENT

Systematic Executions, Village
Destruction and the Flight of Villagers
in Nyaunglebin District

An Independent Report by the
Karen Human Rights Group (May 24, 1999)

Abstract

This report is a detailed analysis of the current human rights situation in Nyaunglebin District (known in Karen as Kler Lweh Htoo), which straddles the border of northern Karen State and Pegu Division in Burma.Most of the villagers here are Karen, though there are also many Burmans living in the villages near the Sittaung River. Since late 1998 many Karens and Burmans have been fleeing their villages in the area because of human rights abuses by the State Peace & Development Council (SPDC) military junta which currently rules Burma, and this flight is still ongoing. Those from the hills which cover most of the District are fleeing because SPDC troops have been systematically destroying their villages, crops and food supplies and shooting villagers on sight, all in an effort to undermine the Karen National Liberation Army (KNLA) by driving the civilian population out of the region. At the same time, people in the plains near the Sittaung River are fleeing because of the ever-increasing burden of forced labour, cash extortion, and heavy crop quotas which are being levied against them even though their crops have failed for the past two years running. Many are also fleeing a frightening new phenomenon in the District: the Sa Thon Lon Guerrilla Retaliation units, which appeared in September 1998 and since then have been systematically executing everyone suspected of even the remotest contact with the opposition forces, even if that contact occurred years or decades ago. Their methods are brutal, their tactics are designed to induce fear, and they have executed anywhere from 50 to over 100 civilians in the District since September 1998.

In order to produce this report, KHRG human rights researchers have interviewed over 50 villagers in the SPDC-controlled areas, in the hill villages, in hiding in the forests and those who have fled to Thailand to become refugees. Their testimonies have been augmented by incident reports gathered by KHRG human rights researchers in the region. The interviews were conducted between December 1998 and May 1999, with the exception of one interview from September 1998. Several interviews were also conducted with villagers who fled Tantabin township of southern Toungoo District in April 1999, because their testimony indicates that the Sa Thon Lon execution units are now operating there as well. KHRG would like to thank the human rights section of the Federated Trade Unions of Burma (FTUB), which contributed interviews #11 and #35. Photographs which relate to the situation described in this report can be seen in KHRG Photo Set 99-A (March 1, 1999) [http://metalab.unc.edu/freeburma/humanrights/khrg/archive/photoreport s/99photos/set99a/index.html]. Some of them are reproduced below. For

additional background see "Wholesale Destruction: The SLORC/SPDC
Campaign to Obliterate all Hill Villages in Papun and Eastern
Nyaunglebin Districts" (KHRG#98-01, April 1998) [http://metalab.unc.
edu/freeburma/humanrights/khrg/archive/khrg98/khrg9801.html].

This report consists of this preface, an introduction, and a detailed
description of the situation including quotes from interviews. In the
appendix is reproduced a list of 151 civilians killed directly by regular
SPDC troops and Sa Thon Lon units since 1997. The KHRG web site
contains an index listing and summarising the interviews used in the
report. The full text of the interviews and field reports upon which the
report is based is also available from KHRG.

Map of Nyaunglebin District

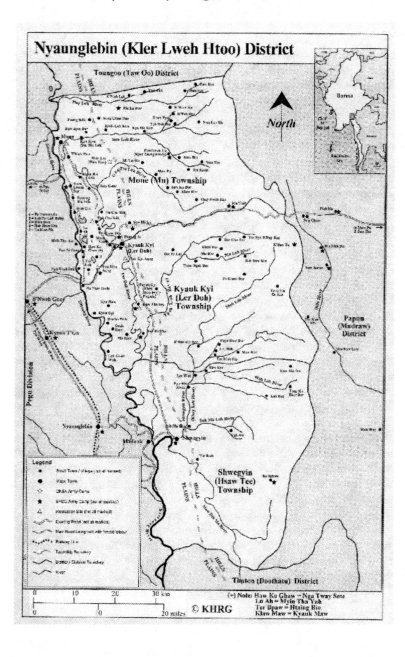

Notes on the Text

In the text all names of those interviewed have been changed and some details have been omitted where necessary to protect people from retaliation. The captions under the quotes used in the situation report include the interviewee's (changed) name, gender, age and village, and a reference to the interview or field report number. These numbers can be used to find the description or full text of the interview or field report in the Interview Index (on the KHRG web site) and the Annex (presently only available by request from KHRG).

The text often refers to villages, village tracts and townships. The SPDC has local administration, called Peace & Development Councils, at the village, village tract, township, and state/division levels. A village tract is a group of 5-25 villages centred on a large village. A township is a much larger area, administered from a central town. The Karen National Union (KNU) divides Nyaunglebin (Kler Lweh Htoo) District into three townships: Shwegyin (Karen name Hsaw Tee) in the south, Kyauk Kyi (Karen name Ler Doh) in the centre, and Mone (Karen name Mu) in the north. Reference is also made to Kyauk T'Ga and Pyu townships, which lie west of the Sittaung River, and Tantabin township, which is just to the north in Toungoo District. The official townships used by the SPDC do not correspond to the Karen townships; in this report we have used the townships as defined by the Karen, though usually referring to them by their more familiar Burmese names. The SPDC does not recognise the existence of Nyaunglebin District, but only uses Townships, States and Divisions. In this region many villages have both a Karen and a Burmese name, and where necessary this is clarified in the text.

In the interviews villagers often refer to '*loh ah pay*'; literally this is the traditional Burmese form of voluntary labour for the community, but the SPDC uses this name in most cases of forced labour, and to the villagers it has come to mean most forms of forced labour with the exception of long-term portering. Villagers, particularly those in the hills, do not keep track of dates or ages, and as a result sometimes different people give different dates for an event or different ages for the people involved. Wherever possible KHRG has attempted to establish and indicate the most accurate dates and ages possible. All numeric dates in this report are in dd/mm/yy format.

Introduction

Nyaunglebin District (known in Karen as Kler Lweh Htoo) is one of the northern Karen districts, straddling the border of Karen State and Pegu Division (see maps at the end of the book). It covers an area about 110 kilometres from north to south and averaging 40 kilometres from east to west, bounded by the Sittaung River in the west and the upper reaches of the Bilin River in the east. To the north lies Toungoo District, to the south Thaton District, to the east Papun District, and to the west the heartland of Pegu Division and the Pegu Yoma hills. The District is divided into three townships: Shwegyin (Hsaw Tee in Karen) in the south, Kyauk Kyi (Ler Doh) in the centre, and Mone (Mu) in the north. The District itself is a Karen designation dating back to colonial times; the SPDC regime no longer recognises districts, only townships and States/Divisions.

The westernmost part of the district is a narrow strip of fertile plains which form part of the Sittaung River valley. Just 10 to 15 kilometres east of the river itself, the hills abruptly begin and cover the eastern 75% of the district. Villages in the western plains tend to be larger and more prosperous, and have a mixed population of Karens and Burmans. Some villages are unofficially divided into a 'Karen section' and a 'Burman section', while in other places one village is entirely Karen and the next village up the road is entirely Burman. Because of the easy terrain, the proximity to central Burma and the roads which already run between Shwegyin, Kyauk Kyi and Mone, this area has been strongly controlled by the SLORC/SPDC military for a long time. As soon as you enter the hills to the east the situation is different; the population is almost 100% Karen, life is harder and based more on shifting hillside rice cultivation instead of flat paddy fields, and there are no vehicle roads except one which goes eastward from Kyauk Kyi into Papun District. Villages are more numerous but smaller than in the plains, averaging only 10 to 30 households in size. In these hills the Karen National Liberation Army [KNLA] is very active in guerrilla operations, and neither the SPDC nor the KNU/KNLA exerts strong control.

Finding itself unable to suppress Karen resistance activity in the hills, in early 1997 the SPDC (then named SLORC) began a campaign to wipe out all Karen civilian villages there. Where villagers could be found they were ordered to relocate westward into the plains; where they could not be caught, their villages were shelled without warning, looted and then burned to the ground, while villagers found afterwards were shot on sight. In 1997 KHRG compiled a list of 35 villages in Shwegyin (Hsaw

Tee) township alone which had been completely destroyed [for this and other details of the 1997 campaign see "Wholesale Destruction", KHRG #98-01, April 1998] [http://metalab.unc.edu/freeburma/humanrights/ khrg/archive/khrg98/khrg9801.html]. A similar number of villages were destroyed in Kyauk Kyi township. Most villagers fled into the hills to live in hiding in small groups of families while trying to grow small patches of rice, and many others moved westward as ordered into SPDC garrison villages in the plains, or to stay with relatives in the comparative safety of larger villages.

Many of those who fled to the plains found they could not survive there; they had no land to plant and there was little work to be found, because villagers in the plains were suffering heavily under the heavy extortion fees and crop quotas imposed by the SPDC military and civilian authorities. At the same time, the hill villagers found they were being used as forced labour by the SPDC much more in the plains, both at Army camps and on local infrastructure projects. Unable to survive under these conditions, many have fled back to their home villages in the hills, only to find that the clampdown on the hill areas is continuing. In most cases the hill villages have not been rebuilt because SPDC patrols continue to move through the area destroying whatever structures they find, destroying rice stockpiles and crops in the fields, shooting livestock and shooting villagers on sight. Those living in the hills and those who have returned from the plains have no choice but to live in hiding in small groups, usually near their home villages or their old hill fields. They try to grow small crops, forage for food in the forest and flee further into the hills whenever SPDC patrols come near.

At the same time, something is happening which has never occurred to such a large extent before: an increasing number of villagers native to the Sittaung River plains, both Karen and Burman, are fleeing eastward into the hills, and some are fleeing southward along the main road through Pegu and Kyaikto, then eastward to the Thai border. In the past the prosperity of the Sittaung valley villages has always made it possible for them to survive even under the burden of SLORC/SPDC demands for extortion money and forced labour, but things have changed in the past two years. The SPDC has increased its military presence in the area in an attempt to increase its control in the hills to the east, and these troops are placing ever-increasing demands for extortion money, crop quotas and forced labour on the civilians. The SPDC in Rangoon is no longer sending them full rations and has ordered them to grow their own food or take it from the villagers; as a result, not only are they taking food from the villagers, but they are also taking their land and forcing them to work to grow food for the Army. At the same time, crop quotas which all farmers must hand over to the SPDC have increased and the corruption of the civilian authorities who collect the crop quotas has grown worse. The farmers might be able to survive this in good years, but most of them have suffered partial or complete crop failures for the past two years running due to droughts when they need rain, followed by floods once the crop is planted. The combination of the crop failures and the increased demands has made it impossible to survive. As though this were not enough, many have found they have to flee a new SPDC force which has been introduced in the area: the Sa Thon Lon Guerrilla Retaliation death squads.

The Sa Sa Sa, or Sa Thon Lon, is the Bureau of Special Investigations of the SPDC's Directorate of Defence Services Intelligence (DDSI), and its Guerrilla Retaliation squads have been handpicked from Battalions based in the region, reportedly under the direct orders of DDSI chief Lt. Gen. Khin Nyunt. They began operations in the region in or around September 1998, and currently operate in the plains area east of the Sittaung River, covering Shwegyin, Kyauk Kyi and Mone townships. The Guerrilla Retaliation squads operate secretively in small groups, but with a clearly stated purpose: to execute without question everyone suspected of any present or past connection with the KNU or KNLA, regardless of how long ago or how slight that connection may have been. Their obvious purpose is to deliver a message to villagers that any contact whatsoever with resistance forces will be punishable by death, if not now then 10 or 20 years from now. They have already executed dozens of villagers both in the plains and the hills, both Karens and Burmans, guilty and innocent, and the terror they create is now driving many to flee their villages even if they have had no contact with the opposition. Recently they have expanded their operations northward into Tantabin township of southern Toungoo District, and they have also begun searching for people on the western side of the Sittaung River. This combined with all the other forms of oppression the villagers are suffering has driven them beyond their endurance, and villages in the plains as well as the hills are now breaking up.

Armies in the Region

In addition to the Sa Thon Lon Guerrilla Retaliation units (which are described in greater detail below), SPDC Battalions operating in the plains and hills of the region include Infantry Battalions #26, 30, 35, 39, 48, 53, 57, 59, 60, and 73, Light Infantry Battalions #264, 349, 350, 351, 361, 362, 364, 365, 368, 369, 439, and 440.

Some of these Battalions are operating as part of Light Infantry Division #77, and some are operating under Strategic Commands #1, 2, and 3; these Strategic Commands have been set up in the area with 2 to 3 Battalions each. All of the regular SPDC troops in the area are under orders of the Southern Regional Command (Ta Pa Ka in Burmese), which is based in Pegu and commanded by Brigadier General Tin Aye. Each SPDC Battalion has approximate fighting strength of 500 troops, though some Battalions operate in several areas so not all of these are employed within the district. Some of their camps and outposts throughout the district are at Mone, Ma La Daw, Gawlawah Lu (Kyet Taung Mway), Aung Laung Say, Thaung Bo, Saw Mi Lu, Mu Theh, Kyauk Kyi, Yan Myo Aung, K'Baw Tu, Kaw Tha Say, Baw Ka Hta, Ko Sghaw, and Shwegyin. Troops from various Battalions are regularly rotated in and out of these camps, and mobile columns also head up from the plains into the hills, using existing camps in the hills as temporary bases or setting up their own temporary bases in and around villages.

The Democratic Karen Buddhist Army (DKBA) is not a significant force in the region, but it has two camps at Payah Gyi in Kyauk Kyi township and Maw Lay (Plaw Haw) in Mone township. In total there are reportedly just under 100 DKBA soldiers in the district under the command of Battalion Commander Po Maung from DKBA Brigade 777. About 50 of these troops are at Payah Gyi, where Po Maung is based, and the remainder at Maw Lay are under the command of Bo Law Plah. The DKBA troops are mainly involved in reconstructing the old Klaw Maw pagoda near Payah Gyi, as well as pagodas at Maw Lay and Kyun Gyi. They also sometimes work together with the SPDC troops on operations. More details on their activities are included below under 'KNLA and DKBA Activities'.

Nyaunglebin District is often referred to as KNLA 3rd Brigade area, and the Karen National Liberation Army (KNLA) is very active here. The 3rd Brigade consists of Battalions #7, 8, and 9; numbers are difficult to confirm, but there appear to be several hundred KNLA troops. These troops no longer firmly control territory in the district, but they hold de facto control over some parts of the hills and engage in extensive harrassment and guerrilla operations. SPDC troops usually do not dare penetrate too far into the hills except in large columns, and when this happens the KNLA and the villagers in hiding clear out of their way until they are gone, then reemerge. In the past the KNLA operated extensively in the plains to the west as well, but while they still make regular forays around the villages on the edge of the plains, they cannot operate as freely as before.

The Sa Thon Lon Guerrilla Retaliation Units

*"They move during the night and they wear short pants most of the time.
They go to houses and ask the names of the people, and if the person is
on the list they kill them. They were given special authority and a license
to kill. They can kill anyone who has helped the KNU. With the authority
that they have, people have said that even Operations Commanders can't
comment on their work. The Operations Commander is under them
because they are directly controlled by Khin Nyunt."* - "Saw January"
(M), KHRG human rights monitor (Interview #1, 1/99)

Villagers in the plains east of the Sittaung River and in the western
reaches of the hills say that at present there is one thing which they fear
more than all the other SPDC abuses in their area, and that this is the
SPDC's new Sa Thon Lon Guerrilla Retaliation force. No information is
readily available on when this special force was first recruited, but it
began appearing in the villages of western Nyaunglebin District in
September 1998. The force only consists of an estimated 200 troops but
they have been handpicked and specially trained. Operating in small
sections of 5 to 10 soldiers, they are very secretive, moving by night
from village to village. Their self-stated purpose is to summarily execute
every villager who has ever had any kind of contact with resistance
forces, whether at present or long in the past. They have been carrying
out this function brutally, shooting, stabbing, and often beheading their
victims and dumping their bodies in the rivers. Operating in Mone,
Kyauk Kyi and Shwegyin townships, estimates on the number of people
they have executed thus far range between 50 and over 100, though it is
difficult to establish any definite numbers. Recent testimonies from
villagers fleeing Tantabin township in southern Toungoo District indicate
that they have now expanded their operations northward into this area,
and they are also going west of the Sittaung River to look for people to
target. This expansion of their operational area is cause for grave
concern.

Structure and Purpose

This force goes by a variety of names, including Sa Sa Sa ['SSS'], Sa
Thon Lon ['Three S'], Sa Thon Lon Dam Byan Byaut Kya ['Sa Thon
Lon Guerrilla Retaliation'], A'Htoo Ah Na Ya A'Pweh ['Special
Authority Group'], Baw Bi Doh ['Short Pants', a name invented by the
villagers because of the civilian clothing the soldiers often wear],
Myanma Ta Oo ['Burmese Eldest', i.e. most senior, troops], and Shwit

A'Pweh ['Shwit group', 'Shwit' being the sound of a knife cutting someone's throat]. All of these names have been used by the troops themselves in front of villagers. Judging by the testimonies of many villagers who have had contact with them and KNLA sources, it appears that their official name is the Sa Thon Lon (or Sa Sa Sa) Dam Byan Byaut Kya, which is translated in this report as Sa Thon Lon Guerrilla Retaliation.

"[P]eople call them Baw Bi Doh ['short pants'], but they don't like that so they ordered people to call them Thad Shin A'Pweh ['killing and clearing group']. Later, they didn't like that either and forced people to call them Shwit A'Pweh ['shwit' group]. They say that the sound of cutting someone's throat with a knife is 'shwit'." - "Saw Tee Ko" (M, 40), xxxx village, Mone township (Interview #19, 2/99)

"I don't dare even go near the [Sa Thon Lon] guerrilla troops. If I looked at their faces I'm afraid they'd kill me. In Meik Tha Lin the village headman is friendly with him [Shan Bpu] so he asked him, 'Teacher! What is your group called?' Then he [Shan Bpu] took out his knife, put it to the headman's throat and said, 'Shwit'. The village headman told him, 'You can tell me the word 'shwit' without having to pull out your knife'. Then he didn't dare ask more." - "Saw Ghaw" (M, xx), xxxx village, Mone township (Interview #29, 1/99)

'Sa Sa Sa' is a Burmese abbreviation equivalent to SSS in English; 'Sa Thon Lon' simply means 'Three S's'. This is an abbreviation for A'Htoo Son Zan Seh Seh Yay Oo Zi Ka Na, which translates as Bureau of Special Investigations (BSI). According to independent Karen sources, this department was first formed by General Ne Win's BSPP regime in the late 1970's or early 1980's with the function of cracking down on the country's black market and investigating some other crimes. Sometime in the mid-1980's it was shifted and placed under the control of the Directorate of Defence Services Intelligence (DDSI). DDSI currently has several branches, including Military Intelligence, Special Branch (the police), and the Bureau of Special Investigations (Sa Thon Lon). The Sa Thon Lon still has the function of cracking down on the black market, but the new Guerrilla Retaliation force has also been placed in this department. The reason may be to keep the force under the direct personal control of Lt. Gen. Khin Nyunt, Secretary-1 of the SPDC and head of the DDSI. According to villagers and KNLA sources, the Guerrilla Retaliation force was created by his direct order and remains under his control. This is the origin of the name A'Htoo Ah Na Ya A'Pweh ['Special Authority Group']. SPDC Battalion Commanders and

Strategic Commanders in the area have said directly to villagers that they have no control over the Guerrilla Retaliation troops, and there are reports that regular SPDC troops in the region have shown some enmity and fear toward them. Villagers in the area consistently state that the regular SPDC troops never come near their village when a Sa Thon Lon group is around and vice versa. According to a KNLA source, the Guerrilla Retaliation force reports to Military Intelligence Unit #3 based in Toungoo, though they also appear to have some contact with the regular Army's Southern Regional Command headquarters in Pegu (commanded by Brig. Gen. Tin Aye). This contact with the Regional Command may only result from the fact that most of the Guerrilla Retaliation troops were selected from regular SPDC units already operating in Nyaunglebin District.

"They told the villagers, 'If you want to report about our guerrilla group, don't bother reporting us to the Operations Commander or the Regional Commander. You should go to the centre, to Saw Maung [former chairman of SLORC] and Khin Nyunt to report about us. If you go there to report about us we'll give you trip expenses.' After they said that, village heads and elders didn't dare do anything." – "Saw Tha Pwih" (M, 38), xxxx village, Tantabin township, Toungoo District (Interview #50, 5/99)

"The villagers went to complain to the Strategic Command Intelligence but they said they couldn't do anything. They said, 'In the past if you came and gave us money we could help you. However, they [the Sa Thon Lon troops] are controlled directly by the regional command so even if you give us money we can't help you.'" – "Saw Htoo Lay" (M, 25), xxxx village, Kyauk Kyi township (Interview #30, 12/98)

"In the past we could run to the Operations Commander or the Battalion Commander for help if someone was arrested and they could help us to buy the lives of those arrested. But now the Operations Commander says he can't do anything about this group [the Sa Thon Lon] because they have been given complete authority." – "Naw Hser" (F, 40), xxxx village, Mone township (Interview #20, 2/99)

"When the Army troops come the guerrilla group [Sa Thon Lon] goes to another village, then when the Army troops leave they come back again." – "Saw Lay Muh" (M, 42), xxxx village, Tantabin township, Toungoo District (Interview #53, 5/99)

"Now IB 39 and the Guerrillas [Sa Thon Lon] don't like each other, even though they are both Burmese. They've said that a battle could occur between them." – "Pu Than Nyunt" (M, 60), xxxx village, Tantabin township, Toungoo District (Interview #52, 5/99)

The Guerrilla Retaliation troops were specially selected from among the Non-Commissioned Officers (Corporals and Sergeants) of the regular SPDC Battalions already operating in Nyaunglebin District. Based on their subsequent behaviour, it appears that they were selected based on their capacity for brutality. According to some KNLA sources, some of the troops were also recruited from among former KNLA soldiers who had surrendered to the SPDC. None of the villagers interviewed by KHRG have confirmed this, but it would make sense given the purpose of the force; former KNLA soldiers would be able to point out many people who had helped the KNLA in the past. In addition, one woman from Kyauk Kyi township told KHRG that a group of Guerrilla Retaliation soldiers accidentally left a leaflet in her house titled 'Training Course of Pado Aung San', which they later came back for. Pado Aung San was the notoriously corrupt forestry minister of the KNU who defected to the SPDC in early 1998; since then, he has denounced the KNU in several statements and appeared to be trying to find a role with the SPDC. It is possible that he gave some portion of the training for the Guerrilla Retaliation troops, possibly in KNU/KNLA strategy or politics.

"They have created the Dam Byan Byaut Kya because they hope people won't dare be involved with the KNU even a little bit. ... They chose 12 people from each Battalion. They only chose Sergeants and Corporals, and they were given training ... Wherever they move there are no other SPDC troops moving. They stay in many different villages in groups of 4 or 5, and they walk during the night. The people that they have to kill, they kill immediately." - "Saw January" (M), KHRG human rights monitor (Interview #1, 1/99)

"The Sa Sa Sa in Kler Lweh Htoo district are special troops. We've received information that the enemy has collected soldiers who have surrendered from the KNLA, as well as P'Doh Aung San's [soldiers], Thu Mu Heh's [soldiers] and the DKBA. These soldiers, along with SPDC soldiers, have received special training and are being sent into each area. They are calling those troops the Sa Sa Sa, but they are also called the A'Htoo Ah Nah Ya A'Pweh ['Special Authority Group']." - "Saw Kaw Doh Muh" (M), who is with the KNLA in Nyaunglebin District (Interview #36, 2/99)

"One day they came to my house and took a rest, and when they left I saw a paper that the government had given them. I opened it and saw the title, "Training Course of Pado Aung San", and there were some things there written by Pado Aung San. They forgot it there in my house and came back to take it later. I read it quickly and secretly before they came back for it." - "Naw Thu" (F, 26), xxxx village, Kyauk Kyi township (Interview #29, 1/99)

"Some of them are SPDC soldiers and some of them are part of the resistance that was living in the jungle but surrendered to the Burmese. They joined the guerrilla troops and guide them. I only know the name of one of the group commanders, his name is Bo Nagah." - "Saw Ta Roh" (M, 37), xxxx village, Shwegyin township (Interview #32, 12/98)

Most available estimates place the total size of the Sa Thon Lon Guerrilla Retaliation force at about 200 soldiers. It is organised along the lines of a regular Army Battalion though using smaller numbers, and is apparently divided into four or five main Companies: 'Mone Thon' ('Monsoon'), 'Mone Daing' ('Storm'), 'Galone' ('Garuda'), and 'D'Pyet Hleh' ('Sweeper'); the fifth is 'Moe Kyo' ('Lightning'), though as yet KHRG has not been able to confirm whether this is a Company or just a Section. The main operational unit of this force is the section, consisting of 5 to 10 men. According to the limited information available, it appears that there are five sections in each company (making it different from a regular Army Battalion, which at full strength has five companies, each consisting of three platoons of three sections each). Several of these sections have taken on their own names, such as 'Nagah' ('dragon'), 'Moe Kyo' ('lightning') and 'Seik Padee' (Buddhist prayer beads). A KNLA source provided the following partial list of Sections and Section Commanders which comes from KNLA Intelligence:

	Commanded by	Battalion of Origin	Section Strength
1	Sergeant Kyaw Tint	IB #39	10 soldiers
2	Sergeant Khin Maung Than	IB #73	10 soldiers
3	Sergeant Wan Kan Dane	IB #26	10 soldiers
4	Sergeant Maung Myo	IB #60	10 soldiers
5	Sergeant Myint Naing	IB #53	10 soldiers
6	Sergeant Tint Lwin	LIB #440	10 soldiers
7	Sergeant Myint Oo	IB #35	8 soldiers
8	Sergeant Khin Maung Myint	IB #57	10 soldiers
9	Sergeant Pa Tee Pyut	LIB #350	9 soldiers
10	Sergeant Soe Win	LIB #349	8 soldiers
11	Sergeant Aung Naing Win	IB #59	9 soldiers
12	Sergeant Zaw Win	IB #30	8 soldiers
13	Sergeant Mya Zaw Tint	LIB #264	9 soldiers

According to the same source, Sections 1 through 5 above are part of the 'Monsoon' Company, which is commanded by Captain Maung Maung (commonly referred to as Bo Maung Maung) and operates in Mone township and the area between Kyauk Kyi and Na Than Gwin. Sections 6 through 10 are part of the 'Storm' Company, commanded by Major Zaw Naing Htun and operating south of the Kyauk Kyi / Na Than Gwin area. The above list is not complete, because according to information available thus far it appears that the force has 4 or 5 companies. Villagers in Shwegyin, southern Kyauk Kyi and Tantabin townships refer to a commander there named Moe Kyo. In Mone and Kyauk Kyi townships, several names recur in the villagers' testimonies as being particularly brutal: Bo Maung Maung himself (commander of 'Monsoon' company), a section commander under him named Sergeant Bo Shan Bpu (also known as 'Bo Shwit'), another Sergeant named Tint Lwin who is subordinate to Bo Shan Bpu, and a section commander named Bo Nagah (note: 'Bo' is simply a prefix attached to the name of a commander). Bo Maung Maung was previously with LIB #351, and Bo Shan Bpu was reportedly with IB #59. According to several accounts, Bo Shan Bpu is ethnically Shan, or at least can speak Shan. Villagers say that several of the Sa Thon Lon troops can speak various languages such as Pa'O, Shan and Karen. Bo Shan Bpu is a pseudonym, as is Bo Nagah ('Nagah' means 'dragon'); Maung Maung may also be a pseudonym. Some of the section commanders use the same names as their sections; for example, Bo Nagah commands the Nagah ('Dragon') group, and Moe Kyo commands the Moe Kyo ('Lightning') group. Many of these soldiers may be using pseudonyms, because the Guerrilla Retaliation troops are very secretive, and they give very little information to the villagers other than telling them that they will kill everyone who has contact with the resistance.

"The bad person who goes and kills people is Shan Bpu, but he calls himself Bo Shwit. He is the worst, and he is a Shan. I asked him, 'Commander, what is your nationality?' and he answered that he is a Shan national, and his wife is Karen. He is about 28 years old and his hair is long, down to here." – "Pu Than Nyunt" (M, 60), xxxx village, Tantabin township, Toungoo District (Interview #52, 5/99)

These units operate as death squads, executing anyone even remotely suspected of having had any contact with the KNU/KNLA, even if that contact ended 10 or more years ago. Their secretiveness, their brutal methods of killing and beheading their victims, in short everything about the way they operate, is intended to terrify the villagers. The overall purpose of this is very clearly to deliver a message to the villagers that even the slightest contact with the KNLA, even involuntary contact such as when KNLA units demand food from village elders, will be punished with a brutal death, if not immediately then whenever this contact is discovered, even 5, 10, or 20 years in the future.

"They are a mobile unit that is trying to cut the connection between the KNLA and the people. They are primarily active during the night, but also during the day. This force is controlled directly by the regional command. The local troops in the area where they are active can't make decisions for them or reprimand them. The regional commander held a meeting and told them they had to kill 30 people each month in each township. They are to kill 20 villagers who support the KNLA and democracy groups, and the other 10 people are to be anyone they find who has weapons. The names of people who support the resistance groups and democracy groups are written in their books. This group has already killed 2 villagers in each village of Ler Doh township. They've also killed villagers in Mone township and Hsaw Tee township. ... Among the people they have killed, only a few of them have actually been in contact with us. Most people they have killed are innocent villagers. The names they have in their books are names of people who helped us a very long time ago and haven't been in contact with us since then, but they look for the people who are listed in their books and they kill them." - "Saw Kaw Doh Muh" (M), who is with the KNLA in Nyaunglebin District (Interview #36, 2/99)

"They came on the first of September [1998]. They said they would patrol for 6 months and make the area A'Pyu Yaung Neh Myay [a 'white' area, SPDC terminology for areas which are completely subjugated]. ... They are abusing the villagers from all areas. They can't fight their enemy [the KNLA], so they say the villagers are their enemy for feeding the KNLA; that if the villagers didn't feed the KNLA then the KNLA couldn't fight them, so they are finding and killing the villagers." - "Saw Htoo Lay" (M, 25), xxxx village, Kyauk Kyi township, talking about the Sa Thon Lon (Interview #30, 12/98).

Initially these units only appeared in the plains east of the Sittaung River of Nyaunglebin District, but testimony from villagers who fled Tantabin township of southern Toungoo District in April 1999 indicates that Sa Thon Lon units are now operating there as well (excerpts from some of these testimonies are included in this report). They also now search for targets in villages on the west side of the Sittaung River. This expansion of their operational area is cause for extreme concern, as it may indicate that Nyaunglebin District has been used as an experimental ground for this type of operation, which if successful will be introduced in other regions as well. The SPDC's major military offensives and mass relocation campaigns have weakened the resistance forces but have not even come close to wiping them out, and the death squad tactic may be an attempt at a new approach. There may also be elements of internal SPDC politics at play. The tension between the DDSI's Lt. Gen. Khin Nyunt and regular Army leaders such as Gen. Maung Aye is well known, and Khin Nyunt's initiative in this case may be intended to prove that his tactics are more effective than those of the other Generals. In addition, the creation of the Sa Thon Lon Guerrilla Retaliation force gives the DDSI an armed wing, which in effect gives Khin Nyunt his own private army. If the force is expanded in numbers and/or in the size of the territory where it operates, it will be important to watch its interaction with the regular Army as well as the dynamics which develop between the Generals in Rangoon.

"You can't expect us to know their names. They never even allow us to look at their faces - when we see them we have to look down, away from their faces. ... They said that the soldiers who came before were supposed to kill the people but they didn't, so they are now showing the people that they can kill. That's why we are always afraid." - "Saw Htoo Lay" (M, 25), xxxx village, Kyauk Kyi township, talking about the Sa Thon Lon (Interview #30, 12/98)

Methods

"They find people who had contact with the KNU in '95 and those who have contact now. If they can find people who have had contact with the KNU at any time in their past, they kill them. Shan Bpu has killed people in Lu Ah, Haw Ko Ghaw, Twa Ni Gone, Myeh Yeh, and Yan Myo Aung too. When we found out that they are going to kill all the villagers who have ever helped the KNU, we knew they would kill us too. Our names are in their books. ... They are the Sa Thon Lon. People said that they don't ask any questions [they kill without interrogation] and they are going to "cut off the tops of all the plants". The second group, Sweeper, will come to sweep up the people and then the third group will come to scorch the earth and "dig out the roots". They will kill all the relatives of the forest people [the KNLA]. The Sa Thon Lon don't look like they will go and fight [go into battle], they are just going around killing members of the general public. They said that they are going to clear the people out of the countryside, that they have to kill all people who support the forest people and people who give taxes to the forest people. They also said that if the KNLA shoots and kills one of them, they will burn down the village closest to where it happened and kill everyone in the village."
- "Saw Tee Ko" (M, 40), xxxx village, Mone township (Interview #19, 2/99)

The operational unit of the Sa Thon Lon Guerrilla Retaliation force is the section. Each section has 5 to 10 soldiers and moves independently from village to village. Between them they cover the villages of the plains east of the Sittaung River as well as the westernmost reaches of the hills. They do not establish their own camps, but stay in the houses of villagers along their way. Usually they stay in a village through the day, then move to other villages by night. They seldom spend two consecutive nights in the same village. They demand their food and money from the villagers, but when in the villages they order the villagers to look at the ground and not to look in their faces. They do not wear standard issue SPDC Army fatigues. Instead, many villagers say that they often wear civilian clothing, such as T-shirts and sarongs, around the villages, and guerrilla camouflage uniforms by night, or various combinations of civilian clothing and guerrilla camouflage. They very frequently wear camouflage short pants, and this brought about the Karen name Baw Bi Doh ('Short Pants') which many villagers call them. Villagers also say that their weapons are not the standard Army-issue G3 and G4 assault rifle but the AK47 and AR assault rifles, which are far better in the jungle. They have also on occasion used M79 grenade launchers, and they do much of their killing with knives.

"They only walk during the night and sleep during the day. ... During the day they sleep in people's houses but they never introduce themselves to the owners of the house, they never make friends with them. They live there with faces of stone and eat whatever they want to. They never look at the faces of the people they are staying with because they are afraid the villagers may be able to recognise them. ... They don't have people staying in every village at the same time, but they move around and sometimes stay in Haw Ko Ghaw, or Thit Cha Seik, or Yay Leh, or Nga Nwah Seit, or Weh Tu, or sometimes in Yan Myo Aung. They move around like that and don't really have a home base. ... They kill people wherever they go." - "Saw Tee Ko" (M, 40), xxxx village, Mone township, describing the Sa Thon Lon (Interview #19, 2/99)

"People are afraid of them because if you're walking on the path and you suddenly see them you're supposed to sit down and you must not look at their faces. If you look at their faces they kick you at once and say, 'Why are you looking at my face? Am I handsome or something?'" – "Pu Nya Thu" (M, 70), xxxx village, Mone township (Interview #4, 5/99)

"As for the short-pants group, the area leader has to collect money for them once a week. Each family has to give 200 to 300 Kyat each week. This money isn't toward any fees, just for the short-pants group's food. Every village in Kyauk Kyi township has to pay that." - "Naw Say Paw" (F, 26), xxxx village, Kyauk Kyi township (Interview #29, 1/99)

According to the villagers, the sections have lists of people to be killed in each village, and some even claim that they are assigned a quota of people to kill in each township. A consensus on this number appears to be 30, though one villager interviewed claimed that Bo Nagah had said that they are to kill 70 people in each township; if this is so, the number 30 or 70 may have been decreed based on superstitious numerology, which is taken very seriously by Khin Nyunt and other SPDC leaders. In addition, a villager from southern Toungoo District who fled in April 1999 said that the Sa Thon Lon have now ordered villagers in his area to have family photos taken and submit one to the Sa Thon Lon and one to the Army Division. The Sa Thon Lon officer told the villagers that the Sa Thon Lon sections will check the faces of people they meet against their set of photos, and if your photo is not in the set for your village you will be killed.

"Now they've said that they plan to kill 30 people per month between Shwegyin and Mone, and 30 more between Mone and Tantabin. Among the 30 that they kill, one will be a bad person and the other 29 will be

good [innocent] people. " – "Saw Lah Thaw" (M), xxxx relocation site,
Mone township (Interview #2, 5/99)

*"They forced people to take family photos. We had to take three pictures:
one to give them [Sa Thon Lon], another to keep in our house and
another to give to the Division. They said that if they see people going
anywhere they will ask their village name, look at the pictures from that
village and if that person isn't in the pictures they'll kill him. Therefore
people were afraid and had the pictures taken. Even if they didn't have
the money, they borrowed it from others and had the pictures taken." –*
"Pu Than Nyunt" (M, 60), xxxx village, Tantabin township, Toungoo
District (Interview #52, 5/99)

In some cases they enter villages and surround the houses of people they
plan to kill and try to catch them that way. Other tactics they use are to
pretend to stop for a rest in a villager's house and then kill him, or to
conscript a villager as a guide and then kill him once they are out of the
village. Many villagers have fallen unsuspecting into these traps, simply
because they have had no contact with the opposition for years and are
completely unaware of any suspicion against them. However, people are
now aware of the Sa Thon Lon's tactics and some have fled the village
rather than face them, even if they have never had contact with the
opposition. In fact, many of the people already killed have been
completely innocent but were killed based simply on a remote suspicion
or unfounded accusation. The Sa Thon Lon units have not only killed
those on their lists, but also people who they encounter outside the
villages at night, who are automatically suspected of working with
resistance forces. At a meeting called by the Sa Thon Lon in Kyauk Kyi
township in December 1998, they told villagers that they are no longer
allowed to leave their villages between 6 p.m. and 6 a.m. Even during the
day, if they encounter people outside of villages they often stop them and
beat them for no apparent reason other than to drive fear into them.

*"They told us not to enter or leave any villages between 6 p.m. and 6 a.m.
or they would kill us. They said for our villagers to call their children
who are in the KNLA to come back and live in the village, or they will
kill the parents. They know, they said the names of all the KNLA are in
their file, and they said they will kill anyone who has contact with the
KNLA." -* "Naw Say Paw" (F, 26), xxxx village, Kyauk Kyi township,
describing what the Sa Thon Lon said at a meeting in her village
(Interview #29, 1/99)

"They are really doing what they've planned to do, they are going to kill every relative of the KNLA in our area. They said that there's only one way for them to win against the Karen and that is to kill all the relatives of the KNU. The Burmese soldiers who are friendly with us and go to the frontline told us that our names are in their book of those to be killed. We don't dare live there anymore." - "Naw Hser" (F, 40), xxxx village, Mone township (Interview #20, 2/99)

"They held a meeting in our village one time, the same morning that they captured my husband. He [Shan Bpu] said that we mustn't contact people on this side [KNLA]. He said, 'If you want to contact them, leave with your whole family. If you don't go, the day that you contact them will be the day you die.'" - "Naw Paw Paw Htoo" (F, 31), xxxx village, Mone township (Interview #12, 3/99)

"I fled because they are killing anyone who has ever had any contact with the KNU. There have been times when we've met them [KNLA soldiers] along our way and spoken to them, because they're all people that we know. They kill people for that. ... During January of this year [1999] they killed one village headman, Mya Htun, from Meik Tha Lin, and dumped him in the Sittaung river. He was 48 years old and has 5 children. He was unable to avoid being friends with the KNLA [the KNLA approaches the village headmen for food and money]. In their book there are names of anyone who has ever been friends with the KNLA, and I've heard that they kill the people whose names are in the book. ... To cut all connections [with the KNU/KNLA]. To threaten the public so they won't dare contact them in the future and won't dare to give them rations. This is the main objective of their killing." - "Maung Soe" (M, 40), Kyauk Kyi town (Interview #21, 1/99)

"They call themselves 'Bo Shwit', because 'shwit' is the sound of thrusting a knife into someone to kill him. They are murderers. ... Huay!! I can't say how many tens of people they've killed. Any place you go you'll hear about the people they've killed, they've killed people in almost every village. They haven't killed anyone in xxxx yet, but they've killed people in Myeh Yeh, Hsi Mu Plaw, Si Pa Leh, and Meik Tha Lin, which is across the [Sittaung] river from our village. Their commander is Bo Maung Maung. I don't know their base, they just travel from village to village. They don't make camps, they just stay in people's houses. They walk the whole night without sleeping." - "Naw Lah Paw" (F, 21), xxxx village, Mone township (Interview #28, 1/99)

The Sa Thon Lon troops sometimes shoot their victims, but more often kill them with knives by cutting their throats or stabbing them in the chest. In most cases it appears that they do not interrogate or torture their victims beforehand, they simply kill them. Some Sa Thon Lon soldiers have even told villagers that Sa Thon Lon stands for 'No Interrogation'. However, after killing them they often mutilate the bodies, presumably to deliver a stronger message to the other villagers. Villagers interviewed for this report described many instances of beheadings, and in some cases the heads were then displayed as a warning to all villagers. In November 1998 they shot dead villagers Saw Aye from Myeh Yeh village and Po Theh Pyay from Ter Bpaw. They then ordered local villagers to build stands of bamboo, one along the path to Kyauk Kyi and the other on the path to Mone, and displayed the heads on these stands; the villagers were forced to guard the heads for a month, under threat that if the heads disappeared they would be replaced with their own. In another incident, after shooting dead Saw San Myint in Baw Bpee Der village on December 27th 1998, they beheaded him, hung his head over the path to Mone town, and stuck a cheroot in his mouth. The Sa Thon Lon troops often dump the bodies of their victims in the rivers, though sometimes they leave them where they lie and forbid the villagers to move or bury them. For many villagers, the mutilation of their relatives' bodies and the inability to give them a proper burial or cremation is almost as much a crime as the killing itself.

"Before they kill people they tie their hands behind their backs. Most of the people are not shot, instead their heads are cut off with a knife and their bodies are thrown in the river. They normally call people on sentry duty from the village to bury the bodies after they kill them." - "Maung Soe" (M, 40), Kyauk Kyi town (Interview #21, 1/99)

"They cut out people's tongues, cut their ears off and cover their faces with their own intestines. They do that so the villagers will be afraid. Now if we hear their voices, our hands and knees tremble and we can't do anything. The women are very afraid of them... all the villagers are afraid of them." - "Saw Htoo Lay" (M, 25), xxxx village, Kyauk Kyi township, talking about the Sa Thon Lon (Interview #30, 12/98)

"The group that kills people now is the short-pants group [Sa Thon Lon]. They have been there since about two months ago. If they think you've done anything wrong they never ask any questions, they just summon you and kill you at once. They said that if they kill anyone the villagers have no right to say anything, to report it or to hold a ceremony for the dead

people." - "Naw Say Paw" (F, 26), xxxx village, Kyauk Kyi township (Interview #29, 1/99)

Many villagers have managed to escape execution by fleeing the village before the Sa Thon Lon comes for them. In these cases the Sa Thon Lon troops come to the village and confiscate or destroy all of the villagers belongings, as well as their house, land, and livestock. If there is a crop in the field they have on occasion ordered the other villagers to harvest it and hand it over. The Sa Thon Lon troops know that many of these people have fled to villages on the west side of the Sittaung River because it is outside their usual area of operations, so they now occasionally go to villages west of the river and check family registrations from house to house, searching for the people they want. As a result, many people living west of the river are afraid to accept relatives or guests from the east any longer.

"Some of the people they tried to arrest fled and escaped. When they can't catch people they commandeer their belongings in the village, such as their land, farmfields, fishponds, cattle and buffaloes. They take everything they see in the person's house and sell it." - "Saw Ta Roh" (M, 37), xxxx village, Shwegyin township (Interview #32, 12/98)

"In Leh Gkaw Wah village of Kyauk Kyi township, they accused Ko Maung Aye and Bee Win of helping the KNU and were going to arrest them. They fled and escaped so they confiscated their cattle, chickens and buffaloes and took all their belongings from their houses. They took those things to Baw Ka Hta camp." - "Saw Htoo Lay" (M, 25), xxxx village, Kyauk Kyi township, talking about the Sa Thon Lon (Interview #30, 12/98)

"Lately, people who don't dare stay in their villages have been going to other places that are safer such as to town or to the other side of the river [to the west of the Sittaung River]. So the Sa Thon Lon have gone to towns and villages on the other side of the river looking for people they want. They are checking family registration lists at each house. When they find people they want, they kill them and make problems for the families that took them in. Because of this, people in towns and villages on the other side of the river don't like to take in villagers from eastern villages when we run to them anymore. They don't even like us to go and visit them." - "Naw Hser" (F, 40), xxxx village, Mone township (Interview #20, 2/99)

The KNLA has tried to attack the Sa Thon Lon force on several occasions but with very little success, and they have tried to target Bo Shan Bpu himself at least once. In late February or early March 1999 the KNLA ambushed a passenger vehicle on the road near Kyun Bin Seik in Mone township, thinking that Bo Shan Bpu was inside because he always forces the drivers of passenger vehicles and motorcycles to transport him around rather than using Army vehicles. The driver and a passenger were killed, but Bo Shan Bpu had already got off the car some time before. The KNLA soldiers ordered everyone out of the car and burned it. Afterwards, the Sa Thon Lon punished the villagers by forcing every family in the villages from Weh Gyi to Kyun Bin Seik to pay 3,500 Kyat, allegedly to pay for the cost of the car. In addition, Sa Thon Lon commanders Bo Maung Maung and Bo Shan Bpu have both told villagers in southern Mone township that for every Sa Thon Lon soldier killed by the KNLA, they will execute 10 villagers.

"When the Sa Thon Lon are in our area they use the villagers as their cover. They said there must be no sounds from weapons. If there is the sound of a weapon that causes one of them to die, they will kill 10 of our villagers. Shan Bpu and Bo Maung Maung both said that." - "Saw Ner Muh" (M, 30+), xxxx village, Mone township (Interview #8, 4/99)

"I've heard that they have already killed 30 people between Shwegyin and Kyauk Kyi. When the group commanded by Bo Nagah came, they said they are supposed to kill 70 villagers in the area between Shwegyin and Kyauk Kyi. They must kill exactly 70 people, then the group that comes when they rotate their troops will also kill 70 people. Each of their groups must kill 70 people. ... They are killing a lot of people in Shwegyin and Kyauk Kyi areas. I've heard that they have also killed 30 to 40 people up in Mone township. They are killing there as they are here. The [SPDC] guerrilla troops are moving everywhere east of the Sittaung river. Usually they kill one person at a time, but they have killed 2 people at a time and also 8 people at a time. I've also heard and seen that they have gone to Nyaunglebin township and Kyauk T'Ga township [west of the Sittaung River] and are killing people there. They are doing in the towns the same as they are doing here [in the villages]." - "Saw Ta Roh" (M, 37), xxxx village, Shwegyin township (Interview #32, 12/98)

Killings of Villagers

"When they came and captured my husband, we were all in the house: my mother, my children and me. When they called him to go with them, I told my husband, 'Don't be afraid, pray to God.' Then Shan Bpu took his

knife and held it to my throat telling me not to speak. He said, 'Don't say anything! Don't open your mouth! Or you will die!' I was afraid and couldn't speak. At first only two Burmese came for my husband, but later Bo Maung Maung arrived and tied my husband's hands behind his back and covered his face with one of his old sarongs. They took a guitar string and tied it around his neck. ... They didn't say anything after that and they killed him that evening. They pulled him from place to place and then killed him at Teh Su while we were still in Yan Myo Aung. ... The sadness I suffer from is so deep I can't describe it. It's like I'm in the dark. When they first captured my husband I couldn't eat for 2 days but still my stomach felt full. I prayed all day and night. We also had the problem of not having any rice at that time so I had to find rice. I have many children and had to find food for them before every meal. My children didn't know what was happening, they were playing and laughing innocently. ... We didn't have contact with the KNLA and we don't have a well known name, the Burmese soldiers had never asked about us before, so how could we have known that they were going to come and kill us?" - "Naw Paw Paw Htoo" (F, 31), xxxx village, Mone township, describing the killing of her husband Saw Mah Htoo (a.k.a. Gah Gyi, age 37) in November 1998 (Interview #12, 3/99)

It is difficult to establish the exact number of villagers already executed by Sa Thon Lon units in Nyaunglebin District, but villagers and KNLA sources estimate somewhere between 50 and over 100. Most victims have been Karen, but there have also been many Burmans killed because there are many Burmans in the Sittaung River plains who sympathise with the Karen resistance. Many of the killings go completely unreported and in some cases people simply disappear so even the local villagers cannot be sure. KHRG has collected information on a number of killings which have been witnessed or are known to have happened, most of which have been corroborated by the testimony of several villagers. A list of 151 of these killings by the Sa Thon Lon and other SPDC units since 1997 is included in the appendix of this book. One factor which is very consistent in the villagers' testimonies and other information is that many of those systematically executed by the Sa Thon Lon have either been completely innocent or have only had some rudimentary contact with the KNU or KNLA which occurred years ago. Many never did more than act as a guide a few times for a KNLA column or give them some rice. Some of those killed have been village elders who had no choice but to have contact with the KNLA, because the KNLA approached them to demand food and taxes from their village.

"Since 1998 the SPDC has been commanding guerrilla troops [Guerrilla Retaliation units]. ... One night at 9 o'clock they entered Shan Su village and arrested Ko Kyi Hmwe, the 43 year old son of U Poh Bin. I saw them kill him outside of the village. They did that sort of thing in other villages also. They stabbed U Than Myint from Ma Oo Bin village [also in Shwegyin township] with a knife, they did it in the middle of the village. While he was working on his pond, they went and called him and then killed him without asking any questions. In Leh Gkaw Wah village [southern Kyauk Kyi township], which is near Ma Oo Bin, they called Maung Ba Aye down from his house and killed him without asking anything." - "Saw Ta Roh" (M, 37), xxxx village, Shwegyin township (Interview #32, 12/98)

"On 22/11/98 they killed a villager from Kya Plaw village who was over 40 years old. They accused him of helping the KNU in the past and killed him between Kya Plaw village and the old village of Ler Wah. They cut out his tongue and cut off his ears. On 27/10/98, they accused another man of being part of the backbone of the KNU. They took him to the top of Po Noh Po village and killed him. They didn't allow people to go and bury that man. ... They also killed two other Burman villagers, U Aung Baw and Khin Win, from A'Tet [Upper] Twin Gyi village in Shwegyin township. They killed them at the same time. U Aung Baw was 52 years old and Khin Win was 32 years old. They slit their throats near the Sittaung river and kicked their bodies into the river. People didn't see the corpses." - "Saw Htoo Lay" (M, 25), xxxx village, Kyauk Kyi township, talking about Sa Thon Lon killings (Interview #30, 12/98)

"In our village they have killed 2 people, a wife and her husband. In Weh Gyi they also killed 2 people at night after the movie had finished showing. They captured them that night and killed them at once. In the morning the village head went to them and asked about the two villagers they had captured, but they told the village head they had not captured them." - "Maung Sein" (M, xx), xxxx village, Kyauk Kyi township, talking about Sa Thon Lon killings in November 1998 (Interview #33, 12/98)

The killings carried out by the Sa Thon Lon units to date can be divided into two main categories: systematic executions of people they have targetted, and ad hoc killings of people they find in farmfield huts or meet along the pathways. When they target a specific person for execution, a Sa Thon Lon section usually enters the village sometime in the night, surrounds the person's house and orders them to come out, then takes the person away and executes them outside the village. On occasion they will have another villager go to fetch the suspect, or will call the suspect to go with them as a guide and then execute him/her once they are outside the village. One typical example occurred in Yan Myo Aung relocation site in November 1998. A Sa Thon Lon section led by Bo Shan Bpu and Bo Maung Maung asked various village headmen at the site for the whereabouts of Saw Mah Htoo (a.k.a. Gah Gyi). One of the Burman headmen said that he knew of him. That night the Sa Thon Lon group surrounded Saw Mah Htoo's house, tied him up and marched him away. When his wife tried to protest, Bo Shan Bpu held a knife to her throat and threatened to kill her. They marched Saw Mah Htoo to Yay Leh village, executed him and threw his body in the Sittaung River. Saw Mah Htoo and his wife never even knew they were under suspicion, because the only contact he had had with the KNLA occurred years ago when he would sometimes act as a guide for them. In a similar example which occurred on the evening of November 15th 1998 in xxxx village on the west bank of the Sittaung River, Sa Thon Lon troops came to kill villager Maung A---, but caught his wife Ma S--- instead. Maung A--- ran to escape and they fired at him but missed. They began beating Ma S--- on the head intending to kill her, then cut off her ears to steal her earrings, slashed part of her mouth off and left her for dead. However, she lived and her brother secretly carried her to a hospital. When the Sa Thon Lon found out about it, one of them went to the hospital and threatened her, after which she had to leave the hospital and now lives in hiding, as do her husband and brother.

"They tied him up, covered his face and forced him to go with them. His wife came down [out of the house] and said, 'My husband is a good person.' The Burmese who captured him said to her, 'He is a good person now, but in the past he was a bad person.' Then they pulled him away. ... When they pulled him out of our village they were beating him, and we heard the next day that they killed him in Yay Leh and threw his body in the Sittaung river. Some people saw it. He shouted loudly and said, 'I am not the leader of the defenders.' ... The rest of the Burmese left in the village called people to come to the school for a meeting. I didn't dare go, I stayed in my house. Many people hid in their houses. They said, 'Let this serve as an example. We won't forgive you next time. In the future, you must live and stand for people on this side [the side of the SPDC], you shouldn't contact the KNU. The day we hear about you contacting the KNU, you will know.' This is really dangerous." - "Saw Kyaw" (M, 34), Yan Myo Aung relocation site, Mone township, who witnessed the Sa Thon Lon unit take away Saw Mah Htoo, whom they later killed, in November 1998 (Interview #23, 1/99)

"They captured her, tied her up with rope and then beat her head until her head was broken. Her husband ran away, and they shot at him while he was running but he wasn't hurt. Then they tried to finish killing her. They were beating her to death with a gun butt, but she wouldn't die so they slashed her with a knife. They cut off her ears. There was a set of ornamental earrings worth over 10,000 Kyat in her ears. They slashed her chin and her face and left her to die, but still she didn't die." - "Maung Sein" (M, xx), xxxx village, Kyauk Kyi township, describing how the Sa Thon Lon tried to kill his sister in November 1998; they left her for dead but he carried her to hospital, and she survived (Interview #33, 12/98)

"I went to see her in xxxx hospital but I don't recall her name. She is a smart woman and speaks bravely. She told us that the Sa Thon Lon soldiers were coming to kill her husband but when they came her husband ran away. She spoke bravely to the soldiers so they got angry at her and cut off her mouth. When the doctors asked her about her story, she answered truthfully and told them that the soldiers had said: 'You're a woman who can speak very well so I'll cut off your mouth.' The doctor sewed her mouth [back together]. They [the soldiers] thought that she was dead but she wasn't. When she was in the hospital, they heard about it so they went to the hospital. They couldn't kill her in the hospital because there were doctors, nurses and police around. He told her, 'You are very lucky! I thought that you died but you are still alive, so if you have to leave the hospital you'd better go somewhere that I can't find you or you're dead.' She is a strong woman, her mouth, ears and skin were cut off but she is still alive." - "Naw Hser" (F, 40), xxxx village, Mone township (Interview #20, 2/99)

"On November 11th 1998, Sa Thon Lon Guerrilla Retaliation troops led by 'Bo Nagah' [a pseudonym] killed Saw Ba Aye and his wife Naw Dah at the same time without asking any questions. They said that this couple had supported the NLD since 1988 [note: the NLD did not even exist until 1989], and that this is why they had killed them. The couple were from Leh Gkaw Wah village in Kyauk Kyi township. When they were killed their son Maung Lay Lay was only 3 months old. Now his relatives have to take care of him and they are living in fear, spending only one day in each place. He is not getting enough milk and is very weak." - incident report from KHRG field reporter.

The Sa Thon Lon have also been killing people in Tantabin township of southern Toungoo District, just north of Nyaunglebin District, which has become part of their operating area since the end of 1998. According to villagers who fled this area in April 1999, the first Sa Thon Lon unit there was from the Garuda company and they were mainly just interrogating people, but after one of their members raped a Burman schoolteacher they withdrew and Bo Shan Bpu's group came in. Since then people have been killed in several villages of southern Tantabin township. The worst case occurred in April 1999, when Sa Thon Lon troops went to Dtaw Gone village and ordered all the villagers to come to the church. They were then ordered to come out two by two, and were beaten when they did. After interrogating and beating all of the Dtaw Gone villagers and 16 villagers from nearby Zee Byu Gone who happened to be there, they selected three men whom they knew had had past contact with the KNU: Hsah Tu Ghaw, age 35, married with 3 children; Pa Bee Ko, age over 30, married with 5 children; and Ka Ni Ni, age 22 and single. They took them into the trees nearby and executed them. From the church the villagers heard the screams of Ka Ni Ni, whose throat had been partly cut and who died slowly. They stabbed Hsah Tu Ghaw twice, then cut his throat and kicked him to the ground, and also stabbed Pa Bee Ko to death, all in front of witnesses from the village.

"They killed two people in Byin Gah and they also killed people in Yay Sha and Taw Ma Aye. In Taw Ma Aye they killed Uncle Pa Thu Po Pah, he is over 50 years old. They called all the villagers of Taw Ma Aye to go and give 'obligation' paddy. When they went, they asked Uncle Pa Thu Po Pah, 'What is your name?' He said, 'Bo Gkay', and then they tied him up, pulled him to Lay Tee and killed him. This group, if they capture anyone there is no coming back." – "Saw Tha Pwih" (M, 38), xxxx village, Tantabin township, Toungoo District (Interview #50, 5/99)

"They killed three people in Dtaw Gone, near my village. They killed them 2 weeks ago. Hsah Tu Ghaw is 30 years old, he has 3 children. Pa Bee Ko is over 30, he has 5 children. Ka Ni Ni is 22, he is single. They captured them in the church, took them to the jungle and killed them. ... Ka Ni Ni was yelling in the jungle because his throat wasn't completely cut. When we were worshipping in church at noon he was yelling, people heard it and went to him but he died when they got there. People buried him after the Short-Pants group left. We couldn't bring him home because all his blood had runout. As for Hsah Tu Ghaw, there was a hole in his side where they'd stabbed him with a knife. And as for Pa Bee Ko, he had been ill almost to death even before they killed him." – "Naw Htoo Say" (F, 22), xxxx village, Tantabin township, Toungoo District, describing a Sa Thon Lon killing which occurred in April 1999 (Interview #51, 5/99)

Many of those beaten and killed are not specific targets, but simply villagers found outside their villages or relocation sites by the Sa Thon Lon troops. Sa Thon Lon units have issued orders that no villagers are to be outside their villages between 6 p.m. and 6 a.m., and that even when they are allowed outside they must have a pass and are not allowed to have any food. People caught outside their village at night or caught with food are generally executed, while those caught without a pass or with an expired pass during the daylight hours are severely beaten. One of the worst killings of this nature occurred in November 1998, when a group of four Twa Ni Gone villagers and two Myeh Yeh villagers had gone from Yan Myo Aung relocation site to fish at some ponds near their home village. They had a pass, but a Sa Thon Lon unit found them in a hut with some rice and accused them of feeding the resistance. The two Myeh Yeh villagers were released, but the four Twa Ni Gone villagers were taken into a patch of scrub and shot dead. The gun jammed when they tried to kill the fourth victim, a schoolboy in his late teens, so they killed him with a knife and then seriously mutilated his body. The four killed were all male: Saw Gka Bweh, Maw Nyunt Po, Saw Lay Heh and Shaw Po Gkeh. A month later, 5 more Twa Ni Gone villagers were executed under almost identical circumstances. On November 18th 1998 in southern Mone township, Sa Thon Lon troops saw Po Theh Pyay from Ter Bpaw village and Saw Aye from Myeh Yeh village along a path because they had returned from the relocation site to fish. They called to the two villagers, but they ran because they were afraid and the troops shot them in the back. The bodies were then beheaded, and the Sa Thon Lon group forced the villagers to display the heads along two nearby pathways for an entire month. On December 27th 1998, Bo Maung Maung and Bo Shan Bpu led Sa Thon Lon troops into Baw Bpee Der village, where villagers were having a volleyball tournament for Christmas. They opened fire on the villagers, killing Saw San Myint, who was in his early twenties. They beheaded him and hung his head along the footpath to Mone with a cheroot stuck in its mouth as a warning to the villagers. These are only a few examples of some of the killings, both systematic and random, which are being carried out by the Sa Thon Lon troops; many more examples are provided in the table in the appendix, the field reports and the texts of the interviews with villagers which appear in the Annex to this report, and even these are only a partial sample of the killings which have already occurred and are still occurring throughout the district.

"When they killed the four Twa Ni Gone villagers at the fishpond hut I was also in one of the fishpond huts. Those people were keeping some rice in their fishpond hut because they were staying there and needed to

eat. They were villagers who had been forcibly relocated but had come back to work at their pond. When the soldiers saw their rice they accused them of feeding the KNLA, so they killed them. First they asked them questions and brought them to our hut. We had a pass to stay in our fishpond hut. ... But the soldiers took the four Twa Ni Gone villagers away to kill them, and then we heard the sound of the gun: Doan, doan, doan, doan. One of the four killed was a schoolboy. He was in 10th Standard [Grade 10], so he was about 20 years old." - "Saw Ghaw" (M, xx), xxxx village, Mone township (Interview #29, 1/99)

"They killed Saw Gka Bweh, Maw Nyunt Po, Saw Lay Heh and my cousin Shaw Po Gkeh. When the Burmese shot at him their gun didn't work, so they dug out his eyes with a knife, cut open his belly and cut open all his intestines. It was Shan Bpu who killed him." - "Saw Tha Doh" (M, 18), xxxx village, Mone township, describing the murder of his cousin in November 1998 (Interview #13, 3/99)

"That first time they killed 2 people who were single and 2 who were married. Then the next time they killed 5 people - they were all Twa Ni Gone villagers as well. That was on December 26th or 27th [1998]. Three of those people were single and two were married. All the people they killed were Karen. ... They killed them for being friendly with the KNU. It's part of their 'dig out the roots' policy." - "Pu Hla Maung" (M, 57), xxxx village, Mone township (Interview #22, 1/99)

"They killed Saw Aye and Po Theh Pyay while they were fishing in their boat [in November 1998; Saw Aye was from Myeh Yeh and Po Theh Pyay from Ter Bpaw]. When they saw them, they demanded that they come to them. When Saw Aye and Po Theh Pyay got to them, they ordered them to raise their hands and then they shot them dead. After killing them, they cut off their heads and took them to Ter Bpaw and Po Thaung Su. They hung one of the heads on the path to Mone and the other on the path to Ler Doh [Kyauk Kyi]. They ordered people [villagers] to guard the heads and said that if the heads were lost they would be replaced by the heads of those who had been guarding them and lost them. People on sentry duty watched them all day and night. They finally threw the heads away when they were decomposing. They had been hanging there for over a month before they finally ordered them thrown away." - "Saw Tee Ko" (M, 40), xxxx village, Mone township (Interview #19, 2/99)

"They hung one of the heads on the path out of the village that goes to Mone and another on the path to Ler Doh. We had to cut bamboo and

weave it into stands like those used for drinking water and then put the heads on them. ... [T]hey ordered people to do sentry duty around those heads and if the heads disappeared, they said the villagers would have to replace them with our own heads. They kept them there for over a month and then another Army group came and forced the villagers to bury the heads." - "Saw Ner Muh" (M, 30+), xxxx village, Mone township (Interview #8, 4/99)

"On October 15th 1998, Sa Thon Lon Guerrilla Retaliation troops entered Thit Cha Seik village in Mone township and burned down the houses of village chairman Nga Soe and secretary Tin Win. Later they fired three M79 grenades into Ter Bpaw village. The grenades hit village headman Po Thaut Kya's house, killing his 2 daughters Naw Mu Lay, age 8, and Naw Dah Dah, age 2." - incident report from KHRG field reporter

"In our area, if we add it up, they are killing 2 or 3 people per day, but we are busy working so we don't have time to listen to that and we don't hear about it. Even though we're not listening for that news, we still hear of people dying every day, because the enemy is killing many people." - "Maung Baw" (M, 30), xxxx village, Kyauk Kyi township (Interview #39, 12/98)

Other Sa Thon Lon Activities

"One of them got married in Nga Nwah Seit. His name is Bo Maung Maung, he is from the Sa Thon Lon. He asked the girl's parents to give him their daughter, and she didn't like him but she had to marry him. People in the countryside are forced to marry them. They wrote letters to each of the villages and the village leaders had to collect enough money from all the villagers to pay for the food that was going to be prepared and for the clothing and jewellery, a necklace and earrings for the bride. The elders from my village of Yan Myo Aung collected money from the villagers and the whole village had to pay 17,000 [Kyats]. I don't know what other villages had to pay but big villages had to give more. He [Bo Maung Maung] showed movies in each village before the wedding to make money. Each person had to pay 50 Kyats for each night the movies were showing regardless of whether they went to see the movie or not. In our village they showed movies on two nights so we had to pay 100 Kyats each. One movie was an English movie and the other was Burmese, but I don't know the titles of the movies because I'm not interested in movies. The village elders couldn't do anything, they could only tell us that we had to pay whether we went or not, so some villagers went and watched

*the movies. After the wedding he [Bo Maung Maung] had a house built
in Nga Nwah Seit. It was a brick house and the villagers had to bring the
bricks as well as build the house. All the expense and labour that went
into that house came from the villagers.* " - "Saw Tee Ko" (M, 40), xxxx
village, Mone township (Interview #19, 2/99)

Though killing is their main function, the Sa Thon Lon units are also
involved in several other activities, some of which are deliberate efforts
to intimidate the villagers and some of which are the random and brutal
acts of undisciplined soldiers. Their overall purpose is to terrify the
villagers so that they will not support the opposition, and to achieve this
they make a point of trying to frighten villagers whenever they see them.
Ordering villagers not to look them in the eyes, refusing to tell them
anything, constantly moving and arriving by surprise in the middle of the
night are all tactics intended to disorient and frighten the villagers. Sa
Thon Lon leader Bo Shan Bpu makes a point of hitting villagers before
he even speaks to them whenever he meets them along the pathways.
One villager told KHRG that he and his teenage friends met Bo Shan
Bpu along a path near their fields - he immediately slapped them all in
the face, then asked them their ages and beat them for being younger and
yet taller than him. Another villager described how his 67-year-old father
was stopped by a Sa Thon Lon unit when going for SPDC forced labour
with other villagers; the leader beat all of them for not having passes, but
gave his father an extra beating because he was the eldest and should
therefore "know better".

*"My uncle asked me to help by pounding his paddy so I went to do that,
and on the way back I and two of my friends met the Short Pants. I was
with my friend M---, he is 16 years old. ... They asked us about our
passes and we showed them to them. Another one, Shan Bpu, came up to
us and he didn't say anything, he just slapped my face 3 times and
punched the three of us in the stomach once each. He asked M--- how old
he was and when he answered that he was 16 years old, Shan Bpu
punched him in the chest and said, 'Why are you taller than me if you are
16 years old?' I couldn't say anything because a soldier held a knife at
my throat and if I'd said anything he would have killed me. He asked
again, 'Why are you this big if you are only 16 years old?' Then he
slapped his face again. ... Shan Bpu said, 'Nga lo ma Kayin myo,
pyang!' [loosely translates as, 'You Karen sons of my whore, get out of
here!']. Then we rode our bicycles home."* - "Saw Tha Doh" (M, 18),
xxxx village, Mone township (Interview #13, 3/99)

"They even beat my father-in-law who is 67 years old. They force villagers to go back [from the relocation sites] and clear the paths in their old villages. Every morning villagers are going back to their own villages to cut the scrub. One morning in December, they came and saw villagers going to clear their old village. They asked for their passes but none of them had a pass, so they beat them all with fresh bamboo they had cut in the area. On that day, my father-in-law went instead of me because I had to go and give my paddy to the central [command]. ... They beat each of them 2 times with the exception of my father-in-law. He [the Sa Thon Lon commander] said that the others were young and had little knowledge, but that my father-in-law is old and should have enough knowledge to show some respect but didn't. So he was beaten 12 times. He is 67 years old and his head shakes all the time. ... When he returned after being beaten he got a fever, and we had to give him an injection of penicillin." - "Saw Ner Muh" (M, 30+), xxxx village, Mone township (Interview #8, 4/99)

"We hadn't done anything, we were just going to carry our paddy and they saw us, called us to them and then beat us. Most of us were Karen, but there were 3 children among us and they were Burmese. Some were 35, 40 or over 50 years old, and the children were about 10 years old. Eight of them called us over to beat us. First they just asked us, 'Where do you live?', and we told them we live in xxxx. They forced us to lie on our stomachs on the ground. They beat us with 8 cane sticks until all but one of the sticks were broken. They beat us here, on our legs. Thirteen of us were beaten, and they beat each of us ten times. The children were only beaten 3 times each, but they beat the rest of us with all of their strength. While they were beating us their officer [Shan Bpu] ordered them, 'If they move, shoot them dead at once'. Two of them were beating us, and the rest were aiming their guns at us." - "Naw Lah Paw" (F, 21), xxxx village, Mone township, describing her beating by Bo Shan Bpu's Sa Thon Lon unit in December 1998 (Interview #28, 1/99)

"When we were sitting and talking about how to get our living, the guerrillas [Sa Thon Lon] came suddenly. My friends saw them and ran away. I didn't run, because the Burmese soldiers always told us not to run when we see them. I stayed, and they came and asked me, 'Who was that running?' Before I answered he hit my head here and it bled. ... He hit me with his gun barrel, my face was cut here and my head was bleeding." – "Saw Tha Pwih" (M, 38), xxxx village, Tantabin township, Toungoo District (Interview #50, 5/99)

In order to preserve their element of secrecy and surprise, the Sa Thon Lon units have also been ordering villagers to kill their dogs. Many villagers keep small dogs which they take with them to the forest, particularly when hunting, and which provide security at night in the village by barking at strangers. Sa Thon Lon units do not want the villagers to know when they are arriving in the night, so when dogs bark at them they order the owner to be brought forward. They then order the owner to kill his dog, and in addition they beat or fine him as punishment. In the villages of T'Kaw Pwa, Way Sweh, Nga Byaw Daw, Twa Ni Gone, Haw Ko Ghaw, Lu Ah, and Weh Gyi, all in Mone township, Sa Thon Lon units issued orders in late 1998 for all villagers to kill their dogs. In T'Kaw Pwa village alone the dead dogs filled two bullock carts, and the villagers had to discard them outside the village. Some villagers tried to hide their dogs, but when these were found later the troops threatened to kill the owners if they wouldn't kill their own dogs, and most people complied out of fear.

"The Sa Thon Lon are moving in the area at night and don't like the dogs because they bark at them when they want to move secretly. They ordered the village headmen to tell people to kill all their dogs or they would beat the owners. They are really doing what they threatened to do. After killing the dogs that bark at them they beat their owners. Some of us loved our dogs and didn't want to kill them, so we tied our dogs in hiding places. It's not easy for them to be tied up all the time for many days, so we untied them sometimes. There was one night that they came and people didn't know they were coming. The dogs barked at them so they asked, 'Whose dogs are these?' People had to go and get the owners of the dogs, and when the owners came they said, 'If you are going to kill your dogs then kill them now, but if you aren't going to kill them then I'm going to kill you.' The dog owners were afraid of dying so they had to kill the dogs they loved. My dog was very good and obedient, so I was very upset but there was nothing I could do. Finally I had to kill it. When I killed it my children were crying loudly, but we had to kill it because we feared for our own lives. Our dog had to die for us. In T'Kaw Pwa village, people had to give them a list of all the dogs and then people had to kill all the dogs in the village. The dead dogs filled two bullock carts, and the people had to take them and throw them away in the fields." - "Naw Hser" (F, 40), xxxx village, Mone township (Interview #20, 2/99)

"They beat the dogs to death and then they beat the owners of the dogs [which bark at them]. If they shoot the dog dead, then they beat the owner and also demand 500 Kyats for the cost of the bullet after they beat him. They have ordered villagers in the area of Way Sweh, T'Kaw

Pwa and Nga Byaw Daw villages to kill all their dogs. ... Now there are no dogs there. I even had to kill my own dog. In Yan Myo Aung 10 dogs were killed, but in Twa Ni Gone, Haw Ko Ghaw, Lu Ah, Weh Gyi and T'Kaw Pwa all the dogs were killed." - "Saw Tee Ko" (M, 40), xxxx village, Mone township (Interview #19, 2/99)

The Sa Thon Lon units have threatened villagers with forced relocation and burned houses on occasion. They have also ordered villagers who have already been forcibly relocated to return by day to their old villages in Mone township to cut down all the fruit and other trees in the village and to clear scrub along the sides of footpaths, presumably to protect the Sa Thon Lon and other SPDC troops from ambush by eliminating cover for resistance forces while also making it harder for the villagers to find food in their villages. (For more information on forced relocations see below under 'Villages in the Sittaung River Plains'.) One villager stated that in March 1999, Sa Thon Lon units in Kyauk Kyi township began ordering villagers to build fences around their home villages, with only two gates for access. Villages in Tantabin township of Toungoo District have also been forced to fence in their villages.

"When we were in Yan Myo Aung, Bo Maung Maung came and told us, 'In this area, if I don't allow you to live here, you can't live here. If I allow you to stay you can stay, so cut down the trees and plants in the village so it looks clear.' Anytime he comes to the village he demands clothing, sarongs and food. When we see a taxi arriving with Shan Bpu inside it, everyone prays and no one feels like eating. He forces taxi drivers to take him wherever he wants to go, and he never pays them. When he came, all the villagers didn't dare move. Some hid in their rooms and others went to hide in their toilets." - "Naw Paw Paw Htoo" (F, 31), xxxx village, Mone township (Interview #12, 3/99)

"In March 1999, when the road construction was almost finished, the intelligence [Sa Thon Lon] soldiers of the SPDC Army ordered villages in Kyauk Kyi township to make fences around their villages. The villages were allowed to have only two gates." - "Naw Ghay" (F, xx), xxxx village, Kyauk Kyi township (Interview #11, 4/99)

"They forced us to fence our village and then they forced us to stick sharpened pieces of bamboo around the fence. People have to do that in every village." – "Saw Lay Muh" (M, 42), xxxx village, Tantabin township, Toungoo District (Interview #53, 5/99)

"Now they've closed everything. They don't allow people to go to farm. They burned every farm hut and ordered people not to go out of the village. They've fenced the village tightly." – "Pu Than Nyunt" (M, 60), xxxx village, Tantabin township, Toungoo District (Interview #52, 5/99)

Like other SPDC troops, the Sa Thon Lon units largely support themselves by looting and extorting money in villages. In Kyauk Kyi township, each family in villages where they operate has to pay 200 to 300 Kyat per week which is supposedly for the Sa Thon Lon soldiers' food. Villagers throughout their entire area of operations have to pay varying amounts of fees to support them. In addition, when they arrive in villages they choose a villager's house, go to stay there and demand that the house owner prepare food for them. One villager claimed that the Sa Thon Lon group that comes to his village demands at least 5 chickens per day; by Karen standards this is a grossly extravagant amount of meat for a group of only 10 people. They also take whatever they like from small village shops without paying, and demand that the villagers weave or buy fancy traditional clothing for them. The villagers often have to pool their money afterwards to pay for the food and goods they have taken. For transport, they commandeer bullock carts and bicycles, often ordering people with bicycles to deliver messages for them or summon people to them. When Bo Shan Bpu goes back and forth to town and along the roads, he never uses military transport, but instead orders local passenger vehicle or motorcycle drivers to take him wherever he wants to go without payment. His preference for civilian over military transport may be for his own safety; he is a KNLA target, so he may feel that he is safer travelling covertly with civilians.

"They commandeer bulls, carts and bicycles [to carry or send things for them]. Two bullock carts and one bicycle must be ready for their use each day. The bullock carts must take them wherever they want to go, and the bicycles have to send messages for them or go to summon anyone they want to see. In the past, although we had to give taxes and fees we could travel when there was no fighting, but since they've arrived people dare not travel or do their work. When people can't dare go anywhere they can't think of what to do with their lives." - "Saw Ner Muh" (M, 30+), xxxx village, Mone township, about the Sa Thon Lon (Interview #8, 4/99)

"They demanded we give them a chicken every day. We had to buy the chickens for them. When they demanded alcohol they didn't like the local rice whisky, they liked the alcohol that people sell in town. They demanded things like that for a long time, until the villagers couldn't

support it any longer. ... They once held a meeting where I heard them say, 'Whenever I go out [on patrol] you will hear that I have killed people.'" - "Saw Dee Ghay" (M, 38), xxxx village, Kyauk Kyi township, talking about the Sa Thon Lon (Interview #9, 4/99)

"When they came to our village, they went to the shops and took everything they liked without paying and then left. The villagers had to take up the cost of that. They did it 3 or 4 times. When they first arrived in our village we had to buy them a jacket which cost 5,000 Kyats and 5 or 6 sets of Karen traditional clothing and sarongs. ... We don't dare to wear watches and we hide our nice clothes. When the Sa Thon Lon enter the village and see you wearing nice clothes or watches, they demand that you give all of it to them. When a person from Tint Lwin's group saw my cousin's watch, he demanded the watch from my cousin but my cousin said, 'This is my mother's watch.' He slapped his face and took his watch anyway." - "Saw Ner Muh" (M, 30+), xxxx village, Mone township, describing the behaviour of Sa Thon Lon troops (Interview #8, 4/99)

The Sa Thon Lon troops are definitely targets of the KNLA, and as a result they are afraid to travel along the road from Kyauk Kyi to Mone because it skirts the western edge of the hills. To protect themselves, in January 1999 they began ordering villagers to build a new road about 5 kilometres further west, running from Na Than Gwin to Mone along the Sittaung River. The length of this road is 30 to 35 kilometres, and forced labour on it has been intensive because they are in a rush to complete it. Thousands of villagers had to rotate shifts of five days to a week building and smoothing a 4½ foot high embankment and roadbed all along its length between January and March 1999. Sa Thon Lon troops have been supervising the construction, which is now mainly complete except for a number of bridges. Villages have been ordered to provide all the timber for these bridges, and are currently being forced to build them. In April, when Sa Thon Lon commander Bo Maung Maung ordered a final intensive labour week to smooth the embankment, he told the villagers that at the end of the week he would ride a motorbike from Na Than Gwin to Mone and back, and that if he ever had to stop his motorbike because the road was too bumpy the villagers would "know about it". (For more information on this road see below under 'Villages in the Sittaung River Plains: Forced Labour on Roads'.)

Several Sa Thon Lon soldiers have also forced local girls to marry them. The most notorious case of this involved Bo Shan Bpu in Mone township. In December 1998 he saw Naw O---, a 19 year old girl from

Lu Ah village, working in her family's beanfield. He grabbed her and tried to rape her, and she fled. Later he went to her village and asked her parents and the village headman for her in marriage, even though there are some reports that he already had a wife elsewhere. When Naw O--- heard this she fled her village and went to Toungoo. Then Bo Shan Bpu threatened that if she did not return he would burn the village and kill everyone in it, so her parents called her back and she was forced to marry him on December 25th. He ordered her to move to Meik Tha Lin but she didn't want to go, so to encourage her he burned down her family's house in early January. Realising that after that he would be known throughout the district as the man who burned down his father-in-law's house, he then burned down all the houses in Lu Ah village. The Lu Ah villagers had to flee, and are now living in small shelters in a field outside Weh Gyi village. All of these details have been confirmed by the testimony of several different villagers from the area. One villager reported that after that time, he arrived at xxxx village with a bunch of pigs he had stolen, intending to use them to buy a girl named Naw L--- in marriage, but when he found out she was away studying in town he forced the villagers to buy the pigs he had brought and then left.

"We saw a girl in Lu Ah treated this way. Shan Bpu asked the village headman, her parents and the villagers to give her to him. Both her parents and the village headman had to tell her to marry him. The villagers told her the same thing. They said, 'If you don't marry him they will kill us all, as the village headman and your parents told you.' Finally, she had to give herself to the Burmese [soldier] because she loves her parents, the village headman and the villagers. ... She was crying when they first got married and after they were married she was still crying because she doesn't like him. Now her husband has called her to go and live in another area but she didn't go, so he said that she was too attached to her house and returned to burn down his father-in-law's house. When he had finished burning his father-in-law's house he was worried that people would say 'He's the one who burned his own father-in-law's house', so he burned down every house in the village." - "Saw Tee Ko" (M, 40), xxxx village, Mone township (Interview #19, 2/99)*

"She told her siblings, 'I feel very sad that I had to sell myself because of all of you. I want to die but I don't know how to die.' So her siblings are very sad for her also. Whenever she sees her siblings she tells them she is very ashamed. We told her not to be ashamed. She asked us how to suffer this kind of life and we told her there's no other option but to suffer like this. Shan Bpu burned the houses of his in-laws and then burned all the houses in the village. He burned all 50 or 60 houses in [Lu Ah] village

plus all the bamboo that the villagers were going to use to build new houses. That happened in early January [1999] ... They built temporary huts in a place near Haw Ko Ghaw, but then they had to move and build temporary huts in the field near Weh Gyi. ... They are living in the fields and can't build [proper] houses because all of their things were burned."
- "Naw Hser" (F, 40), xxxx village, Mone township (Interview #20, 2/99)

"He killed four people after he got married. He got married on December 25th, and on the night of December 26th he called four people out of the village and killed them." - "Saw Ghaw" (M, xx), xxxx village, Mone township (Interview #29, 1/99)

"They raped a woman near Zayat Gyi. She is a teacher and she is Burmese, not Karen. That group calls themselves the Garuda group. Then they had to go back to clear that up so Bo Shwit [Shan Bpu] came to replace them. When the Garuda group was in our area they came and ate in our village and they just interrogated people, they didn't torture them, but when Bo Shwit came we saw killing and beating." - "Pu Than Nyunt" (M, 60), xxxx village, Tantabin township, Toungoo District (Interview #52, 5/99)

Bo Maung Maung and other Sa Thon Lon soldiers have also reportedly forced local women to marry them. Villagers in Mone township repeatedly complain that every time a Sa Thon Lon soldier marries, everyone in the area is forced to give money as a wedding gift. When Bo Maung Maung was getting married, he sent orders to several villages demanding money for the wedding feast, clothing and jewellery; for Yan Myo Aung relocation site alone, the total came to 17,000 Kyat. Bo Maung Maung then arranged for movies to be shown on two consecutive nights in each village, and everyone had to pay 50 Kyat per night for the movies whether they went to see them or not. After each Sa Thon Lon soldier gets married, the villagers have been forced to buy bricks, take them to the village where the soldier wants to live, and build a brick house and surrounding fence for the bride and groom.

"Sa Thon Lon soldiers also liked two female students around the age of 16. Those girls were about to write their examinations, but instead they left the school and fled." - "Naw Hser" (F, 40), xxxx village, Mone township (Interview #20, 2/99)

"In Shan Bpu's section, all the soldiers are stupid and impudent because all of them are NCO's [Non-Commissioned Officers]. When each of them got married, the villagers had to give them money for gifts and money for

pigs. When they gave the invitation to the village headman, it had written on it how much money each village had to give and it also said that everyone must go to the wedding and bring money as a gift. It said those who didn't go must still give 500 Kyats as a forced gift. The villagers had to bring wood and build a house with a fence around the garden for each of them after they got married. They got married one by one and the villagers had to do that each time but they didn't dare to say anything. ... I didn't go but many people had to go to build their houses. They have to live in nicer houses than ours." - "Naw Paw Paw Htoo" (F, 31), xxxx village, Mone township (Interview #12, 3/99)

"You have to work for them all the time. Any time they force you to work, you must go and do it. You have to carry bricks and build houses for their families. If they order you to bring them 30 bullock-carts filled with bricks, you must bring it to them as they say. ... We got the bricks from a place beside Yan Myo Aung village. We had to buy them. ... We took the bricks to Bo Maung Maung, and then he ordered carpenters and others to build brick houses for them." - "Saw Tha Doh" (M, 18), xxxx village, Mone township (Interview #13, 3/99)

Villagers also complain that whenever they have their own festivals, they are under orders to invite the local Sa Thon Lon group, who usually ruin the festival by demanding alcohol and frightening everyone. According to villagers who recently fled the area, villagers in Nyaung Bin Seik village of northern Mone township were having a festival in March in honour of a monk who had died, and Bo Shan Bpu was there. When a young woman was singing on stage people were going up to give her presents. Bo Shan Bpu went up on the stage and tried to grab her, but some local young men drove him off and had to be held back or they would have hit him. Bo Shan Bpu left, but then came back and fired M79 grenades into the crowd without warning, killing one villager and wounding several others. In another example, after killing a villager named U Kyi Hmwe in Shan Su village of Shwegyin township in December 1998, the Nagah section of the Sa Thon Lon came to the funeral ceremony being held by the villagers and started playing cards and drinking as though it were a party. However, in the midst of all these other activities the Sa Thon Lon groups continue to focus on their main function, which is to execute villagers. On December 26th 1998, the day after his wedding, Sa Thon Lon commander Bo Shan Bpu called four people out of Twa Ni Gone village and executed them, and on the 27th he killed and beheaded Saw San Myint, a young man from Baw Bpee Der village.

"In Nyaung Bin Seik people were having a festival in honour of a dead monk, and there was a stage show. While one performer was dancing and singing, people were going up to give her presents. Shan Bpu also went to give her a present, but he acted like he would grab her so her friends got angry and jumped up to protect her from him. He got angry too and said, 'I was giving her a present with good intentions, but you've made a scene'. Then he went and fired shells among the crowd and the performers." – "Saw Lah Thaw" (M), xxxx relocation site, Mone township, describing an incident in March 1999 (Interview #2, 5/99)

"We live not too far from the KNLA, so they call us 'rebels'. They force the villagers to work for them and to give them what they want. They don't like people asking them questions. They don't even like people to look at their faces. They're walking from place to place every day, and if they enter our village we have to prepare whatever they want to eat. They order more than 5 chickens for each meal. ... They said that if the villagers were going to have any kind of party, they had to be invited. We invited them to a wedding in the village when we had pork for everyone. However, they didn't like pork and demanded steamed duck, so we had to steam ducks for them." - "Saw Ner Muh" (M, 30+), xxxx village, Mone township (Interview #8, 4/99)

"He was Burmese, his name was U Kyi Hmwe and he was 45 years old. They accused him of helping the KNU, which he had. They are killing all the villagers who have had contact with the KNU since it was formed, including Burmans. They took him halfway [along a path] and then slit his throat. ... While the villagers were having a [funeral] ceremony for U Kyi Hmwe, they came to play cards and drank alcohol as though the villagers were having a party for them. They were happy, but they kill very brutally." - "Saw Htoo Lay" (M, 25), xxxx village, Kyauk Kyi township, talking about the Sa Thon Lon (Interview #30, 12/98)

KNLA and DKBA Activities

"The enemy [SPDC] persecuted us. My mother and father were in contact with the Nga Pway, because we had to feed them too. We have to be afraid of all of them and feed them all, both Nga Pway and the Burmese." - "Saw Yeh" (M, 19), xxxx village, Kyauk Kyi township; 'Nga pway' ('ringworm') is SPDC slang for KNU/KNLA (Interview #42, 12/98)

The Karen National Liberation Army (KNLA) is very active in Nyaunglebin District, particularly in the hills which cover the eastern three fourths of its area. The KNLA does not have complete control over any area, but they have a form of de facto partial control in the area of villages such as Tee Muh Hta and Tee Nya B'Day Kee in eastern Kyauk Kyi township. SPDC forces do not dare enter these areas except in well-armed and usually large columns. When they do enter, the KNLA soldiers and many of the villagers disappear deeper into the forest and higher into the hills, only to return as soon as the SPDC column is gone. The villagers in these areas, particularly those whose villages have been destroyed and who are internally displaced, sometimes seek shelter or medical help from KNLA units. The KNLA obtains much of its intelligence on SPDC movements from the villagers, and in return warns villagers when SPDC columns are coming into the area. The KNLA units themselves are small and mobile, usually consisting of 20 or 30 soldiers. They engage primarily in hit-and-run ambush and harrassment operations, avoiding large battles. KNLA units also penetrate the Sittaung River plains to ambush SPDC units and to go to villages there to obtain food, taxes and porters, but they cannot stay in the plains for any length of time because there are too many SPDC troops there. In recent months the KNLA has made several incursions into the plains to attack Sa Thon Lon units and they have tried to kill Bo Shan Bpu on at least one occasion, but without success.

The KNLA's weapons are few in number and old but well maintained, and their ammunition supply is severely limited. They get most of their food from the villagers, demanding it as a form of tax from villages which are stable enough to produce a reasonable crop. Cash taxes are also demanded from the elders of such villages. In Nyaunglebin District these demands are mainly levied against those villages in the hills which have not been destroyed and against villages in the eastern part of the Sittaung River plains. The KNLA also asks for porters, but they only have to go for short periods and are not physically abused; only able-bodied men are taken, and households which have no one fit to go are

Whenever their troops are attacked by the KNLA, the DKBA reacts against the villagers. After an attack by the KNLA in late December 1998 in Kyauk Kyi township, DKBA troops called in the local SPDC Battalion and the two groups cooperated in forcibly relocating Kya Plaw and Leh Wain Gyi villages to a forced relocation site in the first week of January 1999. After another KNLA attack on November 12th 1998, the DKBA arrested three villagers from Thu K'Bee village in Kyauk Kyi township and executed them on November 20th. There have also been abuses resulting from lack of discipline among DKBA troops; for example, in March 1999 a drunken DKBA Sergeant named Saw Shwe Min demanded that a young woman marry him in Taw Ko village of Kyauk Kyi township. When she refused, he fired his gun outside the village, claimed he had fired at the KNLA, and fined and robbed the villagers as punishment. The young woman who refused him no longer dares to live in the village.

"On November 12th 1998 the KNLA shot at the DKBA, those who broke with the KNU, but the DKBA didn't have time to fight them. Then the DKBA said that the villagers are feeding the KNLA and that the villagers had asked the KNLA to shoot at them. That's why the DKBA arrested two villagers, Maung Htwe Soe and Maung Kyaw Thaung Klaw, from Thu K'Bee village. They took them to their camp at Klaw Maw Pagoda. Then on 19/11/98 the DKBA arrested an Indian [villager of Indian descent] from Leh Wain Gyi village. The DKBA took all 3 of them to a place near Klaw Maw pagoda and killed them. They said that they were the backbone of the KNU. Battalion Commander Bo Po Maung of [DKBA] Brigade 777 gave the order to Platoon Commander Saw Ku Mu to kill them. People who had to go for 'loh ah pay' saw that when they were on their way back and then came back to tell us about it. The people who saw it said that the 3 of them were killed on 20/11/98 at 8:10 a.m." - "Saw Htoo Lay" (M, 25), xxxx village, Kyauk Kyi township (Interview #30, 12/98)

"On March 7th 1999 at 9 p.m., DKBA Sergeant Saw Shwe Min went to Taw Ko village in the plain area of Kyauk Kyi township. He asked for the love of Naw M---, age 25. She refused because she knows he already has a wife and children, so he got drunk and then left the village and fired his gun. Then he said that he had shot at the KNLA and ordered the villagers of the entire village tract to pay the price of the bullet, 20,000 Kyat [which is at least 50 times the real price of a bullet], as well as 4 watches with metal bands and 4 watches with plastic/leather bands. He said he would ask her to love him again, and that if she refused he would shoot

her dead. As a result Naw M--- is afraid to stay in her village anymore."
- incident report from KHRG field reporter

Despite the forced labour and occasional abuses, the DKBA is perceived by villagers as being much better than the SPDC. In their other areas of operation further south, they sometimes protect villagers from the worst SPDC abuses. As a result, some villagers in Nyaunglebin District have tried to escape the Sa Thon Lon death squads by taking refuge with the DKBA. Some villagers report that this has worked, while others have given examples where the DKBA has handed villagers over to the SPDC for execution. It appears that the DKBA is willing to protect innocent people who are fleeing the Sa Thon Lon squads, but if they are subsequently asked to hand over a specific person by name they will do so. This reflects the complex nature of the relations between the DKBA and the SPDC; while the DKBA is allied to the SPDC and helps the regime in many ways, most DKBA soldiers personally hate and distrust the SPDC. Some DKBA soldiers and commanders are more interested in personal power and loot than anything else, but there are also those who want to protect Karen people from the SPDC's abuses as much as they can. However, when faced with direct demands and orders from the SPDC they have little choice but to comply or face direct punishments and restrictions on their activities.

*"Some people have gone to live in Klaw Maw because the Sa Thon Lon are looking for them to kill them. They don't dare live anywhere except with the DKBA. They've told their friends that they can't run anywhere so they go and take refuge with the DKBA. ... When I went to the DKBA area in Klaw Maw there were more than 50 or 60 households of villagers there. The villagers there hire themselves out to others in the area who are ordered to go for forced labour but aren't able to go [the forced labour is pagoda-building for the DKBA]. They hire themselves out for 200 Kyats per day and use that money to buy food. People living in Klaw Maw said to me, 'We don't know what is going to happen to Klaw Maw after the pagodas are completely finished. If there is no DKBA area then we will have no safe area to live
in, and we don't know of any other place where we can take refuge. We're really afraid of the Sa Thon Lon.'"* - "Naw Hser" (F, 40), xxxx village, Mone township (Interview #20, 2/99)

"His name was Pa Mee and his wife, who is now staying with her siblings, is called Naw P---. He was not a village headman but he had helped the KNU. The Strategic Commander of Infantry Battalion #60 ordered him to meet them at Thaung Bo. He didn't dare go and instead

fled and went to stay with the DKBA. The Strategic Commander told the DKBA that they wanted to see Pa Mee. The DKBA sent Pa Mee to him and he shot Pa Mee dead. After they killed him they took his belongings, such as his cattle, his buffaloes and his sugar cane plantation." - "Saw Htoo Lay" (M, 25), xxxx village, Kyauk Kyi township; Pa Mee was executed in July 1998 (Interview #30, 12/98)

"The [SPDC] guerrilla troops threaten them and they have to hide and sleep in secret places. They face many problems. Some villagers move to the DKBA area for a while. The DKBA has said that if those troops want the people who they are after, they can't stop them." - "Saw Ta Roh" (M, 37), xxxx village, Shwegyin township (Interview #32, 12/98)

Villages in the Sittaung River Plains

*"All of us were forced to relocate to a field near Thit Cha Seik and live in
an open area where there are no [rice] fields and it's very hot. Thit Cha
Seik [village] lies to the east of the car road and the place they kept us
was to the west of the car road. They call the place Gwet Thit ['New
Area']. The Sa Thon Lon came and forced us to go back to our village
and cut down all the trees. We had to burn and clear everything except
the coconut trees. ... They also forced Lu Ah villagers to move to live in
Weh Gyi on the bank of the Bpareh Loh [Sittaung] river. ... All the trees
in Lu Ah village were cut down. ... We are allowed to go back to our
fields but we have to carry a pass. A pass costs 5 Kyats and is good for 3
days to a week. We can't sleep at our fields. We can't leave before 6:00
a.m. and have to return by 6:00 p.m. At first they didn't tell us we needed
a pass, but after they saw people who had no passes and then beat them,
people started to carry passes even when they go for 'loh ah pay'."* -
"Saw Ner Muh" (M, 30+), xxxx village, Mone township (Interview #8,
4/99)

The villages in the Sittaung River plains in the west of the district are
normally fertile and prosperous, so it is the first time that significant
numbers of people have begun fleeing these villages. The reasons which
eventually led to their flight began accumulating several years ago, when
SLORC authorities began forced relocations of many of the villages
between the Sittaung River and the hills to the east. The relocated
villagers could still return to farm their fields but only under heavy
restrictions. In the past two years, demands for crop quotas, extortion
money and forced labour placed on them increased to a point where they
could no longer bear it, particularly when combined with the failure of
rice crops of 1997 and 1998 due to floods and droughts. When the Sa
Thon Lon Guerrilla Retaliation squads began patrolling the area in late
1998, killing people along the pathways and beating and terrorising
farmers in their fields, this was the final straw for many people. They no
longer dared go to their fields, they could not earn a living, and yet they
still faced the constant demands for money, crop quotas and forced
labour from the regular SPDC units and civilian authorities. They saw no
option left to them except flight.

Forced Relocations

*"In December of 1998 they ordered us to relocate from our village of
xxxx to Kaw Tha Say, but I moved to yyyy instead. There are no longer*

any people in xxxx because they only gave us 3 days to relocate. They said if they saw us in our village after 3 days they would kill us." - "Naw K'Ser Tee" (F, 29), xxxx village, Kyauk Kyi township (Interview #10, 4/99)

The first forced relocations in the plains area of the district occurred over 20 years ago in the mid-1970's, when the BSPP regime, predecessor of the SLORC and SPDC, initiated the 'Four Cuts' policy - a policy to cut all supplies of food, funds, recruits and information from the resistance groups by bringing all villagers under direct Army control, punishing villagers for attacks by resistance forces, and pressuring villagers with excessive extortion, looting, and stealing crops and livestock so that they will never have any food or resources to give to resistance groups. This policy is still in effect today. As the initial relocations were not sustainable, most villagers gradually ended up back in their home villages. In 1991, after a battle between SLORC and KNLA forces in southern Mone township, the villages of Myeh Yeh, Ter Bpaw, Po Thaung Su, Twa Ni Gone, Bpa Reh Si, Noh Htaw Hta, and Ta Maw Ma were forced to move to a buffalo-grazing field at Yan Myo Aung, along the road between Kyauk Kyi and Na Than Gwin. Three to four years later some of these villagers were allowed to move back to their villages, but as soon as the SLORC troops rotated they were forced back again and many of them have now been living at Yan Myo Aung relocation site for three years or more. The site itself is a terrible choice; in rainy season it floods and the water can be waist deep in places, while in dry season there is no good water. The SLORC drilled a well but the villagers complain that the water it produces makes people sick unless they purify it first two or three times using sand pots.

"When we first arrived we had to clear the bushes and trees to stay there, because they forced us to move to a jungle area where a nearby village let its buffaloes forage for food. It was rainy season and water was everywhere. The water came up to our waists in places. It was very hard to live." - "Saw Tee Ko" (M, 40), xxxx village, Mone township, describing conditions in Yan Myo Aung relocation site (Interview #19, 2/99)

"When we first arrived at the relocation site they opened a clinic that provided medicine but it was only open for 10 days. They pretended to take care of us but they didn't really. ... In our area people suffer from fever, coughing and diarrhoea. The water there is not clear. They made a pump well for us but the water from that well makes your teeth and gums turn green if you drink it before purifying it. We dug our own well

and it gives water that doesn't need to be purified before using it, but that well only has water in it during the rainy season. Most of the time we have to use water from their pump well and purify it in two steps, using sand pots, to make it clear. 50% of the people there, including me, had goitres because of the water. People there [at Yan Myo Aung] are not healthy. They suffer from fatigue and dizziness, but they have to stay that way because they have no way to solve the problem. There are no healthy looking people there, only skinny people." - "Naw Hser" (F, 40), xxxx village, Mone township (Interview #20, 2/99)

Other relocation sites have been established more recently at Mone, Weh Gyi and Thit Cha Seik in Mone township, and Yan Gyi Aung and Kaw Tha Say in Kyauk Kyi township, and Than Seik/Min Lan in Shwegyin township; there are certainly other sites as well, but KHRG has not yet been able to confirm them. The following list (Table 1) shows 39 villages known to have been forcibly relocated and which are still not allowed to return home, based on the testimony of villagers from the area. Some of these villages have been forced to move two or three times in the past several years, to a relocation site, then back to their villages, then to another relocation site, and so on. This list is far from complete.

All of those listed in the table are currently not allowed to stay in their home villages. Many villages, such as Myeh Yeh in Mone township, have a Karen section and a Burman section; the SPDC accused the village of being "full of rebels" and forced the Karen section to move but not the Burman section. Villages which are primarily Burman, such as Thit Cha Seik, were not forced to move. Ma Bpee Po and Ma Bpee Doh villages (frequently referred to together as Ma Bpee) were previously forced to Yan Gyi Aung site, but have since returned to their village and are currently paying a large amount of money each month to local SPDC troops as a bribe to avert forced relocation. Similarly, Yay Leh village in Mone township and Baw Ka Hta village in Kyauk Kyi township are paying in order not to be relocated; such bribes can be in the tens of thousands of Kyat per month, and as soon as the village can no longer pay or the troops rotate they may be forced to relocate. For example, a former elder from xxxx village stated that his village could not pay the money demanded three to four years ago, so they were forced back into Yan Myo Aung site while Ter Bpaw and Po Thaung Su paid 300,000 Kyat each to the SPDC troops to be allowed to remain in their villages, and Yay Leh had to pay 500,000 Kyat because it is a larger village; however, since that time both Ter Bpaw and Po Thaung Su were forced to move to a field west of Thit Cha Seik, while only Yay Leh in that area continues to pay to be exempted.

Table 1: 39 villages known to have been forcibly relocated and which are still not allowed to return home,

From	Township	To	Order Date	Remarks
Baw Bpee Der	Mone	Mone town outskirts	4/99	
Myau Oo	Mone	Mone town outskirts	4/99	
Aung Chan Tha	Mone	Mone town outskirts	4/99	
Kyaut Bu Daung	Mone	Mone town outskirts	4/99	
Sweh Dtee	Kyauk Kyi	Baw Ka Hta/ Kaw Tha Say	15/1/99	
Noh Nya Thu	Kyauk Kyi	Yan Myo Aung	7/1/99	
Kya Plaw	Kyauk Kyi	Yan Myo Aung	7/1/99	
Leh Wain Gyi	Kyauk Kyi	Pa Hee Ko	3/1/99	SPDC+DKBA moved, then burned
Ma Oo Bin	Shwegyin	Than Seik/Min Lan	1/99	
Kyi Pin Su	Shwegyin	Than Seik/Min Lan	1/99	
Leh Bain (Leh Pa)	Mone	Yan Myo Aung	1/99	
Lu Ah	Mone	Yan Myo Aung	1/99	
Hintha Weh	Kyauk Kyi	Kaw Tha Say	1/99	
Nga Peh Inn	Kyauk Kyi	Paleh Taw	12/98	
Shan Su	Shwegyin	Paleh Taw	12/98	
Kaw Chay Moo	Kyauk Kyi	unspecified	10/98	
Lan Gweh	Kyauk Kyi	unspecified	10/98	
Twa Ni Gone	Mone	Yan Myo Aung	1997/98	Forced several times since 1991
Bpa Reh Si	Mone	Yan Myo Aung	1997/98	Forced several times since 1991
Myeh Yeh	Mone	Yan Myo Aung	1997/98	Forced several times since 1991
Noh Htaw Hta	Mone	Yan Myo Aung	1997/98	Forced several times since 1991

Ta Maw Ma	Mone	Yan Myo Aung	1997/98	Forced several times since 1991
Po Thaung Su	Mone	Thit Cha Seik	1997	First moved to Yan Myo Aung in 1991
Nga Law Der	Mone	Thit Cha Seik	1997	First moved to Yan Myo Aung in 1991
Oo Chit Kin	Mone	Thit Cha Seik	1997	First moved to Yan Myo Aung in 1991
Ter Bpaw	Mone	Thit Cha Seik	1997	First moved to Yan Myo Aung in 1991
Tha Htay Gone	Mone	Thit Cha Seik	1997	First moved to Yan Myo Aung in 1991
Thay Ko Bu	Shwegyin	none specified	1997	No site specified, just driven out
Thein Kyo	Shwegyin	none specified	1997	No site specified, just driven out
Kyaw Ah Gweh Hta	Shwegyin	none specified	1997	No site specified, just driven out
Doh Ko Wah	Shwegyin	none specified	1997	No site specified, just driven out
Bplaw Hta	Shwegyin	none specified	1997	No site specified, just driven out
Meh Theh	Shwegyin	none specified	1997	No site specified, just driven out
Toh Kee	Shwegyin	none specified	1997	No site specified, just driven out
Wah May Kyo	Shwegyin	Than Seik/Min Lan	1997	
Deh Oo Po	Shwegyin	Than Seik/Min Lan	1997	
Saw Theh Kee	Shwegyin	Than Seik/Min Lan	1997	
Bweh Si Kee	Shwegyin	Than Seik/Min Lan	1997	
Maw Pi Yah	Shwegyin	Baw Hta		
Zee Byu Gone	Tantabin	Taw Ma Aye	1999	In southern Toungoo District

"They have forced all the villages around Yan Myo Aung to move to Yan Myo Aung. It is about 2 hours walking from xxxx. The villages that were relocated are Twa Ni Gone, Yay Leh, Bpa Reh Si, Noh Htaw Hta, Myeh Yeh and Si Bpaw Bpaw. Those people have to stay in Yan Myo Aung." - "Pu Hla Maung" (M, 57), xxxx village, Mone township (Interview #22, 1/99)

"Yay Leh, Ter Bpaw, Po Thaung Su and other villages bribed the soldiers with money so they could stay in their old villages. Each village had to pay hundreds of thousands of Kyats to bribe the soldiers. I heard that Ter Bpaw and Po Thaung Su had to pay 300,000 Kyats each. Yay Leh village is large, so they had to give 500,000 Kyats. As for our village, we couldn't bribe them so we had to relocate again." - "Saw Tee Ko" (M, 40), xxxx village, Mone township, describing the second time his village was forced to Yan Myo Aung relocation site, in 1994 (Interview #19, 2/99)

"We returned to xxxx [their home village] over two years ago. We just came back by ourselves. Now they're demanding more money from xxxx than other villages, but we give it to be allowed to live in our village. Some people are still left in Taw Ma Aye [relocation site]." - "Naw Paw Ghay" (F, 34), xxxx village, Tantabin township, Toungoo District (Interview #54, 5/99)

"The Burmese kept coming to the village and demanding money, poultry and pigs. Then they forced everyone out of the village. They forced them to Baw Ka Hta [where the SPDC camp is]." - "Naw Eh Muh" (F, 51), xxxx village, Kyauk Kyi township (Interview #17, 2/99)

Relocation sites are chosen by the SPDC for their ease of control by the Army. Yan Gyi Aung and Than Seik/Min Lan sites are alongside the Shwegyin-Kyauk Kyi vehicle road. The site at Thit Cha Seik is in a field west of the Kyauk Kyi - Mone road, and the site at Weh Gyi is beside a new road from Na Than Gwin to Mone being built with forced labour. Kaw Tha Say and Baw Ka Hta sites are right beside SPDC Army camps. The newest relocation site, created in April 1999, is on the outskirts of Mone town. Conditions at the relocation sites are generally bad; they are often on lowlying land prone to flooding and there is usually no good water available. Nothing is provided for the villagers; they must bring along building materials they have stripped from their houses in their home villages, or find materials around the new site. They must also bring along whatever rice and other food they can, as none is ever supplied by the authorities.

"As for those who are staying in the relocation sites, they have to do day labour and have difficulty finding food from day to day. They can't go back to work in their villages because some of them are from Mah Bpee and Sweh Dtee, which are very far away so travelling is difficult for them. Many of the people from Hintha Weh who went to live in Baw Ler Hta died of illness. Some of those people fled to the west of the Pay Sa Loh river, and many went to live in Ler Doh [Kyauk Kyi town]. ... I have been there and people in Yan Gyi Aung can't live there all together, their lives are very hard. Some have gone to live with their relatives in other villages so in the relocation site there aren't many villagers left." - "Naw Hser" (F, 40), xxxx village, Mone township (Interview #20, 2/99)

Medicine is not supplied either, and many villagers die of treatable diseases in the relocation sites. Those who have been forced to Yan Myo Aung site say that when it was first established in 1991, the SLORC set up a clinic but it was only open for 10 days, and there has been no access to medical help since then. Those who are sick have to go to hospital in towns like Kyauk Kyi, and they have to take along enough money to pay all the costs of treatment and to buy all required medicines, which are expensive. Villagers are not allowed to bring medicines from town to the relocation sites or villages because the SPDC wants to ensure that no medicine can reach resistance forces; as a result, villagers are threatened that anyone caught with medicine outside the towns will be executed.

"There was no medicine and we weren't allowed to carry medicine. When our children were ill, we went to buy medicine for them and had to hide the medicine on the way back. If they [the Burmese soldiers] saw us with medicine, they would have killed us. After the soldiers told us that, no one carried medicine anymore so no one was killed for that reason. When my children were ill I had to give them traditional medicine and if that didn't work I had to take them to the hospital. We couldn't carry medicine but we were allowed to take sick people to the hospital." - "Saw Tee Ko" (M, 40), xxxx village, Mone township (Interview #19, 2/99)

"We dare not go to the government hospital if we have no money. If we don't take money they don't give us medicine. [If it is serious] we have to try hard to find the money to cure the disease. Mostly we treat things using traditional medicines. My children have never had an injection or vaccination. They called us to go and get vaccinations for our children but we were afraid because people said their children got fevers after the injection." - "Naw Mary" (F, 30), xxxx village, Mone township (Interview #15, 3/99)

According to a villager from xxxx who fled Thit Cha Seik relocation site in March 1999, SPDC troops are now registering the names of young men from villages in the area for what she believes will be forced recruitment to the SPDC Army in the near future. This is normal SPDC practice in areas which they completely control; each village is forced to provide a number of recruits per month or per year, the number being set based on the village size. Villagers whose sons are drawn in the lottery can only get out of it by paying a very large bribe.

"Now they [the SPDC Army] are going to collect soldiers and I have two younger brothers who are single. We were worried for them so we moved away from our village. They are registering names and they say the villagers who become soldiers won't have to give any fees anymore." - "Naw Mary" (F, 30), xxxx village, Mone township (Interview #15, 3/99)

There was a spate of forced relocations in 1997, then somewhat of a lull through early 1998. However, in late 1998 and early 1999, there have been more relocations as well as repeat relocations of villages which had previously made their way back home. This is probably connected with the aim of the Sa Thon Lon Guerrilla Retaliation units to bring all villagers under complete control, execute any with past or present KNLA connections as a warning to the others, and make the area into a 'white area', which is SPDC terminology for regions where the population has been completely subjugated. After Sa Thon Lon Guerrilla Retaliation officer Bo Shan Bpu burned all the houses in Lu Ah village in January 1999, the village was forced to move to a field near Weh Gyi, along the new road which is being built by forced labour under Sa Thon Lon supervision. Also in January, Kya Plaw and Leh Wain Gyi villages were ordered to move to Yan Myo Aung and Pa Hee Ko, and immediately afterward the villages were burned by regular SPDC troops. The forced relocation in April 1999 of Baw Bpee Der, Myau Oo and Aung Chan Tha villages, none of which had been relocated before, to a new relocation site on the outskirts of Mone town seems to indicate that the immediate future will probably bring even more forced relocations. Those who are still in their home villages go on living in the hope that they can remain there and in some cases paying heavy bribes for the privilege, while those who have already relocated try to survive by making the dangerous trip back home to farm their old fields whenever they can get a pass to do so from the SPDC.

"Recently, when a battle occurred at Saw Mu Theh involving the DKBA, they [the Burmese] forced the villagers from 2 villages, Leh Wain Gyi and Kya Plaw, to move to a relocation site near the Ler Doh car road.

They called it Pa Hee Ko village. The [SPDC] guerrilla troops were working [on this] together with the DKBA. All the villagers had to move within 3 days starting on January 3rd [1999]. After they finished moving, the villages were burned. They said that if the villagers couldn't move within 3 days they would fine us and cause us pain. If we couldn't carry all of our things they would be happy because they could take them and sell them." - "Saw Htoo Lay" (M, 25), xxxx village, Kyauk Kyi township, talking about the Sa Thon Lon (Interview #30, 12/98)

Returning to the Old Villages

"I will tell you about the people who relocated to Yan Myo Aung. They are going back to eat in their old villages but they aren't allowed to keep their rice there. When they [Burmese soldiers] saw the rice and living place of a Bpa Reh Si villager named H---, they burned down all his rice and paddy just after he had finished putting his harvest in his storage barn. They also burned the rice storage barns of his friends that were near his storage barn. That happened just a few days ago." - "Saw Kyaw" (M, 34), Yan Myo Aung relocation site, Mone township (Interview #23, 1/99)

Many of the Karen villages in the plains east of the Sittaung River currently lie abandoned because their inhabitants have been forced to relocation sites or have fled. Many people spend part of their time in the relocation site and part of their time hiding around their old village or in their farmfield huts with or without a valid pass, leading a tenuous and risky existence. Some Karen villagers have gone to stay in the Burman villages which were not forced to move. In some villages which had a Karen section and a Burman section only the Karen section was forced to move, and some of the Karen villagers have now returned to stay on the fringes of the Burman section. Villagers from Myeh Yeh in Mone township who have done this say that they can stay but that all the passing SPDC columns demand much more food from them than from the Burmans. People can never be sure for how long they'll be allowed to stay where they are, and in such circumstances there is little or no chance to send their children to school.

"The situation is bad and we must move up and down, fleeing and sleeping outside whenever they [SPDC] come and tell us things [i.e. issue a new relocation order], so we can't send them to school. The situation is very unstable. There is a government school but we can't send them there. We learn Karen language at the pastor's house, mostly reading from the Bible. People dare not open a school to teach the

villagers." - "Naw Mary" (F, 30), xxxx village, Mone township (Interview #15, 3/99)

"My eldest child is 10 years old and has never been able to go to school because we have to run every year." - "Saw Kyaw" (M, 34), Yan Myo Aung relocation site, Mone township (Interview #23, 1/99)

The villagers at the relocation sites have no land there and paid day labour is difficult to find, so most of them try to return to their home fields to farm. This requires a pass which must be bought for varying amounts from the local SPDC military. When available, these passes are only valid for 3 days to a week, and they do not allow the villagers to spend the night; people are only allowed to leave the relocation site after 6 a.m. and must return by 6 p.m., and those in Kaw Tha Say relocation site are not even allowed to take a packet of cooked rice with them for lunch. Many people's home fields are 3 hours or more on foot from the relocation site, so these restrictions make it extremely difficult for them to farm properly, especially as they use labour-intensive farming methods which usually require them to sleep in their field huts through much of the planting and growing season.

"They allowed us to go to work but we had to go in the morning and return in the evening. They didn't even allow us to take cooked rice with us for lunch. We had to eat rice in the early morning in our house and could only eat again when we returned in the evening." - "Naw K'Ser Tee" (F, 29), xxxx village, Kyauk Kyi township (Interview #10, 4/99)

However, villagers have little option but to obey the restrictions, because many who have been caught with invalid passes have been seriously beaten or taken as porters, and several villagers have been killed simply for being found in farmfield huts after 6 p.m., particularly since the arrival of the Sa Thon Lon Guerrilla Retaliation units in the area. SPDC patrols also search for any evidence of food supplies in fiel huts or abandoned villages, and take or destroy whatever they find. Any villagers caught together with a hidden supply of rice run a strong risk of being accused of 'feeding the rebels' and summarily executed.

"They took the rice from the villagers of Zee Byu Gone because they thought that the villagers would feed the KNU. There were 69 baskets and 4 bowls of rice. They took them to the Burmese village together with the rice milling machine from Shan Gyi Bo Daing, poured kerosene on the rice and burned it." – "Saw Tha Pwih" (M, 38), xxxx village, Tantabin township, Toungoo District (Interview #50, 5/99)

"They never take care of us. We can't even go and buy medicine from town. If we bring back medicine, even pills, they give us the death sentence. That is one of the problems." - "Saw Ner Muh" (M, 30+), xxxx village, Mone township (Interview #8, 4/99)

Since late 1998, regular SPDC and Sa Thon Lon Guerrilla Retaliation units have begun taking some additional steps to ensure that people cannot go back to stay in their home villages and that resistance forces cannot take cover there. In some villages they have burned whatever remains of the houses. For example, in December 1998 they burned all the remaining houses in Twa Ni Gone village of Mone township, which has been forced to Yan Myo Aung relocation site and is abandoned. However, some Twa Ni Gone villagers were nearby with passes to farm their fields and saw it happen. When Kya Plaw and Leh Wain Gyi villages in Kyauk Kyi township were forced to relocate in January 1999, the villagers stripped their houses of building materials so that they could build huts in the relocation site, and then as soon as they were gone SPDC troops burned what remained of their houses. In addition to burning the remains of villages, they have begun ordering villagers in the relocation sites to return to their villages to cut down all of the trees in and around the village. Sa Thon Lon Guerrilla Retaliation troops forced villagers in Thit Cha Seik and Weh Gyi relocation sites to return and cut down all except the coconut trees in Ter Bpaw, Lu Ah and other villages. According to a villager from xxxx, people from his village who have been forced to Kaw Tha Say now have to return to cut down "all the trees between Sweh Dtee and Kyun Gyi", a distance of several kilometres. People from several villages have also reported being forced to clear scrub along both sides of the paths around their old villages, presumably to protect SPDC patrols from ambush. Villagers who have fled the western plains of Kyauk Kyi and Tantabin townships state that in March 1999 in their home areas the Sa Thon Lon Guerrilla Retaliation troops began forcing people to build fences around their own villages with a maximum of two gates, also to allow tighter control and monitoring of the movement of villagers.

"Before I came here they burned some houses and farm huts in Twa Ni Gone. They burned them without any reason. They said they were ordered to do it. The villagers there were forced to relocate to Yan Myo Aung a few years ago, but there were some old houses still left there. ... They can go back to the village to work, but they need a pass, and if the soldiers see you and call you, you must go to them and answer all their questions. If you don't go to them or if you run they kill you." - "Naw Lah Paw" (F, 21), xxxx village, Mone township (Interview #28, 1/99)

"For 'loh ah pay', we had to cut down the whole forest so they could see anyone who might be walking there. We had to cut 3 or 4 'khah' each day for a whole week. They are trying to clear all the trees between Kyun Gyi and Sweh Dtee." - "Saw Dee Ghay" (M, 38), xxxx village, Kyauk Kyi township (Interview #9, 4/99)

Even people with passes to return to their villages are finding it more and more dangerous to do so, particularly with the Sa Thon Lon forces in the area. These special troops regularly stop villagers on the path and beat them for no apparent reason except simple harassment and to frighten them. According to a villager from xxxx, villagers in Yan Myo Aung relocation site have recently been told that they will no longer be allowed to return to their fields, and that the fine for anyone caught doing so will be 100,000 Kyat. This may also be an initiative of the Sa Thon Lon units. If this is enforced, it will make survival virtually impossible for the people in the relocation sites, and they will have no choice but to attempt to flee.

"We could do that [leave the relocation site to work their old fields] for 3 or 4 years, but since the Sa Thon Lon came into the area we haven't been able to buy passes to go and work anymore. We have to live in fear, and people have to have passes with their exact name and age on them to go to places near their home villages. If the name they give [when stopped by soldiers] isn't exactly the same as the name on the pass they are beaten nearly to death. There was one villager who got a pass from his village elder with his short name on it, the name everyone calls him by. When the Sa Thon Lon asked him his name he told them his real name, which is different from his short name [nickname] on the pass. He was forced onto his hands and knees and then was kicked until he vomited blood." - "Naw Hser" (F, 40), xxxx village, Mone township (Interview #20, 2/99)

"We were forced to relocate [to Yan Myo Aung] but later they allowed us to go back to live beside the Sittaung river and work our fields. When we were working the fields, they demanded we give them 3,000 Kyats per month and they also demanded we give them 1,000 Kyats when any of them got married. Because of this, we went to live in Yan Myo Aung again. Now the orders are that we can't work our fields anymore, and anyone who does must pay a 100,000 Kyat fine. There are 15 farmfield huts in the area, and they will know if we go back to work because more huts will appear. ... People don't dare go back to work in their fields." - "Saw Tha Doh" (M, 18), xxxx village, Mone township (Interview #13, 3/99).

Crop Quotas

"People who have hill fields must give 12 baskets per acre. Whether our fields yield or not we must give them what they order. They told us, 'We don't care if there's a hole in your bucket, just bring us the water.'" - "Naw Thu" (F, 26), xxxx village, Kyauk Kyi township (Interview #29, 1/99)

As in the rest of Burma, villagers in the plains near the Sittaung River all have to hand over a portion of their crops to the SPDC authorities. This applies both to people still living and farming in their home villages and to those living in relocation sites but commuting to farm their own land. For the crop harvested at the end of 1998, the quota rate was 15 baskets of paddy (unhusked rice) per acre of flat irrigated paddy field, and 12 baskets per acre of hillside ricefield (one basket of paddy weighs approximately 20 kilograms, and when milled produces about ½ basket of rice, which weighs 16.5 kilograms). The SPDC paid 300 Kyat per basket for this quota paddy, while local market price at the same time was 520-600 Kyat per basket. In a good year, one acre of flat paddy field can produce only 40-50 baskets, so this is a sizable portion of the crop. However, in the 1998 season many farmers lost over half their crop and some lost almost their entire crop due to early lack of rain followed by floods; others only had enough seed to plant part of their fields because of debt caused by 1997 crop failures and SPDC extortion, and some lost part or all of their crop because of restrictions on movement or fear of SPDC and Sa Thon Lon Guerrilla Retaliation units. No exceptions or reductions were made for any of these farmers, with the result that many had to sell their livestock and valuables or go even further into debt in order to buy paddy at market price and then hand it over as their quota. When they asked for quota reductions because of the failure of their crops some were told by SPDC officials, "We don't care if your bucket has a hole in it, just bring us the water." In the end, many have been left with no valuables, large debts, and nothing to eat but boiled rice soup - a thin gruel which families eat to try to make what little rice they have last longer.

"[W]e had to sell them 12 baskets [of paddy] for each acre of paddy field but they paid a very low price. They paid 300 Kyats per basket, but the market rate is 600 Kyats per basket. They say it's our duty to sell it to them and they don't allow us to sell it in the market. We have 8 acres of field but we weren't able to produce any paddy because it all died, so we had to buy rice from someone else for 500 Kyats per basket and then sell it to them. We didn't even get 300 Kyats per basket, because they said

some was for a donation and then they deducted a fee." - "Naw K'Ser Tee" (F, 29), xxxx village, Kyauk Kyi township (Interview #10, 4/99)

"We work on a field, but this year we couldn't because the paddy died and then the Burmese government asked for paddy. We couldn't give it to them so we had to buy it from outside and give it to them. This year we couldn't eat. This year we could only plant one acre so we didn't even get 40 baskets of rice. We had to give the government 12 baskets of paddy for each acre and now we have none left for us [they own 2 acres so they had to pay 24 baskets even though they only planted one acre]. They pay 300 Kyats per basket of paddy, but if we buy it outside, one basket costs 550 Kyats. They also cheated us on the number of baskets. We took them 25 baskets of paddy but they only paid for 22 baskets." - "Pi Kler Meh" (F, 60), xxxx village, Mone township (Interview #14, 3/99)

"If we don't sell it to them they scold and beat us, so we have to buy some from outside to sell to them. This year I had to buy 30 baskets of paddy which I then sold to them. ... The villagers who can't buy any have to sell their cattle to buy paddy to give them. Those who have nothing are arrested and forced to porter and they beat them. ... Some other people have their fields confiscated. ... We must sell them paddy every year, and they close the accounts on April 1st. ... When we went to the meeting they called, they shouted at us and scolded us." - "Naw Mary" (F, 30), xxxx village, Mone township (Interview #15, 3/99)

To make it worse, the local quota collection officials are extremely corrupt and the Army demands additional quotas from some farmers. The written law in Burma decrees that all land belongs to the state. A farmer from xxxx explained that his field to the west of the Mone - Kyauk Kyi road was designated as property of the Township Peace & Development Council, while his field to the east of the road was designated as property of the Army; for the Township land he had to give 12 baskets per acre at 300 Kyats per basket, but for the Army land he had to give 10 baskets for acre to the local Battalion with no payment whatsoever. In addition, the Township officials use several transparent tricks to steal much of the villagers' paddy and money. When farmers bring their 12 or 15 baskets per acre, the officials often claim that it's not 'clean', i.e. that it contains bits of straw and impurities, and either winnow it a second time or calculate a reduction in the number of baskets to be paid for. They then deduct a portion of the paddy which they say will be a 'donation to the temple', and reduce the payment appropriately, though it is very unlikely that this paddy will ever be given to any temple. An additional 4 bowls (a quarter basket) of paddy or husked rice per acre is then demanded for the Township Peace & Development Council without payment, and a cash service charge is deducted from the amount to be paid to the farmer. Sometimes even more deductions are made. In the end, most farmers are paid for no more than two thirds of the paddy which they are forced to bring, and at only 300 Kyat per basket. The officials take all the paddy, probably log it as all having been paid for, and can keep the extra rice they confiscate for the Township as well as one third or more of the cash for themselves. The villagers are fully aware that this is simply corruption, but they do not dare complain for fear of arrest. They have no choice but to pay the quota as demanded, and they must do so before the deadline of April 1st each year.

"From each basket they took out a 'donation', then they took an extra 5 baskets from my field for the Ma Ah Pa [Township Peace & Development Council] without paying anything, then they took 4 bowls [about 8 kg / 18 lb] for free from each acre of my field, and they also took 25 Kyats out of my money just for themselves. They are just crooks, and I said to them, 'Ma aye loh, tha ko dway!' ['Motherfucker, thief!'] But they didn't say anything back to me, they were just quiet because they're satisfied once they've got their money from you." - "Saw Ghaw" (M, xx), xxxx village, Mone township (Interview #29, 1/99)

"As for my fields, to the west of the car road they have been marked as belonging to the Township and to the east of the car road they have been marked as belonging to the Army. So I had to give Battalion #60 ten baskets and received nothing for it. For my field west of the car road, the government gives me some money, 300 Kyats per basket. However, I didn't get all the money because they said that some of the rice was for donation and some was for other things, so only about half was left." - "Saw Ner Muh" (M, 30+), xxxx village, Mone township (Interview #8, 4/99)

"In the past we had to give them 10 baskets from each acre for free, but we heard that this year they will demand 20 baskets from each acre. We also had to give 10 baskets of peanuts from each acre for free. They don't pay us anything for this because our fields are east of the car road [so it is 'Army land' and not 'Township land']. ... If we grow mungbeans we also have to give 10 baskets per acre, so there's no difference. They said that the land we're working is their land." - "May Oo Mo" (F, 58), xxxx relocation site, Mone township (Interview #3, 5/99)

"We must give [the SPDC] 15 baskets [of paddy] from each acre. They said that if we couldn't give it to them they'd kill us, so we had to finish getting the paddy for them before we came here. They have no understanding that because we had less water the paddy didn't yield as much, they only know that we have to give them whatever amount of paddy they demand. We had to take our paddy to Na Than Gwin. Then they said that the paddy we took them wasn't 'clean', so they winnowed it again using a machine and then took the 'clean' paddy. Some of the grain went to the waste, and they took that themselves to their houses to eat it. If the paddy you give them is supposed to be 30,000 Kyats, before they give you the money they take some for the monastery, and after they winnow your paddy again a lot of grains are lost, so in the end you might get 10,000 Kyat instead of 30,000. Some people brought 3 bullock carts full of paddy but lost [the price of] one whole bullock cart load in the process. I had to give 150 baskets because I have 10 acres. After they took everything out, I was left with 30,000 Kyat [payment for 100 baskets]. On top of that, they also take 4 bowls [about 8 kg / 18 lb] for free from each acre of your field. We had to pound that paddy [to husk it] for them first. Living and working in our place is like working just to feed them." - "Naw Say Paw" (F, 26), xxxx village, Kyauk Kyi township (Interview #29, 1/99)

Villagers face additional food security problems because SPDC Army units in many parts of Burma no longer receive full rations and have been ordered to either produce their own food or obtain it from the villagers. In some areas they simply demand more food from villagers, while in others they have confiscated farmland and force the villagers to grow crops for them (see below under 'Forced Labour for the Army'). Villagers report that near Pay Sa Loh Army camp in Kyauk Kyi township, the families of SPDC LIB 264 soldiers simply walk into the local villagers' fields and pick their vegetable crops without asking any permission. When a farmer from Kyauk Kyi township drove a soldier's family out of his field in January 1999, a group of 4 soldiers led by a Sergeant appeared an hour later, threatened the farmer and beat him until he needed to be hospitalised.

"The families of LIB 264 troops based at Pay Sa Loh do not receive enough rations to live, so they demand food from the villagers. On January 12th 1999, some families of the Battalion soldiers were looking for and taking vegetables from the villagers' fields. ... They arrived at the hill field of Saw T--- near K--- village, Kyauk Kyi township, and started picking the beans in his field. Saw T--- was staying at his field but they didn't ask his permission, so he drove them out of the field. They

went back to the Battalion camp, then over one hour later Sergeant Mya Than and 3 other soldiers came to see Saw T---. They said the villagers must feed the military, that everything belongs to the military and they can take whatever they want. Then all 4 of them beat Saw T--- at the same time. He suffered a cut on his head, his right hand was broken and he fell unconscious. Later his relatives took him to hospital and he has still not returned. His family sold their belongings and sent the money to the hospital so that he could receive treatment. Since then, whenever the soldiers' families come and steal the vegetables from villagers' farms no one dares to stop them." - incident report from KHRG field reporter

Looting and Extortion

"When they enter the villages they tell the villagers, 'The forest people have come to your village, so if you want to live peacefully come and give me money.' Villagers from each village have to bribe them with hundreds of thousands [of Kyat]. What they said about the forest people entering the villages isn't true, they just lie to the villagers to get money. They demand alcohol, bags and clothing. People bought them things worth 2 or 3 thousand Kyat but they didn't like them, they wanted things worth 4 or 5 thousand Kyat. They required 2 bicycles but they didn't want bikes worth 4 or 5 thousand Kyats, they demanded bikes worth 15 or 20 thousand Kyats. If they see business people, like traders of rice, beans and pigs, they rough them up and take their money. Business people have to avoid them if they hear they're in the area." - "Saw Tee Ko" (M, 40), xxxx village, Mone township (Interview #19, 2/99)

Deserters from the SPDC Army have often testified to KHRG that a large portion of their salaries and rations are stolen by their officers, that their officers try to make as much money as they can before being rotated out while the regular troops have to loot villages for food to survive. In the villages of western Nyaunglebin District this appears to be the case, because troops are constantly looting food and livestock and demanding alcohol and clothing from people in the villages and relocation sites. At the same time, the officers are demanding cash and valuables to an extent where many people have fled their villages because they can no longer pay.

"Sometimes we had to give over 2 or 3 thousand each month. Every house had to pay them. If you couldn't give it the police would come and arrest you and put you in prison. Then you have to buy your release for no less than 10,000 [Kyats]. That has happened to many people in my village, but not to my family. Those who don't have the money to pay flee

with their families to stay in other places." - "Pu Hla Maung" (M, 57),
xxxx village, Mone township (Interview #22, 1/99)

*"They don't even like people to go and stay in their farmfield huts. Any
time they see people at their farm huts they fine them in cash. Recently,
one of my nephews was in trouble and was fined over 50,000 Kyats. They
accused him of being friendly with the KNLA soldiers when they come.
The Burmese from Infantry Battalion 351 beat him until he was almost
dead. ... The villagers also had to give 50,000 Kyats for him so the total
cost was 100,000 Kyats. ... [T]he KNLA didn't go to his house. The
Burmese soldiers were just looking for a reason to fine him ... They are
used to looking for faults in people, but it is hard for them to find
someone to accuse who is actually guilty. ... The reason they make
trouble for the villagers is because they want money. Their troops who
stay in the village stay for about a month, and try to make money before
they leave the village on rotation."* - "Saw Thet Wah" (M, 49), xxxx
village, northern Mone township (Interview #34, 9/98)

*"No one likes to live there but they can't do anything about it so they just
have to suffer. Who would want to live in a place where you have to give
fees and taxes until you can't afford to buy food? We were forced to give
things all the time. They demanded money, sarongs, bags, clothes and
Karen traditional clothing."* - "Naw Paw Paw Htoo" (F, 31), xxxx
village, Mone township (Interview #12, 3/99)

Villagers are forced to pay many kinds of cash fees at least once per
month, and often several times per month. These fees are given various
names such as porter fees, sentry fees, pagoda fees, road fees, and
development fees, but the names are simply invented by the officers as an
excuse to extort money. Many villagers testify that whenever the Army
becomes aware of any villagers making any money they immediately
demand fees; for example, ethnic Burman bamboo cutters in Shwegyin
township told KHRG that whenever they return from the forest with a
load of bamboo to sell, the local military demands that they pay half of
whatever they get for it. Villagers in xxxx village of Kyauk Kyi township
testified that the basic monthly extortion fees have recently been doubled
to 1,000 Kyat per family per month by the Army in their area, and
villagers in Shwegyin township are reporting similar fees.

*"We had to give whatever they ordered us to give. We paid fees 2 or 3
times each month. In the past they demanded that we give them 300 or
500 Kyats each time, but now they are demanding 1,000 Kyats each time.
When we couldn't find the money we had to borrow money from other*

people and sell our belongings. Our bullock carts and cattle are all gone. Everything is gone." - "Naw K'Ser Tee" (F, 29), xxxx village, Kyauk Kyi township (Interview #10, 4/99)

"We came because we couldn't bear to pay the porter fees. We couldn't even eat from what we made from work. First the porter fees were 250 [Kyat], then 400, after that 800 and now 1,000 [Kyat per family per month]." - "U Than Myint" (M, 50), xxxx village, Shwegyin township (Interview #27, 1/99)

"If I made 100 Kyats they demanded 50 Kyats, and if I made 50 Kyats they demanded 25 Kyats. They were the Burmese Army. They said it was for the price of a pass from their Army camp. We had to get a pass whenever we went anywhere. If we didn't they caught us and fined us, saying that we were disrespectful of them. Moreover, we also had to give porter fees and 'patrol' fees of 1,000 Kyats every month. In the past we only had to give 500 Kyats, but starting 3 months ago we've had to give 1,000 Kyats each month. If we couldn't give it, the soldiers from the Army camp captured us and tied us up in the camp, then afterwards they forced us to go out to find the money and bring it to them." - "Daw Khin Htwe" (F, 30), Burman bamboo cutter from xxxx village, Shwegyin township (Interview #24, 1/99)

In addition, the villagers face constant demands for various kinds of forced labour, which usually require them to send one person per household. Many don't dare go because of the heavy work and abuse by soldiers, and those without large families cannot go because they need to work to survive, so they have to pay fees for each day or shift of work which they miss. Some Battalions demand more forced labourers than they need for the sole purpose of collecting this money from many of them, and in some cases when villagers arrive for forced labour they are told they are not even wanted, that they were supposed to pay. One villager from Kyauk Kyi township stated that the local Army Battalion demands two villagers for three-day rotating shifts of labour at their camp but actually refuses to accept workers, demanding instead that the village pay 500 Kyat each 3 days to avoid the work; as a result the villagers have named this 'sitting porters'. Villagers throughout the district state that most families now have to pay out 2,000 to 3,000 Kyat per month for the combination of regular fees and fees to avoid forced labour. People who cannot pay the fees are threatened with arrest, beatings and forced labour as porters, so people sell their belongings in order to pay the fees. Many who have nothing left to sell flee their villages rather than face the punishments for non-payment.

"There's no limit. Sometimes 40 Kyats, sometimes 1,000 Kyats. They demand them whenever they want them. Sometimes they demand them once a month, sometimes twice a week. We can't count it all. ... Aaaaay! All there was was porter fees and 'loh ah pay'! You have no chance to eat. It's been that way for many years and it's been getting worse and worse. This year has been the worst of all. If you don't go to porter then you must pay the porter fee. If you do 'loh ah pay', you have no time to do your own work. It seems like we are slaves. ... They are killing us one by one until everyone is gone." - "Pu Htaw Say" (M, 65), xxxx village, Mone township (Interview #7, 4/99)

"They captured us like this: first they ordered every man to come to a meeting where they said they would tell us important things. When all the men arrived, they forced us to get in their truck and then took us to the other side of the road. They told us, 'Anyone who dares not go must pay us a bribe.' The people had to pay 5,000, 6,000, 7,000, 14,000, 15,000 and 20,000 Kyats and then they released them [the price went up as more were released]. They did that twice. They also captured everyone they saw working in the fields. ... People had to leave their working tools behind and follow the soldiers." - "Saw Tee Ko" (M, 40), xxxx village, Mone township, describing how the SPDC takes porters from Yan Myo Aung relocation site (Interview #19, 2/99)

"The army demands two villagers to work at the camp for three days at a time. However, the army camp does not accept villagers to work, instead they demand 500 Kyats for not doing that job. Thus, our village has to pay 500 Kyats every three days. That's why the villagers named that process 'sitting porters'." - villager (M, 45) from Kyauk Kyi township (Interview #35, 4/99)

Some villages are also paying heavy monthly or yearly fees to local Battalions to hold off orders for forced relocation. Ter Bpaw and Po Thaung Su villages in Mone township paid 300,000 Kyat each to avoid being forced to move several years ago but could not pay again, so they were forced to move to Thit Cha Seik. Yay Leh village, a larger village also in southern Mone township, is reportedly still paying to avoid being moved, as is Zee Byu Gone in Tantabin township. Whenever fighting between SPDC and resistance forces occurs, nearby villages are also heavily fined as part of the punishment. In January 1999, Sa Thon Lon Guerrilla Retaliation troops called a meeting and told villagers in Kyauk Kyi township that they would be fined 100,000 Kyat for each gun lost by the Sa Thon Lon in fighting in their area, in addition to other punishments such as executions and forced relocation.

Fees are usually demanded through the village headperson, who must distribute the burden of the extortion fees among the households of the village. Usually only the village head and a few others are exempt, such as the village secretary and the pastor. The burden is so heavy that all other households must pay, even widows and others who have great difficulty supporting themselves. When troops take livestock, food, alcohol and other such things, money is often collected from all the villagers to compensate those who have been robbed, though often it is the village head who must provide these things and pay for them out of his/her own pocket. Whenever demands are not met, it is the village head who is immediately arrested, detained and physically punished. The expense and physical risk of being a village head make it difficult to find people who are willing to do the job, so some villages have implemented a system to rotate the headman's duties every week or every month between themselves. In some Burman or part-Burman villages the situation is more stable for the village head, and here the village heads often become part of the corruption; if the troops demand 1,000 Kyat from each household they will demand 1,200 or 1,500 Kyat and keep the balance for themselves.

"We have a method of selecting the village head and assistant by a rotation system. One term of being village head lasts one month. Within a one month term, a village head has to spend 15,000 Kyats for the SPDC soldiers who demand chicken, rice, other foods, alcohol, cigarettes and so on. Each family contributes 300 Kyats each month toward that expense and the rest has to come from the village head. If Karen guerrillas attack SPDC soldiers around the village, the village head is severely punished and the village has to pay a huge amount of money as punishment." - villager (M, 45) from Kyauk Kyi township (Interview #35, 4/99)

"Every 15 days the village headman changes because nobody dares to be the headman for long. They come and they scold the village headman." - "Pi Kler Meh" (F, 60), xxxx village, Mone township (Interview #14, 3/99)

"They hold the meetings in the monastery. They told us that we have to give fees and the dates when we had to give it to them by. They shouted at us because we couldn't speak Burmese. We have to give them what they want, they don't care if we can eat or not. We have to pay taxes for the house and the people in it. For each person we have to pay 30 Kyats tax. They also collect yearly taxes and taxes for sports. They also collect for the village headman. We work, get money and then we have to give it

to them for tax while we ourselves can't eat. We have to pay porter fees twice a month, sometimes once a month. Sometimes we have to give 50 [Kyats] and sometimes we have to give 100 [Kyats]. If you don't go for 'loh ah pay' you must also give money for that. If you are sick or don't have time to go, you have to give between 100 and 200 Kyats each time. If you add all the taxes together, we have to pay about 3,000 Kyats per month in tax [per family]." - "Naw Mary" (F, 30), xxxx village, Mone township (Interview #15, 3/99)

"There are a few families near my house that don't have enough food for every meal. They have to go and work and sometimes they still don't have any rice to cook to eat in the evenings. There are many families like that. Before I came here there was a 50 year old woman who didn't have any buffaloes, cattle, fields or rice to cook, so when the [village] section leader asked her for porter fees she was crying. She has 4 children, all of whom are girls, the oldest is in her early 20's and the youngest is over 10 years old. All she can do is day labour, and even she has to give. Even though you have nothing to give you still have to pay the fee." - "Saw Ner Muh" (M, 30+), xxxx village, Mone township (Interview #8, 4/99)

"When people can't pay, they mark down their names and then demand that they pay by force. If they still can't pay, they threaten that they will lock them in the stocks at the township, or put them in jail. That's why people are afraid of them, so they try to find the money, and if they still can't find the money they sell everything they own. As for us, we didn't have anything to sell anymore so we had to leave." - "U Than Myint" (M, 50), xxxx village, Shwegyin township (Interview #27, 1/99)

"Many villagers have to drink boiled rice soup this year because we have to give so many taxes and fees. Most of the villagers are suffering from hunger." - "Saw Thet Wah" (M, 49), xxxx village, northern Mone township (Interview #34, 9/98)

"They say we must go as porters or pay porter fees, or if we cannot pay we must flee. I cannot pay any more, so now I've fled." - "U Hla Shwe" (M, 40), xxxx village, Shwegyin township (Interview #26, 1/99)

Forced Labour for the Army

"We also had to go as porters and give them money. ... My children went to do 'loh ah pay', they had to dig the earth and dig out the stumps at the road near their [Army] camp. They had to go for 3 days and take their own food. About one year ago they called one of my sons-in-law [to go

as a porter] for 14 or 15 days. They said he would come back after that, but we haven't seen him yet. His name is Aung Aung, he has 3 children and he is 25 years old. When we asked people they said he would come back, but later we heard that he died. They killed him. ... You see his daughter sleeping over there? At the time he left, her mother was 7 months pregnant with her. When she was born we took care of her, and then the situation worsened so we left the village." - "Pi Kler Meh" (F, 60), xxxx village, Mone township (Interview #14, 3/99)

People in the villages and relocation sites of the plains have to regularly do many kinds of forced labour as ordered by the Army units throughout the area. One of the most common and feared forms of forced labour is portering, which involves both carrying rations and supplies to outlying Army camps and carrying munitions, equipment and rations with SPDC patrols heading into the hills to "mop up" the villagers living in hiding there. Portering assignments to carry supplies between Army camps usually last a few days to a week; villagers have to take their own food, and are not usually treated too brutally as long as they are not kept beyond the originally specified period. However, it takes them away from their farmwork and there is always the risk of being beaten or killed, so people try to pay instead of going if they can. Portering with SPDC patrols heading into the hills can last for months, and people avoid going at all costs because many never return from this brutal form of forced labour. These porters are forced to carry 20 to 40 kilogram loads of shells and rations through the hills, barely fed and left behind or beaten to death if they can no longer carry.

"Both the SPDC and the DKBA force the villagers to do sentry duty and portering. Some people have to go portering for 1 or 2 months, while others have had to go for 14 or 15 days. It is not always the same. Everyone must go for portering and sentry duty, and we don't get paid. If we can't go we must give money. At regular times we have to hire people [to go in their place] for 5,000 or 6,000 Kyats each. When there are military operations it is worse. They demand that we give them 8,000 or 10,000 Kyats per person [or go as porters]. We must pay 30,000 or 40,000 Kyats for the whole year [per family]. They also demand money directly [apart from the context of forced labour]." - "Saw Ta Roh" (M, 37), xxxx village, Shwegyin township (Interview #32, 12/98)

"We always had to go for 'loh ah pay'. Even though my daughter is only 15, she had to go and carry 48 tins of milk [this would weigh about 20 kg / 44 lb]. She couldn't carry it but she had to. She was crying, so the other people who were there for 'loh ah pay' helped to carry it for her. ... We

had to carry 30 viss [48 kg / 105 lb; i.e. one sack] of rice, and we couldn't carry it. I had to go for 'loh ah pay' 4 times, but I fled one time. They didn't pay us, and we had to take our own rice and tea. Some people got sick, and they didn't care for them. We couldn't walk anymore but we had to keep walking, we had no time to rest." - "Naw Eh Muh" (F, 51), xxxx village, Kyauk Kyi township (Interview #17, 2/99)

"I had to go as a porter this year. When I went to watch video, they arrested me on the path in front of the video [the village video cinema]. I had to carry a basket of their rice for about one week, or maybe two weeks, then I fled and escaped from them. I fled at night. I didn't know the place, but it was very far from my village. It took me 15 days to get back home." - "Saw Po Hla" (M, 25), xxxx village, Kyauk T'Ga township (Interview #18, 2/99)

"I had to go 4 or 5 times per month, every month. For portering, I had to carry rice or shells. ... The last time I went I had to carry about 20 viss [32 kg / 70 lb] of shells. ... We also had to go for sentry duty, each turn was 2 days. They forced us to work for them every day." - "Saw Dee Ghay" (M, 38), xxxx village, Kyauk Kyi township (Interview #9, 4/99)

"They have to go for sentry duty for 3 days at a time. Sometimes they force people who are doing sentry duty to go as porters. Just before I left a child from our village was forced to go portering from sentry duty. He's already disappeared for two weeks, but we don't know where he is. His name is Saw Htoo Gkee, he's about 20 years old." – "Pi Naw Htoo" (F, 75), xxxx village, Mone township (Interview #5, 5/99)

"He was called for portering by Battalion 264 and disappeared. Finally, we asked people and they said he is dead. What can we do now that he's dead? Can we say anything more once he's dead?" - "Pu Htaw Say" (M, 65), xxxx village, Mone township, talking about his son-in-law who never returned from forced labour as a porter (Interview #7, 4/99)

Each village also has to send several people on rotating shifts of three to five days to each Army camp in their area for miscellaneous forced labour, which is sometimes referred to as 'patrol'. This labour routinely includes clearing scrub and grass in and around the camp, maintaining barracks, digging and maintaining trenches and bunkers, building fences and man-traps, cutting firewood, carrying water, cooking, cleaning, and delivering messages to other Army camps and order letters to local villages. They also have to do unarmed sentry duty, both outside Army camps and along vehicle roads which are used by the military. Villagers in northern Mone township report that they now have to do nightly sentry duty along the roads from Kyauk Kyi to Mone and northward to Toungoo. Three villagers have to man each sentry post, which are closely spaced along the road, for rotating 24-hour shifts, and are supposed to report any strangers on the road to the local military. It costs 150 Kyat to avoid one 24-hour shift, and villagers are also punished if they are not seen at their post during the shift. Under normal SPDC practice, villages assigned to do sentry duty along a length of road are held fully responsible for any resistance activity (such as landmines or ambushes) which occurs there. In addition, in March 1999 the Sa Thon Lon Guerrilla Retaliation group reportedly began ordering several villages in Kyauk Kyi and Tantabin townships to build fences around their own village, with only two gates allowed for access.

"In January 1999, SPDC battalions IB 60 and LIB 351 from Kyauk Kyi started calling villages to repair their barracks and fences. Our village was ordered to cut down trees, and other villages were ordered to build fences for the battalions. Villagers had to work on that construction for almost 20 days in January." - "Naw Ghay" (F, xx), xxxx village, Kyauk Kyi township (Interview #11, 4/99)

"After the rice harvest season [i.e. starting in January 1999], the army camp at Kaw Tha Say called for 5 to 8 people each day from each village around the camp to rebuild buildings and fences. Villagers had to cut down trees and bamboo for construction, then build and reconstruct the whole camp. ... Two villagers per day have to work in the camp, doing things such as cleaning the compound, carrying water, cooking and so on. ... If SPDC soldiers patrol around the area, they demand 2 villagers from each of the nearby villages. These villagers have to carry food, supplies and ammunition. This is demanded about once a month and it lasts around 10 days. ... Sometimes soldiers demand that villagers carry them to Shwegyin on bicycles for their shopping. Villagers have almost no time to work for themselves and they are getting poorer." - villager (M, 45) from Kyauk Kyi township (Interview #35, 4/99)

"A few months ago in our village they added another duty for us to do - we have to do sentry duty along the road from Ler Doh [Kyauk Kyi] to Taw Oo [Toungoo]. ... If we don't go we have to give 150 Kyats for one day and night. Three people from the village have to go to each place for sentry duty each time. If there are three posts near your village for sentry duty, 9 villagers must go with 3 at each post. There must be 3 at each post. The groups of three have to rotate. Each group of three has to stay for one day and one night. You go at 4:00 p.m. and must stay until 4:00

p.m. the following day. If you are not on the road during your turn [if they pass and you aren't there], they fine you one pig or force you to jump like a frog. ... Most of the Karen people in our village don't go, they pay the fees. It's mostly the Burman people who have to go." - "Saw Thet Wah" (M, 49), xxxx village, northern Mone township (Interview #34, 9/98)

Some SPDC troops are confiscating land and ordering local villagers to grow crops for them; some of these crops are used to feed the Army and some are sold in the market for the cash profit of the military officers. In Shwegyin township, villagers have been forced to grow over 100 acres of beans for Infantry Battalion #57, harvest and then sell the beans and hand over the money to the Army camp. In December 1998 they ordered the villagers to build a storehouse for the bean crop, but before this could happen the KNLA attacked their camp and burned many of the beans and the wood for the storehouse. In Kyauk Kyi township, villagers report that in January 1999, several Battalions began forcing villagers to clear land for Battalion agricultural projects; they were told that each Battalion would clear 1,000 acres. Several villages in the township have already been forced to grow 2 acres of beans per village for the Army since 1997. One villager who had to grow these beans says that they then had to sell the beans and pay the Army 20,000 Kyats per acre for the proceeds; when the villagers asked if they could just pay the money rather than grow the beans they were refused because the local Army needs to show beanfields to their superiors as evidence that they are producing their own food. West of the Sittaung River in Kyauk T'Ga township, villagers are also being forced to travel all the way to Pegu to dig fishponds for another Army food production project.

"This work [clearing the ground at Kaw Tha Say] started in January 1999. Our village had to send 20 people to a place 3 miles away from the village. Those 20 people had to work for 5 days. When they returned, another 20 people went to work on a rotating basis. The village sent males and females between 12 years and 60 years old. They were not paid. No supplies or equipment were provided either. ... We heard that the land was for IB 57, LIB 349 and LIB 350; 1,000 acres for each battalion for army agricultural projects. ... We heard that in Kyauk Kyi villagers have been called to work for IB 60 and LIB 351 agricultural projects at Kya Theh Taw since 1996. Villagers there were forced to work, to plough the fields, to tend the crops and to reap the harvest. Moreover, starting in 1997 the SPDC battalions inKyauk Kyi township forced each village near their camps to grow two acres of beans. Then at the harvest, they let the villagers sell the beans and then demanded that

they give the army 20,000 Kyats per acre. The villagers negotiated with the battalions, offering that they would not grow and tend beans but would give 20,000 Kyats per acre to the army instead, but the army officials refused because they need bean fields to show at inspections." - villager (M, 45) from Kyauk Kyi township (Interview #35, 4/99)

"The Army had called for 'loh ah pay' from the village and we had to sow those beans for them. We had to sow, tend, and winnow those beans and then take them to Shwegyin and sell them for them. This year their enemies burned some, but there are still more because there are more than 100 acres [of forced labour bean crop, on confiscated farmland]. To hold those 100 acres of beans we were supposed to build a storehouse for them." - "U Hla Shwe" (M, 40), xxxx village, Shwegyin township, talking about forced labour growing beans for IB 57 near his village (Interview #26, 1/99)

"We had to go to dig ponds for them to raise fish at Pegu. It is very far from my village. Some went by car and some went on foot. I had to do it for one or two months. Each time 70, 75, or up to 100 people [from his village] had to go. We had to take our own food. Each person was forced to dig 7 or 8 ponds. People who got sick had to keep working, they wouldn't allow them to go back. They could only go back when they finished digging the ponds." - "Saw Po Hla" (M, 25), xxxx village, Kyauk T'Ga township (Interview #18, 2/99)

"Sometimes we have to go and work at Bpaw Hser Ko clearing their [Army] fields, sowing beans or carrying stones. We have to do whatever the soldiers in the battalion force us to do. They don't give us food, we have to bring our own rice from home. Last year, when we went to dig out large rocks for a road for them, a few villagers died of illness when they returned. ... All the people in the village except the very old have to go. Old people who live in separate houses from their children must register separately from their children and so they have to do 'loh ah pay' [each household has to send a person, regardless of how many people live in the house or their ages]. Old people who live together with their children don't have to go for 'loh ah pay'. If there are no men in the family, women must go. The only people in the whole village who are exempted from 'loh ah pay' are the pastor and the village chairman. All the rest have to do 'loh ah pay'. We don't have time to do our own work. ... I had to go to work on the road twice. I came here instead of going to work on it for a third time." - "Saw Ner Muh" (M, 30+), xxxx village, Mone township, describing forced labour on the new road from Na Than Gwin to Mone (Interview #8, 4/99)

"Whenever they went anywhere they called us to go with them. They also called us to work to get them their food. They forced us to do many kinds of work for them. At last when we didn't have any food for ourselves anymore we talked to them about our problems, but they didn't care. They said, 'If we let one of you behave like this then everyone will become like you. So if there is one person in your house then half of that person should work for us, and if there are two people then one should work for us.' ... Now we have to go for 3 weeks out of every month, and if you don't go you must pay 700 Kyats for each week. I couldn't do the work because I had to go to stay with my mother and also with my Aunt for a while. So I didn't go for the work for 3 weeks, and then they came and demanded that I pay 2,100 Kyats for 3 weeks plus 2,000 Kyats for porter fees. I told them that I had no money to pay, and they said they would send me to the Army camp. Then I decided not to stay there any more and I came here." - "Daw Khin Htwe" (F, 30), xxxx village, Shwegyin township (Interview #24, 1/99)

"'Loh ah pay' is unfair. Every villager from every village must do 'loh ah pay'. Even if you don't have food for yourself you must go and do their 'loh ah pay'. They won't care about us until we starve to death." - "U Hla Shwe" (M, 40), xxxx village, Shwegyin township (Interview #26, 1/99)

Forced Labour on Roads

"I had to go 3 or 4 times already. We had to dig dirt to make the embankment for the road. The height [of the embankment] is higher than this roof and it's about 10 cubits [5 metres / 15 feet] wide. People from both the east and the west had to come and work on it. Some people would have gone but they didn't allow them to go and instead demanded that they give money. ... They never give you food, you must always take your own food. Moreover, you have to bring your clothes and sleep there when you work. There are many people so we go in turns and each person must stay for a week. ... They give Karen people the hard parts [of the road] and their own people [Burmans] get the easy parts. ... If you're ill, you must cure yourself. They never take care of you. They never waste their money on you. It's a hard life that gives us no chance to eat what we work to produce." - "Pu Htaw Say" (M, 65), xxxx village, Mone township, describing forced labour on the new road from Na Than Gwin to Mone (Interview #7, 4/99)

Villagers are being forced to work on several roads in the area. People living west of the Sittaung River, and sometimes those on the east side, are regularly forced to work maintaining the main north-south road from

Nyaunglebin to Toungoo. Those in the entire western half of Nyaunglebin District are forced to maintain the roads from Shwegyin to Kyauk Kyi, Kyauk Kyi to Mone, and Kyauk Kyi to Na Than Gwin, all dirt roads which need extensive work after the annual rains. Villagers in southern Mone and northern Kyauk Kyi townships are also being forced to maintain the military access road eastward from Kyauk Kyi to Mu Theh and into Papun district. This is also a basic dirt road through the hills which is washed out and needs to be rebuilt after each rainy season. It was extended through Papun District in 1997/98 all the way to the Thai border, at Saw Hta on the Salween River [for more details see "Wholesale Destruction", KHRG April 1998]. The extension through the hills of Papun District was performed by bulldozers under heavy Army guard, but even then the bulldozers were attacked and destroyed by the KNLA on at least one occasion. Now the road is essentially complete, and all work maintaining it is done by the manual forced labour of the villagers. The road has already been used to increase militarisation with SPDC Army camps dotted all the way along its entire 100-kilometre route, at Kyauk Kyi, Thaung Bo, Saw Mi Lu and Mu Theh in Nyaunglebin District, and at Pwa Ghaw, Plah Ko, Maw Pu, Maw Kyo, Leh Klay Ko, and Saw Hta in Papun District.

"People from the village had to carry stones from Saw Mi Lu and build the road above Ler Doh. The length of road that our village had to build was 1,000 yards. Some villages had to build more and some had to build less, it depended on how big or small the village was. But every village had to finish their assigned length of road. ... They repaired it in order to transport their food and weapons to Pwa Ghaw [to the east in Papun District] and Mu Theh. They forced us to carry the stones and lay them on the road. You must lay them properly." - "Saw Thet Wah" (M, 49), xxxx village, northern Mone township (Interview #34, 9/98)

"We were forced to dig dirt and make a new car road in Yan Myo Aung village. They told us we had to finish the road in 5 days and if we didn't they would kill us. We tried to finish it quickly. Now it is finished except for the bridge." - "Saw Tha Doh" (M, 18), xxxx village, Mone township, describing forced labour on a new section along the Kyauk Kyi - Na Than Gwin road (Interview #13, 3/99)

"I had to go to the place where they were repairing the embankment on the Kanyunt Kwin road [the main north-south road from Nyaunglebin to Toungoo]. That's on the other side of the [Sittaung] river. We had to go and carry dirt. Both men and women had to go, if the women were busy the men had to go in their place. We sometimes had to go for 3 days,

*sometimes 2 days. If there were only a few villagers we had to go for 5
days. We had to go once a month and we had to take our own food. We
usually had to go on foot, but sometimes they took us by car and then
made us pay for travel expenses. They didn't take us for free."* - "Naw
Mary" (F, 30), xxxx village, Mone township, describing forced labour on
the main north-south road from Nyaunglebin to Toungoo (Interview #15,
3/99)

*"I had to go, I had to go. We had to do 'loh ah pay' regularly every 10
days. We had to work on the road, digging the earth. They came to pick
us up and bring us back in the evening with a boat. The work was at
Thein Zayat and Shwegyin. They never gave us rice, we had to take our
own from home. ... It was not well built, so they called us very often to
work on it. Now the young people are saying they have to go and build a
car road at other villages too. That started after I left the village. They
have to go for the whole week and if they don't go they must give 700
Kyats, but how can we do that?"* - "Daw Hla" (F, 48), xxxx village,
Shwegyin township, about forced labour on the road from Shwegyin to
Kyauk Kyi (Interview #25, 1/99)

The road from Kyauk Kyi to Mone skirts the western edge of the hills
and SPDC troops are regularly ambushed near this road. To protect
themselves, in January 1999 the Sa Thon Lon Guerrilla Retaliation force
ordered people from all villages and relocation sites in the plains of
Mone and northern Kyauk Kyi townships to begin construction of a road
further from the hills, following the Sittaung River from Na Than Gwin
north to Mone, a distance of 30 to 35 kilometres. They want this road
built quickly, and forced labour on it has been intensive. People from
every family have had to go, usually for 5 days to a week at a time on
rotation. Each village is assigned a length of road of several hundred
yards depending on village size, and this is divided up by family; for
example, the families in one village of Kyauk Kyi township had to build
54 feet of road each. The family has to send one or more members, who
must stay until their length of road is complete and sleep alongside the
road. The villagers are forced to dig earth and build a road embankment
4½ feet high and up to 24 feet wide, and must also clear the ground along
both sides of the road. Then they must haul sand and pack it on top of the
embankment to smooth the roadbed.

Some villagers have also been forced to make drainage ditches. One
villager from southern Mone township said that he and other villagers
tried to gather money to hire a bulldozer to help them, but when they
asked permission of the Sa Thon Lon officer in charge it was refused.

According to the latest reports provided by villagers from the area, most of the road construction was finished by April 1999, and all that remains to be built are 10 or more bridges. For the bridges, villages in the area have been ordered to cut logs and saw them into timber, and at the same time they have been ordered to pay 500 or 600 Kyat per family to "buy materials for construction", though this is most likely just extortion by the military officers.

According to a villager who just fled to Thailand at the end of April 1999, SPDC troops confiscated all the wood people had cut for their houses, took it away and then forced the villagers to buy it back from them and use it to build the bridges; in addition, the villagers had to supply all the cement and other materials for building the bridge foundations. Currently, the villagers of the area are doing forced labour to complete the bridges. Since March, labour on the road and bridges has been intensified, as the troops probably want the road completed and usable before the first rains. In April, Sa Thon Lon commander Bo Maung Maung ordered villagers to do a final intensive week of labour to finish smoothing the road and threatened that at the end of the week he would go from Na Than Gwin to Mone and back on a motorbike, and that if he ever had to get off his bike because the road was too bumpy, the villagers "will know about it". Given the Sa Thon Lon's record of summary executions and burning villages, he did not need to be more specific.

"[S]tarting in January 1999 the intelligence [Sa Thon Lon] soldiers ordered about 20 villages in Kyauk Kyi township to build a new road from Na Than Gwin to Mone, along the Sittaung river due west of the old Kyauk Kyi-Mone road. The Kyauk Kyi-Mone road has to pass through forest and hills, so the SPDC soldiers feel it is not safe to use. The Mone-Na Than Gwin road construction is under the control of the intelligence units led by Shan Bpu. The road is 15 feet wide, 24 feet wide at the base [of the embankment], and raised by 4.5 feet. It is at least 20 miles long. The work was divided and each family had to dig the earth and make a segment of road 54 feet long. Therefore villagers had to bring cattle, rakes, baskets, hoes etc. and work until their quota was finished. The villagers were even ordered to work at night in February, so the villagers brought lamps, batteries and fluorescent tubes to the work site and had to work nights. There were no materials supplied and there was no payment for the construction. ... In March the earth work was almost finished, except the bridges. For bridge construction, the intelligence soldiers confiscated wood, even small pieces, from houses and ordered villagers to build bridges. Some villagers had to cut down trees in the

forest for bridge construction. Then each family was ordered to give 500 Kyats to buy materials for the construction. Moreover, each family had to send a person for three days for bridge construction. There were around 10 bridges or maybe more. If a family could not work on bridge construction, they had to give 200 Kyats per day to hire a substitute person. " - "Naw Ghay" (F, xx), xxxx village, Kyauk Kyi township, describing forced labour on the new road from Na Than Gwin to Mone (Interview #11, 4/99)

"They started it in March [1999]. For the two months from March to May, we had no time to take a rest. They forced people from Yan Myo Aung and other villages. ... Now they're demanding that we give money for the bridges. They're demanding 600 Kyat from each household. They came and confiscated the wood that people had cut for their houses, they saw it and confiscated it all. Then they demanded that people go and buy that wood from them and use it to build the bridges. For the foundation of the bridges we had to buy bricks, cement, powdered lime and nails. We had to buy everything for them." – "Saw Lah Thaw" (M), xxxx relocation site, Mone township (Interview #2, 5/99)

"We had to go and work on their road to the east of Weh Gyi village, digging dirt. The road goes from the Mone hospital to Na Than Gwin, which is about one day's walk. They ordered us to make the road 10 cubits [5 m / 15 ft] wide with an embankment 3 cubits [1.5 m / 4.5 ft] high. The road also had to have clearings 3 cubits [1.5 m / 4.5 ft] wide on each side, so the total width is 16 cubits [8 m / 24 ft] with the middle 10 cubits being elevated. After building it up with dirt they said we had to carry in sand and lay it down nicely. We started the work in early March [1999] and dug for the whole month. We returned [to our village] once a week for food. We had to bring our own rice, food and anything else we needed [such as tools]. ... We started working at 6:00 a.m. and worked the whole day. We could take a short rest after we ate rice. We had to try to complete the part they ordered us to finish. We all slept there. We slept under the trees on the side of the road beside Weh Gyi village. They didn't build us shelters. When I came here, the part I was working on wasn't complete yet. ... We weren't allowed to use vehicles. We had told a friend in Ler Doh [about the work] and he told us that he could arrange a machine for us but it would cost money. We told each other to gather up our money for the machine. However, when we got the village headman to go and ask Bo Maung Maung's permission for us, we weren't allowed to do it. ... We have to make a drainage pipe with cement and bricks and then lay wood over top of it, and we were going to have to make a bridge. ... It's not finished yet. When I came, people still

had to go and dig. The road has to be finished this year. It's almost finished, all that needs to be done is to make it level. Before I came here they ordered people to take food for 7 days and to completely finish the road. He [Bo Maung Maung] was going to go to Mone and back on a motorbike. He said he will go straight through on the motorbike and that if he ever has to get off his motorbike because the road isn't good, we villagers will know about it." - "Saw Ner Muh" (M, 30+), xxxx village, Mone township, describing forced labour on the new road from Na Than Gwin to Mone (Interview #8, 4/99).

Arrests, Detention and Killings

"In xxxx [Army camp] they interrogated us and accused us. They said that we are the wives and children of men who live outside the village and that they would kill us. They said that the people from our village have radios and landmines. They said we must know about that so we must go and bring these things to them, and that if we didn't go and bring them they would have to kill us. They said they'd had an order from higher up that they must kill us. ... He said that if we lied to him he would kill us, but if we 'gave them our meat' he would release us with our lives. ... He forced us to sleep with him. He asked for love. I told him, 'Captain, I am 51 years old. I am the same age as your mother so you'd better not say that word to me. You should also remember that you are a Christian.' He said, 'I won't suffer in Hell.' ... I apologised but told him not to do that to me because I am old. Then he said, 'Then I must kill you, Mother'. He said it slowly, then he forced me to lay down and hold his penis. I didn't dare hold his penis, but he drew my hands and forced me to hold it, and he grabbed my buttocks. ... While he was doing it he threatened me with a dagger, he touched it to my chest, neck and armpits. Naw H--- told me how they had interrogated and tried to rape her too. She was crying. She came back saying that he wanted to rape her and forced her to hold his penis, and that he kissed her all over her body. ... Another time after that, they called us in at midnight. They said they would kill us, they touched our chests with a dagger and told us to pray." - "Naw Eh Muh" (F, 51), xxxx village, Kyauk Kyi township, describing part of her 15-day detention at xxxx Army camp in May 1998 (Interview #17, 2/99)

Village heads and elders are usually the first to be arrested, detained and tortured whenever their villages fail to comply with demands. Villagers who are suspected of any contact with the KNU/KNLA or who fail to comply with demands for forced labour and extortion money are also regularly arrested, beaten and either sent as porters or detained and tortured. Knowing this, people usually do whatever it takes to pay the fees and either do the forced labour or pay to avoid it, and when they can no longer do so they flee elsewhere rather than face arrest.

Sometimes SPDC troops arrest villagers and accuse them of working with the resistance simply so they can demand money from the other people of the village to secure their release. One particularly brutal case of this occurred in May 1998 in xxxx village of Kyauk Kyi township, when Company Commander Captain xxxx of Infantry Battalion #60 arrested seven villagers and had them taken and detained at xxxx Army camp for 15 days. Most of the detainees were women, including one 70-year-old and one 13-year-old. All were beaten, interrogated, and threatened with knives and other weapons, and at least two women were raped, aged 51 and 28. They were repeatedly told they would be killed, and two of the women were even tied up and sent "down to the river" with some soldiers to make them think they were to be executed. They were accused of knowing where the KNLA stored its landmines and radios. They were robbed of 8,000 Kyat on their arrest, and after 15 days all but one were finally freed when the other villagers paid for their lives. Naw H---, a 28-year-old woman who had been repeatedly raped, was not released but instead was handed over to LIB #349, taken off and imprisoned in Shwegyin town. According to a friend of hers who saw her in detention there, she had been raped again in Shwegyin and was still being held there several weeks later; no information is currently available on whether or not she is still there.

"Her father never came back because he is living in the mountains with the other villagers [internally displaced]. But they think her father is a bad person [KNLA]. She was about 25 years old. I dare not tell you her name. ... She is single. He put a hand grenade in her hand and demanded her love. Every night he called her to his room and demanded love. ... He was asking her love and trying to get money from her. When they arrest many people they can get a lot of money [from the other villagers, to secure their freedom]. They also arrested a girl who was 13 years old. ... They interrogated her and touched her with a dagger. They released her after 8 days. ... They didn't release Naw H---. She was handed over to #349. The #349 troops arrested her, locked her in the stocks and then sent her to Shwegyin. They sent her to their Battalion camp in Shwegyin and put her in a cell. Then a Corporal with 2 chevrons came and called her, he took her to the Battalion [HQ] and turned off the light. He was with her for 2 hours. When the soldiers went to look, he had raped her. ... After that we came to the hills and didn't hear any more about her.

She is still in jail." - "Naw Eh Muh" (F, 51), xxxx village, Kyauk Kyi township (Interview #17, 2/99)

Other incidents regularly occur involving SPDC soldiers firing into villages without cause and killing villagers, sometimes for strategic reasons and sometimes due to drunkenness; in either case the killers are never punished. There have also been killings connected to rape or extortion. For example, on January 4th 1999 in Kyauk Kyi township, Second Lieutenant Soe Myint Aung and 4 other soldiers from LIB 264 based at Pay Sa Loh camp raped and stabbed to death 20-year-old Naw Mu Mu from Htee Pu Lu village. They then placed a landmine in front of her field hut, which killed her brother when he came to look for her the next day. Following the explosion, they appeared in her village again, accused the village elders of laying landmines, beat them and demanded 200,000 Kyat as a fine from the villagers. Such incidents will continue to occur as long as SPDC troops in the region enjoy complete impunity for all their abuses.

"On January 4th 1999, Second Lieutenant Soe Myint Aung and 4 other soldiers came to Htee Pu Lu village in Kyauk Kyi township and demanded food from the villagers. On their way back, at 8 p.m. they saw Naw Mu Mu cooking alone in her farmfield hut and raped her, then stabbed her to death. Naw Mu Mu was 20 years old, single, a Karen Buddhist farmer from Htee Pu Lu village. After killing her, the soldiers laid a landmine outside the hut and then headed back to their camp. Naw Mu Mu's brother Saw Na Dway went looking for her the next day because she hadn't returned home, stepped on the landmine outside the farm hut and was killed. On January 5th, Second Lieutenant Soe Myint Aung and his friends returned to the village. They said they had heard the sound of a landmine explosion but no one had reported it to the Battalion office, so they beat the village elders, accused them of conspiring with the KNLA to lay landmines, told them not to tell this information to their [SPDC] commanding officers, and demanded 200,000 Kyat." - incident report from KHRG field reporter

"On October 13th 1998, IB 59 Column 2nd-in-command Aung Soe opened fire in Aung Chan Tha village, Mone township. When they shot at Ma Lah Myint's house, one of her daughters was wounded. Then they captured Ma Lah Myint, age 45, and Ma Nyunt, age 15, both from the village, and raped them. Then they took them back to their houses and shot both of them dead." - incident report from KHRG field reporter

Villagers are also sometimes killed when they are porters or summarily executed by SPDC troops. However, most of the executions and other direct killings in the plains of Nyaunglebin District are currently being carried out by the Sa Thon Lon Guerrilla Retaliation units, whose methods and activities have already been described above.

Villages in the Hills

"If they see villagers, they shoot them dead or beat them to death. They burn down all the houses. They burned about 15 houses in Thaw Ngeh Der, 30 houses in Dta Kaw Der, about 20 houses in Tee Nya B'Day Kee and some from Oo Keh Kee. They couldn't burn everything because of the rain. In addition, when they see farms and fields they pull up the paddy and destroy it. In the area of Theh Kee they shot and killed villagers, destroyed their paddy, and fired at the houses to set them on fire but they didn't all burn because of the rain. The villagers fled the village and all of their belongings were lost because they couldn't carry them when they left. They have no food and other villagers have to feed them. They [the Burmese soldiers] took all their belongings and killed the chickens and the pigs but didn't eat them. They just cut open one side of all the animals and leave them [to make the meat begin rotting immediately so villagers couldn't come back and use it]." - "Saw Ghay Po" (M, 40), xxxx village, Kyauk Kyi township (Interview #41, 12/98)

East of the Sittaung River plains lie the hills which make up approximately 75% of the area of Nyaunglebin District. They begin abruptly 10-15 kilometres east of the Sittaung River and extend all the way eastward into Papun District; steep and rugged, dotted with small villages and forested except where they have been cleared to make hillside rice fields. The villagers rotate use of these fields, clearing and planting a field one year, then letting the scrub overgrow it until they use it again several years later. The Karen National Liberation Army (KNLA) is active in these hills, and in an attempt to undermine it the SLORC/SPDC began systematically burning villages and shooting villagers in the easternmost regions in early 1997 [for more details see "Wholesale Destruction", KHRG April 1998]. The intent was to undermine the KNLA by driving everyone into the plains or killing them, thus depopulating the entire region. The campaign has driven thousands of villagers into hiding in the forests and hundreds to Thailand as refugees but has failed to undermine the KNLA. Rather than give up, the SPDC has responded by expanding the campaign throughout the hills of Nyaunglebin District and prolonging it indefinitely. In the hills, villagers live in fear in and around their villages, many of which have been destroyed, and flee further into hiding whenever SPDC patrols come around to burn more houses, destroy their food supplies and shoot villagers on sight.

Destruction of Villages and Food Supplies

"It's not possible for us to stay there anymore because the enemy [Burmese soldiers] burned down the village and all the paddy. They came to stay on the hill beside our village at about 1 p.m. on November 16th [1998] and burned all the houses. We ran and stayed in the jungle. Then they were looking for us there so we came here. They didn't see us, but they fired at us near the village when we were out looking around so we ran, they fired at us again and again and we ran." - "Saw Wah" (M, 30), xxxx village, Kyauk Kyi township (Interview #38, 1/99)

When the campaign to depopulate the hills began in 1997, over 30 villages in Shwegyin Township were systematically and completely destroyed by SPDC columns who took up positions on nearby hills, shelled the villages, then entered and burned all houses and sheds in sight [for a list of these villages and other details see "Wholesale Destruction", KHRG April 1998]. Throughout 1998 and thus far in 1999 military columns have continued to set out from bases at K'Baw Tu, Mu Theh, Saw Mi Lu, the Sittaung River plains between Shwegyin and Mone, and Papun District on a regular basis to move through villages in eastern Nyaunglebin District. The columns usually target a specific group of 5 or more villages, which they shell without warning. They then enter the village shooting, kill the livestock, and loot valuables from the houses. When they find plates and pots they smash them or poke holes in them to make them useless. Some or all of the houses are burned. The villagers flee and if seen are either shot on sight or captured as porters. The troops then hunt out rice supplies, and if they find any they take what they want and destroy the rest by scattering it on the ground or burning it. For the period November 1998 to February 1999 in Kyauk Kyi township, villagers interviewed by KHRG have described such attacks on Tee Muh Hta, Kler Kee, Ler Wah, Htaw Ee Soh, Tee Nya B'Day Kee, Dta Kaw Der, Kheh Der, Paya Hser Der, K'Dee Mu Der, Ler Hah, Maw Kee, Thaw Ngeh Der, Oo Keh Kee, Khoh Lu and Po Meh Baw villages. Some villages have been attacked more than once. Villages in the Tee Muh Hta and Kheh Der areas of Kyauk Kyi township have been particularly hard hit because columns have come repeatedly to destroy whatever is left and hunt for villagers in hiding.

"The day after they were shooting in our village, they went to Kler Kee village. The villagers had already fled when they got there but had left their belongings in their houses. They entered the village and shot the pigs and chickens, then they burned the village. After they burned Kler Kee village, they went to stay at Lah Soe. There are 2 or 3 farms at Lah

Soe and they destroyed them all. They pulled out the paddy and stomped on it, they didn't eat it." - "Saw Tee Muh" (M, 37), xxxx village, Kyauk Kyi township (Interview #40, 12/98)

"They told me that SPDC troops arrive at their place 2 or 3 times a month. SPDC troops are always moving around their area so they live in fear and must always be cautious. When I was there on November 17th [1998], the SPDC troops came and shot up Paya Hser Der, K'Dee Mu Der, Ler Hah and Maw Kee [villages]. That was a time of many troubles for the villagers. At that time many people died, including a student in 3rd Standard [primary school, Grade 3], and 3 other schoolchildren were also injured. They [SPDC troops] burned down paddy storage barns and houses. Before burning the houses they took the things inside, such as clothing, blankets, pots, plates, and other things. They took what they could carry with them and destroyed the rest." - "Saw January" (M), KHRG human rights monitor describing conditions in the hills of the district (Interview #1, 1/99)

It is important to note that when the SPDC columns attack villages there are almost never any KNLA troops in the village, and no one fires back at them. The KNLA troops camp in the fields and forests, especially if they know an SPDC column is in the area. The purposes of the attacks are simply to drive out the villagers and to make it impossible for them to survive in the area. In most areas the SPDC would use forced relocation orders for this purpose, but in the hills of Nyaunglebin District the villagers flee as soon as they hear of an SPDC column coming, so the columns have no opportunity to issue relocation orders to them. The columns set out to areas where they have heard of KNLA activity but do not seek out the KNLA, they simply go from village to village destroying everything they can. Whenever there is a KNLA ambush or attack of any kind they also retaliate against the villagers. For example, on February 25th 1999 there was a skirmish between SPDC LIB 351 and the KNLA near Ler Wah village in Kyauk Kyi township. As retaliation, the Battalion shelled Ler Wah village, then entered after the villagers had fled and looted and destroyed their belongings. They also went to Htaw Ee Soh village nearby on February 27th, but they couldn't catch any villagers there so they destroyed the paddy storage barns of 15 families, a total of 715 baskets of paddy. Just 3 months earlier, a combined column of Light Infantry Battalions #351, 361 and 368 had already shot at people in Ler Wah village and burned down 17 of their paddy storage barns.

"There was a firefight and several SPDC soldiers were wounded and killed. As punishment, they fired shells into Ler Wah village. The

villagers had no time to gather their things and fled for their lives. Then the SPDC soldiers entered the village, took some of their belongings and burned and destroyed others. The villagers are now internally displaced, living in hiding in the fields and forests, and have nothing." - incident report from KHRG field reporter

"They don't just shoot at people who have weapons, they kill the general population to clear the area. The following day, the 17th [November], they were shooting around Tee Muh Hta where there are many villages, such as Paya Hser Der, K'Dee Mu Der, Ler Hah and Maw Kee. I saw that with my own eyes." - "Saw January" (M), KHRG human rights monitor describing conditions in the hills of the district (Interview #1, 1/99)

"As we were fleeing we weren't able to take anything with us. We left everything behind in our houses, such as our pots, clothes, blankets and all our rice. They destroyed all the things we couldn't take. They also ate the pigs and chickens and destroyed 2 paddy storage barns in the village that belonged to Uncle W--- and S---. They hacked down and destroyed their paddy barns and all the paddy fell out. Uncle W---had 70 baskets of paddy in his barn and Uncle S-- had 60 baskets of paddy. ... They were shooting in the village for about half an hour and by then all the villagers were gone from the village. There must have been at least one or two hundred soldiers because they were firing a lot of guns. They continued shooting for about another half an hour. There were only villagers in the village, no one shot back at them." - "Saw Tee Muh" (M, 37), xxxx village, Kyauk Kyi township (Interview #40, 12/98)

In order to make it impossible for the villagers to survive or to support the resistance, the SPDC columns are also systematically trying to destroy their food supplies. After villagers harvest their paddy, they winnow it, dry it and then store it in paddy storage barns, which are small sheds measuring about 2 metres square, raised on posts and filled entirely by a woven bamboo paddy storage bin. In recent decades, their fear of Burmese troops and the regular need to flee to the forest has caused most of them to hide their paddy storage barns deep in the forest, only keeping a portion of their supply in the village at any given time. When SPDC columns approach the village, people have no time to save their rice or paddy, so the troops take it or deliberately destroy it when they arrive in the village. They also hunt for the villagers' paddy storage barns in the forest, and whenever they find them they either burn them along with all of the paddy, or tear them down and scatter the paddy on the ground to be destroyed by dirt and animals. Sometimes if the owners return from their hiding place soon afterward they can salvage some of the paddy which is scattered on the ground, but usually only a small portion of it.

"Now these two columns are moving through the hill regions, and when they arrive at villages they burn the houses. When they see paddy storage barns, they burn them and destroy all the paddy. If they can't take it to eat, they destroy it. When they see paddy growing in the fields they pull it up, and when they see paddy which the villagers have already harvested they burn it all. They also burn other plantations, like betelnut, betel-leaf trees, durian and many other kinds of trees, they burn them all. When they see villagers they shoot them dead, or if they can catch them first they abuse and torture them first and then kill them. As for livestock like pigs, chickens, cattle, goats, and buffaloes, they shoot them dead and eat them. If they can't eat it all, they just kill them and throw them away. They also take belongings like clothing, pots, plates, knives and small baskets. If they can't carry them all they cut, poke or shoot holes in them to destroy them. They keep doing it until the situation is like it is now." - KHRG field reporter, Nyaunglebin District (Field Report #FR2, 1/99)

"[T]hey came and burned it all. We got rice from other villages that hadn't been burned, but this latest time they came they burned all the villages so now we can't live there anymore and we left. ... They destroyed paddy storage barns, took everything from the houses and ate all the food from the two fields belonging to Pa W--- and Saw M---. They didn't burn the houses, they only took what was inside. They destroyed all our things which we had hidden in our secret huts [in the forest and fields] such as clothing, blankets, pots, mats and plates. They also took money from me and everyone else. Some people lost 10,000 Kyats and some lost 20 or 30 thousand Kyats. The paddy storage barns contained about 100 baskets of rice each. They belonged to Maw C--- and K---. They didn't burn the paddy barns, instead they tore them down. They ate some of the paddy and threw the rest away. ... Maw C--- was able to collect 10 baskets of his rice off the ground, and another person got 5 baskets. People who have paddy are sharing it with the people who don't. They look after each other this way. People have farms, but I don't know if they can work on them because of the troops moving in the area. ... When they went to Lah Sho they burned 4 sets of farming tools and 4 farmfield huts. They burned over 10 houses in Kler Kee village - only 3 houses were left unburned. They shoot the livestock everywhere all the time." - "Saw Wah" (M, 30), xxxx village, Kyauk Kyi township (Interview #38, 1/99)

"In Htaw Ee Soh village on February 27th they destroyed all the paddy storage barns they could find. Fifteen families lost a total of 715 baskets of paddy. The troops took some of the paddy to eat and destroyed the rest. The villagers fled into hiding in the fields and forests, and some continued on to refugee camps in Thailand." - incident report from KHRG field reporter

The SPDC columns also shoot the villagers' livestock whenever they see it in the village or the fields, and either eat it or leave it to rot. One villager from a hill village in Kyauk Kyi township told KHRG that in his area the troops cut open one side of the cattle and buffaloes they had shot, just to make sure the meat would be destroyed by insects or rot before the villagers could get to it. During the rice growing season, SPDC columns which see rice crops growing in the hills often go into the fields and pull up the plants or beat and stomp them down with machetes and Army boots in order to destroy the crop. In Khoh Lu village of Kyauk Kyi township in August 1998, an SPDC column cut and bundled the entire crop of several farmers, then threshed the unripe grain from the stalks onto the ground to destroy it. Another Column used the same method to destroy much of the crop at Kler Kee village in November 1998. The hillside rice fields are impossible to conceal, though fortunately for the villagers the Columns often do not have the time to stop and destroy more than a portion of the crop. When harvest time comes the Army columns seem to step up their activities, possibly with the intention of driving the villagers away from their crop at this crucial time. It is common for villagers to lose muchof their crop because SPDC Columns are too close to their fields just when the rice is ready for harvest. There have also been several cases of people being shot while trying to harvest, some of which are documented below under 'Shootings and Killings'.

"When we fled and then returned all our paddy was lost. ... Some people were able to harvest their paddy before [the SPDC soldiers came] so they got their paddy. Some people hadn't harvested their paddy yet so when the SPDC came they destroyed all of it. Animals also destroyed some of the paddy, so there isn't enough. ... We can't go and buy rice from the plains because the SPDC are there. If we could, we would have to pay 1,000 Kyats for one big tin of rice." - "Pu Ko Suh" (M, 60), xxxx village, Kyauk Kyi township (Interview #47, 12/98)

"They entered the village while we were harvesting. I had only put 10 or 20 baskets of rice in my paddy barn so far. After we fled we didn't dare go back to work on our fields so all the paddy was destroyed by animals.

Now I have returned to stay on the farm and we got a little bit of paddy, but it's not enough for the year. It's only enough for about one or two months, so I'm going to have to ask some from others. Most of the villagers don't have enough paddy." - "Saw Lay Muh" (M, 48), xxxx village, Kyauk Kyi township (Interview #46, 12/98)

"When I was collecting information on December 5th 1998, commander Min Kyu and his troops from LIB 361 burned 7 of the villagers' hill fields. ... Now these villagers have to live very hard lives, because the SPDC troops are patrolling around there even now. When they see the owners of farmfields they don't distinguish between old and young, they kill them all. If they see villagers' belongings like clothing, pots, plates and knives, they take it all. If they can't carry it they destroy it. People have to suffer many kinds of problems. When I went to see them they were gathering a little bit of their paddy which had been scattered on the ground by the SPDC troops so that they would have something to eat for a short time. ... I asked him, 'How will you get food in the rainy season?' He answered, 'We can't do much in the rainy season. We go to gather some bamboo shoots, we cut it up into small pieces and then mix it with a little rice and cook it. If there are seven of us, we mix it with one milktin of rice [less than enough for one person in normal times] and we eat together.' I asked him, 'Before your paddy crop is ripe, what will you do if you have no more rice and there are no more bamboo shoots?' He answered, 'We won't be able to do anything if there are no bamboo shoots. We'll dig for taro roots and eat that until the paddy is ripe.'" - KHRG field reporter, Nyaunglebin District (Field Reports #FR2, 1/99)

Shootings and Killings

"Both the first and second times they came they killed villagers. The first time they came two villagers died, Saw Bo Kee and Saw Pa Toh [October 13th 1998]. They were in their farm hut with two other villagers. The other two were able to flee and escape. The second time they came [November 16-17 1998] 4 villagers died and 3 were injured. The villagers who died were Saw Ko Pah, Saw Maw Dah, Nat Noh and Naw Tha Paw. Nat Noh and Saw Ko Pah were brothers and Saw Maw Dah and Naw Tha Paw were their cousins. Those who were injured had to treat their own wounds in the jungle. It was very difficult." - "Saw Lay Muh" (M, 48), xxxx village, Kyauk Kyi township (Interview #46, 12/98)

When moving through the hills, if SPDC columns see people in the villages, fields or forests they usually shoot at them with no questions asked. Occasionally they will call to the villager first, but when this happens people usually try to run away in fear and are then shot. However, there have also been cases where they have seen villagers working their fields, concealed themselves along the path and then shot the villagers when they try to head home. Some of the worst cases have happened near Tee Muh Hta village in Kyauk Kyi township. On October 13th 1998, a column of troops from LIB 368 saw a farmfield hut at xxxx where some villagers were weaving a mat. They opened fire without warning, and two villagers were killed while the other two escaped. The two men killed were Saw Bo Kee, age 33, and Saw Pa Toh, age 40, both from Paya Hser Der village. After killing the two men, the troops burned the farmfield hut and destroyed the paddy in the nearby fields. Saw Bo Kee's wife fled to Thailand as a refugee with their child, but Saw Pa Toh's wife is still trying to survive in hiding with their 3 children. Then on November 16th 1998, an SPDC Column from LIB 361 arrived at xxxx to shoot up and loot the village. As they entered the village they saw Saw Nat Noh, a 26-year-old man, and shot him under his house; he managed to drag himself out of the village and died on the path. The rest of the villagers had scattered, and the troops then looted the village, killed livestock and destroyed the villagers' rice, pots, plates and other belongings. Then they set off for xxxx village, burned some houses and camped along a path between the villages.

Twenty-year-old Saw Ko Pah had heard that his village had been shot up, so he was concerned for his parents and set out from Ler Wah village with a group of friends. They were ambushed by the LIB 361 Column along the path and Saw Ko Pah and his 14-year-old friend Saw Maw Dah were killed. Naw Tha Paw, a girl aged 17, was killed as well, though it is unclear whether she was shot or raped and then knifed to death. Three others escaped, but two of them were wounded. Making the tragedy even worse, Saw Ko Pah was the brother of Saw Nat Noh, who had been gunned down the day before. Their father told KHRG that he and his wife had 10 children but only four are now left - two have been shot dead by the SPDC, and four others have died of illnesses when they have had to flee SPDC columns and hide in the forest. After hearing that her two sons had both been killed, his wife cried for several days and then fell seriously ill. Saw S---, the owner of the paddy field where Saw Ko Pah and the others were killed, said that after killing the villagers the LIB 361 troops destroyed his entire paddy crop, and he subsequently fell seriously ill as well.

"We have to cut the weeds and then flee. We have to harvest the paddy and then flee. It's always been that way until now, when they came to shoot my sons. Both of my sons were shot and killed at the same time but

they were killed in different places. Saw Nat Noh died first and then Saw Ko Pah died the following evening. Nat Noh was killed near xxxx village, and Saw Ko Pah was killed in xxxx, which is near xxxx village. Nat Noh had been married for 3 years when the SPDC killed him but he had no children. His wife is now staying with her parents, who are already old. They are poor and have difficult lives. Saw Ko Pah had been living in xxxx, which is a 2 hour walk from xxxx. I wasn't healthy, so when the SPDC came to shoot in xxxx he was worried that I couldn't run and he came to help me. ... On his way back, he met some SPDC soldiers and they shot him dead. They also killed his friend and his cousin at the same time. They shot and killed 3 villagers, and 3 more were injured but managed to flee and escape. ... Since my sons died I can't work and that's causing me problems. Now I only have 4 children. Three of them are single and only one son can work [the others are too young]. ... I have 10 family members if you include those who have died [himself, his wife and 8 children]. The SPDC killed two a month ago, and the others died from illnesses. We fled and had to stay in the jungle, that's why they were sick. They died in the jungle. Now I only have a few children. ... We only have small children left and we can't ask them to help us. ... My wife has been sick for 4 or 5 days. She was mourning her sons and then got sick." - "Pu Ko Suh" (M, 60), xxxx village, Kyauk Kyi township (Interview #47, 12/98)

"I know her [Naw Tha Paw] because she harvested the paddy with us. She is 17 or 18 years old and was wearing a shirt and sarong. She was raped and killed on November 16th by the troops I mentioned before. That column also included some Ko Per Baw [DKBA soldiers]. A porter who had escaped saw it and told us. They stabbed her to death at L---'s farm. As for the boys, they shot them." - "Saw Wah" (M, 30), xxxx village, Kyauk Kyi township (Interview #38, 1/99)

"Saw Ko Pah was the younger brother of Saw Nat Noh - both brothers were killed by the same enemy group. Saw Ko Pah had heard the news about the enemy but he thought that the enemy wasn't on the path. He was going to find his parents where they were hiding. He was worried that they weren't so well. He thought his parents had had to flee and was coming to take care of them." - "Saw San Htay" (M, 40), xxxx village, Kyauk Kyi township (Interview #43, 12/98)

"On October 13th 1998, Burmese troops from LIB 368 at K'Baw Tu killed two villagers: Saw Bo Kee, age 33, married with one child, from Paya Hser Der village; and Saw Pa Toh, age 40, married with 3 children, from Paya Hser Der village. These two men were weaving a

mat in a farm hut at xxxx. There were 4 people in the hut when the SPDC saw them, but the other two escaped. Then the Burmese robbed 1,000 Thai Baht and some Kyat from Saw Bo Kee. Now Saw Bo Kee's wife has fled to be a refugee in Thailand, and Saw Pa Toh's wife is still staying near xxxx and taking care of their 3 children with great difficulty." - KHRG field reporter, Nyaunglebin District (Field Report #FR2, 1/99)

There have been many killings similar to those listed above. In addition, some SPDC columns have deliberately targetted villagers tending their fields and those harvesting rice. Usually villagers harvest in groups, making them an easy target, and during the harvest of late 1998 there were several incidents of SPDC Columns opening fire on people harvesting in the fields. On November 17th 1998, an SPDC Column from Mu Theh camp saw villagers harvesting a hillside field near xxxx village and opened fire on them. All escaped except Saw S---, age 40 from xxxx village, who was hit in the leg and the shoulder. He tried to escape and managed to keep going for two hours before collapsing and later being rescued by other villagers. On November 21st 1998, another SPDC column opened fire with large and small weapons on villagers harvesting near xxxx village in Kyauk Kyi township. Saw M---, age 38, ran to fetch his 9-month-old daughter from the hammock where she was resting and then fled carrying the baby but was hit in his legs. He handed the baby to his wife so she could keep running, but his wife discovered that one of the baby's legs had been blown off and the other was broken. The baby later died.

"I didn't dare stay in the plains so I came up to the mountains. I came to stay with my parents and work on the farm. Then during harvest time they shot at me many times. They came up from Mu Theh. They shot at us at xxxx, on the xxxx [river]. There were two of us, me and S---. S--- is married and Buddhist, he is from xxxx village. He is over 30 years old. They shot at him many times and his arm got wounded." - "Saw Yeh" (M, 19), xxxx village, Kyauk Kyi township, describing how SPDC troops fired on him and his friend while they were harvesting rice on November 17th 1998 (Interview #42, 12/98)

"While they were shooting at the people who were harvesting, a man named Saw M--- ran quickly to his field hut and took his 9-month-old baby daughter, who had been sleeping in a hammock, and ran away. Then he was shot in his leg and hand, and his baby was also hit. Saw M--- couldn't run properly anymore so he passed the baby to his wife. She was running with their other children. ... Then she looked down at her baby daughter, 9 months old, and saw that there was no way that the

child could survive. One of the baby's legs had been blown off by the gun and the other was broken. She put her baby daughter down and ran to safety with her other children." - "Saw January" (M), KHRG human rights monitor describing what happened when SPDC troops opened fire on villagers harvesting rice at xxxx village, Kyauk Kyi township, on November 21st 1998 (Interview #1, 1/99)

SPDC Columns in the hills know that most of the villagers are living in hiding in their farmfield huts and in makeshift shelters, usually along small streams high in the hills. One of their tactics is to fire mortar shells into the forest, stepping the shells up the gullies along the streambeds in the hope of hitting the villagers in their hiding places. As this can be done from a distance, it catches the villagers completely without warning and they have no idea of where the troops are or what is happening. Usually they are lucky enough not to be hit, but there have been several deaths of villagers and their livestock from this practice. On December 3rd 1998, a man from xxxx village was wounded by shrapnel in both his heels when troops from LIB 361 fired mortar shells into the forests in an area of northern Shwegyin Township where displaced villagers are hiding. In Kyauk Kyi township on December 14th 1998, troops from LIB 368 fired mortar shells into the forest near xxxx village and Saw Lay Lay Paw, a 10-year-old boy, was blown completely apart.

"At 6:30 a.m. they shelled the villagers in hiding while they were cooking their morning meal, and Saw M--- from xxxx village was wounded on both his heels. They also destroyed 7 of the villagers' fields, and the crops in 20 other fields were destroyed by animals. These troops regularly fire shells at the streams and into the deep forest just in case villagers are hiding there, so the villagers have to live in fear and can only cook before dawn and after dark." - incident report from KHRG field reporter

"Now the villagers there are living in hiding, but LIB 368 patrols and regularly shells all the places which they think are not secure. At 10 p.m. on December 14th 1998 they shelled the villagers' hiding place near xxxx village, and Saw Lay Lay Paw, male, age 10, was hit by a shell and blown completely apart." - incident report from KHRG field reporter

Survival in the Hills

"They have built huts to live in but these are very small. Some people don't even build huts in the dry season, they say that in the dry season they'll live instead near the stream in the jungle and will build huts again

for the rainy season. If they build huts during the dry season, they're worried that the Burmese will burn them if they see them. [Instead they just build a small split-bamboo sleeping platform under the trees.] Groups of 2 or 3 families live in each hiding place with 2 or 3 pots and their baskets to carry their belongings and their rice. They build their paddy storage barns in the jungle as well, and then they don't go far from where their paddy storage barns are hidden. The Burmese burn their paddy storage barns if they find them. They are living as animals live." - "Saw January" (M), KHRG human rights monitor, describing living conditions of people hiding in the hills (Interview #1, 1/99)

Many villages in the hills are already destroyed or partly destroyed, and those that still exist are abandoned whenever SPDC patrols are anywhere nearby. The villagers lead a very tenuous existence, some staying in their villages when they can but often fleeing to hiding places they have already established in the forest, while many more have forsaken their villages entirely and live in farmfield huts or shelters in the forest near their fields. People from some areas have had to flee the area entirely because too many SPDC patrols are always passing through; for example, many of the people of K'Dee Mu Der have left their village and fields and have tried to reestablish themselves living in the forests further east. Some have also fled westward to the plains, particularly if they have relatives there, but this is a very dangerous move particularly since Sa Thon Lon death squads have begun operating in the plains. Anyone from the hills would be perceived by the Sa Thon Lon as having contact with the KNLA. When the village destructions began in 1997, many people from the hills moved westward into the plains, but many of them have fled back into the hills over the past year, stating that they could not survive in the plains because they had no land, there was no work and the burden of forced labour and fees which must be given to the SPDC was more than they could bear. When they return to the hills they cannot go to their villages, but live in hiding in the forests like the others.

The people in hiding in the forest build small lean-to's from bamboo and leaves or small huts. Some villagers only build open-air sleeping platforms from split bamboo in the dry season because they have to run from place to place so often, or because they are afraid a hut would be too visible and the SPDC troops will burn huts if they find them. They stay in small groups of two to four families, and when SPDC troops are anywhere in the area they don't even dare light cookfires except before dawn and after dark. The young men of the villages often act as sentries, going out to look around and watch for any signs of SPDC Columns so they can give the others advance warning. Even so, the villagers often have little or no time to flee when troops appear, and in the sudden flight essential items like cookpots and clothing get left behind, and families scatter and get separated. When an SPDC Column arrived at xxxx village in November 1998 and started shooting, 16-year-old "Pa Noh" found himself alone because his family were out working the fields. "Pa Noh" is blind, but he managed to run out of the village. Later when he tried to return, SPDC troops saw him and opened fire on him and he ran again. In the end he spent over 2 weeks in the forest, surviving on nothing but water, bamboo shoots and ome jungle leaves; once he fell in a river and had to swim, but eventually by following the riverbank he made his way to xxxx, about 10 kilometres from his home, and found some villagers. At the same time that "Pa Noh" fled, a grandmother in the village who is over 70 years old had to flee with her three small grandchildren because their mother was out harvesting rice. The four of them were in the forest for over a week with no food but what they could find, and the youngest child was constantly crying because it needed to be breastfed, but they couldn' treturn to the village because the SPDC Column was still in the area. When they were finally found they were all extremely weak. There are many stories of such suffering in the forest, particularly from the elderly and the handicapped among the villagers.

"They shot at him when he was running away. The Burmese shot at him Baun, Baun, Baun, Baun, many times. He can run, and he ran down to a lower place. He lost his slipper there. He crossed the xxxx river. He said that when he went to drink the water in the river, he fell in and then he tried to get to the other bank. It was during the rains when he fled. ... He disappeared for about 3 weeks. ... He slept many days on the way. ... He didn't know where he was when he arrived at xxxx village because he had never been there before. ... He didn't have any food for over 10 days, he only drank water and ate wild jungle vegetables. When he returned he had a fever and his arms and legs were in pain." - "Pi Hser" (F, 50+), xxxx village, Kyauk Kyi township, describing how her 16-year-old blind son "Pa Noh" fled alone into the forest when SPDC troops came and was lost alone for over 2 weeks, surviving on water and raw bamboo shoots (Interviews #44 and #45, 12/98)

"I was staying alone in the village at that time. The other villagers were harvesting their paddy beside the village. At that time, the Burmese started shouting and firing their guns. I prepared a small amount of rice and packed my clothes and blanket. I had no friends with me, I was alone. I didn't see my son when he fled, he got lost. I couldn't walk and carry my things for long. I discarded a bottle of salt on the path so I was only carrying my blanket and some rice. While I was walking the

Burmese passed in front of me. I slept in the jungle for 4 nights. I didn't have any good rice to eat and could only eat a small amount of rotting rice when I needed to eat. When people saw me after that, they carried me. If they didn't carry me I wouldn't have been able to walk because I was so weak." - "Pu Tha Muh Htoo" (M, 75), xxxx village, Kyauk Kyi township (Interview #48, 12/98)

"Then on November 16th they came again to shoot in the village. When they came the villagers were threshing their paddy, but everyone fled when they arrived. When they came, the first thing the villagers heard was the sound of the shooting so all the villagers fled from the village. One villager was killed [Saw Nat Noh, age 26] and 2 others were injured. We had no time to take care of each other. At that time an old grandmother named K---, who is about 70 years old and can't hear or see well, was staying in the village with three of her grandchildren. The children's mother had gone to harvest paddy. The youngest child was still breastfeeding, but their mother left them with their grandmother. When the enemy came to shoot in the village, she fled with her three grandchildren in a different direction [than the other villagers]. She couldn't do anything with the youngest grandchild who still required breastfeeding and was crying. When we asked her, she said that she had boiled cucumber and vegetables to feed her grandchildren. They were staying in the forest for a week before some people found them and carried them back. When they were found, the grandmother and the three children were very weak and had to be fed, but they recovered." - "Saw Tee Muh" (M, 37), xxxx village, Kyauk Kyi township (Interview #40, 12/98)

"The villagers are having difficulties doing their work because their farms are near the Mu Theh road, which is where the enemy is staying. The villagers are doing what they can to get food. They have to move amongst the enemy cautiously and keep their eyes and ears open all the time. The villagers post sentries around their area, and if they get careless and don't remember to worry about the enemy then the enemy comes and shoots at the villagers." - "Saw Ghay Po" (M, 40), xxxx village, Kyauk Kyi township (Interview #41, 12/98)

"They have to listen for the Burmese troop movements and if the troops are moving in their direction they must gather up their children and the baskets containing their pots, clothes, rice and salt, and run to hide themselves. Men, women and children are always living like wild chickens. ... Some people don't have enough rice to eat because insects have destroyed their crops, while other people had enough rice but the

SPDC burned and destroyed it." - "Saw January" (M), KHRG human rights monitor, describing living conditions of people hiding in the hills (Interview #1, 1/99)

For the villagers in hiding in and around their hill villages, the key factor is food. As long as they can somehow obtain food they feel that they can survive, even if they regularly have to avoid SPDC patrols. For this reason they try to stay near their farmfields unless it is absolutely impossible, and if they cannot then they try to establish new fields elsewhere. Unfortunately, rice fields are very visible to SPDC patrols and very vulnerable, and the villagers often have their crop destroyed by an SPDC patrol or they have to flee at a crucial point in the crop cycle. Even after the harvest is in, there is always the danger of SPDC troops finding the hidden paddy storage barns and destroying the food supply. For these reasons, villagers in the hills often have little or nothing to eat.

When KHRG was interviewing internally displaced villagers in the hills before the harvest in late 1998, almost all of them said they were surviving on boiled rice gruel, which is made by boiling rice for an extended period of time, then eating it with the water it was boiled in; villagers only do this when they need to make a small amount of rice last a long time. They have little or nothing to eat with the rice; most have no livestock or meat, only a little salt or chillies if they are lucky. Many have nothing but bamboo shoots, taro roots or 'sour cucumber soup', which is just cucumber boiled in plain water, or soup made by boiling jungle leaves. The 1998 crop was already seriously damaged by a severe shortage of rain early in the growing season. Then when the harvest came, some people managed to get a reasonable crop but for most it was a partial or total failure, particularly in areas where SPDC patrols were operating around harvest time. They had to flee, and much of the crop was destroyed by the SPDC troops or by animals. Those who have rice have been sharing it with those who have none, sometimes as simple charity and sometimes with the understanding that it will be paid back next year.

"All the villagers gathered together and we went to harvest the green [unripe] paddy which we then had to dry in a pot over a fire. Then we pounded it to get rice and ate the rice together. If we didn't do it like that, we wouldn't have been able to eat. Our living conditions were very difficult. Those who had plastic sheets made shelters with them. We had to stay under a tree or under bamboo trees, and sleeping was very hard. When we fled it was rainy season and many children as well as old people got sick. We couldn't do anything." - "Saw Tee Muh" (M, 37),

xxxx village, Kyauk Kyi township, describing what the villagers did after
the SPDC raided his village on November 16th 1998 (Interview #40,
12/98)

*"All the villagers from the other villages have fled to stay in the jungle.
They can sleep in their houses for one or two days at a time and then they
have to flee. They have to carry food, rice and paddy. We couldn't get
our rice and paddy because of the troops moving in our area, so we had
to flee and we have to make rice soup with what little rice we have. ... It
is better in the hot season; in the rainy season it is very terrible. ... We
have to go back and get food, cut banana trees and bamboo shoots. We
eat very poorly. The children get sick and there is no medicine. Also
there are no plastic sheets [to protect them from the rain]. The water is
also no good. The villagers don't have enough clothes to wear. There
isn't enough of anything."* - "Saw Ghay Po" (M, 40), xxxx village, Kyauk
Kyi township, describing life in hiding in the forest (Interview #41,
12/98)

*"They [the Burmese soldiers] went to the houses of the villagers who had
fled and ate their pigs and chickens. When they saw buffaloes, they shot
and killed them. When the villagers who have fled to stay in the forest
run out of food, they return to their village [looking for food]. When they
[the Burmese soldiers] see them, they shoot and kill them."* - "Saw Thu"
(M, 33), xxxx village, Kyauk Kyi township (Interview #49, 12/98)

Some villagers have been seeking out their relatives from other villagers
to borrow rice, or trying to find food left behind by villagers who have
fled the area, but these sources have almost all been used up by now.
Many villagers have taken their jewellery and whatever other valuables
or cash they still have and set out on the dangerous trip to try to buy rice
from the plains. However, they are at risk of being shot on sight or
executed by a Sa Thon Lon squad if they do this, and they can only go if
the path is clear of SPDC troops. Some villagers say that they made the
trip but on the way back with their rice they were spotted by an SPDC
patrol and had to flee, and in the process they lost all the rice. They
cannot allow themselves to be caught, because anyone caught carrying
rice from the plains into the hills would be accused of feeding the KNLA.

*"We went into the plains to find rice. We had to pass through the enemy's
area. Sometimes we got one or two bowls [about 4 kg / 9 lb] and
sometimes we got one big tin [about 16 kg / 37 lb]. ... The villagers met
the enemy and lost their rice several times. They [the Burmese soldiers]
shot at them, killing one villager named Saw Shwe Win ... We are living*

day by day. " - "Saw San Htay" (M, 40), xxxx village, Kyauk Kyi township (Interview #43, 12/98)

"The other thing I want to tell you about is when we go to bring food from the lower places [the plains]. The people who carry the food for us, if the enemy sees them they shoot them. The enemy also shoots at us if they see us carrying food. Many of the villagers throw away the rice [when they get shot at] and much rice is lost. The enemy doesn't allow the villagers to carry rice, salt, tobacco, tea, other foods or bread. If they see people carrying those things, they beat and kill them." - "Saw Ghay Po" (M, 40), xxxx village, Kyauk Kyi township (Interview #41, 12/98)

"Here I've had to flee two times. ... Last year I had to flee for the whole year. I've met with many kinds of problems. During the rainy season I couldn't buy rice so I had to eat boiled rice soup the whole rainy season long, for about 3 or 4 months. Getting food was difficult and frightening." - "Saw Lay Muh" (M, 48), xxxx village, Kyauk Kyi township (Interview #46, 12/98)

Villagers taking medicine from the plains into the hills would also be executed as rebels, and for this reason the villagers have no access to modern medicines. Those who are sick can only be treated with roots and herbs. Many have died of treatable diseases such as malaria, diarrhoea and dysentery, particularly children and the elderly. For those who suffer gunshot or shrapnel wounds, the villagers have no gauze or antiseptics, only herbs and sesame oil. Sometimes they are lucky enough to get some help from a KNLA medic, but only if there is one in the area who has any medicine or bandages which he can spare. For the villagers in the hills, going to the plains to go to hospital, particularly for a gunshot wound, would be just as risky as going to buy rice.

"The most common illnesses they suffer from are fever and malaria. People with fevers or malaria who wouldn't normally die are dying because there is no medicine. Most of the people who have died are children, ages 1 to 5 years old. I saw children with fevers, and because they had no medicine the fever never went down. Even though they put sesame oil on the body of the child, they still die. There is no gauze, no cotton and no medicine for when someone is injured. All they have are their traditional healing practices, but those are not perfect without some medicine as well." - "Saw January" (M), KHRG human rights monitor, describing living conditions of people hiding in the hills (Interview #1, 1/99)

"People keep them [villagers with gunshot and shrapnel wounds] in a hiding place and treat them with curry roots and cooking oil. It's difficult to get cooking oil and it's very expensive. Some people pound the curry roots and mix them with cooked rice and then put it in the wounds. Some people make holy water and mix it with curry roots. There is no other medicine." - "Saw Ghay Po" (M, 40), xxxx village, Kyauk Kyi township, talking about how villagers in the forest treat each other for gunshot wounds (Interview #41, 12/98)

"I waited for one or two days and then saw people bring S---. He is about 40 years old. They were carrying him in a hammock and he was bleeding a lot. He was wounded on his leg and his shoulder, and his shoulder was bleeding too much. I asked people, 'Is there any medicine?', and I was told, 'There is no medicine. Those who are hurt always know in their hearts that if they are lucky they will live but if they are unlucky they will die.' I told them, 'It is not good to keep things like that in your heart, you should find medicine.' They told me, 'There is no medicine.'" - "Saw January" (M), KHRG human rights monitor who was there when villagers in hiding tried to treat a villager who had been shot on sight while harvesting rice on November 17th 1998 (Interview #1, 1/99)

The children in the hills have also lost all opportunity for education, because it is not possible to keep a school open in such an unstable situation. When SPDC Columns raid villages, schools and churches are usually the first buildings they burn. In xxxx village of Kyauk Kyi township they managed to keep a primary school open until September 1998, but then had to close it because none of the teachers or students had enough food anymore, and everyone had to do all they could to get enough food to survive. There was a plan to reopen the school in November, but then an SPDC Column shot up the village and everyone had to flee. At present the villagers around xxxx are still fleeing back and forth between hiding places in the forest, and there has been no chance to reopen the school.

"[W]e closed our school on September 13th [1998] because we didn't have enough food. The students and teachers have only a little food left. The paddy that the enemy didn't destroy will be eaten by us all together [shared between all of them]. We thought that we would open the school again later, but then the enemy came on October 13th. That's why we had to close the school until December." - "Saw San Htay" (M, 40), xxxx village, Kyauk Kyi township (Interview #43, 12/98)

"My son who was killed by the Burmese was starting to study but was killed before he could finish school. Some of my other children went to school for 2 years but because of the current problems they've stopped going to school. They are afraid to go back to school. When we are not afraid they will go back. But we are afraid of the SPDC and must lead difficult lives." - "Saw Lay Muh" (M, 48), xxxx village, Kyauk Kyi township; his 14-year-old son Saw Maw Dah was shot dead by LIB 361 on November 16th 1998 (Interview #46, 12/98)

Flight of the Villagers

"The Burmese opened fire on Ler Wah village before dawn and after the villagers had run away they entered the village and burned the houses and paddy storage barns. The villagers told me that they had harvested enough rice for the whole year but the enemy burned their paddy storage barns, so now they don't have any food to eat. They couldn't live in their home area so they went to a refugee camp." - "Saw January" (M), KHRG human rights monitor who met with Ler Wah villagers just after their village was raided on December 26th 1998 (Interview #1, 1/99)

Karen villagers are subsistence farmers and are extremely attached to the land. Many would rather die on their land than flee, and for the vast majority the idea of leaving the only home they have known and the land which is their only source of security is extremely frightening, an insane thing to do. This is why the people in the plains stay on even in the face of constant and inhuman abuse and repression, and thousands of people in the hills continue to hide in makeshift shelters deep in the forest, suffering from disease and hunger and running away every week or every month, rather than leave their land and flee to Thailand. However, for the villagers in the hills and those in the plains there comes a point when they know that to stay means almost certain arrest, death at the hands of SPDC troops, or death by disease or hunger. For many people, the decision comes when they think of their children rather than themselves. Some refuse even to consider it, and say that they will die before they will flee. But for many, they reach a point where flight becomes the only option.

"In the past it was better and now it's getting worse. People can't tolerate it anymore. Some people would like to flee but they don't know how or where to go." - "Saw Dee Ghay" (M, 38), xxxx village, Kyauk Kyi township (Interview #9, 4/99)

It is difficult to estimate the number of people who have been displaced from their villages in the hills and are living in hiding from SPDC forces, though the number is probably 10,000 or more. The vast majority of them are still trying to live in the forests around their own villages or villages further into the hills. Since 1997 some of them have fled westward into the plains, though many of these have found it impossible to survive in the plains and have now returned to live in hiding in the hills. At the same time, since the beginning of 1998 villagers native to the plains have begun fleeing to the hills for various reasons: some are fleeing in fear from the Sa Thon Lon death squads, some can no longer pay the ever-increasing extortion fees and provide all the forced labour demanded of them, some can no longer produce their own food because of all the restrictions imposed on them in the SPDC relocation sites, and for most the reason is a combination of all of these factors. The population in the plains is much higher than in the hills and to date it appears that only a few hundred to a thousand have fled, but the flow is increasing each month. Many have fled to villages west of the Sittaung River where conditions appear safer, but now the Sa Thon Lon squads are looking for them there. As a result, an increasing number are now fleeing eastward into the hills or to Thailand.

"I came here because my name appeared. In the past I stayed in the mountains and worked for the resistance, but when I started getting old I knew I couldn't do that anymore so I went back to live with my children in the village. However, my name was written down and now they are going to kill me so I have to find a place of refuge. ... I couldn't stay in my village or my head would have been cut off." - "Pu Hla Maung" (M, 57), xxxx village, Mone township, interviewed after his arrival in Thailand (Interview #22, 1/99)

"This force [Sa Thon Lon] is made up of people from every battalion. The current leader of the people doing the killing in our area is from Battalion #53. ... They wear simple T-shirts, but at night sometimes they wear guerrilla uniforms. ... They were going around and asking people about me by name. They came 3 months ago. I don't dare to go back and I won't go back until this force leaves the area. I will go back after they move away. I've come as a refugee." - "Maung Soe" (M, 40), Kyauk Kyi town, interviewed after arriving in Thailand (Interview #21, 1/99)

"They said that if they couldn't kill the head of the household they would kill the whole family in the house, so my family couldn't dare stay in the village. They [the Sa Thon Lon] came and looked around our house 3 times, so we headed towards the mountains where the KNLA are. ... We came without even a blanket or a pot and had to ask others for some. Now we are living like this." - "Saw Ta Roh" (M, 37), xxxx village, Shwegyin township, interviewed in hiding in the forest (Interview #32, 12/98)

"I don't dare stay in the village so I came here. None of the villagers are in the village anymore. They are all afraid and don't dare to stay there. They are afraid of Byaut Kya [Sa Thon Lon], who said that if they know of anyone who has joined the people here they will kill them all." - "Pu

Eh Doh" (M, 55), xxxx village, Kyauk Kyi township, interviewed while living in hiding in the hills (Interview #31, 12/98)

For those who can no longer survive in either the hills or the plains, there are few options. Some flee to the homes of relatives in near or distant towns. However, this often doesn't work out because even people in towns are struggling to survive, and the SPDC is always checking house registrations looking for unregistered strangers whom they often arrest or take as porters. The other option is to try to flee to Thailand, though this is also difficult. Most people are afraid to head for Thailand because they have no idea of what awaits them in such an utterly foreign land. In addition, the trip is long and dangerous, and they have heard the stories that refugees in Thailand are still attacked by SPDC and DKBA troops and abused by Thai troops as well. However, some decide that this is their only option. For those in the hills the usual route is to cross overland, eastward across the hills of Nyaunglebin District and then northern Papun District. This is a difficult walk through the hills and would take 4 to 7 days at the best of times, but travelling with children, the elderly and sick, cookpots and basic belongings makes it take two weeks or longer, with no access to food along the way. Since 1997 the SPDC has destroyed all of the villages in the hills of northern Papun District; the villagers there are also living in hiding in the hills and are shot on sight if seen by SPDC patrols [see "Wholesale Destruction", KHRG April 1998]. As a result they have little or no food to share with the people from Nyaunglebin District who are passing through, and the villagers heading for Thailand must often stop for days and hide when SPDC Columns are moving in the area. Many of the paths along the way have also been landmined by the SPDC or the KNLA. Usually the only way the villagers can make the trip is if they gather into a group and are escorted all the way by a KNLA Column, and for this reason they often arrive in Thailand in groups. For example, on January 10th-11th 1999 a group of 107 people, 28 families from the xxxx area in Kyauk Kyi township, arrived together at xxxx refugee camp. There have also been smaller groups of several dozen at a time arriving before and since then, producing an overall total of several hundred since late 1998. Thus far they have been allowed to stay at the refugee camps by Thai authorities; however, because of concerns about arriving in large groups they sometimes split up into groups of one or two families when they reach the border and try to arrive at the camps in small numbers. There are reports that some families crossing the border singly have been forced back if they encounter a Thai Army unit before reaching the camps.

"Over a hundred people came with us, about 150 people. We left on December 31st and arrived here on January 11th. Many children were sick on the way. We had no medicine, but when we crossed the river and arrived here [the refugee camp] people here gave us medicine. ... On the way here the SPDC Army nearly found us. One group of their troops was behind us and another was in front of us. The KNLA in the area showed us the way to evade them. If they'd shot at them they could have killed them, but we told them not to because we were travelling with children." - "Saw Wah" (M, 30), xxxx village, Kyauk Kyi township (Interview #38, 1/99)

"We had problems because we had to avoid them [the Burmese soldiers] in some places. We left the village 15 days ago and arrived here 3 days ago. We spent a lot of money coming here. Some was spent on food and some on travel. We rode [in a vehicle] to the foot of the mountains and then came on foot. We won't go back. My father, 2 of my younger brothers, an elder sister and her 2 small children are still coming but they haven't arrived yet." - "Naw Mary" (F, 30), xxxx village, Mone township (Interview #15, 3/99)

People fleeing the plains in the west of the district have been using a different route, taking commercial passenger trucks southward along the main roads to Pegu, Thaton and Pa'an, then eastward by truck or on foot to the Thai border near xxxx. These people then arrive at xxxx refugee camp, or disappear into the illegal labour market in Thailand. Since early 1999 ten or twenty people per week have been arriving at the refugee camp this way, a mix of Karens and Burmans from the Sittaung River plains. Their numbers do not appear on the camp registers because Thai authorities officially refuse to accept any new refugees. The Burmans are viewed with suspicion by the Karens in the camp and the Thai authorities, so they usually have to leave and find illegal labour somewhere in Thailand. For this reason it is difficult to estimate the total number of people who have arrived by this route.

"The two of us are the first from our village who have ever come to Thailand. There are some people from other villages who have already fled, so they [the SPDC troops] were afraid that we would flee too. That's why they threatened us and said, 'If people go and I find out, I will kill them when they come back.'" - "Naw Say Paw" (F, 26), xxxx village, Kyauk Kyi township (Interview #29, 1/99)

"If the enemy keeps moving around their area, they have only one option, to come here. That is what I've seen; we don't dare go to stay among the

enemy. " - "Saw Wah" (M, 30), xxxx village, Kyauk Kyi township, after arriving in Thailand as a refugee (Interview #38, 1/99)

Future of the Area

"The Burmese are very strong and there is no security here for us. They are staying close to us, so we have to hide and live the hard way. We can only farm a little bit. It's not enough for us. Last year when we had a farm and were carrying our paddy, they were waiting for us on the path and shot at us when they saw us. If we had died, it would all be over for us. The villagers living here have to depend on their luck. We don't know if we will die tomorrow or this evening. I am talking to you now but I may be dead tomorrow. The people who are here are on the path to death. The enemy doesn't differentiate between good and bad people, whenever they see villagers they just kill them. If they see a man, they kill him. If they see a woman, they rape and then kill her." - "Maung Baw" (M, 30), xxxx village, Kyauk Kyi township (Interview #39, 12/98)

The situation in Nyaunglebin District is quite similar to that in Toungoo, Papun and some other Karen districts, with the exception of the Sa Thon Lon death squads. For both Karens and Burmans in the Sittaung River plains, it is the Sa Thon Lon which is the last straw forcing them to flee the area, and people are still being executed every week. For this reason it is very important to watch for developments involving the Sa Thon Lon squads, whether their behaviour continues as it is and whether they expand their operations into other areas or similar units are created elsewhere. The fact that they have now expanded their operations northward into the southern part of Toungoo District is cause for grave concern. At the same time, some villagers say they have been told by Sa Thon Lon soldiers that the force will withdraw in May or June 1999; the soldiers may just mean they will be rotated with fresh troops, as a complete withdrawal of the Sa Thon Lon force appears very unlikely. The use of the Sa Thon Lon in Nyaunglebin District may be an experiment which, if the SPDC perceives it as working, will be recreated in all other regions where they are trying to consolidate their control. The possibility of Sa Thon Lon-style death squads being created all over Burma is frightening.

For the villagers in the Sittaung River plains it appears that the situation will only continue to get worse. The latest wave of forced relocations, when 5 villages in northern Mone township were forced to a new relocation site outside Mone town in April 1999, appears to indicate that the SPDC is not finished with its forced relocations of villages in the plains. As long as the KNLA continues to occasionally come out of the hills to ambush SPDC and Sa Thon Lon troops, the SPDC will continue to forcibly relocate every village which is not under their direct and constant control. At the same time, the continued heavy militarisation of the area will ensure that the triple burden of forced labour, extortion and crop quotas will continue to fall heavily on the villagers. Most people have already sold most or all of what they have and have gone into debt in order to pay these fees and quotas and survive, and if it goes on much longer they will have to flee. Their only hope is that the failures of the 1997 and 1998 crops will not be repeated in 1999; however, many of them do not even have enough seed to plant a full crop and cannot dare go to their fields because of movement restrictions or fear of the Sa Thon Lon squads. When harvest time comes at the end of the year, none of this will be taken into account when the authorities once again demand their rice quota. In the meantime, many villagers will be living on boiled rice gruel to make it to the harvest. If this harvest fails for any reason, there may be a rapid increase in the number of people fleeing the area.

"Everyone is in trouble. People like us only have food to eat when we go to the forest [to earn money gathering bamboo and thatch], but when we come back we have to give fees and taxes to them. Not only do we end up with nothing to eat from our work, but we also have to go and do work for them, so we are living the lives of slaves. People who had bullock carts and teams now have no bullock carts or teams." - "Daw Hla" (F, 48), Burman bamboo cutter from xxxx village, Shwegyin township (Interview #25, 1/99)

For the people in the hills the situation is even more immediately desperate. Most of them are already almost completely out of food and are surviving on rice gruel and jungle vegetables such as bamboo shoots and banana tree stalks. With little or no seed to plant and regularly having to flee SPDC Columns, it is very unlikely that any of them will be able to produce enough rice to support themselves for more than a month or two. They will have to continue moving from shelter to shelter when SPDC Columns come near; some of their shelters will be burned, and some of their crops will be systematically destroyed by SPDC troops. However, their attachment to their land is so strong that most of them will probably continue to survive in this manner for as long as they possibly can. Many will be killed by SPDC troops, many more will die of disease, and some will flee. Regular groups of refugees from the hills of Nyaunglebin District can be expected to arrive at the Thai border, and hopefully the Thai authorities will continue to allow them asylum in the existing refugee camps. At the same time, the flow of Karens and Burmans from the Sittaung River plain to refugee camps in Thailand can be expected to increase as long as the Sa Thon Lon squads continue to operate as they do at present.

"We can't do anything, we have no food. Some villagers are thinking they will go to the refugee camps. Some have said that they will stay in this difficult situation and try to find food in other places. It won't be easy. We have talked about many ideas. We can't do anything and we don't know how to help each other. ... We dare not go back to stay in our village but we will stay near our village. We will have to stay cautiously, because they come to the village and patrol the area. We will stay in our own country here. Some villagers have said that they will go to stay in the refugee camps if they must. If it is at all possible, we don't want to go to the refugee camps." - "Saw Tee Muh" (M, 37), xxxx village, Kyauk Kyi township, interviewed in hiding in the forest (Interview #40, 12/98)*

There is no sign that the killings, abuses and repression by regular SPDC units and Sa Thon Lon squads will decrease as long as the KNLA is active in Nyaunglebin District, and the KNLA shows every sign of remaining active for the foreseeable future. The SPDC tactics have been very effective in wiping out villages and the people in them, but have had very little success in undermining the KNU/KNLA. For its part, the KNU has repeatedly sought ceasefire negotiations with the SPDC, but at present the SPDC is refusing to negotiate any political or human rights issues and is demanding that the KNU renounce its struggle, surrender its weapons and "join the legal fold". The small-scale autonomy and military zones which were offered to other opposition groups in the past are not being offered to the KNU. The KNU is unwilling to accept this because it views surrender to the SPDC as suicide. Most villagers say that they would like to see the fighting stop because they are tired of all the retaliations taken out against them by the SPDC for the KNLA activities in the area, but at the same time they do not trust the SPDC at all. Most of them believe that even if the fighting stops the KNLA should continue to exist and should keep its arms, because otherwise things would only get worse for the villagers; that the SPDC troops would initiate an unrestrained witchhunt to kill all villagers with KNU/KNLA connections, and would then use the villagers as nothing but a captive population of forced labourers. The situation is at a deadlock with little room for optimism, but the villagers have little time to think about the politics of it all. For them, even thinking about life six months in the future is a luxury they cannot afford. They need to survive until tomorrow.

"If the enemy stops moving, the population can survive. If they don't stop moving the villagers won't be able to live. The enemy is not kind, they are killing people like they are dogs or pigs." - "Saw Ghay Po" (M, 40), xxxx village, Kyauk Kyi township (Interview #41, 12/98)

*"The people from the foreign country said the SPDC are coming now.
They said they will come and do good things, but they haven't come to do
good things. They have shot and killed the villagers. We don't
understand what they are doing. Will they clear out all the Karen people
or not? We don't see how they are going to clear out all the Karen
people. We don't know what their purpose is for clearing out the Karen
people. However, they are still killing and eventually we will all be
gone."* - "Pu Ko Suh" (M, 60), xxxx village, Kyauk Kyi township
(Interview #47, 12/98)

In the appendix is reproduced a partial list of villagers killed directly at
the hands of regular SPDC troops and Sa Thon Lon units in Nyaunglebin
District and the area of Tantabin township, Toungoo District which lies
just north of Nyaunglebin District. These killings have been described in
the interviews and field reports collected for this report, and many of
them have been corroborated by several interviews and field reports. Full
texts of these interviews and field reports are available on request from
KHRG.

Photographs

Plate 1: Khoh Lu village, Ler Doh township, which was completely burned down by SPDC troops on 20 August 1998. *[Photo: KHRG]*

Plate 2: Houses in Kya Plaw village, Ler Doh township, after the villagers there were forced to move to a relocation site just outside Ler Doh (Kyauk Kyi) town at the beginning of January 1999. The villagers dismantled their houses to cart the building materials to the relocation site in order to build small huts there. *[Photo: KHRG]*

Plate 3: A woman searches for her belongings in the ruins of Daw Peh village, Papun District, after it was completely burned by LIB 369. SPDC units often landmine villages after burning them, knowing the villagers will return. *[Photo: KHRG]*

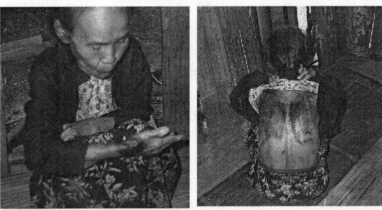

Plates 4, 5: Naw Y---, age 60, a Karen Christian farmer in Toungoo District. On October 20th 1999, troops from SPDC Infantry Battalion #59 set her house alight while she was inside it, and she suffered severe burns to her back and wrist. *[Photos: KHRG]*

Plate 6: Internally displaced Thaw Ngeh Der villagers harvesting rice at the end of 1998, Ler Doh township. Villagers usually work together in groups harvesting each other's fields, making them an easy target for passing SPDC patrols. *[Photo: KHRG]*

Plate 7: Thaw Ngeh Der villager Saw S---, age 40; on 17 November 1998 he was harvesting rice with a group of other villagers at 7:30 a.m. when an SPDC patrol saw them and opened fire on them. Saw S--- was hit in the leg and the shoulder. *[Photo: KHRG]*

Plate 8: Naw P---, age 11, an internally displaced villager in Papun District who was shot on sight by SPDC troops in November 1999 when she and other villagers were carrying the rice they had harvested through the fields. She saw both her mother and father fall dead but managed to escape with a bullet wound on her arm. Three people were killed and two others injured. The troops then destroyed the rice and landmined the fields. Later two other villagers were killed by these mines, and the next month another SPDC patrol came and burned all the farmfield huts and the houses in Naw P---'s home village. *[Photo: KHRG]*

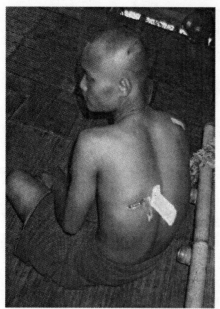

Plate 9: In Baw Bpee Der area of Nyaunglebin district, a *Sa Thon Lon* unit tried to kill Saw K--- with knives after accusing him of contact with the KNU, but he escaped and fled to hide in the hills in June 1999. *[Photo: KHRG]*

Plate 10: Saw P---, age 32, Kheh Der village, Ler Doh township, being treated by a Karen medical team after stepping on an SPDC landmine laid by Column 2 of LIB 368. The front half of his foot was blown off. Saw P--- lives in hiding in the forest with the other villagers, and LIB 368 lays mines on the paths to kill villagers in hiding. *[Photo: KHRG]*

Plate 11: A villager in the hills of Kyauk Kyi township tries to salvage some of his paddy after SPDC troops emptied the entire contents of his paddy storage barn onto the ground to destroy it. *[Photo: KHRG]*

Plate 12: A ricefield in southern Toungoo District, uprooted and destroyed by SPDC troops before it was ripe. SPDC columns are now destroying crops in the fields in several Karen regions. *[Photo: KHRG]*

Plate 13: Saw Ko Pah, a 20-year-old Tee Muh Hta villager who was studying to become a medic. In November 1998 he heard that an SPDC column had shot up his village and rushed back with his friends to help their parents. On the way they ran into the LIB 361 column, who shot them down on the path. Three were killed, and two escaped with injuries. *[Photo: KHRG]*

Plate 14: A father looks on at the graves of his daughter, Naw Mi Mu Wah, female, age 2 (right), and her cousin Saw Ta Plah Plah, male, age 3 (left). On 12 March 1997 SPDC Division 77 troops shelled Doh Daw Kee village without warning. The children's parents were away in the fields, and their grandmother could only flee carrying Naw Mi Mu Wah's smallest sibling. The two small children were left behind alone as the

troops came into the village and began burning all the houses. According to witnesses in the bush just outside the village, the children were running around wailing until they were thrown back into the flames by the soldiers and burned to death. *[Photo: KHRG]*

Plate 15: Ler Doh township. As darkness falls, Thaw Ngeh Der villagers prepare to flee into hiding in the forest after hearing that an SPDC column is coming into the area of their village. *[Photo: KHRG]*

Plate 16: Shelters of a group of internally displaced people hiding in the forest in western Papun District; the young woman is weaving homegrown cotton into cloth. *[Photo: KHRG]*

Plate 17: A woman internally displaced in Ler Doh township spends a night in the forest hiding from SPDC patrols in early February 1999 after part of her village was burned. The split-bamboo platform is her bed. *[Photo: KHRG]*

Plate 18: Ay Pree Paw, age 4, and Si Mu Paw, age 3. When SPDC troops shelled Tee Muh Hta village on 20 November 1998, they fled into the forest with their 80-year-old grandmother and their 17-month-old sister, and the group was alone in the forest for 10 days with no rice to eat before they found the other villagers. In the photo they are still living in hiding in a temporary shelter in the fields. *[Photo: KHRG]*

Plate 19: Families from Ler Doh township flee toward the border with Thailand. *[Photo: KHRG]*

PART II

CAUGHT IN THE MIDDLE

The Suffering of Karen Villagers in
Thaton District

An Independent Report by the
Karen Human Rights Group (September 15, 1999)

Abstract

This report looks at the human rights situation for Karen villagers living in Thaton District (known in Karen as Doo Tha Htoo), which includes part of northwestern Karen State and northern Mon State. The western parts of this district, near the coast of the Gulf of Martaban, are under the strong control of Burma's State Peace & Development Council (SPDC) military junta, and the villagers there face heavy demands for forced labour, crop quotas and extortion money by SPDC troops. The SPDC also has 'de facto' control over the eastern parts of the district, but in this area guerrilla units of the Karen National Liberation Army (KNLA) are also active, as well as units of the Democratic Karen Buddhist Army (DKBA) allied to the SPDC. The villagers are caught in the middle; not only do they have to hand over money and food to all three groups on a regular basis, but they are severely punished by the SPDC and the DKBA every time the KNLA takes any action. Rather than seek out and fight the KNLA, the SPDC forces in the area try to undermine the KNLA by stripping villagers of all of their belongings, detaining and torturing them on a regular basis, committing random killings and occasionally burning houses. These tactics are supposed to make it impossible for the villagers to support the KNLA, but the KNLA continues to operate. According to media reports and both KNU and SPDC sources, on September 5th the KNLA blew up and temporarily crippled a small gas pipeline near Bilin town in Thaton District, which is likely to lead to even further punishments and repression being inflicted on the villagers.

Of further concern is statements by some villagers that units of the SPDC's 'Sa Thon Lon Guerrilla Retaliation' units may be appearing in Bilin Township. These special execution squads have already been responsible for dozens of systematic and brutal executions in Nyaunglebin and Toungoo Districts to the north, which are their main areas of operation [for more information see below under 'The Short Pants' as well as the report "Death Squads and Displacement: Systematic Executions, Destruction of Villages and the Flight of Villagers in Nyaunglebin District" above.

All of these forms of repression are leading many villagers in Thaton District to flee to other villages, or to spend their lives hiding in the forest whenever SPDC forces are around. A few are fleeing to become refugees in Thailand, but the trip is long and dangerous.

In order to produce this report, Karen Human Rights Group (KHRG) researchers and field reporters have interviewed villagers in the SPDC-controlled areas, in the hill villages, in hiding in the forests and those who have fled to Thailand to become refugees. Their testimonies have been augmented by incident reports gathered by KHRG researchers in the region. The interviews were conducted between January and July 1999.

Photographs which relate to the situation described in this report can be seen in KHRG Photo Set 99-B [http://metalab.unc.edu/freeburma/humanrights/khrg/archive/photoreports/99photos/set99b/index.html] (August 18, 1999). Some of them are reproduced below. Order documents sent to villages by SPDC and DKBA units in the area can be seen in "SPDC Orders to Villages: Set 99-B" [http://metalab.unc.edu/freeburma/humanrights/khrg/archive/khrg99/khrg9903.html]   (KHRG #99-03, 19/4/99). Excerpts from the latter report are used in the body of this report where noted. These reports and photos are available on the KHRG website [http://www.khrg.org]. The full text of the interviews and some of the field reports which were used in compiling the report are availabe   at   http://metalab.unc.edu/freeburma/humanrights/khrg/archive khrg99/khrg9907.html.

This report consists of several parts: this preface, an introduction with background, a detailed description of the situation including quotes from interviews, field reports and order documents.

Map of Thaton District

Thaton District

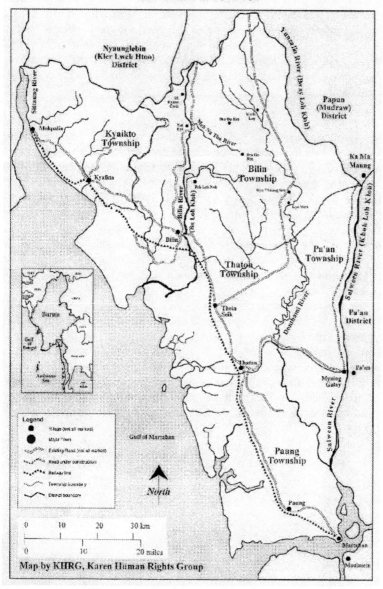

Map by KHRG, Karen Human Rights Group

Notes on the Text

In the text all names of those interviewed have been changed and some details have been omitted where necessary to protect people from retaliation. The captions under quotes used in the situation report include the interviewee's (changed) name, gender, age and village, and a reference to the interview or field report number. This can be used to find the full text of the interview or field reports at the KHRG web site at http://metalab.unc.edu/freeburma/humanrights/khrg/archive/khrg99/khrg 9907.html

The text often refers to villages, village tracts and townships. The SPDC has local administration, called Peace & Development Councils, at the village, village tract, township, and state/division levels. A village tract is a group of 5-25 villages centred on a large village. A township is a much larger area, administered from a central town. The Karen National Union (KNU) divides Thaton (Doo Tha Htoo) District into five townships: Kyaikto, Bilin, Thaton, Pa'an and Paung. The official townships used by the SPDC do not correspond to the Karen townships; in this report we have used the townships as defined by the Karen, though usually referring to them by their more familiar Burmese names. The SPDC does not recognise the existence of Thaton District, but only uses Townships, States and Divisions.

All numeric dates in this report are in dd/mm/yy format. In the interviews villagers often refer to 'loh ah pay'; literally this is the traditional Burmese form of voluntary labour for the community, but the SPDC uses this name in most cases of forced labour, and to the villagers it has come to mean most forms of forced labour with the exception of long-term portering. SPDC officers often accuse villagers of being 'nga pway' ('ringworm'); this is derogatory SPDC slang for the KNU and KNLA.

Introduction

Thaton District (known as Doo Tha Htoo in Karen) straddles the border of Karen State and northern Mon State, bounded in the east by the Salween and Yunzalin rivers, in the north by Nyaunglebin (Kler Lweh Htoo) District, in the west by the Gulf of Martaban, and in the south by the estuary of the Salween River at the town of Martaban. It consists of five townships: from north to south, Kyaikto, Bilin, Thaton, Pa'an, and Paung (note that Pa'an town is not in Pa'an township; the town lies on the east of the Salween River in Pa'an District, while Pa'an township is on the west bank of the Salween). Being close to the coastal road and railway lines, the western part of this district near the towns of Kyaikto, Bilin and Thaton is under quite heavy SPDC control. There is also a significant presence of Democratic Karen Buddhist Army (DKBA) forces allied to the SPDC, particularly in eastern parts of the district. However, in the eastern and northeastern parts of the district, particularly the area of the upper Bilin and Donthami Rivers and the Salween River below Ka Ma Maung, there is extensive Karen National Liberation Army (KNLA) activity.

The east and northeast of Thaton District have always been major areas of activity for the KNLA, and up until the early 1990's they exerted de facto control over some parts of the region. Skirmishes were common between KNLA and SLORC (now known as SPDC) units, and the SLORC attempted to undermine the KNLA by harrassing and forcibly relocating the villagers. Undefended villages regularly suffered retaliatory attacks by SLORC forces; houses were burned, villagers shot on sight and villages forced to move. The largest single forced relocation occurred in 1992-1993, when over 50 villages were issued summary orders to relocate immediately to SLORC-controlled relocation sites, after which their villages were burned and people found there were killed or captured [see "Forced Relocation in Thaton District" [http://metalab. unc.edu/freeburma/humanrights/khrg/archive/khrg93/93_01_09.html] (KHRG, 9/1/93), "The SLORC's New Forced Relocation Campaign: Translations of Some SLORC Orders Received So Far" [http://metalab.unc.edu/freeburma/humanrights/khrg/archive/khrg93/93_01_08.html] (KHRG, 8/1/93), and "Report from Thaton District" [http://metalab.unc.edu/freeburma/humanrights/khrg/archive/khrg93/93_03_10.html] (KHRG, 10/3/93)]. Many people from these villages fled to KNU-controlled areas or to become refugees in Thailand.

Since that time many people have trickled back in to reform those villages, though others had to continue fleeing as SLORC gained more control over KNU territory; in the end many of them have become long-term refugees in Thailand. In 1991-92 and again in 1994-95, it was through Thaton District that the SLORC launched its major offensives attempting to capture the KNU headquarters at Manerplaw, which lies further east in Pa'an District adjacent to the Thai border. The Democratic Karen Buddhist Army (DKBA) was formed in December 1994 during the 1994-95 SLORC offensive. It immediately joined with SLORC and helped the regime to capture Manerplaw, after which Pa'an District and eastern Thaton District became the DKBA's primary areas of operation. The DKBA's headquarters at Myaing Gyi Ngu (a.k.a. Khaw Taw) lies on the eastern bank of the Salween River just above Ka Ma Maung, not far upriver from Pa'an township of Thaton District.

Since 1995 the KNLA has lost the de facto control it had over small parts of eastern Thaton District and has reorganised into small guerrilla units which are still very active in the area. The SLORC, and now the SPDC, have continued the campaign of harassment and retaliations against villagers in an attempt to undermine KNLA activities in the area. SPDC and DKBA units are now based in and around many more villages, and where villages prove hard to control they are forcibly relocated. In 1997 several Karen villages near the Bilin and Donthami rivers were forced to relocate to larger villages, though there has not yet been any repetition of the large-scale forced relocations which occurred in 1992-93. Many of those forcibly relocated in 1997 found it impossible to survive after being moved and have taken the risk of gradually trickling back without permission to reform their villages since then.

When Lo Plah, Dta Leh Gaw Der and Lay Po Kaw Tee villages along the Bilin River were all completely destroyed by SLORC, some of the villagers from all 3 villages fled to this patch of forest and built small shelters. On June 6-7, a SLORC patrol found the site and immediately burned it. Because of the rains not all of the shelters would burn, so they ripped down whatever was left. Fortunately, the villagers knew they were coming and escaped. They have now scattered further into the hills to build even simpler shelters at more remote places.

Throughout the district, SPDC troops intimidate the villagers by regularly detaining, torturing and occasionally executing village elders and ordinary villagers for any failure to comply with SPDC demands or for any suspected contact with the KNLA. They also use the constant threat of burning or relocating villages to keep the villagers in line, and they sometimes carry out that threat. At the same time they subject the villagers to constant demands for frontline porters, forced labour at Army camps, crop quotas, cash, food, livestock and building materials. In the eastern parts of the district, the SPDC is now using DKBA forces to do much of their fighting and suppression of the villagers for them, and villagers report that the tactics of the DKBA have become indistinguishable from those of the SPDC. Many people in the area now resort to living in hiding in the forest whenever SPDC or DKBA troops are around, only returning to their villages occasionally. Some have become permanently displaced in the forest, but only a few have managed to make the long and precarious flight to reach the Thai border as refugees.

In the meantime, the KNLA continues small-scale guerrilla operations against SPDC and DKBA forces, and it appears they will continue to do so for the foreseeable future.

Forces in the Area

The SPDC and its Army

"If the KNLA shoot at them, they torture the villagers. It seems very strange to me. When the KNLA shoot at them, they come to torture the villagers by beating them, forcing them to drink water [pouring gallons of water down their throats], and taking things from them. So we villagers told the KNLA soldiers that if the Burmese are near our village please don't shoot at them. After that, when the KNLA shot at them near H--- village, they told the villagers that if the KNLA shot at them like that again they would throw 3 villagers into the river. When we heard about this we were very frightened." – "Naw Muh" (F, 46), xxxx village, Bilin Township, (Interview #10, 1/99) [see below for the interviews]

As in other areas, the SPDC rules the area through Army battalions under the Regional Command, which work losely intertwined with the regional and local 'Peace & Development Councils'; it is the Army battalions, however, which are really in command. Several battalions operate in the district, including Light Infantry Battalions #4, 8, 9, 308, 355, and 356, and Infantry Battalions #36, 96, 98, 108, and 231; several of these battalions are reportedly under the command of Light Infantry Division #44 in Kawkareik. Several new camps and posts have been added in villages throughout the district within the last 3-4 years; some of these are very small, only having 20 or 30 troops, while others are bases for Company-sized (100 or more) troops which patrol the local area. Troops at SPDC camps throughout the district are rotated in and out of the area regularly every 4-6 months, so villagers often have difficulty keeping track of which unit is in their area. The situation for the villagers can change radically with the rotation of the local soldiers, because some officers are ruthless and demanding while others are more lenient.

"[T]hey ask questions and they touch us with their guns. They force us to search for the KNU. They've come to a KNU place and there are KNU around, but they torture us instead. We always have to flee. When they came to our village they shot dead one of my cows and stole another. They always come and steal the villagers' animals. They come and demand rice from the villagers, and the villagers have to give it to them." – "Saw Po Si" (M, 50+), xxxx village, Bilin Township (Interview #13, 2/99)

The battalions are supported by the local and regional 'Peace & Development Councils' (PDC's), which exist at the State, District, Township, Village Tract and Village levels. Down to the Township and sometimes the Village Tract levels, these are made up of SPDC officials who follow orders from above and work closely with the local military. The local battalions and PDC's usually issue demands for forced labour, cash, food and materials by sending written orders to the Village PDC Chairperson, who is then responsible for gathering people for forced labour or collecting money, food or materials from the villagers to meet the specified demand. Alternatively, SPDC troops simply arrive in the village, go to the Village PDC Chairperson and issue their orders to him or her. Usually the Chairperson divides the demands evenly between the households of the village, demanding a certain amount of money per house or having the households of the village rotate turns in sending forced labourers.

At the village level, the Village PDC is a group of villagers either appointed by the local battalions or chosen by the villagers and approved by the battalions. In many parts of Burma people vie to become Village PDC members because they can get relatively rich off the villagers; when SPDC Battalions and authorities make demands, they add a percentage when they pass these demands on to the villagers and then skim this percentage off the top for themselves. However, in Thaton District, particularly in the east and northeast of the district, no one wants to be Village PDC Chairperson. The villagers are poor and often cannot meet the heavy demands for forced labour, food, materials and cash, and when the demands cannot be met the Village PDC Chairperson is the first to be arrested and tortured. The Chairperson often has to try to pay off the Battalions out of his or her own savings or belongings in order to avoid arrest. This is especially true now that the number of battalions making demands in the area has increased at the same time that up to half of the population of many villages has fled the area. Moreover, whenever there is KNLA activity in the area the Chairperson is the first to be blamed. In order to fill the position of Village PDC Chairperson many villages have adopted a rotation system, appointing a new Chairperson every month or every few months. Many villages consistently choose women for this role, particularly elderly women, because women are less likely to be accused of being KNU members and tortured.

"If you are village headman for the Burmese [i.e. the SPDC-appointed Village PDC Chairman], you have to follow and obey them. When you don't, they accuse you of helping Karen soldiers, and then if one or two [KNLA] people go and shoot at them they make problems for the village.

They say that we didn't inform them that KNLA people were staying in our village. They come and stay in our village many days and shoot and eat our chickens and pigs, then when they leave the village they shoot and kill all the livestock they see along their way." - "Saw Po Thu" (M, 36), xxxx village, Thaton township (Interview #6, 5/99)

"Each month a new village head is elected. We have to do it that way, we don't have someone who always remains as village head. The village head has to change monthly because people don't want to be village head, and the Burmese don't want that [a permanent village head] either. Nobody dares to be a village head for 2 or 3 months."- "Naw Hser" (F, 51), xxxx village, Pa'an township (Interview #2, 7/99)

In the areas of the district where the KNLA operates, the SPDC battalions force the villagers to report regularly on KNLA movements. The villagers usually lie or tell only part of the truth, but they must be careful because the battalions also use other more reliable informers, most of whom are Burmans, Mon and Karens from the plains to the west who come to the area to do logging. However, even when they hear of KNLA movements the SPDC commanders often use the information to avoid the KNLA rather than to fight them, because most commanders would rather focus their energies on making money while in the field and they do not want to take personal risks by fighting the KNLA. There are regular skirmishes when SPDC patrols on their way to and from the villages stumble on or are ambushed by KNLA units, but for the most part the SPDC battalions prefer to undermine the KNLA by threatening, harassing and attacking undefended civilian villages rather than seeking out and engaging the enemy.

"The 'patrol' women have to report to the camp commander about whether or not any Kaw Thoo Lei have come to the village each day. ... Sometimes they tell him that the KNLA have come and headed someplace and that there are 200 or 300 of them, when really there were only 0 to 80 of them. Sometimes people tell them but they don't give chase, they just say to the women 'Let them go, let them go'. Most of the time he says, 'It's enough to inform us about it, as long as we know it's no problem'." - "Saw Eh Htoo" (M, 37), xxxx village, Bilin township (Interview #1, 7/99)

"[T]he Burmese soldiers were shooting at each other [by mistake]. Then the next morning they punished the xxxx villagers for it. They demanded 100 viss [160 kg / 352 lb] of pork. The villagers couldn't give them that much, so we collected 300 Kyat from each household and gave it to the

Burmese instead of the pork. The whole village of xxxx had to give money to them. ... He [the Company Commander] called him [the village headman], slapped his face and kicked him. Then he forced him to lie down and stood on his back with big jungle boots. [Second woman]: They said if we didn't give it, they would kill the village headman the next morning. Then the villagers had to collect the money and give it to them, and they released the headman." – "Naw Wah Paw" (F, 30), xxxx village, Bilin Township (Interview #15, 1/99)

"They just want the villagers to suffer. They think that if they treat us like that then we won't be able to do anything against them." – "Saw Ghay" (M, 36), xxxx village, Bilin Township (Interview #12, 1/99)

The DKBA

"The Burmese [troops around her village] are now staying quietly. They don't disturb us, because they have put their work in the hands of the DKBA. The Burmese are staying in their own place, and the DKBA have been given authority by the Burmese so they can do whatever they want to do. The villagers can't dare say anything. In the past the Burmese also had a camp in the village, but none of the villagers were fleeing. But since the DKBA started the villagers have had to flee to escape. They force us to do a lot. We had to give them leaves and shaved bamboo ties, because they had families but they had no leaves or things to build houses. We had to go and build their houses for them in the village." - "Naw Mu Mu Wah" (F, 29), xxxx village, Pa'an township (Interview #7, 7/99)

Thaton District is one of the main areas of operation of the DKBA, particularly the eastern part of the district near the Salween River. The main DKBA commander near the Salween is Captain Bo Than Htun of the DKBA's #333 Brigade. Their numbers are small, but they appear to be spread in groups of 10 to 20 throughout the region. They have some small camps, but in some villages they have confiscated land in and around the village and forced the villagers to build houses for them and their families. One woman from a village on the west bank of the Salween River told KHRG that the DKBA had taken farmfields, including part of her family's own, from several villagers and divided them up among DKBA families, and that there are now 20 DKBA families living scattered among the 100 families of her village.

"There is not a camp, they stay in their houses with their wives and children. They're staying in the eastern part of the village, in the western

*part, and also in the centre. They don't all stay together; each house is in
a different part. There are about 20 families of them. ... [T]hey give the
villagers' land to their wives and children so they can stay there. They
don't ask the villagers. They've occupied people's land by force, then
they give it to their soldiers and their families. They are giving out much
of our land [to their soldiers]. Soon they will give away the land around
our house. When they built the motor road, it crossed my father's field.
It's a long narrow field along the river. Now my father can't plant there
anymore because they [the DKBA] have shared out that land for their
houses. There is an Indian in the village whose field they have divided up
and shared out to DKBA families. He didn't even get a piece of his field.
He wanted his family to stay there, but the DKBA wouldn't allow him to
stay."* - "Naw Mu Mu Wah" (F, 29), xxxx village, Pa'an township,
describing land confiscation by the DKBA (Interview #7, 7/99)

Most of the DKBA soldiers are not former KNLA members, because
most of the KNLA soldiers who originally formed the DKBA have
already deserted back to civilian life or defected back to the KNLA. Most
of the DKBA soldiers are former villagers, some of whom were
previously loosely connected to Karen National Defence Organisation
(KNDO, a wing of the KNU) village militias, who have joined during the
4½ years since the DKBA was founded. The DKBA forces do not
usually get along well with the SPDC Battalions, but in this area they
often work together and the DKBA soldiers still receive all of their
rations, ammunition and supplies from the SPDC Army. Villagers in
Pa'an township have described to KHRG how they have been used as
porters when DKBA units along the Salween River go to Ohn Daw, an
SPDC Army camp above Ka Ma Maung, each month to receive their
monthly rations such as rice, salt and cooking oil.

*"[T]here is one DKBA who married one of our neighbours. He trades
cattle and buffaloes and his animals came and ate our vegetables, so my
brother told him about it. He became very angry and he said my brother
is stupid, that 'he is exaggerating and is being disrespectful to me'. Then
he called my brother over and tried to slam his head on a rock. My
mother stopped him and told him, 'Nephew, don't do that, we are Karen
people, we should not be unfriendly, we should love each other'. And he
said, 'Hey, we need to love each other? We should stay unfriendly. I
don't know what love is.' Then he grabbed the ladder from my mother's
house and threw it away."* - "Naw Mu Mu Wah" (F, 29), xxxx village,
Pa'an twp. (Interview #7, 7/99)

The behaviour of DKBA units toward the villagers varies by region, but according to all of the villagers interviewed by KHRG the DKBA is quite bad in Thaton district. In most areas they operate partly as adjuncts to SPDC units, with two or three of them accompanying SPDC patrols as guides, and partly on their own. Even on their own, their activities tend to mirror those of the SPDC units. They order villagers to go with them as porters and to do forced labour at their camps, they regularly demand money, food and materials, and they arrest, torture and sometimes execute villagers whom they suspect of having any contact with the KNLA. Though they themselves demand taxes and food and some of them even used to be connected to the KNLA, the DKBA soldiers in the region have shown little mercy to villagers who have paid the taxes and food which are demanded by the KNU/KNLA. They are also active in fighting the KNLA, in some areas more so than the SPDC Battalions.

"They came to the village and summoned me. They were DKBA soldiers. Their commander was Bo Than Htun, and he had over 10 soldiers and a 2nd Lieutenant. They summoned me at 9 p.m. and accused me of helping the KNU and collecting taxes for them. I told them I don't collect taxes or do anything for them. Then they covered and tied my head until I couldn't breathe, and they started interrogating me. I shouted, I told them 'If you do this to me I will die! If you have questions then ask me, I will explain clearly to you!'" - "Pu Hla Maung" (M, 50), xxxx village, Thaton township (Interview #5, 4/99)

"On the 25th of April 1999. They came to arrest me at night, at 10 p.m. ... P--- and M--- [DKBA commanders] came with about 20 DKBA soldiers. They are #333 [Brigade]. ... They covered and tied my head. Then they interrogated me and accused me of contacting the Kaw Thoo Lei, feeding them and collecting taxes for them. I said I didn't know anything, but they said I must know because people had already told them about it. So I told them that Shar Gu [a KNLA commander] had come, and that after the people gave them some rice they left the village. I told them the truth. They nearly killed me. They tied my sarong around my head until I couldn't breathe or speak, and they didn't beat me but they stood on my chest on one foot. Then they poked me with a gun." - "Saw Hsay Hsay" (M, 26), xxxx village, Thaton township (Interview #8, 5/99)

"Sometimes they scold us. Sometimes they say, 'You are staying in this village. If you don't like us to force you, then leave the village.' The villagers are angry with them because the DKBA have power and do not respect the villagers. I know many of them [DKBA]: Maung Shwe Aye,

Klu Gyi, and another who's now dead, Maung Ghaw. Their commander is Bo Than Htun. They patrol in groups of just 10 or 20 people. ... They demand things but more than that, they also steal. Even if you know about it you can't dare say anything. When they come to our houses to steal we can hear the steps of their boots, but if we come down out of the house they run away. ... If we grow fruit or vegetables we don't get to eat them, they come and pick them before we can and take them as their own. If you complain to them they say, 'Who are you to dare speak to us?' These words are painful to our ears and make our hearts beat faster."- "Naw Mu Mu Wah" (F, 29), xxxx village, Pa'an township, describing DKBA activities around her village (Interview #7, 7/99)

According to villagers along the western side of the Salween River south of Ka Ma Maung, this year the SPDC Battalions have spent most of their time around their camp at Ka Ma Maung and have largely left control of this part of Pa'an township to the local DKBA. Villagers in the area say they seldom see the SPDC troops these days and that it is the DKBA who are always patrolling the area, arresting, torturing and killing villagers suspected of contact with the KNU, and demanding their forced labour, money and other contributions. They say that the only thing the SPDC appears to be doing in the area is building a road up the west side of the Salween from Myaing Galay (see below under 'Forced Labour').

"They said, 'No one can say this is their land, this is DKBA land.' Another of them is Maw Nga. He is very bad. When we were milling our sugar cane he did not come to ask us for some. If he said 'Uncle, Aunt, Sister' and asked for some we would be happy to give it, because we are all humans, all the same. But they are not the same as us. He came and broke our sugar cane and then took it back to his commander and soldiers. Then they ate it together. They didn't ask the owner, instead they destroyed the fence around the sugar cane plantation, then they broke off the sugar cane and when they couldn't carry any more, they fired off their guns. These are Karen people!" - "Naw Mu Mu Wah" (F, 29), xxxx village, Pa'an township (Interview #7, 7/99)

There are no reports at the moment of the DKBA restricting freedom of religion in the area, nor is it their usual policy to do so. Most incidents of religious repression by the DKBA in the past have been the initiatives of local DKBA officers, not a systematic policy. Most of the Karen villagers in Thaton District are Buddhist, with Animist and Christian minorities. For the most part, they do not like the DKBA because they see the DKBA soldiers doing all the same things as the SPDC soldiers, even executing innocent villagers. Some villagers interviewed told

KHRG that seeing the DKBA act this way makes them especially angry and sad, because these are Karen abusing and killing Karen.

"I think about how in the time of the Burmese, they forced our father to do 'loh ah pay' and our brother to go as a porter, and sometimes they came back and they didn't even look human. They were dirty and ragged, and sometimes my father said, 'The Burmese are no good, they didn't even feed us rice'. I looked at our father and I was sad, and it hurt my heart. As for the DKBA, they demand everything with anger. If we do good things they still refuse to see any good in us. They are always looking for fault, they are always aggressive. If anyone talks back to them they say we are their enemies. They demand things, and if we don't do it then they accuse us of being their enemies." - "Naw Mu Mu Wah" (F, 29), xxxx village, Pa'an township (Interview #7, 7/99)

The 'Short Pants'

"The DKBA also come, and the Short Pants group comes as well. The Short Pants group is very strong. They come to our village from the direction of K--- and M---. My cousin was returning from town when she met them. They told her, 'You are a very beautiful woman'. She said 'I am beautiful because I am Karen'. Then they tried to grab her, and my cousin ran away. They followed her to her house, and then they said to her, 'You should join the Kaw Thoo Lei' [said sarcastically as a threat to accuse her]. Then they called her parents down, slapped her mother's face once and punched her father's face once." - "Saw Eh Htoo" (M, 37), xxxx village, Bilin township (Interview #1, 7/99)

One of the villagers interviewed for this report in Bilin township mentioned the arrival of the 'Short Pants' group in the area of his village. This is the first report that KHRG has obtained of this group operating in Thaton District, and it has not yet been confirmed. However, if the villager was correct this is a very serious development. The 'Short Pants' ['Baw Bi Doh'] is a name given by villagers to a special SPDC unit which began operating to the north in Nyaunglebin District in September 1998. Known more formally as the Sa Thon Lon Dam Byan Byaut Kya (Bureau of Special Investigations Guerrilla Retaliation) units, these are the SPDC's new execution squads. Reportedly under the direction of SPDC Secretary-1 Lt. Gen. Khin Nyunt and reporting to him through Military Intelligence #3 in Toungoo, they number about 200 men, handpicked from operational battalions in Nyaunglebin District and given special training. Operating in squads of 5 to 10 soldiers, they move between the villages of Nyaunglebin District executing everyone on their 'list', which includes anyone who is suspected of ever having had any contact whatsoever with the KNU/KNLA. They operate covertly but speak openly to villagers of their purpose, and their methods are deliberately brutal in order to intimidate the villagers; they usually cut the throats of their victims, then often behead them. They have executed anywhere from 30 to over 100 villagers in Nyaunglebin District since their inception. The clear intention is to deliver the message to villagers that if they have even the slightest contact with the KNU or KNLA they will die for it, if not now then 10 or 20 years from now. For more information on this group see part 1: "Death Squads and Displacement: Systematic Executions, Destruction of Villages and the Flight of Villagers in Nyaunglebin District". (KHRG #99-04, 24/4/99).

The SPDC Guerrilla Retaliation squads have already expanded their area of operations from Nyaunglebin District up into southern Toungoo District, and for several months there have been rumours and unconfirmed reports that one or more small groups of them had been brought into Pa'an District. According to these unconfirmed reports, they had arrived in Pa'an District but had not yet begun operations. This is the first report of them appearing in Thaton District, and the villager interviewed made no mention of any executions. However, his description of how they tried to grab his cousin and then chased her home and beat her parents is completely consistent with dozens of accounts of their behaviour in Nyaunglebin District, where they have regularly committed rape, sexual harassment and abuse of women, and in some cases have forced women to marry them by threatening their families and villages.

The KNLA

"We don't have any trouble from them [KNLA], but once a year they come and ask for taxes for the year.It is Karen country, so the villagers give the tax. But if the DKBA knew about that, they would make trouble for the villagers." - "Naw Mu Mu Wah" (F, 29), xxxx village, Pa'an township (Interview #7, 7/99)

The KNLA is still very active in Thaton District, particularly in the eastern and northeastern parts of the district: the Salween River below Ka Ma Maung as well as the Yunzalin, Donthami and Bilin River watersheds. They operate in small guerrilla columns, laying low much of the time but springing ambushes on SPDC and DKBA troops on the move as well as military vehicles on the roads and boats carrying soldiers or military supplies on the rivers. Many of the skirmishes are not planned, and occur when KNLA and SPDC or DKBA units stumble on each other along pathways or in villages.

Whenever fighting of any kind occurs, SPDC and/or DKBA forces inflict punishment on the nearby villages. This usually includes heading for a village and grabbing the first villagers they see, interrogating them under torture and sometimes executing them. If the village elders are suspected of not having reported KNLA movements in the area they are also detained and tortured. On some occasions the nearby villages are partly burned or ordered to relocate. In response to all of these punishments, the elders of many villages have requested the KNLA not to attack the SPDC or DKBA near their villages. In some cases the KNLA respects these requests, but in other cases it does not.

The KNLA also demands tax money and food from all villages. The tax is usually collected on a yearly basis, and food much more often than that. There are very few reports of the KNLA physically abusing villagers to make them pay, because the KNLA prefers to keep the villagers on its side. Many of the KNLA soldiers and officers are from the local villages themselves, and the vast majority of villagers are sympathetic to the KNU/KNLA. However, the taxes and demands put the villagers in a difficult position, both because they are barely surviving themselves and have little or nothing to give, and because they face heavy punishments such as torture or execution whenever the SPDC and DKBA forces find out they have given food or money to the KNLA. Sometimes one or two KNLA soldiers are in a village to get food or visit relatives when SPDC or DKBA units arrive, and if they are sighted the entire village is punished. In September 1998, an SPDC Column saw one KNLA soldier run out of Kyu Kee village, and the commander immediately ordered his soldiers to loot and burn all the houses of the village.

"The Karen soldiers had asked her to collect food in our village. They asked for 'ah gyay' ['help fees']. She told the headman, and he said he didn't dare do it at that time, that she'd have to wait for a while. Then she went and showed the [KNLA] letter to the DKBA, and the DKBA told her, 'You are looking to become our enemy. You can go and stay on the outside if you like, but we don't want to hear of any collection and taxes like this in the village.' ... She said to them, 'Before you were living outside [when they were with the KNLA] and we had to feed you like this. Now you are staying here so you need to be understanding about this, because when you yourselves were outside you received our food and ate it too.' But after she said that to them, they tied her up. They took her to

the other side of the Khoh Loh Kloh [Salween River], and they shot her dead. She died for nothing. That was three years ago. Her name was Naw Khu. She was from Noh Aw La village. She was a village head." - "Naw Mu Mu Wah" (F, 29), xxxx village, Pa'an township (Interview #7, 7/99)

Suffering of the Villagers

Village Destruction and Relocation

"They forced the other villages to our village. Lay Kaw Tee village and Tee Pa Doh Kee village. They brought their belongings and their houses. The Burmese drove them from their villages, that's why they came to our village. They gave them 5 days to move. I don't know why. They didn't stay long. Now they have gone back to their villages." – "Naw Hser" (F, 51), xxxx village, Pa'an Township (Interview #2, 7/99)

In most areas where the SPDC is having difficulty bringing villagers under control, they use the forced relocation and destruction of villages as their main weapon. However, in Thaton District the Army has seldom resorted to these since it last relocated groups of villages along the Bilin and Donthami Rivers in 1997. It appears that the military in the area feels that it has enough control to be able to clamp down on villagers without having to destroy their villages. Most of the villages which have been forced to relocate over the past several years have now re-established themselves, at least in part. However, the threat of village destruction and relocation is always held over the head of the villagers, and if KNLA activity in the area continues at its present level it is likely that further forced relocations will occur in the future. It is also likely that the burning of houses will continue to be used as a punishment for KNLA activity near any village. SPDC and DKBA units are always making this threat.

"On September 11th 1998, SPDC soldiers from Column 1 of Frontline #98 Infantry Battalion based at Meh Prih Kee camp entered Kyu Kee village in Bilin Township. They saw one KNLA soldier running away from the foot of the church, so they summoned the lay pastor and village teacher and asked her who it was who had fled from the base of the church. She told them it was a KNLA soldier. Then they accused her of working with the KNU. SPDC Commander Aung Kyaw Htun then gave the order to his soldiers to call everyone in the village down out of their houses. The soldiers then looted everything from the houses, including clothing, blankets and utensils, and then burned down the church and all the houses in the village. They also shot dead all the pigs, chickens and other livestock which they saw in the village, and then returned to their camp. The villagers were left with nothing but the clothes on their bodies, not even any cookpots, and no way of knowing how they would survive in

the future. Some of them have gone to stay in other villages, and others have fled to live in the jungle." – Field report from KHRG Field Reporter (Field Report #FR7)

Detention and Torture

"They tied me up and hurt me. They beat me with a stick and punched me. My teeth still hurt nowbecause of their punches. The Commander in charge of the troops, the Battalion Commander, was drinking alcohol while he was beating me. ... I can't count all the times that they punched me. They beat me with a stick. They tied me up and beat me on my head and my legs. They said I am Nga Pway ['ringworm', derogatory SPDC slang for KNU/KNLA]. I said I am not Nga Pway. They tied my legs, hands and neck. At night they tied my hands behind my back, beat and punched me, and then held me down in the river until I lost consciousness. When I regained consciousness, all the water came out of my nose. They asked me, 'Do you have a gun?' I said I didn't have a gun, I am a villager and I have nothing, and I always went as a porter when asked." – "Saw K'Ler" (M, 38), xxxx village, Bilin Township, describing his detention for 10 days by SPDC troops (Interview #14, 1/99)

Currently the main method being used by SPDC and DKBA units in the district to intimidate villagers and prevent them from helping the KNLA is the arbitrary detention and torture of people in the villages. Usually this occurs when SPDC or DKBA troops have encountered the KNLA or when they have heard that the KNLA has passed through a village or received aid from villagers. It can also occur when a village fails to comply with an order such as a demand for forced labourers, cash, food or materials. Usually the first people to be detained are the Village PDC Chairperson and other village elders. Sometimes SPDC or DKBA troops on the move grab and detain a farmer for no apparent reason, simply because he is out in the fields or forest away from the village and they think he looks like he could be a KNLA soldier, or because they want some information.

"They entered the village at 9 p.m. There were about 70 soldiers, and they arrested me while I was pounding paddy. They asked me, 'Have any Karen soldiers come to the village?' I said, 'Sometimes they enter the village.' Then he asked me, 'When Karen soldiers come do they eat and drink, and whose field do they stay in?' I couldn't answer him so he beat me. The one who beat me was a commander with 3 stars [Captain]. He beat me with a wooden stick as thick as my wrist, and over an armspan long. He hit me 3 times on the head, and the skin on my scalp was broken

so he stopped hitting me there. Then he started beating my shins about 20 or 30 times. After that they tied me up with my hands behind my back and sutured my head. They sutured my head 3 times. After that I couldn't walk for 10 days." - "Saw Thay Htoo" (M, 35), xxxx village, Thaton township, describing his beating by SPDC troops in March 1999 (Interview #4, 4/99)

In the event of battles, as soon as the shooting is over the first act of the SPDC or DKBA column is usually to head for the nearest village to inflict retaliatory punishment on the villagers. On their way, they often grab the first farmers they see and accuse them of being Karen soldiers. On arrival at the village, they sometimes begin firing off their guns or looting houses before seeking to detain the village leaders and others.

"They took things by force from the villagers and shot and killed our poultry. They shot and killed M---'s pig but they didn't give him any money for it. ... [T]hey called for me and came to arrest me at 3 a.m. There were 30 soldiers with one commander. They arrested 5 of us. They didn't do anything to me, but they did to my friend Maung T---. They tied him up, beat and punched him, then they hung him upside down and beat him with a bamboo stick." – "Saw Htoo Kyaw" (M, 33), xxxx village, Bilin Township (Interview #16, 1/99)

If a village fails to comply with an order the order is usually repeated or sent again several times, each time in more threatening language. After a few times, the officers either summon the village chairperson to the camp or take an armed column to the village. The village is usually looted and the Chairperson and others are detained.

Those who are detained are immediately accused of being Karen soldiers, and the captors often also demand that he or she hand over guns, bullets, radios or other military hardware, even when it is obvious that the person is not a soldier and has no such equipment. Sometimes the beating begins before any questions are even asked and before the villager even knows why they are being detained. As the torture continues the methods tend to become more brutal; villagers interviewed for this report described being hung upside down, punched, slapped, kicked, hit on the head and body with rifle barrels and rifle butts, and beaten on various parts of the body with bamboo rods or wooden sticks. One area of the body which is frequently beaten is the shins, which is extremely painful; after a heavy beating on the shins, villagers have said that they could not walk for several days. Some villagers were forced to lay down on their backs or their stomachs while soldiers stood on them in Army boots, had their heads held underwater, or had their heads wrapped so tightly in their sarongs that they couldn't breathe. Another method reported by the villagers involves being forced to lay on their backs and having their nose held shut while litres of water are poured into their mouths; in gasping for air, the person cannot stop gulping the water. If this torture is continued the belly becomes distended and the stomach can burst, killing the victim, though none of the victims interviewed were forced to gulp that much. Detainees are frequently touched, poked or slapped with bayonet blades. One villager interviewed described how SPDC troops poked him with a bayonet, slapped his face with the flat of a bayonet blade, and then put a bayonet in his mouth and shook it around [see Interview #11]. After being beaten or tortured, detainees are often tied to a post with their hands behind their backs in a sitting or standing position and left like that overnight or for periods of up to 12 hours.

"After they arrested me they took me to the village and interrogated me. They told me, 'Your brain is hard [you are stubborn, you won't speak] so I must give you some water to drink'. Then they grabbed me and forced me to lay down, and made me drink water. I couldn't drink it. They asked me, 'Do you have a gun?' Then they held my nose closed and poured water into my mouth. I couldn't suffer it so I told them I would talk. I said I have no gun, I am a villager and have no gun. Then he closed my nose and did it again. He did it 6 or 7 times, until I was about to die. Then he said my answers were strange. He tied me to the post of the monastery, and he told me I'd better think about it and that I'd have to drink more water. One of the commanders came to interrogate me and slapped my face. They punched me one time, and when they brought me back to the monastery they slapped me. After interrogating us, they took me to the hall, and they tied my hands to a post behind my back. I couldn't lay down and sleep, I had to stay like that all night until morning. In the morning, villagers brought rice for us. Some of the others could eat, but not me because of the way I was tied. M--- [another villager] fed rice to me with a spoon. I had to eat like that." – "Saw Ghay" (M, 36), xxxx village, Bilin Township (Interview #12, 1/99)

"The first time they captured me in my hill field. They boxed me in the face. I only remember four punches, and then I fell unconscious. When I woke up I felt my face in pain. I also noticed that they must have kicked me many times with jungle boots on both sides of my body, because when I woke up my sides were aching and I couldn't breathe easily. Then a Burmese came up to me, I think he was a corporal because he had a pistol. He shouted at the soldiers who were torturing me to stop. By the time he came, they had already tied me up. I'd already been hit on my

head, my chest and my back, and my face and body were red with the blood flowing from my head. The one who came with the pistol told the soldiers who were torturing me, 'You should ask if he's a good person or a bad person first.'" - "Saw Eh Htoo" (M, 37), xxxx village, Bilin township (Interview #1, 7/99)

"They come to the village very often. They came when they arrested and beat me, just 4 days ago. ... When I came down out of the house, they beat and punched me. I don't know how many times they hit me, 7, 8, over 10 times, and they hit me 3 times with a gun. Then they took me to the monastery. When we arrived at the monastery, they poked me with a bayonet, they beat me in the face with a bayonet and they put the bayonet in my mouth and shook it around. Then they tied my hands behind my back and I had to sleep like a dog or a pig. ... They released me after 2 days. I had to give 3 baskets of rice and one pig." – "Saw Plaw" (M, 23), xxxx village, Bilin Township (Interview #11, 2/99)

In the cases described by villagers for this report, the period of detention was usually a few hours to a few days, and generally did not end in death; however, many villagers say that they have suffered the after-effects of the torture for months afterwards, and some of them may have permanent physical and psychological damage. In most cases, the soldiers knew they were holding an ordinary villager and not a KNLA soldier. Though some of those detained admitted under torture to having some limited contact with the KNLA, in reality the soldiers know that most villagers in areas such as this have little choice but to have some form of contact with the KNLA, even if it is only complying with the KNLA's demands for food and money. In most cases, the villagers and elders were released in the end when they were 'guaranteed' by a village head or monk and when a fine was paid in cash and/or goods. In many cases, the real reason that soldiers detain and torture villagers is only to obtain this payment for their release. However, the overall objective of this pattern of regular and arbitrary detention and torture is to strike fear into the villagers, to demonstrate to them that their lives exist at the whim of the soldiers, and to intimidate them to a point where they will be too afraid to support the opposition in any way.

"[T]hey beat one of the village women. ... They hit her 30 or 40 times on her head. I saw them beat her. They beat her savagely. They beat her with the same size of stick that they used to beat me. They hit her with the end of the stick." - "Saw Thay Htoo" (M, 35), xxxx village, Thaton township, who witnessed SPDC troops beat a woman because they said

they'd seen her dog near a group of KNLA soldiers and therefore she must be KNLA herself (Interview #4, 4/99)

"Then he accused me of contacting Kaw Thoo Lei. He hit my head with a gun barrel and my scalp was cut open. Look at the top of my head here and you will see the scar where he cut my head open. He hit it with a gun barrel. Then they hit me twice in the chest with a gun butt. He hit the back of my neck with the gun barrel and shouted, "Speak the truth!!" Then they pushed fire against my belly here, and it burned and the wound was there for a long time. ... Then he released us, but he came to capture us again the next evening. I had already fled, the same evening that he released us. ... After we ran, when we were staying at xxxx, I was informed that the Burmese had killed my elder brother and my younger brother. They captured the two of them and killed them. They killed my two brothers because of me."- "Saw Eh Htoo" (M, 37), xxxx village, Bilin township (Interview #1, 7/99)

Killings

"We'd been carrying for 3 days when they beat the first porter to death. They beat him to death at Dta Oo Nee village, on the streambank in front of peoples' houses. The village women saw but they made no sound. The next day at 2 p.m. a battle occurred, and that evening they beat the other man to death at the edge of Ler Ga Dter village, because he couldn't carry things anymore. The first man they killed was Doh Koh and the other was Mya Gyi. Doh Koh was about 40 years old and had a wife and 4 children. ... I think Mya Gyi was my age. He also had a wife and 2 children." - "Saw Eh Htoo" (M, 37), xxxx village, Bilin township (Interview #1, 7/99)

Despite the fact that most villagers who are detained and tortured are not killed, there are still cases in Thaton District where innocent villagers have been killed on suspicion of having contact with the KNLA, and such cases will almost certainly continue to occur. Some torture victims have died after detention from the lasting effects of the torture or from disease brought on by weakness and the other effects of torture. Many villagers have also died during forced labour or from the after-effects of forced labour, particularly portering. Several villagers interviewed for this report saw other porters beaten or shot to death by SPDC troops, or left behind in remote areas when they were too sick to carry any further. This is a regular occurrence, particularly on long portering trips of 10 days or more in duration. One woman described to KHRG how her husband complained of chest pains on returning from forced labour as a porter, and soon after he died. He was over 50 years old.

"All the Burmese who are patrolling force the villagers to go – sometimes they go far, sometimes only nearby. The women also have to go. The oldest whom they force to go are age 40 or more, and the youngest are 14 or 15 years old – as long as you can carry 1 bowl of rice. I heard from my husband that if porters who were carrying heavy things fell down, the Burmese beat them with a stick, or kicked them with boots. ... My husband was old, so he was tired after going as a porter and one time he became sick and died. After he came back [from portering] he told me his chest was in pain. He was in pain for many days until he couldn't tolerate his suffering any more, and then he was dead. He was over 50 years old He died this dry season. He died in January." - "Naw Hser" (F, 51), xxxx village, Pa'an township (Interview #2, 7/99)

Troops on patrol are always ready to fire, and villagers sighted in their fields are always at risk. When villagers see SPDC troops approaching their fields their first instinct is often to run because they fear being interrogated and beaten or taken as a porter. However, when the troops see someone running they often open fire. Even if the person escapes, if his or her friends or family are left behind they are then interrogated about why the person ran. If there has been a skirmish with KNLA troops, SPDC soldiers often take shots at the next people they see in the fields, or enter a village and begin shooting in the air, and this also poses a constant danger for villagers.

The worst case of random killing this year in Thaton District occurred on March 7th in xxxx village of Thaton township. That day most people attended the cremation of an elderly woman at her daughter's house. After dark, just after 9 p.m., the ceremonies were over but several women and children were still outside under the house while "Naw Paw Ler", the daughter of the woman who had died, was in the house putting her children to sleep. Suddenly about 30 troops from Light Infantry Battalion #xx entered the village and without warning started shooting at the people under the house. "Naw Paw Ler"'s younger sister, who was pregnant, fell with a bullet through her shoulder, and the troops then opened fire into the house itself. "Naw Paw Ler"'s small daughter, already asleep, was shot in the head and died, and she and her other child were hit and wounded. The shooting continued, and when it stopped 6 villagers were dead and 9 were wounded, some seriously. The six dead were Ma San Kaing (female, age 24), Naw P'Saw (female, age 17), Naw

Du Paw (female, age 15), Ma Aye Aye (female, age 18), "Naw Ler Paw"'s daughter Ma Aye (female, age 5), and "Naw Ler Paw"'s brother Pa Kaw Naw (male, age 25). The nine wounded included six women aged 17 to 55, two boys aged 12 and 18, and a man aged 27. All were ordinary villagers. After stopping their fire, the troops turned and left the village. They never said anything to the villagers or gave any explanation. The following day when the wounded made their way to a town hospital, they found some of the SPDC soldiers already there, so there may have been a skirmish with the KNLA nearby and the shooting in the village may have been a punishment. The villagers could not give any reason for the shooting. The wounded spent 2 weeks in the hospital, where they had to pay for everything, and during that time the SPDC commander who had ordered the shooting came several times to shout at them, telling them that people in their village are stubborn, that their village is a 'ringworm' (KNLA) village, and that if all the villagers should die, "Good for them".

"My mother had died and we had just cremated her. Then in the evening they entered the village and they didn't say anything, they just started to shoot their guns. They came and fired their guns near my house. They didn't ask for food or alcohol, they asked nothing. ... Many villagers were wounded. Eight villagers were wounded, and six villagers died. The Burmese shot and hit my younger sister first. She is 17 years old, and at the time she was under the house. Her name is A---, she was pregnant. Later when we were taking her and reached M---pagoda, she delivered her baby. The bullet hit her shoulder and came out through the other side. After she fell down, the Burmese fired into the house, TA! TA! TA! TA!! When they fired, one of my daughters was hit in her head and she died in our house. She was sleeping in the house, and the bullet went through her head. I stayed near her and kept her younger siblings near her. As for me, one shot hit my shoulder and another grazed my head. Most of those who got wounded under my house were children, because they were playing under the house and the Burmese fired there a lot. ... Some of those who were wounded were B---'s daughter Naw P---, Pa K--- [a man], and S--- [a woman]. Pa K--- was hit in the leg. He is 23 years old. In my family we are 3 siblings [she has one brother and one sister], and all three of us were hit. My brother was killed. M--- [a woman], M--- [a woman], Naw T--- [a woman], and K--- [a man] were also wounded. M--- is 13 years old, and Naw T--- is 42. M--- is 16 years old, and K--- is 25. A--- [her younger sister mentioned above] is 17. Also my younger sister T---, she was 23 at the time, now she is 24." - "Naw Ler Paw" (F, 28), xxxx village, Thaton township, describing the massacre when SPDC

troops from Light Infantry Battalion #xx entered her village and opened fire on March 7th 1999 (Interview #3, 5/99)

"When the Burmese saw us in the hospital, they said, 'The villagers from xxxx village are stubborn. It's a Nga Pway ['ringworm', i.e. KNU/KNLA] village. If they die, good for them.' I was not happy to hear him talk like that, so I protested. He is an officer, and he often came to shout at us [in the hospital]. The other villagers were afraid and stayed quiet. He said 'Nga Pway stay in your village'. I said, 'There were no Nga Pway. After you shot at us, you went back. We saw you when you came into the village. All of you were Burmese.'" - "Naw Ler Paw" (F, 28), xxxx village, Thaton township (Interview #3, 5/99)

Forced Labour

"[T]hey always force people to go. The villagers have to plant sugar cane, cut wood and clear the forest for them. The villagers have to work very hard for them and never get a single coin of money. We have to pack rice from our house and take our own rice to eat. On top of that, they shout at us while we work. They guard us with guns and sometimes shout at us. They force us to go early in the morning, and let us come back at 4 p.m. ... The youngest ones who go are 15 or 16 years old, and they also force people over 40 years old to go. ... People who are 60 years old have to go, and those who are over 60 also have to go to do 'loh ah pay'." - "Naw Ler Paw" (F, 28), xxxx village, Thaton township (Interview #3, 5/99)

Villagers in Thaton District face a heavy burden of forced labour. The nature of this forced labour varies throughout the district; villagers in the completely SPDC-controlled coastal areas in the west of the district face forced labour on roads, while those in the eastern parts of the district face more forced labour as porters and at SPDC Army camps. The Army usually obtains forced labourers by sending written orders to village heads or dictating demands to them at 'meetings'; the village heads are then responsible for rotating the burden of forced labour among the people of their village. If the specified number of villagers does not arrive on time or if any of them leave before they are given permission to go, the village head and the village itself can face heavy punishments.

"They ordered the village headman to gather the villagers, and the village headman called us to go. The last time we went, they forced us to work in their camp. They forced us to carry bamboo and wood. They didn't feed us. ... Sometimes they force 20 or 30 villagers to go at a time.

When I've gone there have also been many old people, some are 40 or 50 and some are nearly 60. We had to take our own rice, and while we were working they never allowed us to leave." – "Saw K'Ler" (M, 38), xxxx village, Bilin Township, (Interview #14, 1/99)

"U yyyy from xxxx village has returned without permission, so you yourself immediately send 15 viss [24 kg / 52 lb] of pork. Come yourself today with one person to take his place as a volunteer worker. If you cannot get pork, [you] must pay fine money of the value of the pork. You are informed that the village head and the village will be severely punished if they fail." - text of a written order sent to a village in Thaton District by the SPDC Army in December 1998 (Order #T6, "SPDC Orders to Villages: Set 99-B") [http://metalab.unc.edu/freeburma/ humanrights/khrg/archive/khrg99/khrg9903.html]

Portering is the most difficult and feared form of forced labour, and in the villages of eastern Thaton District it takes varying forms and is a constant burden. Both SPDC and DKBA units demand porters for their patrols on a rotating basis, and also take porters for ad hoc short-term portering duty carrying rations and supplies between Army camps; for example, the DKBA along the Salween force the villagers once per month to go with them to Ohn Daw, near Ka Ma Maung, to fetch and carry their rations back. These kinds of porters are demanded in written orders, or sometimes by sending troops to the village. When a demand is made the village head must decide who will fill the requirement, and those villagers must drop all work and other commitments immediately and go. Most village heads rotate the demands through all the households of the village, and when the turn for a household comes, that family must send a person regardless of how many people are in the family. Alternatively they can hire someone else to go in their place, but this costs 100 to 300 Kyat per day depending on the portering assignment, and many people do not have enough money after paying all of the other fees and taxes demanded of them. Even though villagers have to pay 'porter fees' regularly as well, this money is not actually used for porters and they must still go whenever porters are required. Troops on patrol also often grab villagers they encounter along their way and force them to follow them as porters.

"If they see us when we are tending our buffaloes, they order us to go with them. We complain to them that the buffaloes will eat the paddy, but they don't listen to us. They told me to follow them for just a few minutes, but when the Burmese say 'for a few minutes', it takes a long

time!" – "Saw Ghay" (M, 36), xxxx village, Bilin Township (Interview #12, 1/99)

For one or two days of portering villagers take along their own food, but sometimes the shift is much longer than was originally specified and they run out of food. In these cases they must beg food from villagers in the villages which the Column passes or from the soldiers themselves, though the soldiers are usually unwilling to give them more than a few tablespoons of rice per day. There are also longer term shifts of portering when troops are going on longer patrols, and this forced labour is particularly feared. Most villagers do whatever they can to try to pay instead of going, because it is on these trips that many porters are killed. Even so, some villagers are so short of money and food due to all the demands placed on them that they hire themselves out for 1,500 or 2,000 Kyat to take the place of people who have been ordered to go on these trips. On these portering trips, most villagers run out of food while some who are caught along the way by the soldiers have no food with them to begin with. The soldiers feed them next to nothing, allow them little or no rest and force them to carry loads of 30 to 50 kilograms. Porters who fall sick or are unable to carry are left behind, or in some cases killed by the soldiers. As porters die or escape, those remaining are forced to carry heavier and heavier loads. Even those who survive this type of portering sometimes die on their return home from illness brought on by exhaustion, malnutrition and wounds from beatings. They also face the risk of being wounded or killed during skirmishes.

"We laid down on our bellies among the soldiers. They were watching us; some were shooting and some were watching us. If we stood up to run they would have shot us dead." – "Saw Eh Htoo" (M, 37), xxxx village, Bilin township, describing what he and other porters did when battles occurred (Interview #1, 7/99)

"When portering, the Burmese force us to carry rice and other food. Sometimes they force us to carry weapons and bullets. We have to take our own food, and if it runs out we have to ask food from other people. Sometimes they [the soldiers] give some if they have enough, but usually they don't and we have to ask for food from the houses in the villages we pass through."- "Naw Hser" (F, 51), xxxx village, Pa'an township (Interview #2, 7/99)

"I had to go as a porter for them because my turn had come. If you don't go for your turn, you must hire someone else [to go for you]. To hire people, you must give them 2,000 Kyat for 5 days of portering. I didn't

have the money to hire anyone. I had to carry a big basket with two pots in it, and two Army packs filled with rice. It was so heavy that it was hard for me to stand up with it. ... They fed us 2 times each day, at 10 a.m. and 7 p.m. We only got 3 tablespoons each for each meal. They told us, 'Eat this much because there are no rations for you. You should be thankful to get this much.' We didn't dare ask for more, because if we asked they kicked us. I got tired. Some people became giddy and sweaty and fell down but they still kept kicking them. They beat some porters to death. ... When they were portering, their blood pressure got higher and higher until they became giddy, then they fell down. The soldiers yelled at them and they didn't answer, so they beat them to death. They hit them with gun butts on their necks and backs a few times and then they died. They beat people to death heartlessly. They're never afraid to beat people to death. ... Everyone is living in hard times like I am. Some people are rich, but most are poor and have to do everything [demanded of them]. People who are rich take their money and hire people to go for their turn as porters. The price for one trip is supposed to be 2,000 Kyat, but if the rich people only offer us 1,500 Kyat then we have to go for them if we don't have any rice to eat. If we don't eat we can't survive, so I went for that 1,500 Kyat and gave the money to my wife and children. While I was gone she had to give fees, buy medicine for her children and buy paddy from that money." - "Saw Eh Htoo" (M, 37), xxxx village, Bilin township (Interview #1, 7/99)

The villagers say that they also have to go for rotating shifts of forced labour at SPDC Army camps to build and maintain the camp's buildings, fences and other defences. At xxxx village, where there is an SPDC Army camp, the villagers were forced not only to build a fence around the camp but around their village as well. Some villages are also forced to provide unarmed sentries along the motor roads; usually each village is responsible to guard the road halfway to the next village in each direction. The villagers have to rotate 24-hour shifts at each of the assigned sentry posts, and are supposed to report any activity on the road. If any landmines are subsequently found on the road or any fighting happens near the road, the village responsible for that section of road is punished.

"Tomorrow morning at 6 o'clock send 3 emergency servants from your village for repairing the camp. Send [them] without fail to repair the camp. It will be two nights long, so they must bring rations. Without fail. If [you] fail it will be the responsibility of the Chairpersons." - Text of a written order sent to a village in Thaton District by the SPDC Army in January 1999 (Order #T2, "SPDC Orders to Villages: Set 99-B")

[http://metalab.unc.edu/freeburma/humanrights/khrg/archive/khrg99/khrg
9903.html]

*"We had to fence our village, and we also had to build fences around
their camp and work on the road. If several people stay in a house, then
one person has to go from each house. They forced us to work from 8
a.m. until noon. ... Whenever they need the villagers, they come to collect
them. If people are sick, they force them to go when they become better."*
- "Naw Hser" (F, 51), xxxx village, Pa'an township (Interview #2, 7/99)

*"For 'loh ah pay' we have to go and work in the Army camp. ... We had
to go and slice bamboo into small pieces, then sharpen it into spikes for
booby traps. Anyone who didn't go was put in the stocks. They put you in
the stocks and fine you five viss [8 kg / 17.5 lb] of chicken or five viss of
alcohol. You have to give it, you cannot stay [in the village] if you don't
give it. They write a letter demanding one goat as the fine for anyone
who escapes while portering, or 5 viss of alcohol for someone who didn't
go for 'loh ah pay'."* - "Saw Eh Htoo" (M, 37), xxxx village, Bilin
township (Interview #1, 7/99)

*"One person has to go and sleep at each place along the car road as a
sentry, but there are 3 or 4 places between villages. One village has to
send sentries to 4 places. They force 2 villagers to go to the road east of
the village and 2 villagers to go to the road west of the village. There are
4 sentry huts. The DKBA said that people will try to put landmines on the
road, so they force the villagers to stand sentry on it. The Burmese trucks
come up the road to deliver the rations. They also come in the daytime.
The villagers have to do sentry duty day and night."* - "Naw Mu Mu
Wah" (F, 29), xxxx village, Pa'an township (Interview #7, 7/99)

Another form of forced labour is known as 'patrol'. This involves women
from the village going to the local SPDC camp every day to report
whether or not there have been any KNLA movements in their area, and
if so how many KNLA troops were involved, where they came from,
where they went and so on. One villager from Bilin township told KHRG
that 3 women per day must go to the SPDC camp for this each bearing a
bundle of firewood, and that the Army insists that only women go for this
labour. Once at the camp they are also used for any errands required by
the officers.

*"Each day 3 people must also go for 'patrol'. Women must go for that,
the men are not allowed to go. When they go, each of the 'patrol' people
must take them a bundle of firewood. The 'patrol' women have to report*

to the camp commander about whether or not any Kaw Thoo Lei have come to the village each day. ... The camp commander is kind, but still his heart is crooked because he is a Burman. Sometimes he shouts at the 'patrol' women, 'Why don't you inform us when Kaw Thoo Lei come? Do you like Kaw Thoo Lei? Do you like Nga Pway?' ... He threatens the women, 'If you don't inform us truthfully next time we will punish you severely.' ... He has already put many people in the stocks. He puts the women in the stocks if they arrive late for 'patrol'. They are told to go for patrol at 10 a.m., and if you arrive later than that you will be in the stocks. ... The women must talk sweetly to the Burmese. If they don't speak sweetly the Burmese will beat them. They beat one woman from my village. Her name is M---. ... [H]e beat her twice with a bamboo stick as thick as my hand, and she passed urine right then and there. He beat her on her back with the bamboo, Baun! Baun!! ... Bwah!! M--- had to drink holy water [to heal herself] for many days when she got home after being beaten like that. She is almost 50 years old."- "Saw Eh Htoo" (M, 37), xxxx village, Bilin township (Interview #1, 7/99)

People in some villages report that they must also do forced labour growing crops for SPDC troops on farmland which has been confiscated from their village. According to the report of a KHRG field reporter, Light Infantry Battalion #8 has one such plantation in Thaton township on about 100 acres of confiscated land, and each day villagers must come from the villages of Ma Aye Cha, Ka Law Kher, Lah Aw Kher, Ma Ya Gone, Mo Kyaw Eh, Wah Lu, Noh Pa Leh, Kaw Kya Ther, and Kaw Ler to work on it. Land confiscation and forced labour farming has been on the increase throughout Burma since 1998, when the SPDC in Rangoon ordered its Army units in the field to produce more of their own food or take it from villagers.

Villagers throughout the region report having to regularly go for short shifts maintaining local roads. According to one woman whose village is on the western bank of the Salween River below Ka Ma Maung, the SPDC is also building a new road from Myaing Galay (directly across the river from Pa'an) up the western side of the Salween River to Ka Ma Maung. When completed, this road would be approximately 60 kilometres (40 miles) long. She reports that the SPDC has hired villagers in the area to do some of the work, paying 50 Kyat per day for road work and 100 Kyat per day for bridge work. These wages are impossible for a family to survive on. KHRG has not yet been able to obtain any reports on whether villagers on other parts of the route are also being paid or are being used as forced labour.

"They are building roads and bridges around Pa'an Township. They started at Myaing Galay and are coming step by step. At every river they build a bridge, so there are many bridges. They've hired villagers to do it for them, for building roads and bridges. Their aim is to send all their rations by truck. They hire people for 100 Kyat per day for bridge building, and 50 Kyat per day for road building. But as for sentries, they don't hire us, we have to hire ourselves. If you don't dare go as a sentry, you have to hire someone yourself." - "Naw Mu Mu Wah" (F, 29), xxxx village, Pa'an township, describing SPDC road-building along the western bank of the Salween River (Interview #7, 7/99)

According to the villagers, most DKBA units in the district are forcing villagers to do similar types of labour to those which the SPDC is demanding, including portering and camp labour, and is using similar methods to demand it, sometimes sending written orders and sometimes collecting people in their villages. Some villagers pointed out that as people flee their villages to other areas the burden of forced labour is becoming heavier on those who remain. Some villages have lost 30-50% of their population already, yet they must still provide the same numbers of forced labourers and the same amounts of extortion money, food and materials. One villager from Bilin township reported that in his village, this means that the women must go as porters much more than ever before, and that even widows with children to care for must now go as porters [see Interview #1].

"They do it this way: today they collect 4 or 5 people from this part of the village, then tomorrow they go and collect 4 or 5 people from another part of the village, and so on. When they get through the whole village they start again. They collect and force people by turns. Seven, eight, or 10 people at a time, and they have to take along their own food and go as porters." - "Naw Mu Mu Wah" (F, 29), xxxx village, Pa'an township, describing how the DKBA takes forced labour in her village (Interview #7, 7/99)

"[T]hey force us to go for 'loh ah pay' building the motor road and their camp, digging trenches and fencing their camp. They also force us to go portering. Right now they've demanded 6 people. They got 5 people, and they collected money for the one they didn't get." - "Saw Po Thu" (M, 36), xxxx village, Thaton township, talking about forced labour for the SPDC Army (Interview #6, 5/99)

"The above mentioned village, send without fail 10 men tomorrow at 0600 hours NOW to repair xxxx camp." - text of a written order sent to a

village in Thaton District by the SPDC Army (Order #T3, "SPDC Orders to Villages: Set 99-B") [http://metalab.unc.edu/freeburma/humanrights/khrg/archive/khrg99/khrg9903.html]

Looting, Taxes, Extortion, and Crop Quotas

"We worked in our ricefield and we planted sugar cane, but we could not eat because of all their demands. The government also demands 'obligation' rice. We only had a small rice field, and they demanded 6 baskets of paddy from my mother. The paddy all died, but we had to give this to them anyway. ... The sugar cane was also damaged, but we had to pay 'obligation' on that as well. We didn't have a single grain of paddy to eat, it had all died. But we had to give them paddy regardless. We couldn't give them any, so we had to give them money instead. They forced us to give them 200 Kyat for each basket of paddy. We had to pay 1,200 Kyat in lieu of our 6 baskets of paddy. All the villagers who have a field have to pay. We have to give whatever they ask. If you don't pay it, you can't stay there. They will drive you out of the village." - "Naw Mu Mu Wah" (F, 29), xxxx village, Pa'an township (Interview #7, 7/99)

In addition to the forced labour demanded of them, villagers in the district find it almost impossible to live with all the material demands made of them by all of the forces present in the area. The SPDC demands add up to the most and cause them the most suffering. All farmers who have land must pay crop quotas to the SPDC based on the amount of land they own, not on the amount of land they plant or the amount they harvest. Villagers complained to KHRG that even though their rice and sugar cane crops failed this past year due to droughts, they were forced to hand over their quotas of rice, cane and jaggery (slabs of crystallised sugar made by boiling cane juice) regardless. Those who could not gather enough produce to hand over had to pay cash instead, even if they did not have enough to eat for themselves. Failure to pay the quota can result in confiscation of your land and being driven out of the village by the Army. In addition, most of the quota collection officials are corrupt, demanding more than the real quota and paying out less than they are supposed to, even though the price they pay is already less than half of market price. One farmer complained that he regularly has to give over half of his entire rice crop to the Army and the officials without receiving any payment at all. When the quota collection officials visit the villages, the village head is also expected to feed them extravagantly, and after they leave the cost of this is collected from the villagers. One villager reported that the cost for this one meal amounts to 50 to 70 Kyat from every household in the village.

"When we work in our field and get 50 baskets [of paddy], we have to give them 25 baskets. Then there are only 25 baskets left for us, but we still must give taxes and fees so each year we never have enough rice left. Each year I had to borrow from others. There are many taxes, like taxes for pigs and taxes for goats. If they come to the village you can't keep your livestock. They come to take one pig, and if the villagers cannot give them one pig then they fine the village head and torture him. We are just villagers, so we must give to the village head whenever he collects money from us. When we don't have money to give we must sell things from our house." - "Saw Eh Htoo" (M, 37), xxxx village, Bilin township (Interview #1, 7/99)

"If you plant 5 'dter' [the area of a large field] of sugar cane, you have to give them 1 'dter'. ... This year we had to give them money [because the sugar cane crop failed]. I don't know how much money it was for 1 'dter', but my mother also had to give them 100 packets of jaggery. We couldn't give it so we had to pay them. If we sold that much jaggery we would get 8,000 or 9,000 Kyat, but they demanded 5,000 Kyat from us because that is the government price. ... We couldn't eat, we had to pay them so much. ... When they come to tax, we have to run and get it. If you have no money you have to find some you can borrow and give it to them. Many villagers borrowed money and are now in debt. The villagers have nothing to eat, but they still have to help the Burmese. They say that the place where we stay is government land. It's as though we're staying on their land so we have to pay tax to them." - "Naw Mu Mu Wah" (F, 29), xxxx village, Pa'an township (Interview #7, 7/99)

"They also demand donations when their officials come to the village. They call it 'sah kywe' ['eating tax']. They come and eat food in our village, and after they go back we have to pay for them. We have to pay 50 or 60 Kyat each. Now in our village the DKBA are showing videos of their battles, and when you go to see it you have to pay 50 or 60 Kyat each night. Even if you don't go to see it, you still have to pay. That's why the women are very angry, but nobody dares to complain to them and everyone is keeping quiet." - "Naw Mu Mu Wah" (F, 29), xxxx village, Pa'an township (Interview #7, 7/99)

The crop quotas are collected by SPDC officials each year, but the villagers must also face regular and arbitrary demands for rice, other foodstuffs, and livestock by every SPDC Army unit in their area. These demands usually come by written letter, and every household must contribute. When livestock is demanded, an animal belonging to one of the villagers must be sent and then all of the villagers must contribute money to reimburse the owner. Similar demands are also received for building materials such as wooden or bamboo posts, shaved bamboo ties, and roofing thatch. When interviewed, some villagers were in the process of gathering materials to meet SPDC demands for several hundred bamboo posts, or in one case 1,400 sheets of thatch roofing. To make thatch roofing, the villagers must gather a specific kind of leaves in the jungle and gather bamboo, then split the bamboo into sticks and shave some of it into ties. Each sheet requires making a frame from the bamboo sticks and attaching several leaves onto it with the bamboo ties. The process is labour-intensive, yet a typical SPDC order for one or two thousand roofing sheets will only allow the villagers three days to a week to comply.

"Now I am going to send thatch to the Burmese. We have to send seven bullock carts full of thatch. That is 1,400 sheets of thatch. ... They demanded it from all the villages, like D---, K--, L---, L---, K---, and G---. They called the village heads from each village and ordered them to go and meet. They sent us a letter written in red ink. I said that the red pen is very hot for us, we'd better not rest, we have to go 'on the hot' [i.e. 'hotfoot it']. One of the women thought it was an emergency so she carried her child and went 'on the hot' to see them, but when she got there they just asked for thatch. ... I think they will build a storehouse and fix their other roofs. The villagers from T--- and H--- are going every day now to build the storehouse." – "Naw Muh" (F, 46), xxxx village, Bilin Township, (Interview #10, 1/99)

"[T]he Burmese soldiers came to the village. They just came to the village last night ... on the 3rd of May. They came to collect 2,000 pieces of thatch and 1,000 bamboo. They came in the evening and visited the village chairman. ... We can get bamboo in our village, but there are no 'ta la aw' leaves for thatch in our village, so they forced us to give them money instead of thatch. We collected 70 Kyat and 5 bamboo from each household for them. They said the Brigadier had ordered them to collect it." - "Saw Po Thu" (M, 36), xxxx village, Thaton township (Interview #6, 5/99)

"[Y]ou are informed to send without fail 500 wooden planks, length 10 taun [cubits; 10 taun is about 5 metres / 15 feet], which must arrive on 22-11-98 for A'Su Chaung bridge. ... Arrange 'loh ah pay' workers on the day of construction." - text of a written order sent to a village in Thaton District by the SPDC Army in November 1998; the villagers were given only 2 days to make and deliver the planks (Order #T12,

"SPDC Orders to Villages: Set 99-B") [http://metalab.unc.edu/freeburma/humanrights/khrg/archive/khrg99/khrg9903.html]

"[T]he villagers must send them whatever they've demanded, because it's not good to wait until they come for it. If the villagers don't give it until they come, then when they come they beat every villager." - "Saw Eh Htoo" (M, 37), xxxx village, Bilin township (Interview #1, 7/99)

Whenever an SPDC military column arrives at a village, the troops take livestock and other food as well as many of the villagers' belongings. Those who live in villages adjacent to SPDC and DKBA camps complain that the soldiers are constantly coming in the night to steal their chickens and other belongings. Even in broad daylight, the soldiers regularly pick fruit from the trees and vegetables from the kitchen gardens without even asking the owners and with no intention to pay compensation. The villagers usually dare not say anything, because those who complain are often punched or threatened with an accusation of being a KNU sympathiser.

"[T] hey eat a lot of chickens and livestock in the village. They eat without paying. Sometimes they order the village to send it and we give it, and then sometimes they pay something, but usually they do not pay. They also steal it at night. We usually don't dare complain to the camp commander. If people go and tell them they beat those people, so we don't dare complain to them often." - "Naw Hser" (F, 51), xxxx village, Pa'an township, describing the looting of livestock by the SPDC troops based at her village (Interview #2, 7/99)

"When they steal our poultry we don't dare complain to them. If you complain to them, they'll say later that they met the KNLA near your village and had to shoot at them, and the bullets just happened to come right down through the roof of your house. That's why nobody dares to tell them anything." – "Naw Muh" (F, 46), xxxx village, Bilin Township, (Interview #10, 1/99)

Although most villages are populated by subsistence farmers and there is no significant cash economy, the villagers also face heavy demands for cash from SPDC Army units. On average, a family needs to obtain 1,000 or more Kyat per month to pay all of the regular extortion fees demanded by the Army under various names such as 'porter fees' and 'development fees'. This money simply goes into the pockets of the local officers, but the villagers have no choice but to pay it. In addition, they need money to hire people to take their place for forced labour if they are ill or if they need the time to work in their fields. Families must always be ready as well to contribute money to compensate those whose livestock are looted by the soldiers, and to pay 'fines' which are imposed on the village if porters from the village flee their duty or if a skirmish with the KNLA occurs in their area. One villager from Thaton township described how a DKBA commander came to the village and demanded 30,000 Kyat compensation from the village because one of his own soldiers had run away with all of the unit's rations. He gave the villagers less than 3 hours to come up with the money, and the best that they could negotiate was that they pay him the next morning. Even then they could not raise the full amount.

"He demanded 30,000 Kyat the same night that he arrived at the village. He ordered us to pay it by 9 p.m. Some villagers went to see the monk and asked him to go and tell the DKBA that they had problems finding so much money at night. The monk went to the DKBA and 2 or 3 villagers went with him. The monk told him, 'Bo Than Htun, the villagers can't find this money in the night'. Bo Than Htun said, 'This is not the business of a monk.' Then the monk told him, 'This is not my business, but the villagers came to me so I must tell you. You would be better to ask them in the daytime.' Then he made an appointment to give him the money the next morning at 9 a.m. The villagers could only find 27,000 Kyat, they couldn't pay 30,000 Kyat. ... The villagers had to go into debt. Some had to pawn their pots and rings. They demanded it immediately, so we could not find the money. Some villagers had nothing to pawn, so they went to plead with the shopkeepers and the shopkeepers loaned them money. ... If the villagers didn't give it to them, they would beat and kill the villagers and burn their houses." - "Saw Aung Htoo" (M, 28), xxxx village, Thaton township, describing how a DKBA Captain demanded compensation from the villagers after a DKBA soldier defected with his unit's rations (Interview #9, 5/99)

The DKBA in the region is known for making such arbitrary and exorbitant demands and for accompanying them with serious threats. Even so, the burden of their looting and demands amounts to less than the demands of the SPDC on most villages. Even after the villagers give everything they have to these two Armies, they must still pay yearly taxes and supply food to the KNLA. Though these demands amount to far less than those imposed by either the SPDC or the DKBA, it is still one additional burden which the villagers cannot bear.

"We cannot live without giving to the Burmese. They will kill us and burn the village. They told us they won't eat our 4-legged animals but they will

eat the humans. [Second woman]: They said they'll cut off our heads and hang them in front of our [village] leaders." – "Naw Wah Paw" (F, 30), xxxx village, Bilin Township (Interview #15, 1/99)

"They won't like it. They'll come to the village and torture us. They'll accuse us of joining the Nga Pway ['Ringworms', derogatory SPDC name for KNU/KNLA]. If they give us an order and we don't go at once, they accuse us of joining the Nga Pway and they say it was the Nga Pway who didn't allow us to go. They say 'If the Nga Pway can control you they will, but we will also control you as much as we can'." – "Naw Muh" (F, 46), xxxx village, Bilin Township, describing what happens if the villagers fail to send materials demanded by the SPDC camp (Interview #10, 1/99)

Curfews and 'Letters of Recommendation'

"From your village, children, men and all the villagers are absolutely (absolutely) not allowed out of the village on September 27 / 28 / 29, Thadin Kyut Hla Zan 7 / 8 / 9 [the corresponding Burmese calendar dates]. Don't go at all for looking after your cattle, buffaloes, farm affairs or picking vegetables. Inform the village that they will be shot and arrested if the Columns find out [that they have left the village]." - written order sent to a village in Thaton District by the SPDC Army in September 1998 (Order #T1, "SPDC Orders to Villages: Set 99-B") [http://metalab.unc.edu/freeburma/humanrights/khrg/archive/khrg99/khrg 9903.html]

Forced labour and work gathering materials to meet SPDC demands takes a great deal of working time away from the villagers, but in the villages of eastern and northeastern Thaton District they also complain of military-imposed curfews which make it difficult to tend their fields. People in villages near SPDC military camps are not allowed to leave their villages until after 8 a.m. and must return by 4 p.m. in some villages, 6 p.m. in others. Villagers are used to spending much of the growing season living in their 'deh', the simple huts they build in their farmfields, because their farming methods are labour intensive and many of them work fields which are several miles from their village. The curfews prevent them from doing this and make it very difficult for them to produce a full crop, which they desperately need because of all the demands placed upon them. In some villages the villagers can pay 20 Kyat to get a 'letter of recommendation' signed by the village head which allows them to sleep in their deh for one or two nights; in the letter, the village head guarantees that the person is a farmer from his village and has no contact with the opposition. However, villagers using these letters are taking a risk because they are not always accepted by SPDC and DKBA patrols, who view any villager staying in his or her deh with extreme suspicion.

"Whenever you want to go to the forest, you have to get a letter of recommendation. You have to pay 20 Kyat for each one. I don't know if the DKBA or the village head takes that money. You have to go and get it from the village head. After he writes the letter, he gives it to the villager. If the DKBA sees them in the jungle they ask, 'Where do you live?' In xxxx [her village]. 'Do you have your letter?' The villagers show them. If the villagers have no letter, they can kill them." - "Naw Mu Mu Wah" (F, 29), xxxx village, Pa'an township (Interview #7, 7/99)

"We don't have enough time to work. They don't allow us to go out [of the village] until 8 a.m., and we must come back by 4 p.m. on time. They won't let the villagers work any extra time. I don't know what they'd do if you're late. The Burmese camp is right there, so they won't let us stay out for extra time." - "Naw Hser" (F, 51), xxxx village, Pa'an township (Interview #2, 7/99)

Land Confiscation

"[O]ur parents have land, but when the Burmese built the road they built it right through the middle of our field. We are greedy for our land too, because we earn our lives from it. We told them to build it through the village or across the river instead. But they said, 'Don't say anything. It's not your land, it's government land. You don't need to say anything, the government can do as they like.'" - "Naw Mu Mu Wah" (F, 29), xxxx village, Pa'an township (Interview #7, 7/99)

According to the official law in Burma all land is the property of the State, and the SPDC troops in the district constantly remind the villagers that "this is not your land, it's government land". This argument is used whenever the Army wishes to take land or produce for its own purposes. Some of the SPDC Battalions in Thaton District have been confiscating villagers' farmland in order to use it to produce food for the Battalion. Not only have the villagers been paid no compensation whatever, but they are thereafter forced to work on the land growing crops for the Army. One of the worst cases of this has occurred in Thaton township, where Light Infantry Battalion #8 has confiscated approximately 100 acres of land and is currently using the people of nine villages in the area as forced labour to work it [see above under 'Forced Labour'].

DKBA units have also confiscated land in Pa'an township and settled the families of DKBA soldiers on it, in some cases even forcing local villagers to provide building materials and forced labour to build their houses [see above under 'The DKBA', and Interview #7]. A woman from Pa'an township also reported that the new SPDC road from Myaing Galay to Ka Ma Maung was built right through the length of her father's sugar cane field without any compensation being paid, and that when her family complained they were given the usual argument that "It's not your land, it's government land". Her father's field follows the riverbank and is long and narrow, and by traversing its entire length the road and its embankment have rendered the entire field unusable.

Schools and Health

"I have a small brother, and at that time he had gone to find frogs in the fields. He is 15 years old, a young boy. He went to find frogs every night. He was trying to get money to buy his reading books. My mother told him not to go that night because it was very dark and there was thunder, but he wanted to get money and study in the school, so he went to find frogs. At that time, one of them [DKBA] whom we call Maung Shwe Aye went and demanded frogs from the villagers who were gathering them in the fields around xxxx. He stole 8 frogs from each of the adults and from those who had many frogs, and he took 5 frogs from each of the children like my younger brother. He pointed his gun at people while he robbed them. He made the sound of the gun bolt, 'Klaw Kla, Klaw Kla', and he said, 'Do you know what this is?' My brother only had 10 frogs but he stole 5 frogs from him. Then my brother was afraid and came back. If they didn't give him the frogs he would have done something to them, because he was drunk." - "Naw Mu Mu Wah" (F, 29), xxxx village, Pa'an township (Interview #7, 7/99)

With each year, fewer and fewer children in Thaton District are able to go to school. Schools up to 8th or 10th Standard (middle or high school) level still exist in major villages and towns, but these can be a significant distance from most villages and each year fewer and fewer villagers can afford to send their children there; to do so, they must be able to pay for the school fees, all educational materials, and the cost of having their child stay near the school if it is far away. After paying all of the extortion, crop quotas and taxes demanded by the SPDC Army and other groups, most villagers have no money left whatsoever; even just to pay all of the extortion they often have to sell household belongings and livestock. In addition, families which are struggling to survive need their children to help at home. It is often the children or adolescents who are sent to fill quotas for forced labour so that their parents can continue working in the fields.

In the past many villages have pooled their resources and built their own schools to give at least primary level education to their children right in the village. These schools usually go up to 2nd or 4th Standard (Grade 2 or 4), but in some cases they go higher. Those in the village who have had the most education either volunteer or are pressed into teaching and the villagers support them with some rice and a small amount of money; sometimes they teach part time and still work a small farm. However, villagers in Thaton District report that since the beginning of this year the SPDC military has been ordering these schools closed. Habitually suspicious of anything which is not directly controlled by the Army or the SPDC, the officers have told the villagers that they must hire SPDC-sanctioned teachers from town if they still want to keep their schools open. The villagers say there is no way they can afford the salaries of these teachers, so their village schools are closing. With their closure, many village children are losing their only chance for education.

"She can speak Burmese because she finished Grade 8 in Burmese school. After she finished Grade 8, she taught in our village school for 2 years. Then she had to stop teaching because the Burmese said that people in the forest villages should not teach. Our school went up to Grade 9, but starting this year the Burmese won't allow the teachers to teach. They said villagers must go and get teachers from town if they want to teach in the villages. As for us, we couldn't hire those teachers because they want a lot of salary. They won't come to our village. Our village is small. At first there were 70 households, but many people have fled so now there are only 30 households left. There is still a school building, but no one can study. So none of my children can go to school, instead they take care of buffaloes in the rain all the time." - "Saw Eh Htoo" (M, 37), xxxx village, Bilin township (Interview #1, 7/99)

Health care is also severely lacking in the villages of Thaton District. Medicines can be difficult and expensive to obtain, often only available by travelling to town or from travelling medicine sellers, and most villagers have little knowledge of the difference between various modern medicines. Many of them know paracetamol and quinine but nothing else, and most of them believe that if someone is wounded or seriously ill the best medicine to buy is an 'injection', without knowing what they are injecting. Most people do not have enough money to buy more than a few tablets of modern medicine so they largely rely on traditional herbal and spiritual remedies. These are usually the best for minor ailments but are often not enough on their own to treat serious illness, gunshot wounds or the after-effects of serious torture. Villagers also have the option of going to the clinics or small hospitals which exist in the big villages and towns of the area, though it can be very difficult for someone who is wounded or seriously ill to get there. Once they are there, they must provide all of their own food and pay their hospital fees, including all medicines, every day. The villagers who were wounded when SPDC troops opened fire in xxxx village of Thaton township [see above under 'Killings'] say they spent 14 days in hospital and had to pay 1,000 to 4,000 Kyat each day, depending on what treatment they were given on that day. Many villagers simply cannot pay this, or have to sell everything they own and go deeply into debt to pay it.

"I went to get treatment in xxxx hospital. They fed us nothing there, we had to bring it all from home. The nurse at the hospital gave us injections, 2 or 3 injections each day. We had to pay them. Some days, we had to pay over 2,000 Kyat for one day. Some days 2,000 Kyat, some days over 1,000 Kyat, and some days 3,000 to 4,000 Kyat. All the patients have to pay like this." - "Naw Ler Paw" (F, 28), xxxx village, Thaton township (Interview #3, 5/99).

Internally Displaced People

"We fled to stay in the jungle because the SPDC came and tortured us. They asked me questions and beat me. They often beat us. If they didn't beat us, people would dare to stay in the village." – "Saw Po Si" (M, 50+), xxxx village, Bilin Township (Interview #13, 2/99)

Many villagers are so afraid of the arbitrary detention, beatings and torture that they fear ever encountering SPDC troops, so they flee into the forest whenever they hear that an SPDC column is in their area. Others have had to flee because they can no longer do all the forced labour and pay all of the fees. For many of these people life is now a matter of running back and forth, spending much of their time living in the forest or their fields, where they must always be on the lookout for SPDC or DKBA columns, and sneaking back to stay in their villages for brief periods when they think it is safe. If they are found in the forest or living in their field hut they face almost certain arrest, interrogation and torture as suspected KNLA supporters, and they may be shot on sight, taken as porters or executed. While living outside the village most of them still try to work their family fields, but they have no access to schools, medicines or the help and support of other villagers. They have to move often to dodge patrols and this can make it very difficult to grow a sufficient crop.

As a result, many have little or nothing to eat other than what they can collect in the forest. It is more difficult for villagers to remain hidden in Thaton District than in an area such as Papun District, because the terrain here is less rugged and the SPDC and DKBA are much more in control. Otherwise, more villagers would probably choose the option of living in hiding, but as it is most of them still try to survive in their villages or flee to entirely different areas. The number of people currently in hiding in Thaton District is difficult to estimate, but most likely numbers a few thousand.

"There are children, old people, and many villagers living in the jungle. They have already been staying there for over 4 years. Since the DKBA began working together with the SLORC and SPDC, they have fled from the north, up to the source of the xxxx river. They tortured the villagers until the villagers could not suffer it any more, so they fled and are staying in the jungle until now. The villagers are staying in the jungle very poorly. They are sick but they can't get medicine. The villagers who have fled are from xxxx, xxxx, xxxx, xxxx and xxxx villages." – written report by KHRG field researcher (Field Report #FR8, 2/99)

There have been some efforts to deliver some help to these displaced people and to the people in the villages who are the worst off, mostly in the form of rice and money to buy food and pay off debt. Most of these efforts have been delivered by agencies originally set up by the KNU, and the villagers have benefitted from this help. However, according to reports from KHRG field reporters the SPDC military in some areas has become aware of these efforts and has begun punishing the villagers for it. On May 19th 1999, troops from SPDC Light Infantry Battalion #355 demanded rice and other food from Ta Rer Kee village in Bilin township and the commander told the villagers they would be increasing their demands now that they knew the villagers were supposedly receiving money from the KNU. On May 22nd, the same troops arrested and beat to death Saw Bah Yay, the village head of Naw K'Toh village in Bilin township, accusing him of failing to report that the KNU had given money to his villagers. Three days later, the same troops detained a villager named Saw Nu Nu from Naw K'Toh village on his way to his fields, interrogated him about money allegedly given to the villagers by the KNU, and tortured him to death [for more details on these events see Field Reports #FR4-FR6 at http://metalab.unc.edu/freeburma/ humanrights/khrg/archive/khrg99/khrg9907.html].

Flight

"When we were coming here we had to flee secretly because their camp is right at our village. They wouldn't allow us to come here. If they saw us, they would ask 'Where are you going?' and we couldn't dare tell them that we were coming here. First each family had to flee into the jungle, and then we had to come here secretly."- "Naw Hser" (F, 51), xxxx village, Pa'an township, after arriving in Thailand as a refugee (Interview #2, 7/99)

Anyone who cannot pay all the demands or do the forced labour has little choice but to flee the village, and many also flee after being arrested and tortured or in fear of being tortured. While some manage to live internally displaced for months or even years, for villagers whose fields are near SPDC or DKBA camps this is next to impossible. Many villagers who do attempt to live in hiding eventually find that they cannot produce enough food to support themselves. In the end, many villagers find that their only option is to leave their land and their village and flee elsewhere.

The first choice for most of these people is to flee to the homes of relatives in other villages not so far away. They may have relatives in a village which is further from an SPDC camp and therefore faces fewer demands, or in a large village where there is a certain amount of safety in numbers. If this is not possible, people often move westward into the coastal plains, becoming itinerant labourers in the large villages there, in towns like Thaton, Bilin or Kyaikto, or even further away in cities like Moulmein or Rangoon. When fleeing, villagers usually gravitate toward any place where they have some kind of contact, such as a distant relative or even just a friend from their village who already lives there.

"[S]ome villages are forced to do things a lot and some villages aren't forced as much, so they've gone to stay at those kinds of villages. Some also go to stay with their relatives in other villages. But no one dares to stay in farmfield huts." - "Naw Mu Mu Wah" (F, 29), xxxx village, Pa'an township (Interview #7, 7/99)

Some villagers know of relatives or people from their village who have already fled eastward to refugee camps in Thailand, so this is where they choose to flee. This is the most difficult option, so very few villagers have made this choice so far. Most of them do not know the way, and can only get to the border if Karen soldiers are headed that way or other villagers know the way. The journey can take 4 days to several weeks, depending on whether the family has children and belongings and how often they have to detour or lay low to avoid SPDC or DKBA forces. The villagers themselves say that if the SPDC or DKBA knew they were heading to Thailand they would stop them. Because of this, most of them carry few or no belongings, so they can tell any troops they encounter that they are just on their way somewhere to visit a relative. They need money to pay for road or river transport, buy food, pay off any checkpoints they encounter, and sometimes to hire a guide for part of the journey. Only a few families per month from Thaton District manage to make the journey and arrive in refugee camps in Thailand, but it is becoming an increasingly steady trickle.

"We came as only one family. Before we came here, others asked to follow us. I told them 'Don't come with us. If you want to go, go later one by one.' If we came in a group and the Burmese saw us, they wouldn't allow us to come here. We had to come secretly." - "Naw Hser" (F, 51), xxxx village, Pa'an township, after arriving in Thailand (Interview #2, 7/99)

"If I told you everything in detail it would take a whole day and night and we still wouldn't be finished, because the Burmese made problems for us in every way. We just had to tolerate it because we had nowhere else to go, until I found the soldiers who were headed this way and so I followed them. I knew that I could not stay in the village anymore. I knew that they would make problems for me again and again until in the end they would kill me, and my wife and children would be left alone and in trouble. That is why I came here. If I died there, my wife and children would face problems with food, taxes and forced labour. The widows in our village all have to pay taxes and go as porters, all of them. Because there are now few people left in our village, the women also have to go as porters. ... It took us 6 days to come here. We walked the whole way, and twice we had to walk through the night." - "Saw Eh Htoo" (M, 37), xxxx village, Bilin township, after his arrival in Thailand (Interview #1, 7/99)

Future of the Area

"I am so thankful for all your help, the food and everything else you gave when our Battalion was in xxxx. I hope that all of you will understand and forgive us for what we said, ordered of you and did to you. These were our duties and were done under orders. I do apologise for our previous deeds. Actually, we and all of you are brothers and sisters." - text of a letter dated December 1998 from an SPDC Army Captain to villagers in Thaton District after he had been rotated out of the region (Order #T39, "SPDC Orders to Villages: Set 99-B") [http://metalab.unc.edu/freeburma/humanrights/khrg/archive/khrg99/khrg9903.html]

There is no sign that all of the demands for forced labour, extortion money, materials and crop quotas imposed upon the villagers are about to decrease. If anything, the trend in other Karen regions would indicate that the SPDC will only continue to increase militarisation of the area and the villagers will face even heavier demands as a result. The future of villagers in this area will also depend on the amount of activity conducted by the KNLA; assuming that the KNLA continues to operate there as at present, it is likely that the SPDC will continue to arbitrarily detain, torture and execute villagers, use them as porters under brutal conditions, and may eventually clamp down further on the villagers by conducting further forced relocations. There are no indications that the KNLA plans to cut back on its guerrilla operations in the region, and it definitely has the ability to continue these for the foreseeable future. The villagers will most likely continue to ask the KNLA not to attack SPDC or DKBA units near their villages, but even if the KNLA does not actively seek confrontation with the SPDC or the DKBA, skirmishes will occur and the villagers will be forced to pay the price.

Another factor which will play a strong role in determining the future of the villagers will be the relationships between the DKBA and the SPDC and between the DKBA and the KNU. The DKBA and the SPDC have never trusted each other, and in fact many DKBA members openly state that they hate the SPDC. However, they are completely reliant on the SPDC for arms, ammunition, food and logistical support, not to mention that the SPDC could capture and disarm most of the DKBA in one quick surprise sweep should it decide to do so. At the same time, the DKBA is useful to the SPDC in several ways: as guides and informers, to do some of the dirty work in the villages, as a front to attack refugee camps and other sites in Thailand, and because they pit Karen against Karen. The SPDC and DKBA tolerate each other because they are useful to each other, but it is not a smooth relationship. The DKBA was formed in

December 1994, and since 1996 the SLORC/SPDC has gradually cut down the material support given; the salaries paid to DKBA soldiers and officers were cut and then eliminated, the rations given to non-DKBA families at the DKBA's headquarters were eliminated, arms and ammunition supplies were cut back to a minimum, and food rations to DKBA soldiers and their families were cut back. The SPDC even threatened to cut all food support to the DKBA by December 1998, but this has not happened. In Thaton District, SPDC units still use DKBA soldiers as before, and the DKBA appears to have been given limited control over some parts of Pa'an Township along the Salween River. Given the SPDC's distrust of the DKBA, it is unlikely that they will be given control over more areas like this. DKBA units operating on their own in Thaton District behave very much like SPDC Army units, though this could change if relations between the two groups deteriorate. The DKBA has a weak command structure and very little idea of where it wants to go politically anymore, and this makes it volatile.

At present, DKBA and KNLA units in the area fight each other regularly, and there is little sign of any improvement in relations. However, some higher-level KNU leaders have recently become more open to the idea of talks with the DKBA, and some factions within the DKBA have always wanted this to happen. If the KNU and the DKBA were able to forge even the beginnings of an agreement, this would greatly strengthen the hand of the KNU/KNLA in Thaton District, but it would certainly cause the SPDC to turn against the DKBA. The result for the villagers would probably be an escalation of the civil war in the region, widespread forced relocations by the SPDC and a general increase in SPDC repression and the internal displacement and flight of villagers.

It is also very important to watch the region for any further evidence of the possible presence of 'Short Pants' Guerrilla Retaliation units [see above under 'The Short Pants']. If it is true that these units are about to begin operations in Thaton District and if they operate as execution squads as they are doing further north in Nyaunglebin District, villagers throughout the district will begin scattering in fear. In Nyaunglebin District many have fled eastward into the hills, but the villagers of Thaton District do not have this option so their situation would be even more desperate.

Even under present conditions, an increasing number of people are likely to flee their villages to the plains, to internal displacement, and to Thailand as refugees over the next year. Some villagers interviewed for this report say that their villages have already lost 30-70% of their population, and this trend is only likely to continue. In Bilin township, SPDC troops have now begun trying to block outside aid from reaching internally displaced villagers by demanding more from villages and torturing village leaders who are supposedly responsible [see above under 'Internally Displaced People'], and if this continues it will become even more difficult for people to live in hiding without fleeing to other areas. Most villagers will still try to brave it out in their villages for as long as they can, particularly in the western parts of the district, but it is hard to say just how much longer most of them can continue to suffer as they are now.

"My mother and father are dead, and now my brother is also dead. I have only one younger sister. The Burmese shot to kill. Now my relatives are almost all gone. If they do this for much longer, all of my relatives will be gone. They've done this to us, and still they accuse us that we are 'Tha Bone' ['rebels']. Even while we were going to get treatment in hospital, they were still accusing us of being 'Tha Bone'." - "Naw Ler Paw" (F, 28), xxxx village, Thaton township, who lost a daughter and a brother and was wounded herself in a massacre by SPDC troops on March 7th 1999 (Interview #3, 5/99)

.

Photographs

Plate 20: "Sein Myint", age 12 (right) and his 16-year-old friend (left) just before boarding a boat to go for 15 days of forced labour building the T'Gu-Ta Po Hta road in Tenasserim Division. One person from every house in their village has to go on the boat, which the village headman had to arrange and pay for to send them to the labour. "Sein Myint", an orphan, has to go because his 30-year-old sister (who has a 4-year-old of her own) is too sick to go. Just 2 weeks earlier, he'd already done 12 days of forced labour digging ditches along the road. He has no chance to go to school. *[Photo: KHRG]*

Plate 21: Villagers in Thaton District taking sheets of thatch roofing which they were ordered to deliver to the local SPDC Army camp for building purposes at the beginning of 1999. In this case they were ordered to deliver 7 bullock-cart loads, a total of 1,400 sheets of thatch. Gathering the materials and weaving the thatch shingles is time-consuming, but they were paid nothing; they received a threatening order in red ink telling them to go to the camp, and when one of them went the officer dictated the demand and the deadline. *[Photo: KHRG]*

Plate 22: The men of a Burman village on their way to do a shift of forced labour on the Boke-Ka Pyaw-Kyay Nan Daing road in Tenasserim Division, together with all their food. They had already been walking 5-6 hours, and still had close to an hour to walk to get to the worksite, where they were to work for a 5 day shift. *[Photo: KHRG]*

Plate 23: A SLORC/SPDC 'government' middle school in Noh Aw village, Tenasserim Division - until the village was ordered to move, the 'government' teacher fled, and SLORC/SPDC troops came and burned the school and much of the village. Though it was a 'government' school, the villagers had to pay for the construction, build it, pay for and support the teacher, and pay for all school supplies. Since 1999, SPDC troops have also been forcing all non-state run schools in rural areas to close. *[Photo: KHRG]*

Plate 24 (previous page): Karen villagers run for their lives with whatever they can carry across the Thai border in 1997. A SLORC/SPDC attacking force was only half an hour's walk distant when these photos were taken. The villagers were fleeing from villages throughout the Lay Po Hta-Saw Hta (Azin)-Kyaikdon plain in Dooplaya District, and crossing the Thai border at Lay Po Hta. As these villagers ran, distant mortar explosions were audible from Kwih Kler and Meh Tharoh Hta, an hour's walk away. Thirty minutes later, SLORC/SPDC troops began shelling Lay Po Hta, just 15 minutes' walk away. *[Photo: KHRG]*

Plate 25: Villagers who made it to KNU-controlled area in far southern Burma after SLORC/SPDC troops burned their villages in 1998, then had to flee a SLORC/SPDC offensive in the area to Thailand. They set up these makeshift shelters in a narrow gully just 1 km. inside unprotected Thai territory, very vulnerable to attack but not allowed by Thai authorities to move further inside Thailand or to build more permanent shelters until several months later. Thai forces in the area are positioned further inside Thailand than the refugees - stopping the refugees from escaping, but doing nothing to defend the Thai border. *[Photos: KHRG]*

Plate 26: A family flees. SLORC/SPDC troops destroyed their village in Papun District in March 1997, so they fled and built a shelter in the forest. In June, a SLORC/ SPDC patrol was passing near their shelter so they had to flee further into the hills in fear. The baskets on their backs contain all that they still possess. *[Photo: KHRG]*

PART III

BEYOND ALL ENDURANCE

The Breakup of Karen Villages in
Southeastern Pa'an District

An Independent Report by the
Karen Human Rights Group (December 20, 1999)

Abstract

Pa'an district forms a large area in the central heartland of Karen State. Much of the eastern part of the district used to be under at least partial control of the Karen National Union (KNU), but after troops of the State Law & Order Restoration Council (SLORC) military junta captured the KNU headquarters at Manerplaw in 1995, they progressively exerted increasing control over the entire eastern part of the district.

Pa'an district is covered by a large central plain in the west, bounded by the Salween River and the town of Pa'an (capital of Karen State) in the west and north and by the Myawaddy-Kawkareik-Kyone Doh road in the south. In the east of the district lies the Dawna Range, a line of mountains running north-south parallel to the Thai border, which form a steep natural boundary. Currently the activities of the Karen National Liberation Army (KNLA) are concentrated in these mountains.

No longer trying to hold territory, they operate as a guerrilla force and regularly penetrate into the plain to the west. In its determination to gain complete control over all of Pa'an district, the army of the current State Peace & Development Council (SPDC) military junta is now trying to undermine the KNLA throughout eastern Pa'an district and the Dawna Range by intimidating the Karen villagers who live in the region, increasing their burden of forced labour and extorting money and food from them until they can no longer survive. The Democratic Karen Buddhist Army (DKBA), a Karen group allied with the SPDC, is helping them in these operations.

At the same time, the KNLA, SPDC and DKBA forces have all been unceasingly planting landmines throughout the region, and the SPDC and DKBA troops have been using villagers as human minesweepers, resulting in the deaths and maiming of many. As a final straw, in August 1999 the SPDC made it known that it planned to force everyone in the hill villages of southeastern Pa'an District into Army controlled sites, and it has begun actively pursuing this operation. Villages have been emptying out as people flee into the fields and forests to escape the combination of intense abuses, landmines and the certainty of forced relocation. Unable to survive in hiding in the hills, many have begun trying to reach the Thai border, only to find the Thai Army determined to prevent them from entering Thailand.

KHRG first documented this new exodus and its causes in Information Updates   #99-U3   (27/8/99)   [http://metalab.unc.edu/freeburma/

humanrights/khrg/archive/khrg99/khrg99u3.html] and 99-U4 (29/9/99) [http://metalab.unc.edu/freeburma/humanrights/khrg/archive/khrg99/khrg 99u4.html]. This report follows up and expands on those updates, analysing the human rights situation for these villagers in eastern Pa'an district and how they are affected by the current activities of the SPDC, DKBA and KNLA. It looks in detail at specific issues of concern to the villagers, such as forced relocations, forced labour and the landmines which are now being laid all over the region by all parties to the conflict. For additional background, see "Uncertainty, Fear and Flight: The Current Human Rights Situation in Eastern Pa'an District" (KHRG #98-08, 18/11/98) [http://metalab.unc.edu/freeburma/humanrights/khrg/ archive/khrg98/khrg9808.html], "Abuses and Relocations in Pa'an District" (KHRG #97-08, 1/8/97) [http://metalab.unc.edu/freeburma/ humanrights/khrg/archive/khrg97/khrg9708.html], "Interviews from Northern Pa'an District" (KHRG #96-33, 4/8/96) [http://metalab.unc.edu/ freeburma/humanrights/khrg/archive/khrg96/khrg9633.html], and "The Situation in Pa'an District" (KHRG #96-17, 15/5/96) [http://metalab.unc. edu/freeburma/humanrights/khrg/archive/khrg96/khrg9617.html].

In order to produce this report, Karen Human Rights Group (KHRG) researchers and field reporters have conducted detailed interviews with villagers who have fled to Thailand to become refugees, villagers stranded in camps of internally displaced people in Burma because Thai authorities will not allow them to cross the border, and people in hiding around their home villages. The interviews used directly in the report were conducted between April and November 1999, with additional background provided by KHRG interviews conducted in the months preceding that period. Most of the interviews are with people in and from T'Nay Hsah, Myawaddy and Kawkareik townships of southeastern Pa'an District, though there are some interviews with people living slightly further north in Dta Greh, Hlaing Bwe and Lu Pleh townships, and one interview with a woman from far to the east in Mon State whose husband died as a porter in eastern Pa'an District. Their testimonies have been augmented by incident reports gathered by KHRG researchers in the region. Photographs which relate to the situation described in this report can be seen in KHRG Photo Set 99-B (18/8/99) [http://metalab.unc.edu/ freeburma/humanrights/khrg/archive/photoreports/99photos/set99b/paan. html]. Order documents sent to villages by SPDC and DKBA units in the area can be seen in "SPDC Orders to Villages: Set 99-B" (KHRG #99-03, 19/4/99) [http://metalab.unc.edu/freeburma/humanrights/khrg/archive/ khrg99/khrg9903b.html] and "SPDC and DKBA Orders to Villages: Set 99-C" (KHRG #99-06, 4/8/99) [http://metalab.unc.edu/freeburma/ humanrights/khrg/archive/khrg99/khrg9906.html].

This report consists of several parts: this preface, an introduction/summary, a detailed description of the situation including quotes from interviews and order documents. The full text of the interviews can be seen at [http://metalab.unc.edu/freeburma/humanrights/khrg/archive/khrg99/khrg9908a.html].

Map of Pa'an District

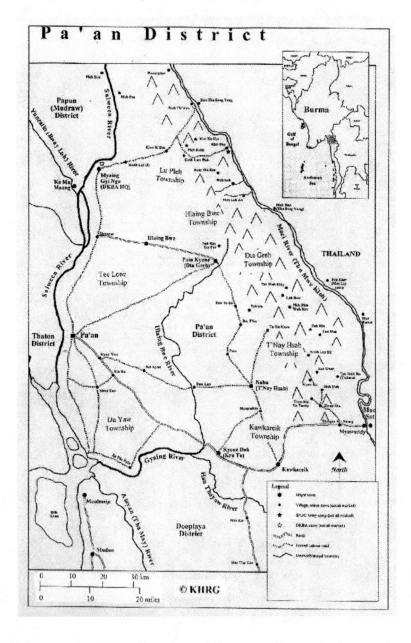

Notes on the Text

In the text all names of those interviewed have been changed and some details have been omitted or replaced by 'xxxx' where necessary to protect people from retaliation. The captions under quotes used in the report include the interviewee's (changed) name, gender, age and village, and a reference to the interview number and date. These numbers can be used to find the full text of the interview in the KHRG web site at [http://metalab.unc.edu/freeburma/humanrights/khrg/archive/khrg99/khrg 9908a.html].

The text often refers to villages, village tracts and townships. The SPDC has local administration, called Peace & Development Councils, at the village, village tract, township, and state/division levels. A village tract is a group of 5-25 villages centred on a large village. A township is a much larger area, administered from a central town. The Karen National Union (KNU) divides Pa'an District into five townships: Lu Pleh in the northeast, Dta Greh in the central east, T'Nay Hsah in the southeast, Tee Lone in the northwest, and Du Yaw in the southwest. The official townships used by the SPDC do not correspond to the Karen townships; for example, the SPDC uses Myawaddy, Kawkareik and Hlaing Bwe townships. This report primarily uses the KNU townships, except where a village is closer to the SPDC township centre. The SPDC does not recognise the existence of Pa'an District, but only uses Townships, States and Divisions.

All numeric dates in this report are in dd/mm/yy format. In the interviews we have translated as '*paddy*' the term for rice which has been threshed and winnowed but still has a husk, and '*rice*' to mean husked rice ready for cooking. It takes about 2 baskets of paddy to make 1 basket of rice; villagers usually store it as paddy and only pound or mill small quantities into rice at a time. Villagers often refer to '*loh ah pay*'; literally this is the traditional Burmese form of voluntary labour for the community, but the SPDC uses his name in most cases of forced labour, and to the villagers it has come to mean most forms of forced labour with the exception of long-term portering. '*Set tha*' is forced labour as messengers and "errand-boys" for the soldiers. Villagers often refer to the KNU/KNLA as *Kaw Thoo Lei*, the DKBA as *Ko Per Baw* ('Yellow Headbands'), and SPDC troops and officials as 'the Burmese'. SPDC officers often accuse villagers of being '*Nga Pway*' ('ringworm'); this is derogatory SPDC slang for KNLA soldiers. Villagers' exclamations such as '*Pwah!*' and '*Der!*' are transliterated in the text as they are pronounced.

Introduction

*"Being a villager is the very worst because we have to feed both sides.
You can't give to only one side, because if you give to just one, the other
side hates you. If the Burmese force you, you have to go. If the Kaw Thoo
Lei [KNLA] force you, you have to go. If DKBA forces you, you have to
go. So it is the worst being a villager."* - "Naw Ther Paw" (F, xx), xxxx
village, T'Nay Hsah township (Interview #32, 8/99)

Located in central Karen State, Pa'an District is bounded in the west and
north by the Salween River and the town of Pa'an (capital of Karen
State), in the east by the Moei River which draws the border with
Thailand, and in the south by the motor road from Myawaddy (on the
Thai border, west of Mae Sot) westward to Kawkareik and Kyone Doh.
The region referred to as the southeastern part of the District extends
from the Moei River westward to the town of T'Nay Hsah (Nabu), and is
bounded in the north by Dta Greh (Pain Kyone). While the western part
of Pa'an District has been controlled by the SPDC for over 10 years, the
KNLA has maintained a steady influence over the eastern strip near the
Thai border including the Dawna Mountains and the narrow strip of land
between them and the Moei River, which forms the border with Thailand.
The KNLA also regularly penetrates partway into the plains west of the
Dawna. Pa'an District is also known as the KNLA's 7th Brigade area.
All of the villagers in this region are Karen rice farmers, predominantly
Buddhist with Animist and Christian minorities.

Since the capture of the KNU headquarters at Manerplaw in northeastern
Pa'an District in January 1995, the SPDC has intensified its presence in
the area in order to undermine the KNLA's loose but steady grip on the
region. Under-manned and lacking both arms and ammunition, the
KNLA has compensated by using 'landmine warfare' in order to prevent
the advance of SPDC columns in the area. The SPDC has responded by
continuing to increase its troop presence in the region despite heavy
landmine casualties, and the Army is ever increasing its own use of
landmines and rounding up of porters to walk in front of the columns to
detonate any mines. The DKBA has also begun extensive use of its own
landmines. As a result, eastern Pa'an District is probably now the most
heavily landmined area in Burma. All armies involved in the conflict
plant landmines, but innocent villagers are often the ones to detonate
them, either accidentally as they come and go from their fields and
villages, or intentionally when they are used as human minesweepers by
the SPDC and DKBA. Though the KNLA warns villagers about the
location of its landmines, the DKBA and the SPDC do not, and in some

cases deliberately place them in areas where they know villagers will detonate them. Fear of stepping on landmines while portering, being used as human minesweepers, or simply farming their fields has caused many people to flee their villages.

Villagers interviewed by KHRG for this report cite many reasons for flight from their villages, beginning with forced labour imposed by both the SPDC and DKBA. Often patrolling together, these armies enter villages and occupy homes for indefinite periods of time; villagers rarely know when troops will come, and live in fear of a military presence in their village. Villagers no longer have money to pay bribes to avoid forced labour, so they must personally fulfil the village's quota for forced labourers at worksites near their villages or at Army camps. Poorly rationed troops relentlessly loot from villagers, who can also no longer afford to replenish lost food and belongings. With the demands for forced labour always increasing, overtaxed villagers also cannot find time to work their own fields. The Army constantly loots their rice supply, demands burdensome rice quotas from farmers, and in at least one area is now burning the villagers' paddy and placing landmines in their fields so farmers cannot continue harvesting their crops. All of these factors are making hunger the villagers' chief preoccupation. Ultimately they know that if they fail to meet the Army's impossible demands, they face severe punishment in the form of arrest, physical abuse, and potentially death.

"We left because we couldn't tolerate the persecution anymore. We felt it from all sides. Even if we stayed in the village and used a flashlight at night, they would shoot us and not be punished for it [SPDC units regularly issue orders that villagers are only allowed to carry firebrands to light their way around the village at night, and that they will shoot at anyone carrying a flashlight]. This year before the rainy season they shot a villager named Pa B--- and his two friends who were looking after their elephants, but even then we dared not say anything. Whenever we had to go to porter for them and had no money to pay the fee, we worried that we would die. We dared not complain when they stole our chickens and pigs, or they would glare at us. When the owners weren't in the houses, they took our belongings too. Then they demanded rice and told us they would give it back, but they didn't. If they needed it they took it as they liked. If the owner wasn't home when they came, they looted the paddy and carried it off to eat. If your paddy was gone you would starve. So we didn't have enough, and we had to leave." - "Pa Kyaw" (M, 40), B'Naw Kleh Kee village, T'Nay Hsah township (Interview #22, 8/99)

The SPDC's strategy in southeastern Pa'an District, as in other parts of Burma, is to squash the remaining presence of the opposition army by intimidating villagers into renouncing all connections to the KNLA, systematically impoverishing villages so they cannot provide material support for the opposition, and bringing villagers under direct Army control. Since 1996 the Army's main tactic in this strategy has been to forcibly relocate remote villages in the Dawna Mountains region to SPDC and DKBA Army bases and forced labour sites. This accomplishes two goals simultaneously: villagers are more easily guarded which prevents KNLA contact, and the Army has a ready supply of villagers to draw upon for forced labour projects such as the building of military access roads. The Army increased its presence throughout the Dawna, and in 1998 it attacked and destroyed several villages on the eastern slopes of the Dawna without warning, causing all the villagers to flee (see "Uncertainty, Fear and Flight", KHRG #98-08, 18/11/98) [http://metalab.unc.edu/freeburma/humanrights/khrg/archive/khrg98/khrg 9808.html]. This year the militarisation and resulting abuses have continued to increase, and to deliver the final blow to the villagers the SPDC has issued an order to clear out all remote villages in southeastern Pa'an District, primarily in the Meh Pleh Toh area, before the end of 1999. They have told villagers that anyone left after the deadline to move has passed will be shot. Villagers have been ordered to move to two main sites, one at a DKBA Army base in Ker Ghaw, and one at Tee Wah Blaw. Villagers fear relocating to the designated sites because they know that in most cases they will not be able to return to their fields because they are quite far away, the villagers are guarded at all times, and outside movement is severely restricted. The Army does not supply families with a rice ration, nor are they allowed to plant gardens or forage for food elsewhere. Due to the grim conditions of the relocation sites and the mounting presence of abusive troops in their villages, many choose to flee into the jungle rather than wait to be forcibly moved.

"There are about 100 Burmese soldiers who stay in Taw Oak. Before that, their troops were only staying in Ker Ghaw. The commander's name is Kyaw Zay Ya [commander of the troops from LIB #118]. It might be his soldiers who come to our village, but people said he does not come himself. The Burmese are working with the DKBA. After I came here, the people said there are many Burmese soldiers in Pah Klu village." - "Naw Mu Mu Wah" (F, 50), Taw Oak village, T'Nay Hsah township (Interview #30, 8/99)

Pa'an District is the headquarters of the Democratic Karen Buddhist Army (DKBA), and it maintains a strong presence in the southeast. Since its founding in 1994 with the backing of the SLORC, the DKBA and the SLORC/SPDC have collaborated on the common goal of ridding the area of the KNLA. Trust between the two armies is minimal to nonexistent, however, and the DKBA reluctantly works with the SPDC mainly because Rangoon supplies its food, arms, and ammunition. In return, the DKBA helps the SPDC by acting as guides, fingering villagers with KNLA connections, doing much of the actual fighting with the KNLA and providing convenient cover for cross-border incursions into Thailand. The SPDC stopped paying cash salaries to DKBA soldiers 3 years ago and threatened to cut off the DKBA's provisions by the end of 1998, but it appears that this has not in fact occurred. It is clear that the DKBA and the SPDC continue to work together in the region, to the extent that villagers often confuse which soldiers belong to which army. They inflict the same abuses on the villagers, from forced labour to heavy fees, and they share the strategy of purging the KNU from the region by starving their support base—the villagers who supply them with food and necessary materials.

"In the month of October their commander's name was Captain H---, and the troops were from #207 [SPDC Battalion]. They came and said that they will behave peacefully. They came and said that they will gather all the villagers together and do good things. They said that we must not stay in the forest, that we must all come back and stay together in the village and then they wouldn't beat or torture us. Then after the villagers came back to stay together in the village, they gathered 30 villagers and forced them onto a truck, and forced them to go with them back to the Moei River [as porters to the Thai border]. All of them were from our village. One of them died by stepping on a landmine, not on the way but on the way back. He died when he ran to escape at Thay K'Yah." - "Saw Tha Wah" (M, 32), xxxx village, T'Nay Hsah township (Interview #3, 11/99)

Aside from the dominating presence of the SPDC and DKBA, there are other smaller groups of troops in southeastern Pa'an District. Of particular note is a group of troops staying in Pah Klu village who bear a strong resemblance to the Sa Thon Lon Guerrilla Retaliation Units that began operating in Nyaunglebin District in September 1998 (see part 1, "Death Squads and Displacement: Systematic Executions, Village Destruction and the Flight of Villagers in Nyaunglebin District"). Commissioned as the SPDC's special execution squads, the Sa Thon Lon move from village to village executing anyone suspected of connections with the KNU/KNLA. The villagers' name for the Sa Thon Lon is 'Baw Bi Doh' ['Short Pants'], which describes the soldiers' civilian dress, but residents of Pah Klu call the troops staying in their village 'S'Ker Po' ['Short Skirts'], a sarcastic reference to their attempts to rape women villagers. These troops have yet to execute any villagers in the brutal way associated with the Sa Thon Lon—usually by cutting the civilian's throat—but the dress and manner of these soldiers have made some villagers suspect they could be one of these feared units. A villager from northeastern Pa'an District also reported that in that area the SPDC is forcibly recruiting people in their villages to serve in village-based militias. By letter to the village head, the SPDC conscripts a certain number of male villagers whom the other villagers are then instructed to support with a salary and rations. The Army outfits the militia members with weapons and charges them with guarding the village from enemy contact, but the SPDC often finds their greatest use for such villagers as cannon fodder in battles with the KNLA.

The villagers remaining in this area are struggling against all odds to survive. Villagers in the Pah Klu, Taw Oak, and B'Naw Kleh Kee area claim that most of their villages are already cleared out as people have fled before being forcibly moved. Villagers have been enduring the extensive abuses just to make it to the harvest of October/November 1999, only to have the harvest fail because they were busy doing forced labour or hiding from patrols. One villager from the hills of T'Nay Hsah township told KHRG that while harvesting in November, SPDC troops came while people were harvesting, burned the rice already harvested and landmined the crop still remaining in the fields. Many villagers are either joining the thousands still displaced in the jungle without adequate food, medicine or shelter, or they are braving the journey to the Thai border where they find their hopes for safety thwarted by full refugee camps and aggressive Thai soldiers. For these villagers, their past is destroyed, their present is unstable, and their future is ominous

"If I go back I won't even have a pot. I sold all my pots and plates. If I stay here, I have no pots, plates, or a house. I have no one to help me. I don't know where to go." - "Naw Bway" (F, 29), Pa Noh village, Kyaik Mayaw township, Mon State (Interview #27, 8/99)

Suffering in the villages

Forced Labour

"When they entered the village the Burmese collected porters and other people for forced labour. Each month they demanded 5 porters to work for them, and if you could not go you had to give them money. We had to pay 2,500 Kyat per person for 3 days. They also demanded that for every 10 houses we send 4 people for 'set tha' [forced labour as messengers and doing other errands]. We could never stop to take a rest. Someone had to go every day and if we could not go we had to give money, 800 Kyat per day. A group of villagers had to be there every day to porter, and we would take turns going in groups for 5 days at a time." - "Pa Kyaw" (M, 40), B'Naw Kleh Kee village, T'Nay Hsah township (Interview #22, 8/99)

Widespread, relentless forced labour is the most common complaint among villagers from southeastern Pa'an District, who commonly cite it as the primary reason for fleeing their villages. The most common type of forced labour has traditionally been road construction, and from 1995-96 villagers were used to build and upgrade a network of roads linking the main towns of Kyone Doh, Kawkareik, Nabu, Pain Kyone, Pa'an and Myaing Gyi Ngu. As the Burmese Army presence in the region intensifies, building and maintaining new roads remains a priority to facilitate transportation between SPDC Army camps. In this area there are only dirt roads, so villagers are forced to repair them every year after the rainy season washes away the work accomplished the previous year.

"Last year before I went to porter, I also had to dig a road at B'Naw Kleh Kee. It was horrible. I had to go for 5 days and take my own food. Five villagers at a time had to go from each of Toh Thu Kee, Kwih Lay, Kyaw Ko, Ker Ghaw, and Thay K'Dtee [villages]. We dug a road from Lay Kaw Tee to Meh Pleh and Kway Sha. We had to work the whole day except for time to cook rice and eat it. We dug out logs and bamboo stumps and carried rocks." - "Pa Ghaw" (M, 35), Toh Thu Kee village, T'Nay Hsah township (Interview #38, 7/99)

"The villagers have to go to fetch water, find firewood, and carry rice for them. On each turn we had to carry 10 times. Two villagers would go every day, and one person has to carry 2 big tins each time [about 32 kg / 70 lb]. It is very far, about 1 furlong [220 yards] distance. Once they had enough water, they forced us to carry firewood. If they didn't need

firewood, they forced us to send letters. If we didn't send the letters, they punished us. I also had to cut and clear alongside the car road [the Myawaddy/Thingan Nyi Naung road]. We even had to fence the bridges where the cars pass." - "Saw Ler" (M, 36), Paw Baw Ko village, T'Nay Hsah township (Interview #29, 8/99)

"We didn't have any more money for 'set tha' [to avoid forced labour as messengers] and so we had to go in person. If we went for 'set tha' and also portering, we would come back from 'set tha' one day and the next day have to go as porters. Then we would porter for 3 days and there would be no replacement because they had come to our homes to collect people for 'set tha' or 'loh ah pay' already. So we had no time to do it all in person because if we went then we had to pay money too, and so we couldn't tolerate it." - "Pa Kyaw" (M, 40), B'Naw Kleh Kee village, T'Nay Hsah township (Interview #22, 8/99)

"...they are still clearing the place to plant rubber. I think they are planning to plant rubber between Toh Kaw Ko and Dta Weh Dah. They are building a road between those places this year. Last year it still didn't reach Toh Kaw Ko, only Dta Weh Dah, but this year they will continue it. Last year we had to dig the road, but this year the Toh Kaw Ko villagers will have to do it." - the mother of "Nan Paw Oa" (F, 18), xxxx village, Kawkareik township (Interview #42, 7/99)

All the types of forced labour are too numerous to mention, but they can be grouped into 3 general categories: 'loh ah pay', 'set tha', and portering. When villagers refer to 'loh ah pay', the work required usually entails a 1-3 day commitment and relates to general jobs like construction of Army bunkers or fences at the camp, road-building, and cutting firewood or bamboo. 'Set tha' is the term used to describe chores like serving as a messenger between Army camps, or simply being on call to meet the random demands of officers. Portering is often classified in a category of its own, and is discussed at length in the following section. Villages located nearest the Army camps bear the greatest burden of forced labour, since their proximity makes it convenient for troops to round them up quickly. In addition to roads and facilities, the greater concentration of troops in the area also necessitates a greater food supply; since troops receive only meagre rations at best from Rangoon, the Army confiscates fields near the camp and orders the villagers to work them. An officer will usually issue orders to a village head demanding a quota of villagers for forced labour who must report to the camp or worksite at a specified date and time. The village head then decides which villagers must go, usually implementing a rotation system calling for one person per family. Villagers are never safe, however, from the threat of capture by Burmese and DKBA soldiers looking for people to perform everything from trivial chores to intense physical labour. The next page shows the direct translation of a typical order issued to a village by an SPDC officer and illustrates the type of demands placed upon villagers on a regular basis [see Order #9, "SPDC Orders to Villages: Set 99-C" (KHRG #99-06, 4/8/99); a copy of the original order is included on page 59 of this report].

Stamp: #97 Infantry Battalion
#97 Infantry Battalion   Kawkareik
Military Control Command   Reference: 1000 / 97 / xxxx

Date: 1999 June 12th

To: Chairpersons
      xxxx / yyyy village groups
      Village Peace & Development Council

Subject: To send volunteer servants

For cultivation at #97 Infantry Battalion [camp], send 5 cattle (with plough) and 15 people (with mattocks) to xxxx on 13-6-99, you are hereby informed.

[Sd.]
(for) Battalion Commander

Copies to:
      Office Copy
      File
xxxx

The informal rotation system implemented by many village heads theoretically disperses the burden so that each family will have time to tend their own fields, but with the demand for labourers ever increasing, villagers are finding it more and more difficult to make time for their own work. As the above order reveals, the villagers are often instructed to bring along their own oxen, bullock carts, and tools to use while working, eliminating the possibility of family members tending the fields while they are gone. As one villager bluntly describes it, *"We had to pay four different ways: our own labour, fees, our bullock carts, and our cattle."* ["Kyaw Soe" (M, xx), xxxx village, Myawaddy township (Interview #31, 8/99)] Due to the increasing and constant demands for forced labour from both the DKBA and the SPDC—which can amount to several times per month, or even half the work week—the villagers must neglect their fields, leaving little possibility of harvesting enough rice to sustain them throughout the year. Hunger is thus an ever-present worry among villagers. Following last year's drought, villagers were hoping for a good harvest this year, but the call for forced labour, often at great distances from their villages, obligates them to remain away from their fields for days on end at crucial times in the crop cycle. When they return they are often too exhausted to satisfy the demands their own fields require.

"They did that near their battalion camp. They have 2 paddy fields that the villagers have to go and work on for them. They don't do it themselves. The villagers have to do it every year." - "Saw Lah Baw" (M, 31), Paw Baw Ko village, T'Nay Hsah township (Interview #28, 8/99)

"At the Burmese camp now there is a farm, so we must go to plough, sow, and transplant paddy in their field. If you have buffaloes and a plough, you must go to plough, and if you have nothing you must go to dig the earth, sow, and transplant. At harvest time, they force people to reap for them until it is finished. As for us, we don't even have enough food for our family, and no time to work for ourselves...[Also] the road that leads from Kawkareik to Mya Pa Deh [Myapadine] and T'Nay Hsah. The width of the road is approximately 10 cubits [15 feet]. We had to dig earth and put it on the road to build its height to 4 or 5 cubits [8-foot high embankment]. People from the whole village had to go. If you had money you could hire others, but if you didn't have money you had to go. People who had bullock carts had to go with bullock carts. We had to take our own rice, fishpaste, and chillies from our house. We even had to take our own machetes, axes, mattocks and spades." - "Maung Hla" (M, 30), Kru Bper village, Kawkareik township (Interview #44, 4/99)

"I went twice and had to plough the field. The other villagers went during the time of transplanting the seedlings and harvesting. They even forced us to do it in the rainy season. I was not free to do my own work." - "Saw Ler" (M, 36), Paw Baw Ko village, T'Nay Hsah township (Interview #29, 8/99)

"I always had to go for 'loh ah pay' every day. They forced people who live in the fields to go, and if they didn't the soldiers chased them and captured them. The fields are destroyed because no one is working on them." - "Pa Po Doh" (M, 24), Tee Hsah Ra village, Myawaddy township (Interview #39, 7/99)

The rainy season, usually a time of respite from forced labour for the villagers, was particularly stressful this year, as the Burmese augmented their demands and forced the villagers to work in the very worst conditions. Villagers who chose to hire people rather than work in dangerous conditions on slippery roads and elsewhere paid so much money in fees that they depleted all their savings, sold their possessions or went into debt. Both the SPDC and DKBA collect forced labour fees from villagers who cannot or choose not to go. Seldom are the villagers excused from forced labour shifts if they are sick or have other legitimate reasons, so instead they must pay a fee—typically 500 Kyat per day—to hire someone else to replace them. Villagers may hire replacements in three ways: by personally seeking out a fellow villager or an itinerant day labourer to hire, by paying the village head the fee and leaving it up to him/her to hire a replacement, or the most common way, which occurs when villagers hand over the fee to the village head, who then pays the SPDC Army. This last option especially creates a distressing cyclical pattern for the villagers, who hand over a sum of money intended for hiring substitutes. The soldiers pocket these 'fees', then go to other villagers demanding 'volunteer workers'. These villages in turn pay their obligatory fees instead of going in person, until eventually the soldiers have accrued a substantial amount of money from the villagers but are left with no workers. This prompts them to capture villagers while they are working in their fields; villagers have the option of running and being shot at, or being captured to serve as porters or forced labourers. This is why many villagers complain of paying twice, once in fees and once by their work.

"If the men don't stay in the village they force the women to go and carry rice whenever they run out. They force one villager per house to go. If the villagers are not free to go, they have to hire someone for 500 Kyat per day. We have to pay the village head and then the village head repays the one who goes in the villager's place." - "Naw Lay Wah" (F, 25), Pah Klu village, T'Nay Hsah township (Interview #36, 7/99)

"Der! All of the villagers have to give, and the people who can't give have to sell their rice and paddy to give money to them. Each family has to hire someone for 1,000 Kyat or more per time; some families have to give 2,000 Kyat. They don't care about young or old people; young and old all have to go. They force children as young as 10, and some people who go are 50 or 60 and have grey hair already. Some people who went came back and told us that they hadn't eaten for 4 or 5 days. As for me, I was afraid and I didn't go, also because I am a woman and mostly men go. In our village other women have gone, but I never went." - "Naw Paw Htoo" (F, 27), Taw Oak village, T'Nay Hsah township (Interview #9, 9/99)

One of the most alarming consequences of the increased demand for forced labour is the rise of child labour. With a diminishing supply of able-bodied adults to satisfy the Army's demands since men and later women flee to avoid portering shifts, or are already working for the Army, families must resort to sending their children, especially when other adults must stay to work the fields. Children as young as 10 have been sent by their families, or even captured by troops, to work as forced labourers, and many drop out of school because they have to go on a regular basis. Similarly, elderly family members must fulfill the quota if no one else in the family can work. It is now quite common for women to go for 'loh ah pay' more often than men, who either remain to work the fields or flee to avoid capture as porters. One villager succinctly explained, *"Mostly they need men but the men hide, therefore the girls have to go."* ["Saw Daniel" (M, 70), Dta Greh village, Hlaing Bwe township (Interview #41, 7/99)] Particularly in the Ker Ghaw area, the site of a large DKBA camp and relocation site, villagers of all ages and physical ability are forced to do labour of some kind.

"The youngest are children, as soon as they can work. Children who are over 10 years old. The oldest who have to go and make fences are old enough to be grandparents. Women too. Recently P--- worked for them and she is over 50. My wife and children had to carry water for them, they couldn't avoid it." - "Pa Noh" (M, 45), B'Naw Kleh Kee village, T'Nay Hsah township (Interview #12, 9/99)

"If the village head couldn't collect us, they arrested people themselves. Even women and children have to go, some as young as 12 and 13 years old. If their parents are sick, the children have to go. People 40 and 50 years old have to go if they are strong and can work. They forced us to dig the road and build bunkers beside it in Hsah Htoo Gone, between Myawaddy and [Thingan] Nyi Naung. They also forced us to weed the road, cut the grass, haul bamboo, build fences, and cut small trees and bamboo to build their bunkers." - "Pi Ghaw Paw" (F, 51), Meh K'Neh village, Myawaddy township (Interview #40, 7/99)

"For 'loh ah pay' we had to do many kinds of work like plough the fields, clean the roads, cut down trees and bamboo, make fences, and build bridges. Also we had to build their bunkers, since they set up their camp only 30 yards from our village. Villagers had no time to rest; both men and women had to work for them. They demanded one person from each house each day, but because we couldn't finish our own work that way the village head arranged for 10 villagers to go per day. The old people asked their children to go for 'loh ah pay', and the youngest one was just

over 10 years old. We had children around 12 and 13 working also.
Children under 10 had to carry water for them." - "Saw Po Doh" (M,
36), B'Naw Kleh Kee village, T'Nay Hsah township (Interview #23,
8/99)

"Ah, ah! Do not talk of 'loh ah pay'! I had to buy food from the Burmese
soldiers' wives who sold it for 200 Kyat, but I only brought 100 Kyat
with me. I worked very hard. I carried earth on my head like this. They
came and took a video of us and I thought to myself, 'Go ahead, if you
want to take a video of a tall woman carrying a load on her head!'" - the
mother of "Nan Paw Oa" (F, 18), xxxx village, Kawkareik township
(Interview #42, 7/99)

The conditions for forced labour vary by the type and frequency of work
required, the length of the duty, and especially by the treatment of the
labourers by the troops. Often the village head is called upon to supervise
the villagers at forced labour, which in some villages obligates him/her to
serve every day, leaving no time for personal work. Because of this
demand and the severe punishment that the village head faces if the
forced labour requirements are not met, villagers dread the appointment
as village head. Many villagers report that verbal and physical abuse are
prevalent at the work sites, particularly if soldiers think that villagers are
not working fast enough. Villagers usually work a full day with only one
break to eat, though sometimes they are required to stay overnight at the
worksite or Army camp. They must bring all their own food and are often
denied water and permission to rest, even when working in the midday
sun. These conditions vary, however, and some troops are kinder on
villagers than others; the DKBA, for example, usually requires villagers
to do 'loh ah pay' for shorter periods of time under better conditions than
the SPDC. The villagers attribute the heavy demands for forced labour in
southeastern Pa'an District as a major cause of flight from the area. They
remain in their villages as long as they are physically able to do so, but
the threat of physical abuse combined with the lingering fear of
starvation leaves them with flight as their only viable option [see "Flight
and Internally Displaced People" below].

"They did not guard us, but they came to look at us sometimes as they
forced us to work. The children who couldn't speak Burmese were
beaten, but people who could speak Burmese weren't beaten. I saw them
beat Pa N--- with my own eyes. They slapped his face. He slapped him
twice with his right hand. He told him he was stupid because he couldn't
speak Burmese. Pa N--- is married, he is from B'Naw Kleh Kee." - "Pa

Noh" (M, 45), B'Naw Kleh Kee village, T'Nay Hsah township (Interview #12, 9/99)

"The DKBA don't collect money, but they force us to do 'loh ah pay'. The villagers have to go and stay with them and cook rice and fetch water. They force us to do it once a month. As for the Burmese, they don't even care if they force us to go twice or three times a month. The Burmese are always forcing the villagers to go." - "Saw Lah Ku" (M, 21), Pah Klu village, T'Nay Hsah township (Interview #18, 8/99)

"I had to plant rubber. They have already planted many rubber trees in lines. Many people had to go, so we had to do it for 2-3 days, then we went home. They didn't give us anything to eat. We had to take our own food there too, but they gave medicine to the workers who were ill, and if they couldn't work anymore they sent them home." - "Maung Hla" (M, 30), Kru Bper village, Kawkareik township (Interview #44, 4/99)

"They didn't give us anything [money] and they didn't feed us rice. They didn't give us water to drink, either. They were always very angry. If I look back on my life, this was the very worst time. My heart was gone." - "Naw Ther Paw" (F, xx), xxxx village, T'Nay Hsah township (Interview #32, 8/99)

Portering

"My husband died 15 days ago. The Burmese forced him to do 'loh ah pay' [she means portering]. They said that he would only have to go for a few days, but they forced him to go for 10 days. We couldn't hire someone to go for him because we had no money. They said that the villagers who didn't go had to pay them money, that's why we had to go. He had not even been gone for 10 days when people sent me a message that he had died. I didn't know anything. I went to ask the Burmese soldiers and they said he died on the borderline. One of his friends said, 'I saw him when they arrested him, but I don't know where he carried because I didn't see him again'. I went to find him at Ka Daung and Mudon, but I couldn't find anything. After that I didn't know where to go. I thought that I would go to his younger brother, but I couldn't. In the past I stayed in the village, but I have no parents or siblings there. We left the village 10 days after we heard that he died. I have a younger brother who stays in Thailand, but I don't know where. That's why I came up to my Uncle's house, but my Uncle hasn't seen him and can't find him. When I arrived at my Uncle's place, I didn't know where to go

next." - "Naw Bway" (F, 29), Pa Noh village, Kyaik Mayaw township, Mon State (Interview #27, 8/99)

Portering is technically classified as forced labour, but to villagers it falls in a category of its own. The KNLA regularly demands young and middle-aged men for shifts of portering usually lasting one to several days. In the past, the SPDC and DKBA troops primarily targeted male villagers as well, but the influx of troops in southeastern Pa'an District leaves all villagers living in constant fear of being arrested for portering. While serving as porters for SPDC or DKBA troops villagers must remain with the troops for days on end and endure extremely demanding work while they are routinely denied food and often beaten. Young men flee the village immediately upon hearing that troops are in the vicinity, running as fast as they can into the jungle to avoid capture. Villagers try to warn each other when troops are roaming the area looking for porters, but this informal communication network proves only partially effective. Soldiers capture porters if their demands from a particular village for forced labour have not been met, or if they happen to pass men working in their fields while on patrol. If seen running to escape, villagers are shot on sight. Those captured must drop everything to serve as porters often for unspecified periods of time. Men who manage to avoid capture hide out in the jungle, sometimes with no food or shelter, until the troops have moved on - which may take weeks.

"Then they came out of the forest, they entered the village in the night and the dogs didn't even bark at them. They arrived and fired their guns for a while. He captured me and touched me with his gun. He wouldn't even let me urinate, he ordered me to go so I had to go. Some people who could run to escape didn't need to go, but the people who they captured in the group all had to go. If you had 2 or 3 people in your family, they all had to go. They beat and kicked the people they captured before us. Then they went to Tee Hsah Ra, and they forced us to send them there. They forced me to go and carry bullets and shells for them." - "Saw Ghay" (M, 36), Tee Hsah Ra village, Myawaddy township (Interview #7, 9/99)

"The Burmese came to stay at Ker Ghaw when they went to the Lay Ta Play and Ko Ko areas to look for porters. The village head went around the village and told every family to come to a meeting. He said, 'Now the Burmese have arrived, so my dear children, if you do not want to be a porter, wrap up your sarong around your legs and run as fast as you can.' The village head dared not hand us over [to the Burmese], so we ran. Because our village is on the frontline, the Burmese often needed

porters when they came before." - "Saw Kee" (M, 21), Ker Ghaw village, T'Nay Hsah township (Interview #11, 9/99)

"In our village, the men always have to flee from the village. If they don't flee, the soldiers chase them to capture porters. One troop of Burmese stays in the village, and the other is ordered to capture the men. If they couldn't collect porter fees, they would capture the men." - "Saw Nya" (M, 60), Ker Ghaw village, T'Nay Hsah township (Interview #37, 7/99)

"The people who dare to stay in the village are captured by the Burmese. Many who try to flee have no food outside the village, so they must come back. When the Burmese are leaving the village, they capture the villagers as they like [to go with them]." - "Pa Kyaw" (M, 40), B'Naw Kleh Kee village, T'Nay Hsah township (Interview #22, 8/99)

When troops camp in or near a village for a significant period of time, the male villagers are forced to set up shelters in the jungle where they remain in an exiled state indefinitely, tending hill fields to survive. Occasionally the men will sneak back to the village secretly to visit their families and to get food and supplies, risking arrest if troops are still in the vicinity. If the SPDC or DKBA comes through looking for porters and finds few men in the village, they will often capture women, older people, and even children big enough to carry a sizeable load. Whereas villagers used to believe that women would be treated less brutally if they served as porters instead of men, now women are particularly terrified of portering because they constantly fear the possibility of rape. One villager from Dta Greh reported that SPDC 'Bpay Pwet', or 'payroll troops', head up into the hills each month to deliver salaries to soldiers, and that they usually collect women porters to follow them. As the 'Bpay Pwet' troops are not carrying heavy supplies, their specific demand for women is probably to use them as human minesweepers or for purposes of rape.

"Bpay Pwet [payroll troops] bring a salary once a month for the Burmese who stay in the mountains. ... they come and call the women to go with them." - "Saw Daniel" (M, 70), Dta Greh village, Hlaing Bwe township (Interview #41, 7/99)

"This year we had a lot of people who carried food for them. Even women had to carry for them, and this year mostly women did it because the men were afraid and ran away, but the women dared to stay for a bit, and they forced the women to porter. They were forcing us and touching

us with guns, so people had to go." - "Saw Maw Htoo" (M, xx), Pah Klu village, T'Nay Hsah township (Interview #34, 8/99)

"Ah! I saw a lot of older people with white hair whom they forced to go portering. The village head collects us but nobody dares to go. Therefore, the Burmese take the money and have to hire the porters. But if they can arrest us instead of hiring us, they can use all the money for themselves. If you give money to the Burmese they say that they have hired the porters, but we never saw them hire anyone. You can't do anything about that." - "Saw Nya" (M, 60), Ker Ghaw village, T'Nay Hsah township (Interview #37, 7/99)

The only recourse for captured villagers is to pay a "portering fee"—typically 500 Kyat a day—rather than going in person, which few villagers can afford anymore after repeated heavy taxation, crop quotas, and forced labour fees. This year the porter fees are steadily increasing as fewer people are available for hire, mainly because the risks of portering are so high that many villagers refuse to hire themselves out anymore. As with the forced labour fees, the portering fees are only squandered by the military, who then turn around and capture more porters. Villagers are now testifying that troops force villagers to porter even though they have already paid the "portering fees", in effect penalising them twice. Soldiers often break agreements with villages over the terms of portering by refusing to release them at the designated time, or in some cases holding porters hostage until the village head will pay for their release.

"Now people have to hire porters [to go in their place] for 3,000 Kyat because people dare not go for less than that." - "Pu K'Ner" (M, 60), Pah Klu village, T'Nay Hsah township (Interview #20, 8/99)

"They come and capture porters when their new friends [replacement troops] come. Every month they collect 7 porters from B'Naw Kleh Kee and Paw Baw Ko. We had to go for 3 days, then after 3 days those 7 people go home and another group has to go. They demanded that the village head collect people for portering. If people could not go they had to give money - 2,500 Kyat for 3 days. They didn't hire other people with the money, they just took it for themselves." - "Saw Po Doh" (M, 36), B'Naw Kleh Kee village, T'Nay Hsah township (Interview #23, 8/99)

"When I arrived there, I thought that they would release me, but they didn't. They released me when the village head came to pay them 1,500 Kyat. I had to carry for over one month but they still demanded 1,500

Kyat [to release him]." - "Pa Ghaw" (M, 35), Toh Thu Kee village, T'Nay Hsah township (Interview #38, 7/99)

After the fear surrounding arrest, they face the threat of abuse if caught and forced to serve as porters. If villagers cannot pay the fee to hire a replacement, they must typically porter on 5-7 day shifts to accompany SPDC or DKBA troops on patrol through the Dawna Mountains. Sometimes they are also called for shorter shifts to carry rations between Army camps. They carry immense loads of food, ammunition, and the soldiers' personal gear, and are often denied adequate food and drinking water. One porter described the food deprivation as so desperate that *"We had to steal from each other to eat enough."* ["Saw Maw Hla" (M, 30), Maw Goh village, Lu Pleh township (Interview #43, 7/99)]. In addition to malnourishment, they receive hardly any rest and no medical attention for injuries. A portering shift will often so debilitate a villager that s/he will spend one month or longer rehabilitating.

"They fed us twice a day, but it was not enough for us because they started early in the morning and we weren't fed until 10 a.m. Then we ate again at 4 p.m. For 5 people they spooned out just enough rice to cover the lid of the pot, then divided it into five and fed you. It was about the same as 2 eggshells full of rice and a spoon of beans, so it was not enough for us. I asked for more but we couldn't get anything more. If we asked for more again and again they glared at us, so we dared not stay close to them. They had enough rice to fill them, but the porters did not. I told him, 'Der! You do not feed us enough, so we cannot carry for you', and he told me, 'Don't argue with me. I feed you well enough already.' Then I said, 'Yes, it is delicious to eat rice with beans, but it is too little.' When you carry loads like that you become more hungry and tired, but if we ate like them we would not have been hungry." - "Saw Mo Aung" (M, 39), Pah Klu village, T'Nay Hsah township (Interview #13, 9/99)

"They gave me only a little rice and a little bit to drink twice a day. They fed us the same amount as the head of a cat [a small ball of rice]; it was not enough for us. They fed us only salt with rice and we didn't get water to drink, while they ate good food which they had brought for themselves. They didn't care if we ate enough or not. When I came back from portering, I was in so much pain that I had to drink many gallons of spirit water [traditional medicine]. I rested for one month." - "Pa Ghaw" (M, 35), Toh Thu Kee village, T'Nay Hsah township (Interview #38, 7/99)

"...the last time was during the rainy season when I had to climb the mountains to Meh Pleh. It was the time to plant paddy and it was raining a lot, so there was flooding. I climbed up the mountain for 3-4 days from Sghaw Ko and B'Naw Kleh Klee to Dta Thu Kee. We had to carry many kinds of loads, and even if you were already carrying bullets and shells they gave you food to carry as well. It must have been more than 20 viss [32 kg / 70 lb] because we could barely walk. They kicked you if you couldn't carry it, so you wouldn't dare tell them if you couldn't carry it. We couldn't take a rest except when they let us. Even if we were so tired that our sweat filled our nostrils, we could not rest or they would kick our behinds." - "Pa Kyaw" (M, 40), B'Naw Kleh Kee village, T'Nay Hsah township (Interview #22, 8/99)

DKBA and SPDC troops both treat their porters horribly, beating them at the slightest provocation. Because the porters are fed less than the troops while carrying heavier loads, they often have trouble keeping up and are severely punished if they lag behind. Porters who have returned to their villages tell stories of others who simply could not continue, and were savagely beaten before being left for dead by the soldiers in the middle of the jungle. Some are killed outright and left on the path without burial, while some die from wounds inflicted from landmines or physical abuse by the soldiers. Another disturbing trend of which villagers recently informed KHRG after their portering shifts is the distribution of Methamphetamines to porters in order to curb their appetites and numb their pain. The porters have no idea what drugs they are forced to consume, just that they leave them in mind-altered states with strange physical side-effects, often lasting well beyond their portering term.

"They gave me medicine, the kind that does not make you sweat but makes you happy to walk. In Kywe and Ta months [around April 1999] there was no shade in Lay Gaw, but because of our medicine we were not sweating. I don't know what kind of medicine it was, but when I arrived in Maw Pleh the people told me that you need a certain kind of medicine to counteract the medicine I had taken. But they didn't give us that one, so I became very sick." - "Saw Mo Aung" (M, 39), Pah Klu village, T'Nay Hsah township Interview #13, 9/99)

"One day one of us died and the Burmese told us he was their friend, but we didn't know if he was Burmese or not. He got sick from the rain and not enough food or sleep. He didn't have a shirt on, and they left him uncovered; we didn't know if he was dead yet, but we knew he would soon die if they left him. We thought he was a villager like us, because we came from different villages and didn't know everyone. I think if he was

their servant they would have treated him and taken him with them;
people said he was their friend but I can't believe it." - "Pa Kyaw" (M,
40), B'Naw Kleh Kee village, T'Nay Hsah township (Interview #22,
8/99)

"They beat me on the temples once. I tied up my load to the baskets and
the soldier asked me, 'Is that tied tightly?' and I answered him, 'It is
tight.' But when we were marching the shells fell down, so he beat me on
the temple. Another time he kicked me with his jungle boots when I was
picking up the fallen rice grains on the ground to eat. When we arrived
at a place where people had lived and recently left, I picked up some rice
to eat to curb my hunger since I hadn't eaten enough rice. He asked me,
'Why do you pick up that rice to eat? If they have poisoned it, you will
die.' And he kicked me with his boots on the head." - "Maung Hla" (M,
30), Kru Bper village, Kawkareik township (Interview #44, 4/99)

"They were Htay Htay Po, Pa Lone Tin, Pa Kyaw Wah, Sah K'Lin, and
Pa Oo Ngeh. The Burmese killed all of them because they couldn't carry
their loads when portering. They couldn't walk, so they fell down and the
soldiers kicked them. They stabbed them and beat them to death; they
didn't shoot them dead. " - "Saw Lay Htoo" (M, 42), xxxx village,
Hlaing Bwe township (Interview #10, 9/99)

One of the most frightening aspects of portering is the danger of stepping
on landmines. The KNLA lays landmines to compensate for being under-
manned and poorly equipped, and the SPDC/DKBA responds by planting
landmines of their own. As a consequence, Pa'an District is the most
densely mined area in Karen State. The fact that many porters would
rather risk escape through a heavily mined jungle than continuing to
serve as porters testifies to the desperation of their condition. Some
porters do escape successfully, but the dangers they face once in the
jungle prove very daunting. Weariness and disorientation are nothing
compared to the possibility of stepping on a landmine and losing life or
limb. Soldiers cultivate this fear in order to prevent escape, often telling
porters that they will die if they run, either from their bullets or from
landmines.

"They told us not to run because there were a lot of landmines, and also
we didn't know where to run to because we didn't know where we were.
They said that if I stepped on a landmine they wouldn't bury me but
would shoot me dead and throw me in a valley. If you listened to them
you were afraid, so we dared not run. ... During the time we were there 3
porters ran to escape, but they were killed by landmines. People said that

they were from Maw Toh Ta Lay and had been porters for over a month."
- "Saw Mo Aung" (M, 39), Pah Klu village, T'Nay Hsah township
(Interview #13, 9/99)

"The places where we ran were full of landmines. We didn't know the direction to run, but we ran ahead and reached Pah Klu even though we'd never been there before. When we arrived at Pah Klu, the Sgaw [Sgaw Karen] women asked us, 'How could you dare to come back this way? Landmines are everywhere. We are surprised to see you arrive here safely.' Some people ran into Burmese soldiers, though, so the soldiers tortured them." - "Maung Hla" (M, 30), Kru Bper village,
Kawkareik township (Interview #44, 4/99)

"One porter stepped on a landmine when he was carrying and they shot him. They didn't bring him back to the village. A villager from Pah Klu witnessed it." - "Naw Lay Wah" (F, 25), Pah Klu village, T'Nay Hsah
township (Interview #36, 7/99)

"Last year one porter died. His name was Hsah Po Dee, about 25 years old. He stepped on a landmine... He was going to hire someone to replace him, but he missed the car at Dta Greh Bridge, and so he had to go. Two groups of people came to replace the group he was in, but he didn't come back. Later the porters who were captured by the Burmese and went together with him returned to the village and said he had been injured by stepping on a mine. He shouted, but the Burmese didn't take care of him. He didn't die right away, but they couldn't go any further with him. No one carried him. His wife is still living in the village... The Burmese didn't come to tell her anything. After people knew about it they went and asked for compensation, but the Burmese refused to listen." -
"Saw Daniel" (M, 70), Dta Greh village, Hlaing Bwe township
(Interview #41, 7/99)

Landmines

"Many villagers' legs have been blown off from stepping on landmines. I foraged for food until I dared not forage any more. The last time I went foraging with other villagers, a girl's legs were blown off by a landmine and two of her sisters were hurt. They are over 20 years old and married. One did not lose her leg, but the other did. Two of my grandchildren also lost their legs. About 12 villagers from Ker Ghaw have been injured, and 3 have died. Kyaw Per died, he was about 50 years old. Also Lin Noh, who was about 30 years old, died this year. The villagers don't know if it is the Burmese or the KNLA who plants the landmines. We don't follow

them so we don't know. One of the villagers was shooting squirrels near his house and stepped on a landmine. Now no one dares to go on the upper side of the pagoda. They plant them near the village, by the pagoda and monastery, where the villagers go to take care of their cattle. When I went to find bamboo shoots there, one cow stepped on a mine. Boom!! It blew its front leg off, and it died." - "Saw Nya" (M, 60), Ker Ghaw village, T'Nay Hsah township (Interview #37, 7/99)

Landmines are being laid in ever-increasing numbers in southeastern Pa'an District by the SPDC, the DKBA and the KNLA. While the KNLA attempts to notify villagers of where they have laid their mostly hand-made mines, the SPDC and the DKBA never do so, and the SPDC often deliberately mines pathways to villagers' fields in order to kill or maim internally displaced people who are hiding in the forests. The number of civilian victims is increasing, and most die before they can be carried to any medical help. SPDC and DKBA columns are now regularly ordering villagers to march in front of their columns as human mine detonators, and fear of this form of forced labour has caused many people to flee their homes.

"I stepped on a landmine near our village one month ago. It was a Burmese landmine, and they put it beside our village. I was going to my hillfields with 5 friends of mine. ... Right after I got wounded people carried me to my farmfield hut and I slept one night in my hillfield. Then the next day people came and carried me back, and I got treated by a Burmese medic at xxxx. Then people carried me here and I slept 5 days on the way. We worried that the Burmese would come and question me about what happened, so I dared not stay." - "Naw Hser Paw" (F, 28), Tee Law Thay village, T'Nay Hsah township (Interview #26, 8/99)

"My daughter and grandchild stepped on landmines and died, so we dared not stay. If we had stayed longer, all of them would die because they tortured us a lot. My daughter stepped on a Ko Per Baw [DKBA] landmine and died 2 rainy seasons ago. She was 20 years old, and her name was Naw Sher Pa. They set up landmines at Kwih Baw Nee, not so far away, about one hour's walk. They set them along the villagers' path to trap their enemies. She died on the path and we went to see her. She had gone with her friend and her older sister, but her sister just got a wound on her leg under her knee. My daughter and my two-month-old grandson and a guest from Tee Hsah Ra village died right away. The guest was named Naw Shu, and she was around 50. They were coming back to the village at the time. It was at the time when the Burmese came to attack this side [to attack the KNLA east of the Dawna Mountains,

near the Thai border] that my daughter was killed by a landmine." - "Pu Tamla" (M, 60+), Taw Oak village, T'Nay Hsah township (Interview #8, 9/99)

The SPDC used to rely mainly on imported mines, but over the past few years China has provided them with factories and technology to produce most of their antipersonnel landmines themselves. The two main mines used by the SPDC are the MM1 and MM2, both made in Burma in factories supplied by China. The MM1 is a copy of the Chinese-made PMOZ-2 or 'corncob' mine, and the MM2 is a copy of the Chinese-made PMN mine; both of these Chinese models have been heavily used in Cambodia. They sometimes mount the MM1, more powerful than the MM2, on a post at waist level in long grass or scrub and rig it with a tripwire; in this way it will kill the villager who trips it and possibly several others rather than just blowing off his or her leg. The MM2 is modelled on a cheap Chinese-made mine which is flat, round and partly made of plastic; however, the Burmese version is made of metal. The SPDC Army has extensive stockpiles of Chinese-made mines and a few old U.S.-made mines, including the M76, but is increasingly reliant on the mines they manufacture themselves.

"A lot of women have to carry for the Burmese too. Der! Last year the Ko Per Baw forced women to go in front of them [to step on landmines] but the women didn't dare to go, so they forced the village head to go. He didn't dare to go either, but they pointed a gun at him and he had to. He went and he died. His name was P---. It happened at T---, next to xxxx." - "Naw Ther Paw" (F, xx), xxxx village, T'Nay Hsah twp. (Interview #32, 8/99)

The KNLA uses mines to shield certain areas from SPDC troops, and also lays them along pathways used by SPDC columns. These improvised mines are usually made of steel pellets and explosives encased in bamboo or other readily available materials, although the KNLA does have access to some landmines from Cambodia and Vietnam bought on the black market. Heavy casualties of SPDC soldiers in the past year from KNLA landmines have prompted the SPDC and DKBA to use villagers as human minesweepers. They often collect villagers in the area specifically to walk in front of a column of troops, to become human mine detonators and human shields against ambush. Most often, however, they require porters to march in front of troops, threatening to shoot anyone who refuses to go ahead. Soldiers frequently force porters to serve as guides if the territory is unfamiliar to them, in order to avoid KNLA landmines. The villagers have sometimes been told by the KNLA which pathways are mined, but they do not know exactly where the mines are and they are constantly afraid of triggering mines as they forge their way through the jungle. Some villagers told KHRG that even when they told SPDC troops that the KNLA had mined the path, the soldiers ordered them to proceed regardless.

"I was carrying a backpack, and he grabbed the backpack and pushed as strongly as he could. Der! He beat me because they forced us to walk and show the way but we dared not go in front of them. People had planted landmines there! I told him that people said there are landmines there, so we dared not go there anymore. If our legs disappeared, we would have nothing. One of my son's legs was blown off by a landmine. It was a Ko Per Baw landmine that had been planted a few years ago. But the soldiers only said that some people had warned us, so why were we so afraid? But they dared not go either, because they worried that their own legs would be blown off. I dared not go, but they went step by step. We thought it would be suicide to go like that. If I stepped on a landmine, maybe I would die or my legs would be blown off, so my life would be useless." - "Pu Than Nyunt" (M, 55), B'Nweh Pu village, T'Nay Hsah township (Interview #15, 9/99)

"I portered for them [SPDC troops] when they patrolled the area between Pah Klu and Ker Ghaw. They guarded us from behind and forced us to go in front of them and walk among the landmines. Four of us had to go in front of them and all of us were villagers. If the landmines were there, they would have liked us to die by them. We were afraid to go because we could not see where the landmines were buried underground. If I went and stepped on a landmine and my leg was blown off, how could I earn my living? My family would be broken-hearted, but I wouldn't dare to hang myself, even though it would break my heart." - "Saw Maw Htoo" (M, xx), Pah Klu village, T'Nay Hsah township (Interview #34, 8/99)

"They arrested us and tied us up, then they accused us of being Kaw Thoo Lei [KNU/KNLA], but we told them that we are not Kaw Thoo Lei and they shouldn't kill us. Then they forced us to go and give directions [serve as guides] for them because they don't know the way in the mountains. I went carefully along the way. If you didn't know the way, you would lose half your leg. We had to go with them for 7 days in the hills with landmines. We dared not go, but if we didn't go they would have shot us with their guns. We were afraid but had to go." - "Saw Lah Ku" (M, 21), Pah Klu village, T'Nay Hsah township   Interview #18, 8/99)

Landmines are one of the most prevalent and feared causes of death for villagers. The KNLA's notifications regarding which pathways they have mined are clearly insufficient, because villagers continue to detonate KNLA landmines. The SPDC and DKBA lay them covertly, often at night without informing villagers of their number or location, causing villagers injury or death when coming and going from their hill fields, or when taking their cattle to graze outside the village. Neither the SPDC nor the DKBA ever offers any compensation for injuries to people or animals as a result of landmines. Villagers are often left on paths to bleed to death, and if they manage to make it back to the village, the chance of medical attention is slim given the lack of trained medics or supplies in the villages. The villager would have to be carried to the nearest medical facility, a journey almost guaranteeing death for a seriously injured landmine victim.

"That morning he wanted to go and tend his hill field and he asked me to go with him and check the path. So I went and was checking [with a stick] along the way, but the landmines were buried beside the path. He was following me, he turned and stepped off the path and a landmine exploded. I turned and looked and saw him running without one foot, and I called to him, 'Don't run!'" - "Saw Lay Mu" (M, 33), xxxx village, T'Nay Hsah township, talking about what happened after SPDC troops mined their fields during this year's harvest (Interview #1, 11/99)

"During the night they sometimes encircled the village with landmines. They planted them surrounding the houses, and if they had sentry duty they planted them around themselves. They planted them surrounding Pah Klu village, but when morning came they took them out." - "Pu K'Ner" (M, 60), Pah Klu village, T'Nay Hsah township (Interview #20, 8/99)

Q: *"Are there landmines around Pah Klu village?"*
A: *"Yes, KNLA landmines. If the Burmese came to sleep in the village, they planted landmines at night near the village. Mostly the cattle stepped on the landmines, but two villagers died from stepping on landmines. They were Pa Kyaw Lu, who was about 30 years old, and I don't remember the name of the other one."* - "Naw Lay Wah" (F, 25), Pah Klu village, T'Nay Hsah township (Interview #36, 7/99)

"The DKBA laid the landmines near the village and along the way that the villagers take to go to their hill fields. Two villagers stepped on landmines and died. One was named Pa Plah Po. He was about 40 years old and has had many wives. Another one was a woman named Peh Peh,

who was also about 40 years old and had many children. She stepped on a landmine and then people brought her home. Then they sent her to Ra Ma Tee [Myawaddy] hospital, but as they were carrying her on the bullock cart she died halfway there. So they carried her back home. It happened in July [1999], when the villagers sow the seed paddy. The man also died in the same month." - "Naw Mu Mu Wah" (F, 50), Taw Oak village, T'Nay Hsah township (Interview #30, 8/99)

"In Taw Oak the DKBA set up a lot of landmines at the top of the village and beside the bank of the river. Just 2 months ago 2 women stepped on landmines when they were going fishing. One of them named Nga Bla Ree died; she was about 30 years old. The other one lost her leg; her name is Y--- and she is over 30. She still stays in the village. Her brother came here and said that they didn't take the pieces of shell out of her leg, and no one sent her anywhere." - "Taw Lay" (M, 41), Kwih Lay village, T'Nay Hsah township (Interview #6, 9/99)

The following order by Commander Chit Thu of DKBA Brigade #999 illustrates how the DKBA's response to the KNLA's planting of landmines in the area hurts innocent civilians more often than the combatants they were intended for. In this order sent to a village head, Chit Thu warns the village that the DKBA will plant landmines because the KNLA had already mined the area, but he does not specify the locations of the landmines, nor accept responsibility for the consequences the villagers may suffer. Instead, he implicitly threatens to shoot all villagers who run away. [See Order #P1, "SPDC Orders to Villages: Set 99-B"   [http://metalab.unc.edu/freeburma/humanrights/khrg/archive/ khrg99/khrg9903b.html] (KHRG #99-03, 19/4/99). This order was typed in Karen and signed with a signature stamp of Chit Thu, a well-known DKBA commander. 'DKBA' is spelt out phonetically as 'Dee Kay Bee Ay' rather than its Karen or Burmese equivalent. Similarly, 'KNU' is spelt out as 'Kay Eh Yu'.]

Democratic Karen Buddhist Army   Stamp:
Brigade #999   D.K.B.A. Brigade 999
Dee Kay Bee Ay   Special Battalion
                                  Ba Ma/0169, Lt. Col. Chit Thu

                                  Number - 999 / Ah Ta Dta Ya / 002
                                  Date: 2/2/99

To: _____ village tract / village
Subject: Distributing information

Regarding the above subject, xxxx area / village tract / village elders
/ all the people, as the KNU has informed the xxxx area, [they will]
place landmines 3 cubits [4½ feet] from the pathways so you cannot
go. They are not placing them to hurt their enemies like us, but to
give more problems to the people's / villager's belongings [meaning
livestock]. As the KNU can do it, mothers, fathers, siblings in the
villages, we inform you that we have the right to do it too. We are
full of love for you but we cannot take care of all.

Notes: 1) On 20/2/99 we will start placing landmines and small-scale
             fighting.
         2) Villagers we see when we enter villages anywhere must
             not run away.
         3) If anything happens to the people who run, we will not
             take responsibility.

                        [Sd. / Chit Thu]
                       Battalion Commander
                        Special Battalion
                          #999 Brigade
                        Dee Kay Bee Ay

Many villagers are terrified of going for forced labour shifts because of
the potential to encounter landmines while working. The SPDC/DKBA
uses villagers as "dispensable" labourers in high-risk areas where they do
not wish to send soldiers, particularly in places that were formerly
controlled by the KNLA, such as a logging site near Kawkareik where
villagers cut logs in a heavily mined forest. Villagers are also being used
as minesweepers at Army camps to clear mines laid by the KNLA,
particularly when an SPDC or DKBA column stays for a long time in the
village and could be the target of a KNLA ambush. A villager from
B'Nweh Pu reported that the SPDC ordered villagers to Tee Wah, where
they the Army tried to force them to be human minesweepers, and when
they would not go the soldiers beat them. The SPDC military has
involved villagers in landmine warfare in the area for at least 2 years by
using them as minesweepers and mine detonators, but soldiers are now

treating mines as deadly tools in a terror campaign targeted at villagers. In villages that the SPDC is relocating, soldiers now deliberately plant mines in areas where they know only villagers will go, such as private homes of people with suspected KNU/KNLA connections. The SPDC's warfare tactics against villagers are the same ones used against the resistance army, reflecting the Army's view that innocent villagers are their enemy.

"We were afraid because the KNLA went and placed landmines around the logging sites. The KNU had protected the woods for hundreds of years, but when the DKBA and the Burmese were planning to log them, the KNLA placed landmines there. We heard about this and were very afraid of doing forced labour there. I had to go to do it, and we helped each other roll the logs or carry them in the cart." - "Nan Paw Oa" (F, 18), xxxx village, Kawkareik township (Interview #42, 7/99)

"I went to cut trees for them because the Burmese wanted to build a bridge and needed wood. When I started to cut down a tree, I stepped on a landmine. Three of us went. One of my friends got a small wound and the other one had dirt sprayed in his face. But I got hit worse than them." - "Saw Lah Baw" (M, 31), Paw Baw Ko village, T'Nay Hsah township; both of his legs were blown off but he survived (Interview #28, 8/99)

"One time a woman from Pway Taw Ro was found dead in her hut, but we didn't know who had killed her. She and her husband were both stabbed to death. She was cut around her neck. At the foot of her ladder there was a landmine, and also in her kitchen there was a landmine. It was lucky that a dog went in there first and lay down, so it exploded that landmine. We don't know who put the landmines there. In the house above the ladder [which serves as the front steps] there was a landmine in the water jug [a pot with drinking water for visitors and passersby]. Since she had died, many people had gone to her house and passed under her ladder. Suddenly somebody knocked the water jug, and it fell down and exploded. Then no one dared to move and walk around her house. Her mother told us this when she was visiting a relative in Pah Ka. I don't know if it was the Ko Per Baw or the Burmese. Her mother told us that her daughter's 4 necklaces were stolen, also 3 rings and 2 pairs of earrings. They also took 20,000 Kyat." - "Naw Kyaw" (F, xx), Pah Ka village, Dta Greh township (Interview #33, 8/99)

Arrests, Torture and Threats

"The village head has responsibility for all people who are sick and cannot go or pay the fee for portering. This is why no one wants to be the village head. Our last village head, D---, fled already, and nobody wanted to be the village head after he left. He was elected by the villagers to cooperate with them to solve their problems, but he did not want to cooperate with the Burmese. If the Burmese demanded things from the villagers which we couldn't give, the village head had to take responsibility. The Burmese punish him if he can't give them what they want. Sometimes they asked for money, but they would also beat him for punishment. My older brother was the village head and I saw the Burmese slap his face and head, just like they do to the villagers who go and work for them every day. His name is xxxx and he is 40 years old. The Burmese hit him when they were angry because they saw the villagers running from them, and when they asked the village head, he told them that they were running to escape from being captured as porters. So they punished the village head. This year at the start of the rainy season the Ko Per Baw ordered a village head to collect porters but he would not go at first and nobody dared to go. They arrested him and put him in jail for 2 or 3 days but he escaped. He is my nephew, only 20 years old. His name is Saw xxxx." - "Pa Kyaw" (M, 40), B'Naw Kleh Kee village, T'Nay Hsah township (Interview #22, 8/99)

The village head serves as a liaison between the village and the military authorities. While ordinary villagers are routinely detained and tortured by SPDC troops, village heads are usually the first ones targeted for failing to comply with the Army's many demands. To the SPDC it is a moot point whether the village can actually meet the monetary, forced labour, portering, and other demands inflicted upon them. A dissatisfied officer will order his troops to arrest and often torture the village head, then hold him/her for ransom while the villagers raise enough money to secure his/her release. Sometimes the forced labour fees, arbitrary taxes, and other demands must come out of the village head's pocket if villagers cannot afford to pay the Army themselves. Traditionally men have been elected to serve as village heads, but now villagers tend to elect women in hopes they will be treated less brutally. Most villagers are terrified of becoming the village head, so many villages now elect their leader on a short-term, rotating basis so s/he will not have to face repetitive punishment. Village heads, even women, are often beaten and tortured when the village fails to raise enough money or fulfil the demands for forced labour, and the killing of village elders is not a rare occurrence.

"If we didn't have the money when the Ko Per Baw came to collect it, they captured the village head. Then if we didn't collect the money for them, they wouldn't allow the village head to come back. They would capture him and keep him in jail. Then the villagers had to collect money until we could give them enough. If you have a goat or a hen you have to sell it. Before some people had money, but with more and more collections they sold all their belongings, even their cattle, pigs and goats." - "Saw Maw Htoo" (M, xx), Pah Klu village, T'Nay Hsah township (Interview #34, 8/99)

"There are about 100 houses in the village. They elect the village head for two or three months at a time. Sometimes in the past they elected one village head for 6 months, but now they always change the village head. If the villagers think that someone can do it, they ask the person to do it. If you ask the villagers to do it, nobody wants to. The villagers all have their land and fields to work." - "Saw Nya" (M, 60), Ker Ghaw village, T'Nay Hsah township (Interview #37, 7/99)

"He is an old village head, and he argued with the Burmese [soldier] so he slapped him. He ordered the village head to buy alcohol for him, but the village head wouldn't do it so he slapped him twice on the back of his neck." - "Pa Noh" (M, 45), B'Naw Kleh Kee village, T'Nay Hsah township (Interview #12, 9/99)

"They beat the villagers, which is why nobody wants to be the village head. This May they beat one of the village heads, who was a temporary headman. ... One time when they tortured him, he didn't want to be the village head any more. He told me that the DKBA beat him. They wanted villagers to go immediately, but he told them that they could not find anyone right away. They said, 'The villagers are bad, and we already told you to get them.' Then they beat him. He told me, 'Brother-in-law, I cannot suffer anymore.' He could not bear it anymore and so he fled from the village. ... Now the villagers are working together with 'Dta Lah Lu Gyi' ['monthly village head'], who is always a woman. The villagers elect her every month. The villagers work for Dta Lah Lu Gyi throughout the year, and each house gives 1 basket of paddy to them for taking care of us. They would elect men but they dare not. When the DKBA or the Burmese come to the village, it is a different matter with a male village head. Once in the past they came to collect emergency porters and the headman couldn't find any for them. Then they beat the headman and the people dared not complain." - "Saw Daniel" (M, 70), Dta Greh village, Hlaing Bwe township (Interview #41, 7/99)

The SPDC and DKBA soldiers often beat, threaten, and intimidate ordinary villagers if they resist handing over their food or belongings on demand. Villagers are routinely arrested for random reasons, for which no explanation is offered before, during, or after their detention. Often villagers will complain to DKBA troops about looting or other injustices on the mistaken assumption that the DKBA will act as allies and confront the SPDC on the villagers' behalf. The DKBA immediately informs the SPDC, and the plaintive villagers are punished for their disobedience. The motivations for torture are too numerous to mention here, but the incidents are becoming more commonplace as the military presence in the region intensifies, resulting in more demands and more interactions with reluctant, weary villagers.

"[talking about the village headwoman] She complained to the Ko Per Baw leaders at Ko Ko and the Burmese beat her very badly. It was after we fled here, because the other group that came after us told us. She was telling the truth, but they didn't like that. She said that the Burmese are raping women and stealing belongings. The Burmese beat her with a stick because they accused her of complaining to the Ko Per Baw about what the Burmese have done. She only reported it to the Ko Per Baw, but they cooperate with the Burmese so the Burmese found out, and they beat her. They accused her of being an informer and they tried to kill her." - "Pu K'Ner" (M, 60), Pah Klu village, T'Nay Hsah township (Interview #20, 8/99)

"Yes, they beat one married woman named P---. She is around 70 years old. When they were looting her children's paddy she told them, 'It will all be gone, then we will have no paddy to eat.' Then they took a stick and beat her once and kicked her once. She dared not complain [to the commander] because the commander and the soldiers are the same." - "Saw Nyo" (M, 50), Pah Klu village, T'Nay Hsah township (Interview #25, 8/99)

"Yes, they frightened us when they demanded food. If people didn't give it to them, they threatened us and touched us with their guns saying, 'Will you give it to me or not? If you don't give, I will shoot you.' We were afraid so we gave to them. We didn't know if they would fire at us or not, and if they did we would die." - "Saw Maw Htoo" (M, xx), Pah Klu village, T'Nay Hsah township (Interview #34, 8/99)

"I was carrying paddy to my house, and when I arrived he came up into the house and demanded alcohol. I told him that we didn't have any alcohol. He called me down to the ground with two of my friends, and

then he told me that whether I found it or not he would tie our hands behind our backs and also tie our legs. Der! He accused me of being a Karen soldier. They saw that I had only one foot, so they couldn't tie it. They tied the hands and legs of the other two with me and demanded that we lie down, but because I couldn't do it quickly they kicked me once on the back with their big boots. They hit my chin with the butt of a gun, then they punched my friend and split his forehead open." - "Saw Tha Suh" (M, 45), Tee Wah Klay village, T'Nay Hsah township (Interview #14, 9/99)

"One time they shot at the village children who were looking after the cattle in the hills, and they captured many children. It was around 20 people. There were children and women, some of whom were carrying their babies. They called them back to their Battalion and forced them to spend the night. Then they released them." - "Saw Baw" (M, 29), Tee Law Thay village, T'Nay Hsah township (Interview #24, 8/99)

Aside from failing to meet demands, the other most frequent cause for detention and torture is the suspicion that a villager has KNU contacts. The SPDC intimidates villagers by physical torture who they suspect have 'rebel' affiliations, though their suspicions are hardly ever based on concrete evidence. Often if villagers fail to comply with their demands, soldiers will automatically accuse them of being KNU members. Although the KNLA does depend on villagers' contributions of food and supplies, any villagers with real allegiance to the KNU stay silent for fear of drawing the SPDC's attention, while most simply wish to distance themselves from all sides of the conflict. Those who happen to know about KNLA activity dare not reveal their information when interrogated unless soldiers literally beat it out of them. DKBA and SPDC soldiers usually make completely arbitrary accusations against villagers, sometimes spurred from personal grudges or a selfish hope for a promotion. Soldiers often detain villagers whose innocence they have never doubted simply as an excuse to demand a significant bribe from the village for his/her release, often totaling 20,000-30,000 Kyat. Whatever the provocation, villagers understand that any known or suspected connection to the KNU will cost them, their families, or their fellow villagers great personal harm. If a villager is arrested, he or she will not receive a fair trial, and will be held indefinitely, possibly serving as a frontline porter or as a forced labourer at an army camp, until village elders can 'vouch' for their innocence. No one is spared from this 'witch hunt' process, and many villagers report savage beatings of women, elders, and children. Through arrest and torture, the SPDC has managed to instill both tremendous fear and the unwilling compliance of villagers.

"Yes, they beat and tortured a villager named P---, who is around 30 years old. The commander ordered it and the privates beat him. They accused him of being Kaw Thoo Lei [KNLA] and working with them. He was never Kaw Thoo Lei, and he told them that but they did not accept it, so they sliced his ears. They beat him horribly with a stick in the village, and we dared not go to look because we were staying outside the village. Now he is not strong enough to carry anything." - "Naw Paw Htoo" (F, 27), Taw Oak village, T'Nay Hsah township (Interview #9, 9/99)

"He asked me, 'Maung xxxx, where are you from?' and I told him 'I stay at T---.' [Where his farmfield hut is.] He said, 'What do you do there, and where do you keep your gun?' He told me that I wasn't telling the truth, so he kept me tied up with rope. After they had kept us tied up at that place for 4 or 5 hours, he said, 'Tie them separately.' The rope was 40 handspans long, but it wasn't long enough for him so he untied a rope from someone's pig and tied me on the back with that rope, too. They tied my friend to me so we were like a ball. You don't need to ask how tight it was. I couldn't sit down so I didn't know what to do. As for my friend, when the Burmese tied him he shouted out and they threatened him with a gun and told him, 'Be quiet. You are real Nga Pway [SPDC slang for KNU/KNLA].' We told them, 'We are not Nga Pway, we are workers and if you don't believe us, go look at our huts.' Pwah! Then we couldn't do anything, so we told the other villagers to go and tell the village head that the Burmese had us tied up. We had done nothing wrong." - "Saw Kee" (M, 21), Ker Ghaw village, T'Nay Hsah township (Interview #11, 9/99)

"Der! They beat my husband's cousin. They chased and captured him and stabbed him with a bayonet. Then they twisted it inside him and he yelled loudly because it was so painful. They accused him of having a gun and radio and making contact with T'Bee Met ['closed-eyes', DKBA slang for KNU/KNLA], but he never had. All of the people they capture they beat a lot. The time they captured my husband they captured 7 people and they slapped their faces until they were bruised. They accused them all of having guns and radios, so they interrogated and beat each of them in the fields. They tied them all and beat and kicked them. Later they released them all because people gave guarantees for them. I was very afraid and my feet were trembling, and I was so afraid that I couldn't go to guarantee him [her husband]. But I had to go to give the guarantee because they kept telling me that they were going to kill him. They said that he and his cousin, B---, were most at fault." - "Naw Ther Paw" (F, xx), xxxx village, T'Nay Hsah township; her husband S--- was

later shot dead by the DKBA, though he was innocent of any contact with the KNLA (Interview #32, 8/99)

"Yes, the Ko Per Baw [DKBA] arrived one time and touched us with guns. The Burmese were also involved. When they arrived at the hut, they pointed their guns and ordered us, 'Don't run away.' We dared not run because they were close to us. Then they said, 'Have you seen T'Bee Met?' ['Closed-eyes', DKBA term for Karen soldiers] I said I hadn't seen them. They started to frighten me and said that the day before they had passed through our area. I told them that they hadn't come, but they continued, 'Uncle, tell the truth. If you do not tell the truth you will face many problems.' So I told them the truth that they had not come, and then they pulled me down toward the path, and when we arrived on the path they asked me again, 'Do they [KNLA] come often?' I told them, 'We haven't seen them', but we were lying to them because some people from here were our friends and sometimes they did come. They told me again, 'Tell the truth', and they kicked me one time on my back and slapped my face twice. I fell down into a gully. We said, 'They do not come often. Sometimes once a month or once a week.' Then they didn't beat me anymore, and they released me and told me to go up to the house." - "Pu Tamla" (M, 60+), Taw Oak village, T'Nay Hsah township (Interview #8, 9/99)

Rape and Sexual Abuse

"They tried to steal women to sleep with, so the women had to gather and sleep together in the same house at night. They had to close the door tightly and each of the women had their own big knives. They dared not sleep at their own houses because the Burmese were staying in their houses, so 4 or 5 families would sleep together in one house. The men dared not guard them. Der! In the morning they would go back home. They asked my wife to have sex because she stayed with just one or two others, and she scolded and shouted at them. We dared not stay without many people. I cannot explain how great the fear was. I have a daughter who is a teenager, so I dared not let them meet her. Two or three years ago they didn't do things like this, and my wife and I didn't want to run too hastily. My wife is an especially strong woman and she faced the Burmese treatment until she couldn't face them anymore. One time my wife visited me in the farmfield hut and whispered, 'We have to move. We dare not stay anymore because now in the night we have to sleep in one big group with big knives.' So people fled because they couldn't tolerate the Burmese treatment. Now they have all fled." - "Pu K'Ner" (M, 60), Pah Klu village, T'Nay Hsah township (Interview #20, 8/99)

On the rise in southeastern Pa'an District are incidents of rape and sexual abuse of women by SPDC troops. While men flee their villages as soon as the military approaches, women usually remain to take care of the house and surrounding fields. Without a male presence to prevent their advances, troops more easily take advantage of the women's vulnerable position. Knowing they will encounter less resistance if the male owner of the house is absent, soldiers boldly enter houses at will, looting belongings and making sexual advances towards women. Some women have been able to ward off intruding, often drunken soldiers, but many have not. Soldiers will often try to convince women to return to their camp when they enter a village at night. In one case, the village headwoman of Pah Klu was forced to become the sexual servant of Captain Toe Aung, a Company Commander with Light Infantry Battalion #120, for the duration of his stay in the village. The other village women, afraid of a similar fate, gathered to sleep in groups and carried knives to protect themselves against soldiers who stormed their houses at night. In the end the women of Pah Klu were largely successful in warding off their attackers because they threatened to tell the soldiers' commanding officer if they were raped. Privates know that rape is one offense they can actually be punished for, though the punishment is almost always minor. In the Burmese military, rape is considered an officer's privilege, and most privates are afraid of overstepping their bounds. In some regions the local commanding officers who commit rape will also be afraid of their superior officers finding out about their own transgressions. The threat of punishment, however, is often not daunting enough to deter soldiers from trying to rape women, especially if they observe the example of their commanding officers. In general, and certainly in southeastern Pa'an District, the Burmese military creates an atmosphere of impunity around rape, just as it does with the torture and killing of villagers.

"He said, 'A'Mo pay! A'Mo leh saun!' [literally: 'Mother, give! Mother, a present!'] I asked him, 'What kind of present?', and he came near to me so I was afraid. He said 'A'Mo pay! Pay!' and I said, 'Give what?', and I moved away from him little by little because I was afraid. I told him, 'Go back. It is dark, go back.' And I moved away from him. I spoke to him in Karen, but he spoke to me in Burmese. After I asked him to go back he went back. ... As for me they couldn't rape me, but they did it a lot to my friends and my nieces, so I couldn't stay anymore. I was afraid and sometimes our hearts become cold and sometimes hot [angry], and we couldn't sleep until morning. In the night my heart and hands became cold with fear of them. My husband was not sleeping beside me." - "Naw Paw Mo" (F, 42), Pah Klu village, T'Nay Hsah township (Interview #21, 8/99)

"There were 3 or 4 women and the people told me they were married. They are older than me. The Burmese soldiers went to the women's houses; they didn't call them [to the Army camp]. They couldn't sleep with the women, but they could hold their hands and legs. At that time I was together with them because the Burmese had arrested and tied me up at the time when they slept with the women. They are the same troops who tied me. I didn't see it because they kept me in another place and in the morning we heard the village head complain to their commander that his soldiers had slept with the women. They punished the soldiers, but they are still doing it." - "Saw Lah Ku" (M, 21), Pah Klu village, T'Nay Hsah township (Interview #18, 8/99)

"...her husband ran at night because they came to kill him so they could have sex with his wife. They couldn't, because she can speak Burmese, so she spoke to them and avoided it while her husband fled in the night. Her name is Ma T--- and she is 30 years old. This was not a long time ago, only 10 days or so." - "Pu K'Ner" (M, 60), Pah Klu village, T'Nay Hsah township (Interview #20, 8/99)

"[about the village head, who is a widow:] He took the village headwoman to sleep with him, and he kept her beside him and slept with her. ... The children go with her and stay with them. She has two children and one is 7 years old. I can't tell what he does with her because he never lets her out, and she has to stay there both days and nights. If he went somewhere, she had to go with him day or night." - "Naw Paw Mo" (F, 42), Pah Klu village, T'Nay Hsah township (Interview #21, 8/99)

The whole village will feel the consequences of a woman's rape. Fear of being violated, and shame experienced after the fact, will drive women out of the village to join their husbands in hiding until soldiers have left, or until the family can flee to a safer location. Rape and the threat of it is often the trigger for a mass exodus from the village, since fear quickly spreads to all women left unprotected, and because no family members are able to remain in safety any longer. The villagers are reluctant to leave their homes unattended because they know that soldiers will raid them, but many women would rather lose everything than face aggressive soldiers.

"Once a Burmese soldier entered a married woman's house. When she tried to go into her room [to escape], he caught her by the leg and pulled her back out of the room. The Burmese was drunk so the woman became afraid and came back out...Now not many women are staying in the village. Mostly they go and sleep in the jungle or in their field huts. They

[Burmese] don't try to find them, because whenever house owners flee they are happy because they can steal freely." - "Saw Maw Htoo" (M, xx), Pah Klu village, T'Nay Hsah township (Interview #34, 8/99)

"They walked around the whole night and went into people's houses. They stole people's belongings and questioned women. They asked the women to sleep with them, and so some women dared not stay and ran away because they couldn't face it. I did not hear that they raped women in the village, but I heard that they harassed women. They asked to have sex and the women got angry and moved away. They harassed 2 or 3 women like that. After people knew about that, only a few people remained in their houses. Most people ran away." - "Saw Nyo" (M, 50), Pah Klu village, T'Nay Hsah township (Interview #25, 8/99)

Killings

"...they killed one of my nephews. They didn't allow the people to go out at night. He was foolish and went outside the village at night to find frogs in the rainy season. It was in Lah Ghoh [August] before people transplanted their paddy seedlings. We had already sown the seed paddy and the seedlings were growing long. Then DKBA soldiers who were staying in the village killed him. His name was Saw Eh Kweh, and he was about 20 years old, younger than my daughter. At that time the KNLA came to fight the DKBA in Taw Oak, and when the KNLA entered the village they met him. Some soldiers arrived and started shooting in the village. When he heard the shooting he was afraid and dared not return to the village, so he ran and followed the KNLA. After they [KNLA] finished shooting, they went back to Pah Klu village and took him there, too. But he was not a soldier, so the KNLA soldiers left him there and went away from Pah Klu. The next day when DKBA went to Pah Klu, they killed him and threw his body in the river. The villagers from Pah Klu saw them do it. They stabbed him through his clothes. Maybe they tied him, too, but we didn't go to see him. It was raining then and the river was in flood. Later when the river went down his body appeared, and the villagers from Pah Klu took him out and buried him." - "Naw Mu Mu Wah" (F, 50), Taw Oak village, T'Nay Hsah township (Interview #30, 8/99)

Villagers in the Pah Klu area have recently reported encounters with troops who bear a strong resemblance to Sa Thon Lon Guerrilla Retaliation Units. These units are special execution squads which the SPDC has employed in Nyaunglebin District, where the villagers call them the "Short Pants" ("Baw Bi Doh") in reference to their civilian clothes. The units there are known for their brutal execution techniques and sexual harassment of women. In Pah Klu they are called "S'Ker Po", or "Short Skirts", apparently a sarcastic reference to their attempts to sleep with all the village women. In Nyaunglebin District, the Sa Thon Lon have a clearly stated mission to execute on sight anyone they believe has had past or present contact with the KNU, but they are also notorious for their unceasing harassment of village women. (For a history and description of 'Sa Thon Lon' units, see Part 1: "Death Squads and Displacement: Systematic Executions, Village Destruction and the Flight of Villagers in Nyaunglebin District", KHRG #99-04, 24/5/99). Until now there have been no confirmed reports of Sa Thon Lon activity in Central Karen State, but there have been several reports that the SPDC planned to bring some Sa Thon Lon execution squads into Pa'an District. KHRG has not found any evidence to confirm these rumours. Rape and looting are rampant in the village, but villagers have not yet reported executions of the type associated with Sa Thon Lon units. It is possible, however, that several units have moved south in order to terrify villagers and facilitate the SPDC's relocation of villages to Army camps with the goal of eliminating the KNLA's support base.

"We heard about them [Sa Thon Lon] but we could not figure out if these belong to the same group, because they are doing the same things as those groups." - "Naw Paw Mo" (F, 42), Pah Klu village, T'Nay Hsah township (Interview #21, 8/99)

"They [the soldiers] already went back to their camp at Ker Ghaw but we heard that they will come back again. I don't know their unit number but there are 80 soldiers. They wear the same clothes as villagers. They wear short pants and shirts...People told me that it is Baw Bi Doh, but we called them S'Ker Po ["short skirts"]... they do not carry guns. They bring knives. They walk around day and night. They are going after women, not men." - "Saw Nyo" (M, 50), Pah Klu village, T'Nay Hsah township (Interview #25, 8/99)

As with torture and detention of villagers, the DKBA and SPDC continue to kill indiscriminately in all areas of southeastern Pa'an District. They are known to blame each other for acts of killing in order to avoid confronting village elders or compensating relatives. Both armies will seek out villagers to accuse of KNU affiliations, but legitimate proof of guilt is never necessary before killing a villager. When summoned by troops, many villagers run in hopes of avoiding interrogation about the KNLA, which may or may not involve torture, and/or an inevitable porter shift if captured. Soldiers shoot anyone running to escape, justifying their actions by claiming that running implies that the villager does indeed have KNLA connections. They seldom offer explanations to relatives of victims either, and never report them as civilian casualties. If recorded at all, the dead are considered KNLA soldiers killed in battle, numbers which are used to boost the SPDC's claims of crushing opposition groups.

"The #120 [Battalion] troops killed a villager named Du Lay Loh. They didn't tell anyone when they captured him, and then they killed him the same day. Later people found his body in a hole and buried him. They didn't tell any of the village elders why they killed him." - "Saw Than" (M, 43), xxxx village, T'Nay Hsah township (Interview #5, 11/99)

"They are always shooting their guns in the village, both big weapons and small guns. If they see the people run, they shoot them all. They starting shooting last year, and they didn't think beforehand whether they're aiming at villagers or the KNLA. The Burmese accuse the DKBA of doing the shooting and the DKBA accused the Burmese of doing it." - "Naw Lay Wah" (F, 25), Pah Klu village, T'Nay Hsah township (Interview #36, 7/99)

"...one of my brothers was shot to death by the Burmese. ... The Burmese didn't say anything afterwards, because they couldn't do anything since he was shot already. Maybe they could have done something, but the Burmese are like that - they shoot first and think later, and you can't bring people back to life. After the people ran away, they took the belongings that they had left. My brother's friend was with his wife, and she was shot. They took all the woman's belongings, like shirts, clothing, pots, and other things. " - "Naw Paw Htoo" (F, 27), Taw Oak village, T'Nay Hsah township (Interview #9, 9/99)

"...they come to my village often and whenever they come they shoot villagers. The other time they came they shot a man named Htay Lah. He is Karen and a villager. He was eating rice at his wife's parents' house when they shot him. He wasn't wearing clothes while he was eating, only short pants. They started shooting into the house, so he stopped eating and ran down to the ground. He ran and they shot him to death. They accused him of being Nga Pway [KNLA soldier]. People told them, 'He is not Nga Pway; he is a villager. Look in his house—there are no weapons!'...When their commander asked them they said that a small battle had occurred with the KNLA and they had accidentally hit a villager. For sure there was no battle, because there was no KNLA there.

They just shot at a villager who was running." - "Pu Dta Ler" (M, 50-60),
Pah Klu village, T'Nay Hsah twp. (Interview #45, 4/99)

*"He went into the forest to find some vegetables to eat, but he didn't
know that the Burmese [LIB 331] were staying along the path waiting for
them, so he went down to enter the village and when the Burmese saw
him and his friend, they shot the two of them dead. My uncle's name was
Per Ta Lu and he was 32 years old. His friend was Pa Mu Dah, who was
only 15 years old. ... We knew it because they came carrying their bodies
in blankets and bags. They said that they made a mistake by shooting
them, but they were dead already, and these dead people were villagers.
They were carrying vegetables when the soldiers shot them dead." -*
"Naw Paw Htoo" (F, 27), Taw Oak village, T'Nay Hsah township
(Interview #9, 9/99)

As the SPDC concentrates its offensive against the KNLA in Pa'an
District more villagers are forced to suffer the consequences, usually not
by being caught in the crossfire but by facing SPDC reprisals after the
shooting stops. Villagers often become scapegoats when a battle occurs
near the village, forced to placate troops by clearing away the dead
soldiers, treating the wounded, and providing them with food and
supplies. This is often is not enough, however, and soldiers vent their
rage by killing civilians whose only fault was being too close to a battle
site. Villagers have no idea how to approach unpredictable and dangerous
soldiers, so without a better alternative many opt to flee deep into the
jungle, becoming internally displaced.

*"In the plain area [west of the Dawna Mountains] they beat all of the
villagers who live near to places where battles have occurred. One battle
occurred at Kaw Suh, near Ler Dah, only 20 minutes' walk from Ta Plaw
Pu. It happened between the villages. There were only a few soldiers
from the Karen side, so they shot for a while and then ran away. I was
involved there too, and when the Karen soldiers ran and shot at them,
one or two of them were wounded and they were upset about this. So they
accused the Kaw Suh villagers of feeding Kaw Thoo Lei [KNLA]. They
killed two women because the Kaw Thoo Lei had shot at them. They
weren't village heads. They were married women, and they ran from
fright when the Burmese arrived. They shot 5 or 6 cows at the same time;
it was not a mistake, they aimed at them and shot them. The Karen
soldiers had already run far away from the village, but the Burmese
came to shoot the two women anyway. They were around 45 years old;
one of them has 4 children and the other one has 2 children." -* "Saw Lay
Htoo" (M, 42), xxxx village, Hlaing Bwe township (Interview #10, 9/99)

Looting, Extortion, and Demands

"If they tax us, we have to give to them. We can't stay without giving to them. Both the DKBA and the Burmese tax us. Last year they taxed us until we could not pay them. This year they taxed us too, and we couldn't pay them anymore. That's why we fled from them. They collected once a month from every house to buy their food. Each time we had to give 1,000 or more Kyat [per house], and sometimes they collected 2,000 or 3,000 Kyat. We had to pay the Burmese less than the DKBA; we usually had to give the Burmese 500 Kyat [each time]. They collected irregularly, twice or three times a month. They made problems for the villagers who could not pay. If there were villagers who couldn't pay, each house would have to give until they collected 10,000 or 30,000 Kyat. The next time the villagers would have to find enough to pay them again." - "Maung Shwe" (M, 36), Pah Klu village, T'Nay Hsah township (Interview #19, 8/99)

Villagers in Southeastern Pa'an District have been the victims of relentless looting of food, livestock, belongings, and money by SPDC and DKBA forces. The SPDC has been gradually reducing rations to its soldiers nationwide and directly ordering them to live off the land or the local villagers. Similarly, DKBA forces cannot depend on Rangoon for any supplies at all anymore. SPDC officers have been known to take the rations and sell them, then inform their privates to loot from nearby villages. Additionally, the quality of the rice rationed to rank-and-file SPDC soldiers is now so poor that most soldiers refuse to eat it, so many simply take the villagers' good quality rice. The SPDC, DKBA and KNLA armies are all therefore dependent on resource-strapped villagers for food and supplies, which they take at will. Villagers are forced to hand over their food to troops who demand them and are threatened in various ways if they do not comply. Most villagers cite looting as a primary reason for flight from their villages, as hunger becomes less of a fear and more of a reality.

"During this last rainy season the rice [ration shipments] didn't come for them, so they didn't have enough rice. Then they demanded rice from the villagers. They demanded it from the village head, and he had to give it to them because he was afraid of their guns. So the villagers had to give and then they had to buy rice for themselves in order to eat." - "Saw Baw" (M, 29), Tee Law Thay village, T'Nay Hsah township (Interview #24, 8/99)

"If the house where they are staying doesn't have rice, they look at other houses to see if they have rice, and they steal it in the night. Villagers sometimes didn't have enough rice and so they couldn't eat. They take our livestock, mostly pigs and goats. If you add up the livestock that they eat during one night, it is at least 3 pigs. They steal it during the night and don't give any money." - "Saw Maw Htoo" (M, xx), Pah Klu village, T'Nay Hsah township (Interview #34, 8/99)

"At my mother's house, where 2 of my sisters were also staying, they [soldiers] came and touched them with guns and looted some rice. Then they threatened my sisters with a firebrand and cut up my mother's bed." - "Naw Paw Mo" (F, 42), Pah Klu village, T'Nay Hsah township (Interview #21, 8/99)

"Don't ask if they eat or not! They ate a lot. We dared not complain to them. If we complained, they said, 'I eat your poultry. If I ask from you, give. Don't talk too much.' The villagers are afraid of them and feed them. But the villagers don't want to feed them in their hearts." - "Saw Lah Baw" (M, 31), Paw Baw Ko village, T'Nay Hsah township (Interview #28, 8/99)

"When they enter the village they eat pigs and hens, and they come and steal all the villager's belongings. They don't ask for it, and if they ask the owner and the owner doesn't give it to them they kill it for themselves and nobody dares to complain. If you talk back to them they point their guns at you. They ate one of my hens but I dared not say anything to them. I stayed quiet, and their commanders also scolded us the way they do. Der! The privates and their commanders eat together. They eat the villagers' pigs and chickens and they don't pay for it." - "Naw Paw Htoo" (F, 27), Taw Oak village, T'Nay Hsah township (Interview #9, 9/99)

"Even though I didn't raise livestock, they took my pumpkins. If I complained, they told me 'You have no legs. You shouldn't say anything.'" - "Saw Lah Baw" (M, 31), Paw Baw Ko village, T'Nay Hsah township, who lost both legs to a landmine doing forced labour for the SPDC (Interview #28, 8/99)

The looting is actively encouraged by commanding officers, who demand large quantities of food and money for themselves and have no objection to their troops obtaining all their food from the villagers. Many villagers report that extortion takes many forms; for example, troops demand that the villagers feed them pork, leaving them the burden of buying livestock outside the village, or the burden of monetarily reimbursing a villager whose pig they must sacrifice. Soldiers also loot in order to provide for their wives and children if their families stay with them in or near the village. It is widely known among villagers that SPDC soldiers, eager to supplement their humble earnings from the military, steal from the villagers and send the money and clothing they steal back home to their families in other parts of Burma. Officers can make millions of Kyat extorting money from the villages in their area in the course of a year's posting, money which their families can use to start businesses back in Rangoon or other towns.

"They took 4 or 5 baskets of paddy from L---'s house. From other women they looted rice and touched the women with their hands. Then there was only a bit of rice left, and they shat in it and then left." - *"Saw Mo Aung"* (M, 39), Pah Klu village, T'Nay Hsah township (Interview #13, 9/99)

"They demand to eat in the village as well. We have to find money to pay for 2 meals of pork per month, which is 20 viss [32 kg / 70 lb] of pork each time, or 40 viss in total. One viss of pork costs 500 Kyat, so that makes 20,000 Kyat monthly just for pork. If we do not have pigs in the village we have to go outside the village to find them." - *"Pa Kyaw"* (M, 40), B'Naw Kleh Kee village, T'Nay Hsah township (Interview #22, 8/99)

"They collected money, for example we have to pay for their batteries and pork. We had to collect money recently so that they can eat pork twice a month. For each month that costs each family 1,000 Kyat or more. Including everything, like porter fees, batteries for their torchlights and radios, and monthly 'set tha' fees, each family has to give 3,000 Kyat or more. We have to give that every month because they demand it every month. If we don't give it to them they just glare at us. You can't stay there without giving, so you have to give all you can." - *"Pa Noh"* (M, 45), B'Naw Kleh Kee village, T'Nay Hsah township (Interview #12, 9/99)

"Der! They will do what they want and send it to their families. It is the way of earning respect from the family by sending them money." - *"Saw Maw Htoo"* (M, xx), Pah Klu village, T'Nay Hsah township (Interview #34, 8/99)

"They did not ask to buy it [rice], they looted it from the owners. The owners saw it but dared not say anything, and if they [the soldiers] were carrying their guns the women were afraid and said, "take as you will".

They took it and put it in sacks that hold 3 big tins each [50-kilo rice sacks], then they pounded it themselves with the villagers' mortars. Then they walked into the village and sold it for 1,000 Kyat per sack. Some people bought it, because if people didn't buy it they couldn't live. Some people can't [afford to] buy it but others can. People bought it to eat because in the village there is rarely enough rice, so we have to go down to buy rice from the plains. The Burmese came to stay in the village, and then the Ko Per Baw took the Burmese rice while it was on its way, and didn't send any of it on to them. [The DKBA stole a Burmese Army rice ration shipment.]" - "Saw Mo Aung" (M, 39), Pah Klu village, T'Nay Hsah township (Interview #13, 9/99)

Now that the demands for portering and forced labour are increasing, many villagers are forced to leave their homes for periods of time, either to escape forced labour shifts or to fulfil them. The soldiers take advantage of the owners' absence by freely entering homes and eating rice, stealing belongings, trashing whatever possessions they cannot use or carry, and in some cases occupying the houses for the duration of their stay in a village, effectively forcing the villagers out of their own homes. Soldiers never offer compensation for stolen pots or clothing, items which are difficult for villagers to replace, nor do soldiers care if they loot the villagers' main food supply. Villagers are frequently left with nothing after soldiers come through their village, without any means of replacing stolen or damaged goods. Despite this, they are still forced to pay extortion fees to the military.

"They took everything that they saw, like gallon jugs and containers and as much as they could carry. Someone from Gkah Deh said, 'They are like gorillas, even if they see pumpkins or pumpkin leaf they take it, and if they see just one aubergine they take it and put it in their basket and you can't keep it.' Even if they saw half a knife [a broken machete] they would take it. Just recently they went and took O---'s saw, and when he went and asked for it back the Burmese pushed his chest with the butt of a pistol and slapped him once on the face." - "Pu Than Nyunt" (M, 55), B'Nweh Pu village, T'Nay Hsah township Interview #15, 9/99)

"Those troops shit into people's mortars [for pounding paddy] and cookpots. There were a lot of people who had to face this in Pah Klu; the married women there said that you dared not open your cookpots because they were full of shit, and so were their [rice container] tins. ... they didn't stay in our village, they just came and stayed one night and I said to him, 'Son, don't shit in our mortars.' He asked me, 'Where did you hear that?' and I told him, 'I heard from Meh Pleh that you shat in

their mortars.' ... Both their leaders and their private soldiers do it,
because their leaders are no good and it is like rain dripping down from
the roof of the house [the example of the officers trickles down to the
men]. People say 'When the head goes, the tail is pulled along' [a Karen
proverb]. I told them we would go to their battalion base at Moh Ta Ma
to do our own shit, and I told them, 'You have very rude habits! You
should know a toilet, can't you tell a toilet from a mortar or a cookpot?'
He said, 'Mother, who told you this?' I told him I heard it when I was in
Meh Pleh, and all the married women in Pah Klu were also talking about
it. They did it in Pah Klu just for spite." - "Naw Hsah Paw" (F, 47), xxxx
village, T'Nay Hsah township; the mortars are large wooden mortars
people keep under their houses for pounding and husking rice (Interview
#2, 11/99)

In addition to theft, the SPDC and DKBA constantly demand fees from
the villagers for everything from replacement of forced labourers to
arbitrary taxes on personal possessions. Sometimes the villagers are fined
for circumstances completely unrelated to them, such as an incident in
B'Naw Kleh Kee when the DKBA commander charged the villagers
70,000 Kyat to compensate for a soldier's desertion. A villager from
T'Nay Hsah township told KHRG how an SPDC officer demanded
316,000 Kyat per month in 'porter fees' alone from the 5 villages around
hers, then kept all the money for himself and demanded porters as well.
Often the villagers have no idea what they are paying for, but they have
no choice but to meet the demand. Typically the village head collects the
various fees from the villagers on a monthly basis, but often the troops
demand random fees without prior warning. Sometimes the village head
establishes a sliding scale system, taxing the richest villagers more than
the poorest. Villagers try to cooperate and help each other meet the
demands, but all have problems meeting the heavy fees imposed on
them. Most villages in southeastern Pa'an District have been so heavily
taxed that villagers simply have no money left, and are forced to take
their turns for forced labour or portering instead of hiring replacements.
This only reinforces their debt, however, as villagers have no time to
work on their fields to produce rice. Instead of remaining caught in this
relentless cycle of fees, more and more villagers are opting to flee their
villages and take their chances on surviving in the jungle.

"For each month our village had to give 14,000 Kyat for each of 2 people
[to not send 2 porters], so we gave them 70,000 Kyat in 3 months. He
took the money from every village. Our village is only small, he
demanded more from the bigger villages. From Ker Ghaw he collected
for 6 people [porters] at 12,000 Kyat each, 6 people from Tee Wah Blaw,

six from Tee Law Thay and six from Sghaw Ko tract, all at 12,000 each. He just took money, not people [he didn't want the porters, it was just an excuse to demand money; in total, the 5 villages listed had to pay a total of 316,000 Kyat per month for 'porter fees' alone, not counting other fees]. There are other village tracts too, like Pah Klu tract, Loh Baw, Meh Pleh Wah and so on as far as Tee Wah Klay and Day Law Pya. He also beat people, and a lot of villagers from our village ran away. ... Sometimes he demanded 10 people or 30 people from each village, took the money for that all for himself and then still called for 'loh ah pay'. He demanded people as well as money. Sometimes when they were going to patrol to Meh Pleh and come back he took more than 10 villagers from our village." - "Naw Hsah Paw" (F, 47), xxxx village, T'Nay Hsah township, talking about a commander from SPDC #116 Battalion (Interview #2, 11/99)

"They collect 2,000 Kyat once a month from each house. They told us that it is for porters' fees, and since villagers dare not go to porter, they give money. If [the Burmese] can't get it, they trouble the village head. They beat him, so the village head has to come back and ask the villagers again until they can raise the money. Then we take it to the village head, and he takes it to them. The village head has no time to rest." - "Saw Mo Aung" (M, 39), Pah Klu village, T'Nay Hsah township (Interview #13, 9/99)

"They often demanded between 70,000 and 80,000 Kyat from each village. If the Burmese demand it, the DKBA will demand the same. There are only 83 houses in our village so each house must give more than 1,000 Kyat at the least. Some families, like ours, have to give 3,000 or 5,000 Kyat, and some even give 10,000. The poorest family in the village must give 1,500 Kyat. But you have no time to go out and work for money, so how can you give that much money so often? You go for 'loh ah pay' every day, so how will you get money?" - "Nan Paw Oa" (F, 18), xxxx village, Kawkareik township (Interview #42, 7/99)

"We paid the big fees 3 or 4 times a month and the small fees 4 or 5 times a month. Some months we had to pay 2,000 Kyat total, but some months we paid 3,000 Kyat [per family]. If we couldn't pay the village head might take away our precious things, such as cooking pots and other things that he could sell to get enough to pay the fee. He is the Burmese village head [the village head appointed by the SPDC]." - "Maung Hla" (M, 30), Kru Bper village, Kawkareik township (Interview #44, 4/99)

"Ah! If they saw a house with a tin roof, they collected at least 5,000 Kyat per month. I don't know what they do with that money. People can't stay [in the village] without giving to them. If you have chickens or cows you have to sell your livestock. They collect 5,000 Kyat from villagers who have belongings, but from people like me they collect 2,000 Kyat per month. They always collect, but for what I don't know. " - "Saw Kee" (M, 21), Ker Ghaw village, T'Nay Hsah township (Interview #11, 9/99)

"After we sold all our belongings we all had to run away and come here. I don't know what would happen if we still lived in the village, if they would kill us or not. But now a lot of people cannot pay them, and this year there is not enough rice or paddy either, so maybe the villagers will have to steal. " - "Naw Ther Paw" (F, xx), xxxx village, T'Nay Hsah township (Interview #32, 8/99)

Challenges for Farmers

"They confiscated our fields but forced us to work on those fields for them. They only sat around and ordered us while we ploughed, sowed, and transplanted. When we finished the harvest they took all the paddy. They didn't give us anything even when we reaped, gathered, winnowed and put the paddy in the [milling] machine. We had to go and sell things like oil, onions, and beans on the other side of the mountain. We bought rice from them [SPDC soldiers] with the profit, but they sold us old rice that smelled bad." - the mother of "Nan Paw Oa" (F, 18), xxxx village, Kawkareik township (Interview #42, 7/99)

To compensate for their depleted rations and those which have been hoarded or sold by the commanders, SPDC officers often encourage their soldiers to simply confiscate farmers' crops when they enter villages. The villagers have little if any rice to spare since last year's poor harvest gave them barely enough to store for their own consumption. After taking more than enough for themselves, the Army sometimes sells the villagers' own rice back to them at half of market price, or tries to sell them their own extremely poor quality ration rice. After paying forced labour fees, rice quota service charges, and other extortion money to the SPDC soldiers, the villagers have no money left to buy back their confiscated rice. In the end, many have been left with large debts and nothing to eat but boiled rice soup—a thin gruel which families eat to try to make what little rice they have last longer. Many are facing starvation.

"They have their own rice but they said it was not white. They wanted to eat the villagers' rice, but they don't give their rice to the villagers. They

just took ours." - "Saw Lah Baw" (M, 31), Paw Baw Ko village, T'Nay Hsah township (Interview #28, 8/99)

"Paddy and rice. They demanded it often and we always had to give. Last year we had only a small amount of paddy and rice [the crop was very bad]. For every basket or big tin of rice we ate, they looted one basket or big tin. We had to collect rice for them too, and Pa N--- from the Ko Per Baw told me to complain to them so I did, but they didn't respond. He said that they would give it back to us because he is the one who takes care of their rations, but they gave us nothing. I know that the name of the chief commander of the Burmese is Pu P'Na Wah, and he has to send rations to all the soldiers, including the Ko Per Baw." - "Pu Than Nyunt" (M, 55), B'Nweh Pu village, T'Nay Hsah township (Interview #15, 9/99)

As in the rest of Burma, villagers in hills of the Dawna Mountains have to hand over a portion of their crops to the SPDC authorities as 'Ta Won Gyay' ('Obligation') paddy, the official state-sanctioned rice quota. This applies both to people still living and farming in their home villages and to those living in relocation sites but commuting to farm their own land. In a good year, one acre of flat paddy field can produce only 40-50 baskets, yet the quota is often 10 baskets of paddy or more per acre. No exceptions are given during bad crop years, and the quota is calculated on the acres registered to the farmer, not however many they have planted. The 1997 and 1998 crops were both dismal, leaving many farmers without enough seed paddy to plant more than a fraction of their fields; yet during this time period the quotas have actually increased. SPDC officials justify crop quotas by citing the written law in Burma which decrees that all land belongs to the state. It is not only the Army but also the local quota collection officials who are corrupt, and they find ways to steal additional paddy and money from villagers. When farmers bring their 12 or 15 baskets per acre, the Township officials often claim that it's not 'clean', i.e. that it contains bits of straw and impurities, and either winnow it a second time or calculate a reduction in the number of baskets to be paid for. They then deduct a portion of the paddy which they say will be 'donations' to local temples, the Township PDC, etc., and reduce the payment accordingly, though it is very unlikely that this paddy will ever be given to any temple. Many also demand an additional cash service charge, and the villagers must put on a banquet for them when they come. Sometimes even more deductions are made. In the end, most farmers are paid for no more than two thirds of the paddy which they are forced to bring, and at half or less than half of market price (about 250 Kyat per basket [market price is 500-600], though a farmer from Dta Greh told KHRG that he only received 3 Kyat per basket once the officials had finished their 'deductions'). The payment per basket is not adjusted to the rapidly increasing market prices, even though much of the inflation is caused by this very quota system. The money not paid to the farmers is either pocketed by the officials or kept by the state. The villagers are fully aware that this is simply corruption, but they do not dare complain for fear of arrest. They have no choice but to pay the quota as demanded each year, and many years the only way they can do so is to go into debt by buying rice at full market price just to hand it over to the authorities.

"...they collect one basket of rice from each farmfield hut. We have to give one basket of rice regularly every month. Even if we have no rice to eat, we have to feed them." - "Saw Lah Ku" (M, 21), Pah Klu village, T'Nay Hsah township (Interview #18, 8/99)

"This year they announced that the government will gather all the paddy that we get from the fields, and then we have to go and buy it from the government. According to them, Pah Klu and Kwih Lay are ruled by them so they have the power to do this. For example, if the villagers would sell each other a basket of rice for 500 Kyat, we will have to buy it from them for 250 Kyat." - "Taw Lay" (M, 41), Kwih Lay village, T'Nay Hsah township (Interview #6, 9/99)

"They taxed us three times this year and were very strict. Every year they collect Ta Won Gyay ['obligation' quota paddy] from the farmers, 5 baskets for every 100. It has been very hot and dry there, so there is a lot of chaff, and when we take 5 baskets to them, they blow off the chaff with a fan and it becomes less. Last year there was no paddy because it was so hot and dry, so they asked for money instead. The government's price is 3 Kyat per basket [actually it is several hundred Kyat per basket, but the officials steal most of the rice quota payouts and give almost nothing to the farmers who are forced to hand over the rice]. They gave three Kyat for one basket and then you had to give more than that to the owner of the bullock cart who carried the paddy for you. But we had to pay 1,000 Kyat three times because we had no paddy, and we couldn't stay without paying them [in lieu of giving paddy]. After collecting the first time, the village head took all the money and fled the village. Then they elected a new village head and he collected again. But that time there wasn't enough money, and so we had to give a third time. We gave 3,000 Kyat in total last year. The last two years there have been droughts and we didn't get enough paddy for seed, so we had to sell the cows and buy paddy seed from Maw Goh village. One basket of paddy is 500 Kyat. Before for one basket of rice [after husking] we had to pay 1,400 Kyat,

*but now we have to pay 1,600 Kyat. That's why we're bitter. If we suffer
any more than this, we'll all die."* - "Saw Daniel" (M, 70), Dta Greh
village, Hlaing Bwe township (Interview #41, 7/99)

In Dta Greh Township villagers have described "double-cropping"
projects presented by SPDC officials as ways to promote their crop yield.
These projects are always devised by SPDC officials in Rangoon as part
of the regime's nationwide agricultural plan, often with the help of the
UNDP (United Nations Development Programme) and other
international agencies. SPDC officials come to villages and call a
meeting with the farmers, where they inform farmers that they are
expected to grow 2 crops per year with the use of fertiliser and other
modern agricultural equipment. Often they insist that farmers donate the
entire second crop to the state, but other times farmers are allowed to
keep the harvest if they pay a significant quota on it to the local SPDC
officials. Guaranteeing that they will donate fertiliser and sophisticated
tools, which are unavailable resources for Karen farmers, the officials
leave without delivering the products or following through on their initial
demonstrations. The second crop inevitably fails because the farmers
never receive their promised fertiliser, which has most likely been sold
by the SPDC officials in charge, but farmers are still forced to pay a
quota on the failed second crop. Farmers go into debt buying rice for a
quota on this nonexistent second crop, or simply never plant it and try to
find the money to pay off the officials.

*"They are not always Burmese soldiers. Sometimes officials come to town
and talk about agricultural development and the villagers have to feed
them too. They come to talk about how to plant and fertilise the rice.
They came to tell us but they didn't do as they said. We never saw
fertiliser or anything else. We have been doing the fields in Dta Greh for
a long time, and it is not productive to fertilise the fields in that area. We
were tired of doing what they taught us with the fertiliser; there was no
improvement. Sometimes when they came to the village, we wanted them
to help us because we don't have anything and our living condition is
poor. They came to tell us that they understand, but we don't understand
them. If they understood, they would come and show us new methods. But
they just come and tell us about them. They already knew that the earth
wasn't fertile, but they came to check. Here the earth is better for
planting mangoes and other fruit. Instead we transplanted 10 baskets of
[paddy] seeds and some years we harvested only 30 or 40 baskets, which
was not enough for us. We had nothing to give to the civil servants [rice
quota collectors], but they also have to give to the government [they must*

collect their given quota with no excuses]. " - "Saw Daniel" (M, 70), Dta Greh village, Hlaing Bwe township (Interview #41, 7/99)

Another challenge to farmers is the SPDC's restricted movement policy for villagers. In order to prevent villagers from being able to contact or supply the KNLA, the military has instituted a policy that villagers must obtain permission to leave the village. All villagers who plan to stay in their field huts must carry a permission letter from a commanding officer or the SPDC village head. Any villager caught outside the village without such a letter is assumed to be affiliated with the KNLA, and may be interrogated, tortured, or even killed. This policy affects farmers with fields far from the village, since they are no longer allowed to stay overnight in their field huts, which farmers traditionally do during most of the labour-intensive growing season from July to November and at various other times during the rice cycle. If they must return to their villages every night they lose a substantial amount of time which they could be devoting to their fields. Restricted movement is a main complaint among farmers who are faced with the dire choice of neglecting their fields or being arrested. With or without a permission letter, if they are working in their fields when an SPDC or DKBA patrol comes by, they are often grabbed as porters.

"They didn't allow the villagers to stay in the farmfield huts. They told us to dismantle our farmfield huts and not to keep them. They said if you keep the field huts, the Kaw Thoo Lei [KNLA soldiers] will come to stay and rest there. The village head went to talk to them, but we had to take them down. They didn't even allow us to tie our cows there. They told us that if they saw us staying in the farmfield huts they would shoot us dead. They think we are all Kaw Thoo Lei. ... The Kaw Thoo Lei never come and the Burmese said they didn't see Kaw Thoo Lei, so the villagers said, 'You don't see them and you still force us to dismantle our farmfield huts. If we go to the field to harvest our paddy, what will we do? Where will we stay? We have no place to stay.' The Burmese said to stay under the shade of the trees and bamboo." - "Saw Ler" (M, 36), Paw Baw Ko village, T'Nay Hsah township (Interview #29, 8/99)

"They dislike people going out to find food and vegetables. They force the married women to stay together [in the village]. They make us stay just in the village, and if we can't find any vegetables in the village we have nothing to eat. You can't sleep in your field hut near your crops or gardens. We have to come back and sleep in the village within the same day. They haven't written [passes for villagers] yet." - "Saw Kee" (M, 21), Ker Ghaw village, T'Nay Hsah township (Interview #11, 9/99)

"If they see the villagers in their huts or fields without passes, they capture them. You can sleep there [in your field hut] for 3 days if you want to, but after that the village head needs to write a permission letter again." - "Naw Hser Paw" (F, 28), Tee Law Thay village, T'Nay Hsah township (Interview #26, 8/99)

Many people have been holding out in or around their villages just hoping to bring in a reasonable harvest this year. However, a villager from the hills of T'Nay Hsah township told KHRG that SPDC troops came in early November while people from his village were harvesting their fields. The farmers fled, and the troops gathered all the paddy they had already harvested into stacks and then burned it, then planted landmines around the fields to prevent the harvest from being completed. On attempting to return to finish their harvest, 2 farmers stepped on mines and were killed and the interviewee was wounded. This type of SPDC activity has also occurred in other Karen districts further north, and could be a final gesture intended to drive the villagers out of their fields and homes. The few villagers who have remained near their homes with the expressed purpose of waiting for the harvest are now forced into hiding, not daring to complete their harvest and unsure where to go next. Most of those who previously fled to the border with Thailand hoping to return for the harvest are now too scared to do so, and remain in a similar state of anxious indecision.

"The Burmese closed the way to the fields, and last year there was no rain. We couldn't plant the paddy so we got no rice. We planted the paddy this year, but we don't know yet if we will dare to harvest the paddy at harvest time. We dare not go back to harvest because we will die. I think that if I dare to go back I will go alone and leave my wife and children here. I am very afraid." - "Maung Shwe" (M, 36), Pah Klu village, T'Nay Hsah township (Interview #19, 8/99)

"The owners were harvesting it, and when they arrived the owners ran. Then they went and gathered it [the paddy they had already cut] in one place and burned it when they were about to leave. They gathered the paddy from P---'s hill field as well as some paddy from other villages and some sticky-rice; they gathered it from 6 hill fields and 4 flat fields, 10 fields altogether. ... Then they laid landmines around there so the villagers wouldn't dare go back. On the day when we went to check on things, one of us was wounded by a landmine. Altogether two people have stepped on landmines. So after that no one has gone back." - "Saw Lay Mu" (M, 33), xxxx village, T'Nay Hsah township; when he tried to

return to the fields in mid-November 1999 he was wounded by a landmine and his friend was killed (Interview #1, 11/99)

DKBA

"They fired guns continuously and children were running and crying. They fired guns before they arrived in the village, and when they arrived on the hill they fired their guns, and when they entered the village they fired their guns again. They frightened all the women in the village, and they laughed at the women who ran with trembling feet. That is their manner and way of thinking." - "Naw Ther Paw" (F, xx), xxxx village, T'Nay Hsah township (Interview #32, 8/99)

The DKBA in southeastern Pa'an District, though under-manned and poorly equipped, have stepped up their campaign to intimidate villagers in order to cripple the KNLA. Founded in December 1994 by a monk named U Thuzana with the backing of the SLORC, the DKBA holds its largest support base in Pa'an District, headquartered at Myaing Gyi Ngu (Khaw Taw) on the Salween River in northern Pa'an District. [For a more comprehensive background on the DKBA, see "Uncertainty, Fear and Flight", KHRG #98-08, 18/11/98, http://metalab.unc.edu/freeburma/humanrights/khrg/archive/khrg98/khrg9808.html] The DKBA is known as the 'Ko Per Baw' ('Yellow Headbands') by villagers because they always wear yellow coloured scarves. The number of their troops is difficult to estimate, but there are probably between 1,500 and 2,000 soldiers at present thinly spread throughout Pa'an, Dooplaya, and Thaton Districts. The DKBA has not received cash salaries from the SPDC in 3 years and they receive very little rations or ammunition, but in some regions their troops are better equipped than in others. It was rumoured that at the end of 1998 the DKBA's rations would be completely cut off by the SPDC, but this has yet to occur; a likely explanation is that the SPDC holds the threat of cutting off support over the DKBA as a means of coercing them to follow SPDC commands. Due to their limited provisions, the DKBA continues to operate in the area by demanding food and money from the villagers. Their lack of support from the SPDC and the tenuous relationship between them has motivated the DKBA to seek out profit-making ventures. In addition to regular extortion from villagers, the DKBA runs checkpoints on major roads demanding money from all passing vehicles, and is deeply involved in the logging business. They forbid logging except for their own purposes, then force villagers to cut logs which they sell primarily to Thai businessmen.

"The people who went out and found money on the black market [selling goods, sometimes back and forth across the border] came back and then they [the Burmese and the Ko Per Baw] demanded their money. Before we came here my husband won 50,000 Kyat in the lottery at the same time that our child was sick. Then the Ko Per Baw asked for that money to rent video equipment, so he didn't get any Kyat for himself. Before my husband left the village he had traded cattle once or twice and the Ko Per Baw knew about it, so when they captured him along the way they stole his money, and now he is in debt for one million Kyat." - "Naw Kyaw" (F, xx), Pah Ka village, Dta Greh township (Interview #33, 8/99)

"The DKBA soldiers came to stay in my village. They are planting landmines to protect their logging, and they are shooting at each other, so we dared not stay." - "Naw Mu Mu Wah" (F, 50), Taw Oak village, T'Nay Hsah township (Interview #30, 8/99)

"They never collected them [fees] before, but now they have started to. From our village of 30 houses they collected 400,000 Kyat. I don't know and didn't ask what they would do with it. Last time they came and asked us through the village head, and the village head gathered us and told us that the Ko Per Baw were demanding it so we had to give it to them. He asked us if we could or would pay them, and if we didn't want to pay them we had to go and leave the village." - "Saw Kler Eh" (M, 30), xxxx village, T'Nay Hsah township (Interview #16, 9/99)

Most of the DKBA soldiers are not former KNLA members, because most of the KNLA soldiers who originally formed the DKBA have already deserted back to civilian life or defected back to the KNLA. Most of the DKBA soldiers are former villagers, some of whom were previously loosely connected to Karen National Defence Organisation (KNDO, a wing of the KNU) village militias, who have joined during the 5 years since the DKBA was founded. The DKBA forces do not usually get along well with the SPDC Battalions, but in this area they often work together, patrolling together and often camping side by side in villages. SPDC Columns in the area almost always have a few DKBA soldiers with them to act as guides, round up villagers as forced labour, and point out villagers as suspects. Both armies demand fees and forced labour from villagers in the area, though in both cases the DKBA's demands are more sporadic and unpredictable; for example, an SPDC Company demands fixed amounts of money weekly or monthly, while a DKBA group may demand nothing for 2 or 3 months and then suddenly demand 100,000 Kyat all at once. Villagers have reported to KHRG that the DKBA requires them to porter, usually carrying rations to troops in neighbouring villages or outposts, and the soldiers have forced them to walk in front of the columns as human minesweepers. As a result, most civilians despise the DKBA as much or more than the SPDC, and often speak of the two groups as one.

"Our village is small, but he demanded porters. He said, 'My son's mother-in-law, I don't ask much of you but it is emergency 'loh ah pay', so give me 15 people.' And after we gave them to him, some have been gone for months and years [died as porters] so we can't do anything. How can we replace them when they are all we have?" - "Naw Hsah Paw" (F, 47), xxxx village, T'Nay Hsah township, talking about demands for porters by DKBA commander Moe Kyo (Interview #2, 11/99)

"They [SPDC] used to come but they don't come any more, now that the DKBA has started controlling the village. Only the militia stays in the village now, but they are working with the Burmese. The DKBA patrol the village, but they rarely force us to work. The Burmese forced us all the time. In the past the Burmese burned the villagers' rice barns, but since the DKBA started patrolling I haven't seen them do it. Before the DKBA came we had to flee quite often. The Burmese arrested porters, so we had to flee or they forced us to work and beat us. Now the DKBA have camps at Lar Ni and Kaw Say Ko. They forced us to go and build the camp, as well as a pagoda and their bunkers. We walked for one day and slept there for 2 or 3 nights, then came back. The DKBA want to kill their enemies, but they haven't killed any villagers. Since the DKBA came the situation has improved, but if they meet us they also treat us badly." - "Saw Maw Hla" (M, 30), Maw Goh village, Lu Pleh township (Interview #43, 7/99)

Because most of the DKBA soldiers are Karen, can speak the villagers' language, and even come from some of the same villages, some hope that the DKBA will treat them more mercifully than the SPDC, but the DKBA in this region have been known to be equally if not more ruthless than the SPDC in their treatment towards villagers. The DKBA has a tenuous relationship with the SPDC, relying on them for rations but in most cases openly distrusting and even hating them; their economic dependence on the SPDC creates an artificial alliance that manifests itself in cruelty towards villagers. Most villagers respond to them in the same way that they do to the SPDC—with fear and compliance—and many speak of a deep resentment for the DKBA because they are Karen people abusing fellow Karen. In Pa'an District villagers have tried to complain to the DKBA about the injustices suffered under the SPDC's occupation of their villages, hoping that the DKBA will act as an ally on the villagers' behalf. They usually have little success winning sympathy; for example, when the village head of Pah Klu pleaded with the DKBA to help stop the raping of village women and extensive looting, she was turned over to the SPDC and savagely beaten. While patrolling with the SPDC, DKBA soldiers have been witnessed torturing and killing innocent villagers accused of having KNU connections, as well as shooting farmers who run from the troops.

"They can't do anything, and if we ask them they say, 'Our footprints are not as big as theirs and we don't dare rebuke them strongly for that'. So they just deal with them gently and softly." - "Naw Hsah Paw" (F, 47), xxxx village, T'Nay Hsah township, describing the reaction of DKBA soldiers when the villagers ask them to intervene with the SPDC (Interview #2, 11/99)

"But during the time when they came and beat people the Ko Per Baw were involved with them. Not one of the Ko Per Baw opened their mouths when they saw the Burmese beating people and shooting people dead." - "Pu Than Nyunt" (M, 55), B'Nweh Pu village, T'Nay Hsah township (Interview #15, 9/99)

"We had to go for both of them [the DKBA and the Burmese] because they are staying in the same place. They didn't hire us, they just came and captured people. Sometimes the Burmese came and ordered it and if the place was near, we went with them. But when the Burmese could not capture people because the villagers ran to escape, the Ko Per Baw came and captured villagers. Since the Ko Per Baw had never captured villagers before, the first time the villagers just stayed in their homes and the Ko Per Baw captured them and handed them to the Burmese." - "Naw Kyaw" (F, xx), Pah Ka village, Dta Greh township (Interview #33, 8/99)

"The Ko Per Baw are staying on the east side of the village and the Burmese are staying on the west side. They stay separately, but they work together. When the Burmese go anywhere, the Ko Per Baw have to go with them. The Ko Per Baw have to spy for them and go in front of the Burmese." - "Saw Nya" (M, 60), Ker Ghaw village, T'Nay Hsah township (Interview #37, 7/99)

"She [the village head] complained to the Ko Per Baw leaders at Ko Ko and the Burmese beat her very badly. It was after we fled here, because the other group that came after us told us. She was telling the truth, but they didn't like that. She said that the Burmese are raping women and

stealing belongings. The Burmese beat her with a stick because they accused her of complaining to the Ko Per Baw about what the Burmese have done. She only reported it to the Ko Per Baw, but they cooperate with the Burmese so the Burmese found out, and they beat her. They accused her of being an informer and they tried to kill her." - "Pu K'Ner" (M, 60), Pah Klu village, T'Nay Hsah township, describing what happened when the village head complained to the DKBA about abuses by the SPDC (Interview #20, 8/99)

A widely feared DKBA commander named Moe Kyo [Burmese for 'Lightning'] has encouraged his troops to generally terrorise villagers and destroy those villages he suspects of having KNU liaisons. He and his troops move throughout much of the Dawna region. Between February 10th and 14th 1999, a DKBA group commanded by Moe Kyo burned 56 houses in the 4 villages of Tee Bper, Dta Wih Ko, Dta Greh Ni and Tee Pa Leh in Dta Greh township after accusing the villagers there of being 'relatives of KNU'. These troops also burned all the family paddy supplies they could find and the piles of rice straw which are used as fodder for the cattle. The villagers have fled into hiding in the forests. Three villagers interviewed by KHRG said they had heard that Moe Kyo recently died from stepping on a landmine, but this report is still unconfirmed. Another notorious DKBA commander in the area is named Chit Thu, also known as Dter Gweh [Sgaw Karen for 'Rainbow'], who commands the 'Special Battalion' of DKBA Brigade #999 and issues many of the orders. These commanders earn their ruthless reputations because despite occasional skirmishes with the KNLA, they—like the SPDC—spend much of their time driving people out of their villages, interrogating and torturing villagers, demanding forced labour and extorting money, with the dual aims of supporting their own operations and destroying the KNLA's support base among the villagers.

"Yes, the DKBA shot 6 people on the 10th of July [1999] in Tee Hsah Ra. I was sleeping at night but I heard it, though I didn't go and look. It was near my house, only a 2-minute walk away. They came at night to shoot people in the fields, then they came back [into the village] to shoot people in the houses. They shot them because they accused them of casting spells over people. But they were villagers, just simple people who cannot do magic or cause harm to people, but only work in the fields. They didn't belong to the opposite side [KNU], they only worked in the fields.... The DKBA [officer(s)] came to look after this happened, but they didn't say anything about it. They didn't accept the fact that they had killed them, and so they're trying to say that it was an accident, that no one killed them. They are going to make the case disappear and make

peace between each other. Commander Maung Chit Thu's soldiers killed them, but he told us it was an accident. But he knew about it because his soldiers had to get permission from him to arrange it, since if he doesn't give permission they can't do anything." - "Pa Po Doh" (M, 24), Tee Hsah Ra village, Myawaddy township (Interview #39, 7/99)

"When Moe Kyo arrived in our village he said that if the people [KNU] attacked them, they would burn down the whole village. He said he would shoot dead all the villagers and burn down all the houses. That is what Moe Kyo said and his soldiers repeated to us. They burned one sugar cane field and also some huts and straw. You can't count all the huts and gardens which they've partly burned. The people who do things like that have envious and jealous hearts, and resent all the people." - "Saw Maw Htoo" (M, xx), Pah Klu village, T'Nay Hsah township (Interview #34, 8/99)

"Before I came here, the people told me the name of the commander was Lin Yone, and people called him "Moe Kyo" [Burmese for 'lightning']. Now he is dead from a landmine. Their chief commander's name is Dter Gweh [also known as Chit Thu]. His troops were shooting between Pah Klu and Loh Baw village. They had a camp in the village. I know because I saw their place and dug the bunkers. At that time the Burmese soldiers also came up and worked with the DKBA. After that, most of the DKBA left the village to go and fight, so few were left." - "Naw Mu Mu Wah" (F, 50), Taw Oak village, T'Nay Hsah township (Interview #30, 8/99)

"They surrounded my daughter's house where I was sleeping, and they interrogated us about whether any Kaw Thoo Lei [KNU/KNLA] were there and if they had laid landmines. The Ko Per Baw were angry and threatened us that they would come and shoot into our wives' vaginas." - "Pu Than Nyunt" (M, 55), B'Nweh Pu village, T'Nay Hsah township (Interview #15, 9/99)

Education and Health

"...they close the school when the children go to work [for forced labour]. If the parents have time to go, we go, but if we have no time, our children must go instead of us. The teachers get a salary from the governor, so they can't do anything about it. They are supposed to get 1,500 Kyat each month but sometimes they only receive 1,500 Kyat for 6 months." - "Saw Maw Hla" (M, 30), Maw Goh village, Lu Pleh township (Interview #43, 7/99)

Among the villagers' many burdens, demands for forced labour and heavy fees are the main factors preventing children from receiving a proper education. Children are often required to fulfil a forced labour shift in lieu of their parents, who must tend the fields to earn enough food. In Pa'an District villagers have reported that children as young as 10 years old are called on to carry water and rations for both SPDC and DKBA troops. Throughout Karen State, the SPDC military places Burmese teachers in villages as a way of phasing out Karen language instruction and cultural history. In some areas the government pays the Burmese teachers' salaries, though they are notoriously underpaid and sometimes receive no money at all for months at a time. In some areas of Pa'an District villagers must pay the Burmese teachers' salaries at a level disproportionate to their own income, while Karen teachers—if they are allowed to teach at all—work on a volunteer basis. In addition, villagers are expected to supply the Burmese teachers with a rice ration. The military even forced villagers in Dta Greh Township to pay for the materials and labour to construct a Burmese school for their children. The greatest irony is that many school-aged children are forced to work for the Burmese instead of attending school, yet their families must pay monthly fees and rations to support the village teachers. If this trend continues much longer, a generation of children in Karen State will lack an education.

"We have a Burmese school with 4 grades. One teacher they gave us, two are from the west of Burma, and one is from the village. Two are paid by the Burmese government and two are Karen volunteers." - "Pa Kyaw" (M, 40), B'Naw Kleh Kee village, T'Nay Hsah township (Interview #22, 8/99)

"I couldn't send them to school. I had no money. It would cost 1,000 Kyat to send the oldest one. When her friends went to school and came back home, she could learn 'Gka Gyi, Ka Kway' ['A, B'; letters of the Burmese alphabet] from them." - "Naw Bway" (F, 29), Pa Noh village, Kyaik Mayaw township, Mon State (Interview #27, 8/99)

"One is a Karen teacher and one is Burmese. I don't know if the Burmese give them money or not. I don't understand and I can't guess. The villagers have to help them by paying with rice. They collect one bowl [about 2 kg] and 10 Kyat from each house per month. Even if you don't send them to school, you have to give." - "Saw Lah Baw" (M, 31), Paw Baw Ko village, T'Nay Hsah township (Interview #28, 8/99)

"Once I saw them ask the villagers to build a school. The villagers also had to pay to build it, and if it wasn't finished by a certain time they said they would fine us. Even if they do something good like that, the villagers have no time to rest. It may have 7 or 8 Standards [up to Grade 7 or 8]. The schoolteacher is from Rangoon. For one year they [the villagers] pay the teacher 10-20,000 kyat." - "Saw Nya" (M, 60), Ker Ghaw village, T'Nay Hsah township (Interview #37, 7/99)

Health care in the villages is in an equally poor state. Some villages have a Karen or Burmese medic qualified to administer basic first aid, but the majority have no medical facilities or supplies at all. If villagers are seriously ill or hurt they have to be carried many kilometres to the nearest clinic, usually in the closest sizeable town. When villagers are injured while doing forced labour or portering, they seldom receive proper medical attention. If the SPDC or DKBA does help them to a nearby clinic or hospital, they are usually left there to cover their own medical expenses. At Myawaddy Hospital, several villagers have reported being forced to leave after their money runs out, even if they are not yet healed. No treatment is given without full payment. Villagers often accrue substantial debts to remain in hospital until their health returns, especially landmine victims whose recovery is typically lengthy.

"We have a medic but we don't have any medicines, only Para [paracetamol]. Ah! If we'd had enough medicines, I don't think those two would have died." - "Saw Lay Mu" (M, 33), xxxx village, T'Nay Hsah township, talking about 2 villagers who stepped on landmines in November 1999 after SPDC troops mined their fields (Interview #1, 11/99)

"After I got injured, my friends carried me to the Burmese. They looked at me, then took me to [Battalion] #356, then sent me to Ra Ma Tee [Myawaddy hospital]...they didn't take care of me...They helped [pay for] only one injection. When I stayed in the hospital they didn't give me any money. I had to spend my own money and eat my own rice because they didn't feed us. I stayed there for over a month before the water festival last season [April 1999]. I spent 45,000 Kyat in the hospital." - "Saw Lah Baw" (M, 31), Paw Baw Ko village, T'Nay Hsah township; both his legs were blown off when he stepped on a landmine while doing forced labour cutting wood for an SPDC bridge project (Interview #28, 8/99)

"I arrived at the other side of the river, I didn't know that the Burmese had arrived. ... I was outside the village, but they were inside the village

when they shot at me. The young man from my village who had come with me ran from behind me and passed me. The Burmese shot at him but hit my leg instead, so I fell down. They didn't come to look at me, and they went away. I was left alone for a while until I saw a young woman who was coming back from gathering firewood. I told her to go back and tell my son to come and get me. ... When I arrived at Ker Ghaw, they gave me 3,000 Kyat and told me to go to Myawaddy Hospital. How would 3,000 Kyat be enough? I stayed there for 10 days and they took care of me while I still had money, but when my money ran out they stopped taking care of me. When it was gone, I had to go back to my village again. Then I asked people to treat it with traditional medicine and holy oil. I can't stand up yet because it is painful." - "Pu Dta Ler" (M, 50-60), Pah Klu village, T'Nay Hsah township (Interview #45, 4/99)

Forced Relocation

"I couldn't stay near my place because they are going to stir up our place. I heard them say that they are going to drive all the villagers out to the same place. They didn't tell us where or when they will drive us out, but they said that they would. They will gather and force out all of the villagers that are living around Meh Pleh Toh. They will block every path that passes or goes through Meh Pleh Toh until nothing can move, even food and other things. I heard that they will make trouble for people who stay in the mountains, that especially if they see men they will kill them at once. Our village head alerted us. If they see them, they will shoot dead all villagers as far as they can see." - "Saw Baw" (M, 29), Tee Law Thay village, T'Nay Hsah township (Interview #24, 8/99)

Forced relocation of villages has become the chief means by which the SPDC military exerts control over villages which are not fully under its influence. In the past the Army has primarily targeted villages with past or present connections to the KNLA, villages located within KNU-controlled territory and/or too far away to supervise in regular patrols from an SPDC Army camp, and villages who have resisted SPDC demands for forced labour and extortion fees. In late 1998 KHRG reported that the SPDC Army had issued an order that villages between Taw Oak and Kyaw Ko would be forcibly relocated to Ker Ghaw, Kwih Lay, or Kyaw Ko at the end of the rice harvest. While some villagers scattered or moved, most managed to hold off from being relocated. However, SPDC columns have been acting directly to enforce the forced relocations since August 1999. One of the final relocation sites is indeed Ker Ghaw, the site of a DKBA Army camp, where the villages Kwih Lay, Pah Klu, and Taw Oak are now being forced to move. The villages

Thay K'Dtee, Toh Thu Kee, and Kyaw Ko are being relocated to another site at Tee Wah Blaw, where SPDC columns temporarily camp while patrolling the area, and where they may be planning to establish a permanent camp once they have relocated all villagers. SPDC troops also destroyed all of the villagers' farmfield huts in the area of B'Naw Kleh Kee village right in the middle of the rice-growing season when villagers need to live in their farmfield huts. SPDC Light Infantry Battalions #310 and #120 have occupied the area of Pah Klu and Taw Oak villages, and Light Infantry Battalions #9 and #2 have occupied the area of Ker Ghaw and Kyaw Ko villages.

"I heard that the Burmese would drive all the villagers to a relocation place. They said they would force ten villages. The name of the villages are Thi Wah Pu, Toh Thu Kee, Pu Wee, Tee Wah Klay, Meh Pleh Wah Kee, Day Law Pya, and Po Thwee Mu. They will surely force them to Ker Ghaw. As for us, the DKBA already tried to force us to Ker Ghaw one time, but we didn't go because our monk pleaded for us." - "Naw Mu Mu Wah" (F, 50), Taw Oak village, T'Nay Hsah township (Interview #30, 8/99)

"...the villages like Thay Wah Pu and Wah Klu Pu and others are all going to be forced down to the lower places, maybe to Ko Ko. Then they will send their Army to that place so there will be one Army unit to guard every village. ... we heard it from the Ko Per Baw secretly. They said that 2 Divisions of Burmese Army troops will come here. A unit of troops will guard each village. All the villages: Toh Thu Kee, Thay K'Dtee, Loh Baw, Pah Klu, Tee Wah Klay, and Wah Klu Pu they will move to a place near Ko Ko, but we don't know where exactly because they did not tell us where. Then they will guard us." - "Pu K'Ner" (M, 60), Pah Klu village, T'Nay Hsah township (Interview #20, 8/99)

"I heard that the villages of Day Law Pya and Meh Pleh Wah Kee will move along with Pah Klu village if there are still people in these villages. They will force us to Ker Ghaw, according to a villager from Loh Baw. Der!! We were afraid that they would drive us to the lowlands [the plains to the west] and make us go among the landmines. The Loh Baw villager told us 'They will force us together', but I was not optimistic about this because I worried about the landmines. I heard people say that they would start driving us out after this month." - "Saw Nyo" (M, 50), Pah Klu village, T'Nay Hsah township (Interview #25, 8/99)

The DKBA also came through the Meh Pleh Toh area to warn villagers that two SPDC Light Infantry Divisions are planning to clear all villagers there before the end of this year. They told the villagers that they will be forced into the centre of the villages, where they will be guarded by soldiers. According to KNU sources, troops from as many as 5 different SPDC Light Infantry Divisions have been sent into the area for an operation to run from August to December 1999, intending to subjugate the area with a special focus on clearing landmines by using villagers as human minesweepers. The operation seems to be a final push to obliterate the KNU hold on the Dawna mountains in the southeastern part of the district. In B'Naw Kleh Kee villagers were ordered to dismantle their houses and field huts which could later be used as KNLA shelters. The Army made it clear to all villagers in the are that anyone remaining in the relocated villages after the deadline passed would be shot on sight, no questions asked.

"They already forced them down [out of the hills] one time, then the villagers pleaded with them and they allowed them to go back. They will force them to Meh K'Neh village near the main road. We think that they forced the villagers away because recently the Kaw Thoo Lei [KNU/KNLA] came to shoot them and they were angry, so they forced the villagers out in order to starve the Kaw Thoo Lei." - "Pi Ghaw Paw" (F, 51), Meh K'Neh village, Myawaddy township (Interview #40, 7/99)

"Htee Klay village and all the villages at the foot of the mountains were all forced to relocate before I came. The reason was because their villages are at the foot of the mountains, so the Karen soldiers could stay there, and sometimes they shot at the Burmese soldiers who went near them. They forced them to move to Noh Ta Bweh and Klaw Kla, or to other villages near the foot of the mountains. They gave the village heads an order on paper saying they had to relocate within 15 days. They could take along their houses and things." - the father of "Nan Paw Oa" (F, 18), xxxx village, Kawkareik township (Interview #42, 7/99)

The motivating factors behind the forced relocation of villages are firstly to eliminate the possibility of KNU contact with villagers, thereby weakening their hold on the district, and secondly to concentrate the population of villagers so that they can conveniently be drawn upon for forced labour and portering. Once relocated to sites close to Army garrisons, villagers can no longer escape forced labour shifts, and the Army relies on them to work rice fields confiscated by the military. Villagers are not given any rations, and in many relocations they are forced to hand over their own rice to the Army and then receive a small ration of it back every few days. If they are lucky they can get passes to go and farm their own fields, but these passes usually require them to return by sunset and their fields may be too far away. The restricted movement policy also prevents them from foraging for food away from the site. KHRG has spoken with several villagers who have also expressed great fear of being used as human minesweepers if they live in close vicinity to the soldiers. Rumours of the dangers and threat of starvation at the relocation sites have reached villagers who have yet to leave their villages, and these stories persuade many to flee rather than relocate or wait for soldiers to forcibly move them. As of late August, Pah Klu village was entirely empty save for a few families and monks at the monastery, because all villagers had chosen to flee before the ordered deadline. For many villagers who have struggled to remain on their land, the relocation order is the last straw in a series of abuses. Most are choosing to head for the jungle rather than wait to be forcibly relocated to an Army-controlled site.

"They said they would drive us all out of the villages in the Meh Pleh Toh area. When I stayed with them, the Burmese told me themselves that they were ordered to clear the place and drive the villagers to a relocation site. I asked them, 'Where will you force us to go?' and he told me, 'I don't know. You have to ask the commander.' I had to stay with the soldiers who arrested me, and they joked together. I said to them, 'If you drive us to a relocation site, we will have no rice to eat.' He said to me, 'I don't know, because we were ordered to do it, so we have to. We wouldn't do it if we weren't ordered to do it.' They are Karen people." - "Saw Lah Ku" (M, 21), Pah Klu village, T'Nay Hsah township (Interview #18, 8/99)

"When we fled there were only one or two households left, but they already took their belongings to their huts in their fields. We have a lot of villagers staying in the jungle now, but I don't know how many exactly. Just a few villagers arrived here, and the rest ran to K--- and to T---. Some also arrived at D--- [on the Thai border]." - "Saw Nyo" (M, 50), Pah Klu village, T'Nay Hsah township (Interview #25, 8/99)

"I heard that the Burmese would drive us out so we dared not stay and came here. I don't know when or where because they didn't tell us. Also I don't know how many villages they will drive out. They just said that if we are still staying in the jungle [i.e. in remote villages] then we are surely feeding the Kaw Thoo Lei [KNU/KNLA]. They say that if they drive the villagers from the area, they will starve the Kaw Thoo Lei. I think that they will drive out all the villages. We stayed in the jungle at our fields. If they drive us out, they will drive out all." - "Maung Shwe" (M, 36), Pah Klu village, T'Nay Hsah township (Interview #19, 8/99)

Flight and Internally Displaced Persons

"We didn't bring anything with us when we fled, just only the clothes we were wearing. I couldn't bring other things because I had to carry my 3 year old son. No one knows what the Burmese will do because if they see people in the mountains they shoot them dead, and if people stay in the village they force them to do 'loh ah pay'. We couldn't do anything. I think all of the villagers left the village after I left; there were 17 households left and I think all have fled to the jungle." - "Pa Kyaw" (M, 40), B'Naw Kleh Kee village, T'Nay Hsah township (Interview #22, 8/99)

The SPDC's operation to clear villages and undermine KNLA activity in southeastern Pa'an district has resulted in thousands of villagers fleeing to hide in their farmfield huts or in the hills, where they risk arrest or being shot on sight by SPDC forces. At first they try to hide outside the village and return whenever SPDC columns are not around, but more and more SPDC troops are now basing themselves in the villages so many people are staying outside their villages permanently. Many of them are finding it too dangerous to do this for long and they have no more food, so a steady stream of refugees has been heading for the Thai border. A new flow of villagers began in mid-August; the first groups were allowed into existing refugee camps in Thailand, but by the end of August the Thai Army began blocking them, leaving them stranded at makeshift and vulnerable sites on the west bank of the Moei River, just on the Burma side of the border. The villagers have fled secretly, travelling through heavy rains along washed-out and treacherous pathways which can best be compared to mudholes, making it almost impossible to cross the Dawna mountains. Shelter along the way is scarce, as is food and medicine. Villagers from areas further from the border often have to resort to car travel, which is expensive and requires paying off every DKBA and SPDC checkpoint along the way. Because of these factors, flight during the rainy season is avoided at all costs, so their decision to face these dangers testifies to the desperate situation facing them in their villages. Flight is the very last option for Karen villagers, who cannot imagine living far from their fields or outside the village network.

"We have to pay money if we dare not go, and if we can't give money we have to run. If we run we don't need to pay because the village head can't find us when we run into the mountains. People who live in the village have to give it, and the villagers who don't want to give it have to run and stay in the mountains like my family. I had to run because I had no money to give, and we just didn't have enough money to buy food." -

"Saw Baw" (M, 29), Tee Law Thay village, T'Nay Hsah township (Interview #24, 8/99)

"In the past there were 40 households, but the villagers all fled. Now there are only 15 households left in the village." - "Naw Mu Mu Wah" (F, 50), Taw Oak village, T'Nay Hsah township (Interview #30, 8/99)

"We arrived here 4 days ago with 4 families, and another 3 families are arriving today. If we came in front of the Burmese, they would not have allowed us to come, so we had to come secretly. They would have arrested us and tied us up. If they can't catch you and you run, they shoot to kill. The Burmese always came to shoot the villagers who stay in the village, so we always had to flee. You must flee. If you didn't flee and they captured you, they wouldn't release you." - "Maung Shwe" (M, 36), Pah Klu village, T'Nay Hsah township (Interview #19, 8/99)

"We had to come during the rainy season so we had many problems on the way. We got sick and had no medicine and not enough food. We slept in the mountains for 5 days and arrived at the Moei River on the 6th day. We stayed at Tee Ner Hta for one day, then came here." - "Pa Kyaw" (M, 40), B'Naw Kleh Kee village, T'Nay Hsah township (Interview #22, 8/99)

"On the way I had to pay for car fare, but I had no money left. I had only 1,000 Kyat left and I didn't have a citizen card, so I dared not come here. They asked me to pay 1,000 Kyat in Tha M'Nya, so I had to give it all to them. I had only little coins left. I asked my Aunt for a little money for car and boat fare. When I arrived at Myawaddy, it was all gone. On the way my children didn't get rice to eat." - "Naw Bway" (F, 29), Pa Noh village, Kyaik Mayaw township, Mon State (Interview #27, 8/99)

The actual number of those who have fled is impossible to estimate because most remain inside Burma, hiding in the jungle near their villages and struggling to survive by planting hill fields and foraging for food. Of those who have braved the dangerous journey to Thailand, only some have been able to cross safely into refugee camps. At the end of 1998 over 2,000 refugees arrived at the site called Meh La Po Hta, on the Burma side of the border, after the SPDC burned 5 villages; now their population has swollen to over 5,000 as people continue to flee from eastern Pa'an District. They remain there in a state of fear, unable to return to their villages after the SPDC Army destroyed the rice harvest. The current flow of villagers from southeastern Pa'an District began in mid-1999. The first 37 families from five villages including Pah Klu,

B'Naw Kleh Kee, Htee Wah Klay, Htee Law Thay, and Day Law Pya were admitted to Beh Klaw refugee camp, while others made it to Huay Kaloke refugee camp. However, at the end of August the Thai Army and police stopped new arrivals from heading to the camps, telling them they would have to go back across the border. Since then over 500 people have gathered at two main sites on the Burma side of the Moei River: Law Thay Hta, across the river from the Thai Karen village of Dta Lah Oh Klah (35 kilometres north of Myawaddy and Mae Sot), and Tee Ner Hta, across the border from Beh Klaw refugee camp.

"Most people have already left the village. More than a hundred people fled to Beh Klaw [refugee camp]. People were leaving day after day. They started leaving in July and August. First they went to stay in their farmfield huts, then they went on further." - "Saw Than" (M, 43), xxxx village, T'Nay Hsah township (Interview #5, 11/99)

Although some are staying on the Burma side of the river by choice, still hoping to return home for the harvest if the situation improves, many refugees interviewed by KHRG have said that the Thai authorities have pushed them back across the border when they tried to enter Thailand. The majority of the 500 villagers at those sites expressed desire to the Thai Army to enter a refugee camp, but they claim that the soldiers refused them access to the camp and forced them to return to the Burmese side of the river. Over 70 families who had arrived at Tee Ner Hta tried to enter Thailand in August and were not allowed to go to a refugee camp, so they tried to stay around the villages on the Thai side of the border but were then ordered back across to Tee Ner Hta by the Thai Army in late August. They had no option but to remain at Tee Ner Hta. The SPDC forces soon discovered their location and heavily shelled it in early September, at which point they scattered in different directions in the jungle. Some of them managed to join those presently at Law Thay Hta, though the whereabouts of the majority are still unknown. There are additional reports that more than 80 other families have managed to enter Thailand and are currently seeking admission to Beh Klaw refugee camp, though their future remains uncertain.

"Their [SPDC] aim is to destroy our Karen nationals until we disappear. I heard this from the village head, who said it is because the Karen villagers who stay in the mountains and work the hillfields are all considered as their enemies. If they see women they rape them, and if they meet men they kill them. It is better to stay in the village but there is too much forced labour there. The village head told us, 'If you cannot stay here anymore and need to go you can go, because there are people

who will look after you'. " - "Saw Baw" (M, 29), Tee Law Thay village,
T'Nay Hsah township (Interview #24, 8/99)

In September there were 61 families (244 people) clustered at Law Thay
Hta, most of whom arrived between four and eight months ago. The
majority of these families are from villages in the area around T'Nay
Hsah and Myawaddy townships. With their food supply rapidly
dwindling or already exhausted, the villagers decided to cross in late
August/early September to the Thai Karen village of Dta Lah Oh Klah to
work as hired farm labour with the intent to buy rice. In early September
they set up a temporary camp near Dta Lah Oh Klah, but remained there
only 5-6 days before the Thai Army discovered their location and forced
them to cross the border again, on the grounds that their "camp" was
illegitimate. In the move back to the Karen side, at least six families
disappeared into the Thai illegal labour market or attempted the
dangerous journey back to their villages. In the days of early September,
SPDC forces patrolled the border area near Law Thay Hta, and the
villagers once again fled to safety in Thailand. That time they dispersed
in the area around Dta Lah Oh Klah, taking day labour jobs and staying
in surrounding villages. Again the Thai Army discovered them and
forced them back to the Karen side once the danger of attack by SPDC
forces had passed. Soon after this, the SPDC Army and KNLA engaged
in fighting north of the villagers' location. Warned by the KNLA of an
imminent SPDC attack, the villagers again crossed to Thailand on
September 25th, returning to the Karen side on September 28th when
KNLA soldiers warned them they were in danger of re-discovery by Thai
authorities, and because the imminent threat of attack by SPDC forces
was over.

All of the villagers interviewed by KHRG expressed a desire to enter Beh
Klaw refugee camp, but insisted that the Thai Army had denied them
access to the camp and forced them to re-cross the border twice. The
villagers stranded on the Karen side of the border have little choice but to
continue on in their present situation, waiting and hoping that Thai
authorities will allow them entry to refugee camps. In statements to Non-
Governmental Organisations and the UNHCR (United Nations High
Commissioner for Refugees) the Thai Army has denied blocking access
to the refugee camp to any new arrivals, but this contradicts the
testimonies of many of the villagers themselves.

The refugee camps in Thailand are already full beyond capacity, but the
Thai authorities are determined to further decrease the number of camps
through camp consolidations, and they flatly refuse to consider the

possibility of creating any more space for refugees - instead, they state that it is time to begin planning the forced repatriation of the refugees already in the country. Therefore they do not want to allow any new refugees, regardless of the situation in Burma. The UNHCR is currently holding closed-door negotiations with the Thai Army and government on the future of the refugees, but refuses to disclose any of the content of these negotiations to the non-governmental organisations who work with the refugees. Most agencies, including the UNHCR, say that they are not allowed to cross the border to see or speak to the internally displaced stranded on the other side. Meanwhile these families have little or no food and medicine and are in great danger of attack by SPDC forces who regularly patrol the area. Frightened of both the Burmese and Thai Armies, and protected by only a handful of KNLA soldiers, they are holding out for the unlikely scenario that the persecution in their villages will abate, or that the Thais will admit them to refugee camps.

"The [Thai] police. They came just a few days ago and told us, 'You can't stay here anymore and you have to go back and stay there.' They forced us to move within one day, so people separated into groups and ran. We stayed on the bank of the river until our Karen leaders here told us to come back and build our huts here, and they took care of us. We don't have new arrivals from my village because they have all gone to Beh Klaw [refugee] camp already. They dared not stay and face all of the demands and torture, so they fled here, too. Some villagers still stay there because they are working on their paddy fields and can't leave. But after they finish working more villagers will flee here...Right now we dare to stay here, but if people send us to the refugee camp we will go. If the Burmese come and shoot at us, we'll have to run to the other side of the river, and when the dry season arrives [in November/December] we dare not stay here because we will be afraid of the Burmese again." - "Saw Ghay" (M, 36), Tee Hsah Ra village, Myawaddy township (Interview #7, 9/99)

"The only problem is that sometimes the Thais come and chase us [when they cross the river into Thailand], so we always have to run. I don't know if they are Thai police or Thai Army, but people are frightened and always tell us to run. They are around 10 soldiers and they sleep on the other side of the river. All of them wear a uniform. They told us that we can't go and stay there because we don't have Ta Gaw Koe [a Thai ID card]. So we couldn't stay at xxxx, and we came back and built our huts here. After that the leaders here went and told them something, I don't know what, and since then we can go back and work there. We hire ourselves out for 60 Baht [per day] to pull up beans for them. If we

didn't do it we wouldn't have food to eat so we have to do it. We buy rice in M---. They [the Thais] like it a lot if we buy things there." - "Saw Lay Htoo" (M, 42), Ler Dah village, Hlaing Bwe township (Interview #10, 9/99)

"...they just told us that because a lot of people had fled there [to Thailand] it was causing trouble, and they ordered the villagers to move back. They came and stayed for 3 or 4 days, and when they left we went back, too. They don't want us to stay there. When we first arrived back there they didn't know about us, but after a while more and more of our friends came. Now they know about it, so they drove us back here again because a lot of people came to stay there. They said it is messy so we had to move. They said, 'Don't come and stay here for a long time' because it is their land." - "Naw Paw Htoo" (F, 27), Taw Oak village, T'Nay Hsah township (Interview #9, 9/99)

Future of the Area

"When I was trying to find my husband, T--- told me to go and find him for them, and if I couldn't find him he was going to kill me and my children and my mother. Myself, I thought if he wants to kill me then kill me. Being a villager is the very worst, so if he wants to kill me, go ahead. I would be happy to die." - "Naw Ther Paw" (F, xx), xxxx village, T'Nay Hsah township; T--- is a local DKBA officer, and his troops later shot her husband dead (Interview #32, 8/99)

There are no indications that conditions will soon improve for the villagers of southeastern Pa'an District. The brutality of the current SPDC offensive indicates their commitment to eradicating the KNLA's presence in the area, but the KNLA has always been strong in this area and it is very unlikely that the SPDC could succeed in this objective. The KNLA, furthermore, has vowed never to surrender, and reports from KNLA soldiers in the field and independent sources suggest that morale is good despite being under-manned and ill-equipped. The guerrilla tactics of the KNLA, including landmine warfare, still manage to deter the SPDC and DKBA from completely controlling the district. There is no indication that any of the parties to the conflict will cease laying mines, and their proliferation is a serious and growing concern; when interviewed by KHRG, villagers from the region now speak of landmines as one of their greatest fears and concerns, which was not the case 2 to 3 years ago. Most local SPDC units fear KNLA landmines as much as villagers do and therefore try to keep their patrols to a minimum, but when ordered to clear villages they mobilise in large numbers and seize villagers to walk in front of them. Villagers depend on the KNLA to alert them about SPDC columns passing through, and in return villagers continue to provide the KNLA with necessary supplies and porters, whether voluntarily or by coercion. In the past six months the SPDC and DKBA have collaborated in the area with the resolve to purge the KNLA by waging war against innocent villagers. So far they have spared no one.

"They did not come to do the best thing for the villagers. They came to break the villagers. I do not feel good since the Burmese came to the village. I suffer always. I eat in the morning and have to think for the evening, then I eat in the evening and have to think for the morning. We have no food to eat and no money to pay the fees, and we could not suffer anymore. That's why we came here." - "Saw Lah Ku" (M, 21), Pah Klu village, T'Nay Hsah township (Interview #18, 8/99)

"I could support my family if we didn't need to fear them, and if they didn't disturb us. But in this messy situation, I had no time to work." - "Saw Baw" (M, 29), Tee Law Thay village, T'Nay Hsah township (Interview #24, 8/99)

"How can I feel when they come and rape our daughters and ask to have sex with my wife? And they loot all of our belongings and our paddy. Last year we could not plant paddy, so we have to buy paddy but then they come and take it. They don't have any rations and their leaders don't send them rice, only alcohol. So they eat all of ours." - "Pu K'Ner" (M, 60), Pah Klu village, T'Nay Hsah township (Interview #20, 8/99)

In the past Thailand has offered sanctuary to Karen refugees, but the villagers are the overlooked victims of the recently tense political situation between Rangoon and Bangkok. Following the armed attack on the Burmese Embassy in Bangkok in early October by a fringe group of Burmese exiles, Thai-Burmese relations soured, resulting in the Burmese closure of 'legal' border trading for 2 months. Beginning in early November, Thai authorities were ordered to round up all illegal migrant Burmese workers in Thailand, numbering in the hundreds of thousands, and deport them to Burma. Thousands of these workers fit the international criteria for refugees but had joined the Thai illegal labour force because they could not or did not want to go into refugee camps. Many of them have been forced to return to their villages, many of which have been destroyed or relocated during the time they have lived in Thailand. This eliminated any possibility of earning a living to support their families, as jobs are few in Burma and do not pay enough to survive. Given the danger of return to their villages through heavily mined areas and SPDC/DKBA controlled territory, many workers were forced to pay huge extortion fees to stay in Thailand to Thai authorities, which sent them into debt, or flee into the jungle to avoid capture. Stranded on the border for weeks, most workers have now dispersed on the Burmese side or returned to factories in Mae Sot and other border towns, where they run the risk of re-arrest.

"The Burmese closed the way to the fields, and last year there was no rain. We couldn't plant the paddy so we got no rice. We planted the paddy this year, but we don't know yet if we will dare to harvest the paddy at harvest time. We dare not go back to harvest because we will die. I think that if I dare to go back I will go alone and leave my wife and children here. I am very afraid." - "Maung Shwe" (M, 36), Pah Klu village, T'Nay Hsah township (Interview #19, 8/99)

This dry season does not bode well for Karen villagers in the area. It is very likely that most or all villages will be relocated by the SPDC Army, and those that choose not to go to the relocation sites will have to flee into the hills. Most, however, will not be able to survive there due to the landmines, poor nutrition and health standards, and danger of attack. The few left in their villages hesitate to leave their fields, which are their only source of income and food, but their families and friends at the Thai border report that many have been waiting until the end of the harvest before fleeing. This means that there will be probably be an increase over the next month in the number of people joining fellow villagers on the banks of the Moei River. Most will be unable to cross into the refugee camps because of current Thai policy, but the lucky few who manage to cross will either sneak into refugee camps and swell the already burgeoning numbers there, or attempt to find an illegal job somewhere in Thailand. The fate of these people depends to a large degree on the policy of the Thai authorities. The closure of the refugee camps and the recent move of two long-standing camps to a location far from the border are both ominous signs for those seeking sanctuary in Thailand. New arrivals will be forced to become unregistered refugees—and therefore receive no rations—hiding at Beh Klaw (Mae La), or attempt to reach Umpiem Mai, a new camp combining the old camps of Huay Kaloke (Wangka) and Maw Ker, which is also at capacity. However, Umpiem Mai is over 50 kilometres from the crossing point of refugees from Pa'an District, so it is almost impossible for new refugees to reach it without being stopped and arrested as illegal migrants by Thai authorities. Villagers inside Burma have heard rumours of full camps and pushbacks by Thai authorities, and are reluctant to make the dangerous journey without the assurance of refuge across the border. Meanwhile, the Thais are trying to appease Rangoon after the embassy crisis by mounting pressure on the UNHCR to speed up the repatriation of refugees, so even those in camps may soon be at risk of losing sanctuary.

"We couldn't deal with the forced labour and fee collections, so we fled and came here for a better future. We still have people there who will come here. Some villagers still have their fields and are waiting to finish the harvest before they come. I came here alone but my wife and children arrived yesterday." - "Pa Po Doh" (M, 24), Tee Hsah Ra village, Myawaddy township (Interview #39, 7/99)

"If I go back to my village, I'll have no rice to eat. My children have been working in the fields, but since there was no rain we didn't get enough rice. My daughter has two small children, and my daughter-in-law also has two small children who are still breastfeeding. My daughter-in-law is

ill in the hospital. When we are cured, we would like to stay here as refugees with all our children, but we don't have any money to build a house." - "Pu Dta Ler" (M, 50-60), Pah Klu village, T'Nay Hsah township (Interview #45, 4/99)

"It is not easy to go back. It will be many long years before the situation gets better. I think it will not change for a while. Some people say that the situation will become peaceful, but that will not be easy. It made my heart unhappy that I had to work for them, which is why I came here. I couldn't suffer anymore. After 2 or 3 years I'd had enough of working like that. The other villagers with fields and cattle want to come here too, but they can't. The rich villagers have to stay because they cannot leave their fields and cattle, but we could come because we had nothing. But if all our people go back, I wouldn't dare stay here alone." - "Saw Maw Hla" (M, 30), Maw Goh village, Lu Pleh township (Interview #43, 7/99)

"[when asked if he thinks the SPDC has come to do good things] I am very afraid that they will come to do 'good things' like that. I think that they have not come to do good things. I don't know if the situation will get better. If our country gets freedom, I will go back. But Karen people said to stay here [displaced on the Burma side of the border] for the moment, and that they will plan a place for us [implying that they will arrange admission into a refugee camp in Thailand]. If they do not send for us, we don't know where we'll go." - "Maung Shwe" (M, 36), Pah Klu village, T'Nay Hsah township; shortly after he was interviewed, the internally displaced camp where he was staying at Tee Ner Hta was shelled by SPDC troops (Interview #19, 8/99)

The full text of the interviews quoted in this report is available at: http://metalab.unc.edu/freeburma/humanrights/khrg/archive/khrg99/khrg 9908a.html

Photographs

Plates 27, 28: Some of the anti-personnel landmines increasingly being used by SPDC troops in Pa'an district. SLORC/SPDC used to rely mainly on imported mines, but over the past few years China has provided them with factories and technology to produce most of their landmines themselves. Plate #27 (above) shows, from left, a Burmese-made MM-1 mine, an old U.S.-made M76A1 mine, a Burmese-made MM-2 mine, and another U.S.-made M76A1. Plate #30 (right) shows a Burmese-made MM1 mine rigged on a post with a tripwire, found along a path used by villagers in Pa'an District. Both the MM-1 and MM-2 are made in Burma in factories supplied by China. The MM-1 is a copy of the Chinese-made POMZ-2 or 'corncob' mine, and the MM-2 is a copy of the Chinese-made PMN mine; both of these Chinese models have been heavily used in Cambodia. The SPDC has stockpiles of Chinese-made mines but now mainly uses the Burmese-made models. *[Photos: Plate 32: FTUB, 33: KNLA]*

Plate 29: A 15-year old girl from Papun District who was taken as a porter by SLORC troops. She was finally released at Kyauk Nyat, but while trying to make her way home she stepped on a landmine which blew off her lower right leg. This photo was taken only a few hours afterward. *[Photo: KHRG]*

Plate 30: A Karen farmer, taken by force from his fields near Myawaddy town in southern Pa'an District to porter supplies for an SPDC column. After being badly mistreated for 2-3 days and seeing others brutalised, he escaped on 26 February 1999 with a friend. He heard his friend being captured and tortured, so he fled through the forest in the dark and stumbled over a tripwire rigged to a landmine. He suffered serious wounds to his entire left side, including his left eye. He managed to continue, bleeding and in pain, reached the Thai border and a refugee clinic where he received treatment. *[Photo: KHRG]*

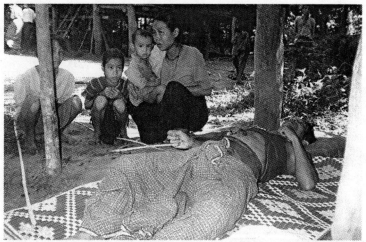

Plate 31: Neh Shway Lay, age 42, a Karen animist farmer of Thi Wah village, southeastern Pa'an district. After fleeing his village because of abuse and forced labour inflicted by both SPDC and DKBA, he returned with two friends to his home one last time in order to complete animist ceremonies connected with leaving his house. On arriving, he and his friends stood talking when a column of SPDC LIB 356 troops saw them and immediately opened fire. Neh Shway Lay was shot in the back with an exit wound in his belly, and his friend M--- was hit in the thigh but managed to escape. While Neh Shway Lay was on the ground moaning and dying all night, his wife, who was in the house, tried to go to him but the SPDC and DKBA troops would not allow her. The photo shows his family and his body the following day, after the troops had left. At the time his wife was 8 months pregnant. *[Photo: KHRG]*

Plate 32: Saw A---, age 17. On April 20th 1999, LIB 106 engaged the KNLA near Win Yaw village in Dooplaya district. As a punishment for the villagers they then fired shells into the village, and one of the shells broke the right calf and penetrated the belly of Saw A---. He is still alive in the photo. *[Photo: KHRG]*

Plates 33, 34 (above): Villagers in T'Nay Hsah (Nabu) township on their way to the local SPDC Army camp. They were ordered to each bring 2 pieces of bamboo and do forced labour building a security fence around the camp. Plate 35 (below): Going for forced labour cutting and clearing a road. One person per household has to go on a regular basis. As the photos show, parents who have to work for their family's survival often have no choice but to send their children. *[Photos: KHRG]*

Plate 36: A girl looks at the burned ruins of her house after it was burned by DKBA troops commanded by Moe Kyo in February 1999. Moe Kyo's unit burned 56 houses in the 4 villages of Tee Bper, Dta Greh Ni, Dta Wih Ko and Tee Pa Leh in Dta Greh township after accusing the villagers of being 'relatives of KNU'. First the troops scattered each family's paddy supply under their house and then burned it with the house. [Photo: KHRG]

Plate 37: SLORC deserter, age 14, Pa'an District. He was taken as a soldier when aged 13, given short training and sent to the frontlines of KNLA 7th Brigade in Pa'an District. He ran away in March 1997 because he said he was not strong enough to carry his G3 [SLORC assault rifle, much bigger and heavier than most assault rifles] and 200 rounds of ammunition as ordered. [Photo: Karen source]

Plate 38: Internally displaced villagers at Meh La Po Hta, a site adjacent to the border with Thailand, in January 1999. They did not want to go to a refugee camp in Thailand because they still hoped to return to their fields to harvest, and then Thai forces began blocking the border. The population of this camp swelled to over 4,000, and smaller IDP camps were formed at Tee Ner Hta and Law Thay Hta. In September 1999 the SPDC shelled and destroyed Tee Ner Hta, then in March/April 2000 they shelled and destroyed Meh La Po Hta and Law Thay Hta. The villagers from all the sites scattered, most of them into Thailand, but Thai authorities do not want to accept them into refugee camps so many have no choice but to return. *[Photo: KHRG]*

Plate 39: New refugee arrivals in Beh Klaw refugee camp, August 1999. At the time, new arrivals from Pa'an District were held in the school by Thai authorities for months with no proper living conditions. When this photo was taken, the Thai Army had already begun blocking all new arrivals from crossing the border in the area. *[Photo: KHRG]*

Appendix: Table of Killings by SPDC Troops

The following list has been reproduced from the report "Death Squads and Displacement" published by KHRG in May 1999 (see Section 1 of this book). It is included here to give an idea of the systematic nature of SLORC/SPDC killings of villagers in rural areas. This is a partial list of villagers killed directly at the hands of regular SPDC troops and Sa Thon Lon units between January 1997 and April 1999 in Nyaunglebin District and the area of Tantabin township, Toungoo District which lies just north of Nyaunglebin District. These killings have been described in the interviews and field reports collected for the report "Death Squads and Displacement", and many of them have been corroborated by several interviews and field reports.

There are 151 people in this list who have been killed since 1997, but it is important to emphasise that this list is far from complete because it is only based on interviews and field reports gathered by KHRG; the true number of those killed is most likely double or triple this amount. Furthermore, this list does not include those shot at, wounded without being killed, or the hundreds who have died of starvation, disease and accident caused by having to flee their villages. Due to the amount of time it takes to travel in these areas and obtain information, there are few accounts of killings which have occurred over the past few months; this does not reflect a decrease in the rate of killing, just a difficulty in obtaining reliable information. Under 'Twp.' (Township), S = Shwegyin, K = Kyauk Kyi, M = Mone, P = Pyu township west of the Sittaung River, and T = Tantabin township, Toungoo District. Under 'Source', FR indicates Field Reports from KHRG field reporters, and 'Ix' indicates interviews with villagers, 'x' being the interview number used in the report.

Date	Name	Sex	Age	Home Village	Twp.	Remarks	Source
4/99	Hsah Tu Ghaw	M	30	Dtaw Gone	T	Interrogated and beaten with other villagers, then pulled into forest and knifed to death by Sa Thon Lon	I50, I51, I54
4/99	Pa Bee Ko	M	>30	Dtaw Gone	T	Interrogated and beaten with other villagers, then pulled into forest and knifed to death by Sa Thon Lon; he was very ill when they killed him	I50, I51, I54
4/99	Ka Ni Ni	M	22	Dtaw Gone	T	Interrogated and beaten with other villagers, then pulled into forest and throat cut by Sa Thon Lon	I50, I51, I54
4/99	Saw Htoo Kee	M	20	Myeh Yeh	M	While doing forced labour as sentry, taken away as a porter and never seen since	I5
3/99	Unknown	?	?	Nyaung Bin Seik	M	Killed at festival when Bo Shan Bpu of Sa Thon Lon fired M79 grenades into the crowd; several others wounded	I2, FR
1/99	Mya Htun	M	48	Meik Tha Lin	P	Village headman, killed by Sa Thon Lon and body dumped in Sittaung River	I21
1999	Two villagers	M		Byin Gah	T	Executed by Sa Thon Lon	I50
1999	Pa Thu Po Pah, a.k.a. Bo Gkay	M	>50	Taw Ma Aye	T	Headman, executed by Sa Thon Lon	I50
1999	Two villagers	M		Shan Gyi Bo Daing	T	Executed by Sa Thon Lon	I50
27/12/98	Saw San Myint	M	25	Baw Bpee Der	M	Killed when Sa Thon Lon entered village and opened fire on people playing volleyball for	I1, FR

Date	Name	Sex	Age	Village		Description	Sources
					M	Christmas; they beheaded him, stuck a cheroot in his mouth and hung head on path to Mone	I22, I29
26/12/98	Five villagers			Twa Ni Gone, now at Yan Myo Aung	M	Found near their home village by Shan Bpu of Sa Thon Lon, executed; 3 were single, 2 married	I41, FR2
16/12/98	Nay Lah Mu	M	?	Tee Nya B'Day Kee	K	Shot on sight, robbed, then disappeared	FR
15/12/98	Maung Soe Myint	M	?	Shah Ku	K	Executed by Sa Thon Lon after warning his neighbour they were looking for him	FR
15/12/98	Ko Kay Mweh	M	?	Shah Ku	K	Executed by Sa Thon Lon	FR
14/12/98	Saw Lay Lay Paw	M	10	Kheh Der	K	Blown apart when LIB 368 shelled the villagers' hiding place in the forest without warning	FR2
3/12/98	Maung Htun Myaing	M	?	Tha Say	S	Shot dead by Sa Thon Lon	I43
12/98	Saw Shwe Win	M	?	Tee Muh Hta	K	Shot on sight by troops who saw him trying to carry rice from the plains up into the hills	I32
12/98	U Than Myint	M	?	Ma Oo Bin	S	Stabbed to death in middle of the village by Sa Thon Lon	I30, I32, I35
12/98	Ko Kyi Hmwe	M	43	Shan Su	S	Executed by Sa Thon Lon 'Nagah' group	I35
12/98	Ko Kyi Myint	M	40	Ma Oo Bin	S	Executed by Sa Thon Lon 'Nagah' group	I35
12/98	Two villagers	M		Zee Taw section,	S	Executed by Sa Thon Lon 'Seik Padee' group	I35

Date	Name	Sex	Age	Shwegyin town		Description	Ref
12/98	Two villagers	M		Kyi Pin Su	S	Executed by Sa Thon Lon	I35
12/98	Three villagers	M		Inn Palah	S	Executed by Sa Thon Lon	I35
12/98	Fourteen villagers	M		Than Seik	S	Executed by Sa Thon Lon	I35
26/11/98	Saw Htoo Yay	M	30	Goh Nee	M	Executed by Maung Maung and Shan Bpu of Sa Thon Lon	FR
22/11/98	Saw Mya Sein	M	30	Meh Praw Hta	S	Shot dead at farm hut by IB 96	FR
22/11/98	Unknown	M	>40	Kya Plaw	K	Sa Thon Lon executed, then cut off tongue and ears	I30
21/11/98	Po Muh Si	F	9	mos. xxxx	K	SPDC Column opened fire on parents while harvesting; her leg was blown off while father carried her, she died, father Saw M--- wounded	I1, I41, FR
20/11/98	Maung Htwe Soe, a.k.a. Maung Htwe	M	20	Thu K'Bee	K	Arrested on 12/11/98 by DKBA, detained and then executed near Klaw Maw pagoda	I30, FR2
20/11/98	Maung Kyaw Thaung Klaw, a.k.a. Kyaw Thaw	M	30	Thu K'Bee	K	Arrested on 12/11/98 by DKBA, detained and then executed near Klaw Maw pagoda	I30, FR2
20/11/98	Saw Gawla Thu	M	25	Leh Wain Gyi	K	Arrested on 12/11/98 by DKBA, detained and then executed near Klaw Maw pagoda	I30, FR2

Date	Name	Sex	Age		K/M	Description	References
20/11/98	Saw Maung Aye	M	?	Leh Gkaw Wah	K	Village headman, executed by Sa Thon Lon	I30, FR
18/11/98	Saw Aye	M	50	Myeh Yeh	M	Shot on sight with Po Theh Pyay in fields by Sa Thon Lon, beheaded, head hung along path near his village for 1 month	I1, I8, I12, I19, I29, FR
18/11/98	Po Theh Pyay	M	36	Ter Bpaw	M	Shot on sight with Saw Aye in fields by Sa Thon Lon, beheaded, head hung along path near his village for 1 month	I1, I8, I12, I19, I29, FR
17/11/98	Saw Ko Pah	M	20	xxxx	K	Returning from xxxx to help parents after his village shot up; ambushed and shot dead on the path by LIB361, who had killed his brother Saw Nat Noh the day before; Saw Maw Dah and Naw Tha Paw also killed, and two others wounded	I37, I38, I40, I43, I45, I46, I47, FR, FR1, FR2
17/11/98	Saw Maw Dah	M	14	xxxx	K	Shot on sight together with Saw Ko Pah and Naw Tha Paw	I37, I38, I40, I43, I45, I46, I47, FR, FR1, FR2
17/11/98	Naw Tha Paw	F	17	xxxx	K	Ambushed together with Saw Ko Pah and Saw Maw Dah, either shot or raped and stabbed	I37, I38, I40, I43, I45, I46, I47, FR, FR1, FR2
16/11/98	Saw Nat Noh	M	26	xxxx	K	Shot on sight under his house by LIB 361 troops who came to destroy the village, tried to flee and died on the path; brother Saw Ko Pah	I37, I38, I40, I43, I45, I46, I47, I48, FR,

Date	Name	Sex	Age	Location		Description	FR1, FR2
15/11/98	Saw Myint Si	M	40	Tee Blah	S	Shot on sight by IB 96, friend Saw P--- wounded	FR
13/11/98	Pa Naw Htoo	M	18	Saw Theh Hta	S	Shot on sight by LIB 351	FR
11/11/98	Maung Ba Aye	M	36	Leh Gkaw Wah	K	Arrested by Sa Thon Lon 'Nagah' group, accused of 'supporting the NLD' and killed together with his wife Naw Dah, leaving a 3 month old child	I32, I35, FR
11/11/98	Naw Dah	F	?	Leh Gkaw Wah	K	Arrested by Sa Thon Lon 'Nagah' group, accused of 'supporting the NLD' and killed together with her husband Maung Ba Aye, leaving a 3 month old child	FR
9/11/98	Saw Per Kaw	M	40	Ma La	M	Taken as porter, couldn't carry anymore so shot dead	FR, FR2
9/11/98	Saw Kah Ko	M	?	Ma La	M	Taken as porter, couldn't carry so killed by SPDC troops	FR
11/98	Saw Mah Htoo, a.k.a. Gah Gyi	M	37	Yan Myo Aung relocation site	M	Taken away from his house by Maung Maung and Shan Bpu from Sa Thon Lon, executed in forest and threw body in Sittaung River	I12, I13, I23
11/98	Tee Sweh	M	?	K'Dee Mu Der	K	Shot dead when SPDC troops shot up K'Dee Mu Der village	I45
11/98	Wah Ku Mu Pa	M	?	K'Dee Mu Der	K	Shot dead when SPDC troops shot up K'Dee Mu Der village	I45
11/98	Wah Ghay Paw Pi	F	?	K'Dee Mu Der	K	Shot dead when SPDC troops shot up K'Dee Mu Der village	I45

Date	Name	Sex	Age	Village		Description	Ref
11/98	Mu Ghay Paw	F	?	K'Dee Mu Der	K	Shot dead when SPDC troops shot up K'Dee Mu Der village	I45
11/98	Ta Kweh Mo	F	?	K'Dee Mu Der	K	Shot dead when SPDC troops shot up K'Dee Mu Der village	I45
27/10/98	Unknown	M	?	Po Noh Po	K	Executed by Sa Thon Lon	I30
22/10/98	Saw Lay Heh	M	?	Twa Ni Gone	M	Sa Thon Lon arrested at fishpond hut, took away and shot dead	I1, I12, I13, I19, FR
22/10/98	Saw Gka Bweh	M	?	Twa Ni Gone	M	"	I1, I12, I13, I19, FR
22/10/98	Saw Maw Nyunt Po	M	?	Twa Ni Gone	M	"	I1, I12, I13, I19, FR
22/10/98	Saw Po Shaw Gkeh	M	~20	Twa Ni Gone	M	Arrested with his 3 friends above and taken off for execution but gun didn't work, so stabbed to death	I1, I12, I13, I19, FR
15/10/98	Naw Mu Lay	F	8	Ter Bpaw	M	Daughter of village head, killed along with her sister Dah Dah when Sa Thon Lon fired M79 grenades into the house	FR
15/10/98	Naw Dah Dah	F	2	Ter Bpaw	M	Daughter of village head, killed along with her sister Mu Lay when Sa Thon Lon fired M79 grenades into the house	FR
13/10/98	Ma Lah Myint	F	45	Aung Chan Tha	M	Raped and killed by IB 59, daughter wounded by gunfire during IB 59 village raid	FR
13/10/98	Ma Nyunt	F	15	Aung Chan Tha	M	Raped and killed by IB 59	FR

Date	Name	Sex	Age	Location	K/S	Description	Ref
13/10/98	Saw Bo Kee	M	33	Paya Hser Der	K	LIB 368 surrounded farm hut and shot dead together with Saw Pa Toh	140, 143, 145, 146, FR, FR1, FR2
13/10/98	Saw Pa Toh	M	40	Paya Hser Der	K	LIB 368 surrounded farm hut and shot dead together with Saw Bo Kee	140, 143, 145, 146, FR, FR1, FR2
10/98	Po Naw	M	?	Kaw Chay Moo	K	Headman, killed by SPDC during forced relocation	130
Late 98	U Aung Baw	M	52	A'Tet Twin Gyi	S	Sa Thon Lon cut his throat and threw him in the Sittaung River	130
Late 98	Khin Win	M	32	A'Tet Twin Gyi	S	Sa Thon Lon cut his throat and threw him in the Sittaung River	130
Late 98	Saw Heh Bo	M	?	Lu Ah	M	Killed by Sa Thon Lon	119
21/9/98	Saw Maw Lay	M	63	Khoh Lu	K	Shot dead then beheaded by Sa Thon Lon	FR
19/7/98	Saw Muh Kaw	M	30	Ler Klah	M	Killed by LIB 367/703 column	FR
19/7/98	Saw Ta Bpu Lu	M	45	Khoh Pu	M	Killed by LIB 367/703 column	FR
19/7/98	Saw Eh Doh Wah	M	12	Khoh Pu	M	Killed by LIB 367/703 column	FR
7/98	Pa Mee	M	37	Leh Yo Poh	K	Summoned by IB 60 to camp at Thaung Bo and executed	130
27/3/98	Hsah Tee Dray	M	20	K'Pah Hta	M	Killed by LIB 703	FR
26/3/98	Maw Ray Heh	M	30	K'Dee Mu Der	K	Killed by IB 59	FR
25/3/98	Naw Thay	F	38	K'Dee Mu	K	Killed by IB 59	FR

Date	Shwe			Der			
24/3/98	Naw Law Htoo	F	45	K'Dee Mu Der	K	Killed by IB 59 together with the 3 listed below; Naw B--- (F, 18) escaped with injuries	FR
24/3/98	Naw Shwe B'Dee	F	47	Ler Hah	K	Killed by IB 59	FR
24/3/98	Naw Mo Reh	F	40	K'Dee Mu Der	K	Killed by IB 59	FR
24/3/98	Naw Mu Ghay	F	10	K'Dee Mu Der	K	Killed by IB 59	FR
16/3/98	Mo Loh Ko	M	30	K'Waw Ko	M	Killed by LIB 703	FR
13/3/98	Saw Shwe Yoh	M	27	K'Kyay Hsay	M	Killed by IB 26	FR
13/3/98	Soe Kyi	M	35	Leh Bpa	M	Killed by IB 26	FR
Early 98	Aung Aung	M	25	Ter Bpaw	M	Taken as porter, never returned	114, 115
16/12/97	Saw Lah Wah	M	17	Nga Law Der	M	Killed by IB 48	FR
11/97	Saw Maw Ko	M	12	Tee Blah	S	Shot on sight while harvesting rice	KHRG*
20/10/97	Saw Maw Gu	M	20	Tee Blah	S	Killed by LIB 440	FR
11/9/97	Naw Deh Deh	F	60	Saw Mu Hsay Day	S	Killed by LIB 350	FR
30/7/97	Saw May Lway	M	20	Aw Bp'Lah	S	Killed by LIB 440	FR
30/7/97	Pa Lay Po	M	45	Aw Bp'Lah	S	Killed by LIB 440	FR
27/7/97	Saw Pah Lee	M	55	Blaw Hta	S	Killed by IB 96	FR
20/7/97	Saw Soe Myint	M	37	Meh Praw Kee	S	Killed by IB 96	FR

Date	Name	Sex	Age	Place		Notes	
22/6/97	Saw Thay Nee	M	25	Meh Praw Hta	S	Killed by IB 96	FR
22/6/97	Saw Cha Po	M	28	Blay Blaw Soe	S	Killed by IB 96	FR
25/5/97	Saw Mah Ner	M	50	Shwegyin	S	Pastor, killed by IB 20	FR
22/5/97	Saw Maw Aye	M	50	Saw Theh Kee	S	Killed by LIB 349	FR
22/5/97	Saw Pah Dee	M	30	Khaw Hta	S	Killed by LIB 349	FR
2/5/97	Way Thay	M	25	K'Pah Hta	M	Killed by LIB 439	FR
2/5/97	Saw Eh Muh	M	25	Nya Mu Kee	M	Killed by LIB 439	FR
27/4/97	Pa Ti Bu	M	32	Ler Hah	K	Killed by joint column of IB 101, 105, & 107 under Division 77	FR
27/4/97	Pa Mah Mu	M	43	Paya Hser Der	K	Killed by joint column of IB 101, 105, & 107 under Division 77	FR
27/4/97	Naw Yweh Ray	F	19	Paya Hser Der	K	Killed by joint column of IB 101, 105, & 107 under Division 77	FR
23/4/97	Saw Way Bpa	M	63	Kheh Der	K	Killed by joint column of IB 101, 105, & 107 under Division 77	FR
23/4/97	Saw Yeh Nyu	M	15	Tee Kay Loh	S	Killed by LIB 440	FR
21/4/97	Pa Taw Thu	M	28	Tee Kay Loh	S	Killed by LIB 440	FR
21/4/97	Saw Tah Lee	M	80	Toh Thu Kee	S	Killed by LIB 440	FR
18/4/97	Saw Ner Kaw	M	40	Tee Blah	S	Killed by IB 20	FR
17/4/97	Saw Tee Muh	M	20	Shwegyin	S	Killed by IB 57	FR
12/4/97	Saw Thi Oo	M	33	Tee Blah	S	Killed by IB 20	FR

Date	Name	Sex	Age	Location	Cause	Description	Source
11/4/97	Saw Eh Muh	M	25	Kheh Der	K	Killed by joint column of IB 101, 105, & 107 under Division 77	FR
9/4/97	Saw Pah Rah	M	23	Wah Kah Der	S	Killed by LIB 440	FR
6/4/97	K'Lah Nga Way	M	35	Baw Bpee Der	M	Killed by LIB 439	FR
6/4/97	Saw Bo Ghay	M	72	Kheh Der	K	Killed by joint column of IB 101, 105, & 107 under Division 77	FR
3/4/97	Naw Paw Htoo	M	50	Maw Soh Ko	K	Killed by joint column of IB 101, 105, & 107 under Division 77	FR
29/3/97	Maw Aye Kyi	M	70	Mu Kee	K	Killed by joint column of IB 101, 105, & 107 under Division 77	FR
20/3/97	Po Lah Heh	M	45	Suh Mu Hta	S	Killed by LIB 440	FR
17/3/97	Saw Mu Kaw	M	32	Ta Ghaw	M	Killed by IB 60	FR
17/3/97	Saw Hsah Kah Htoo	M	20	Ta Ghaw	M	Killed by IB 60	FR
13/3/97	Pa Saw Gkeh	M	50	Wah Peh Kwih	S	Killed by IB 107	FR
13/3/97	Saw Ah Gker	M	37	Wah Peh Kwih	S	Killed by IB 107	FR
13/3/97	Saw Pah Drah	M	45	Wah Peh Kwih	S	Killed by IB 107	FR
12/3/97	Saw Ta Plah Plah	M	3	Doh Daw Kee	K	Division 77 troops shelled village without warning and everyone fled, leaving him and his sister Mi Mu Wah behind. Troops found	FR

Date	Name	Sex	Age	Place	Type	Description	Source
12/3/97	Naw Mi Mu Wah	F	2	Doh Daw Kee	K	Division 77 troops shelled village without warning and everyone fled, leaving her and her brother Ta Plah Plah behind. Troops found them walking around crying and threw them into their burning house	FR
12/3/97	Saw Sah Lway	M	32	Ter Bpaw	M	Killed by combined column of IB 26, LIB 351 & DKBA	FR
3/2/97	Naw Khi Lah Paw	F	17	Toh Kee	S	Killed by IB 96	FR
1996-98	Say Sai	M	?	Yay Leh	M	Killed by SPDC troops at Yan Myo Aung relocation site	119
1996-98	Maw Kaw Gwee	M	?	Twa Ni Gone	M	Killed by SPDC troops at Yan Myo Aung relocation site	119
1996-98	Maw Peh Yah	M	?	Thay Ghee Lu	M	Killed by SPDC troops at Yan Myo Aung relocation site	119
1996-98	Lah Kaw Wah Pa	M	?	Thu Boh Lu	M	Killed by SPDC troops at Yan Myo Aung relocation site	119
1996-98	U Gah Lu	M	?	Bpa Reh Si	M	Killed by SPDC troops at Yan Myo Aung relocation site	119
1996-98	Unknown	M	?	Ta Maw Ma	T	Killed by SPDC troops	119

* indicates source was KHRG Report #98-01, "Wholesale Destruction", interview #52